# THE SOUND OF
## Their Music

# THE SOUND OF

## Their Music

*The Story of Rodgers & Hammerstein*

BY FREDERICK NOLAN

**APPLAUSE**
THEATRE & CINEMA BOOKS

THE SOUND OF THEIR MUSIC
THE STORY OF RODGERS & HAMMERSTEIN
BY FREDERICK NOLAN
Copyright © 2002 by Frederick Nolan
All rights reserved

Library of Congress Cataloguing-in-Publication Data

Nolan, Frederick W., 1931-
The sound of their music : the story of Rodgers and Hammerstein / Frederick Nolan.
    p. cm.
Includes bibliographical references (p.   ) and index.
  ISBN 1-55783-473-3
  1. Rodgers, Richard, 1902-1979. 2. Hammerstein, Oscar, 1895-1960. 3. Composers--United States--Biography. 4. Librettists--United States--Biography. I. Title.
  ML410.R6315 N64 2002
  782.1'4'0922--dc21

                        2002004626

British Library Cataloguing-in-Publication Data
    A catalogue record for this book is available from the British Library

ISBN: 1-55783-473-3


APPLAUSE THEATRE & CINEMA BOOKS
151 West 46th Street, 8th Floor
New York, NY 10036
Phone: (212) 575-9265
Fax: (646) 562-5852
E-mail: info@applausepub.com
Internet: www.applausepub.com


SALES & DISTRIBUTION

| NORTH AMERICA: | UK: |
| --- | --- |
| HAL LEONARD CORP. | COMBINED BOOK SERVICES LTD. |
| 7777 West Bluemound Road | Units I/K, Paddock Wood Distribution Centre |
| P. O. Box 13819 | Paddock Wood, Tonbridge, Kent TN12 6UU |
| Milwaukee, WI  53213 | Phone: (44) 01892 837171 |
| Phone: (414) 774-3630 | Fax: (44) 01892 837272 |
| Fax: (414) 774-3259 | United Kingdom |
| Email: halinfo@halleonard.com | |
| Internet: www.halleonard.com | |

This book is dedicated to you, the reader,
because you love the subject as much as I do.

# Table of Contents:

# Preface

When this book first appeared in 1978, there had been no biography of Richard Rodgers for almost twenty years, and no book at all existed that fully examined all three phases of his songwriting career. Nor, then, had there been any meaningful biography of either Hart or Hammerstein, so it could be said that mine was in its own way a pioneering effort. With the continuing growth of interest in musical theater, however, that situation has been comprehensively remedied, and a number of fine books on the subject have been written by such authors as William Ryland, Hugh Fordin, Ethan Mordden, and, recently and most notably, Meryle Secrest, whose biography of Rodgers will surely be considered definitive.

The impetus behind my original examination of the lives and careers of Rodgers, Hart, and Hammerstein and the world of musical theater in which their talents flourished was not so much to write definitive biographies of the men themselves as to generate a sense of what it was like to be there during the creation of their most memorable shows. It did not occur to me then that I was recording theatrical history. I was just so filled with enthusiasm for the subject, the people, the stories, and the music, that I felt privileged to be allowed to ask my questions and eager to share what I learned.

Now, with so many of the people I interviewed in the 1970s gone, their recollections have become even more valuable, not to say poignant. So, once again, my grateful thanks to every one of them: George Abbott, Larry Adler, Muriel Angelus, Lucinda Ballard, Irving Berlin, Irving Caesar, Sammy Cahn, Jan Clayton, Agnes de Mille, Howard Dietz, Irving Eisman, David Ewen, Ted Fetter, Dorothy Fields, George Ford, Helen Ford, Bennett Green, John Green, Nanette Guilford, Hildegarde Halliday, Dorothy Hammerstein, James Hammerstein, William Hammerstein, Rex Harrison, June Havoc, Celeste Holm, Gene Kelly, Philip Leavitt, Alan Jay Lerner, Joshua Logan, Mary Martin, Samuel Marx, Jessie Matthews, Edith Meiser, James A. Michener, Henry Myers, Milton Pascal, Irving Pincus, Arthur Schwartz, Vivienne Segal, Leonard Spigelgass, Benay Venuta, Harry Warren, Alec Wilder, and, most especially, Richard Rodgers.

To this starry list I have been fortunate in being able to add the recollections of Sheldon Harnick, Penny Fuller, Cy Feuer, and Martin Charnin, who worked with

Rodgers on his last two shows; it was heartwarming to hear them all speak so affectionately about him. For assistance and encouragement in other ways, I wish to offer my warmest thanks to: Ken Bloom; George E. Boziwick, Music Division, Performing Arts Center, New York Public Library; Liz Calder; Reg. Fulton; Dr. Philip Furia, University of North Carolina at Wilmington; Kitty Carlisle Hart; Marty Jacobs and Marguerite Lavin, Theatre and Arts Collection, Museum of the City of New York; Robert Kimball; Prof. Joseph Kissane; Kristine Krueger, National Film Information Service, Academy of Motion Picture Arts and Sciences; Lynn Lane; Ron Mandelbaum of Photofest; Hugh Martin; Anne Kaufman Schneider; and Sherman Yellen. My publishers, John Cerullo, Mark Glubke, and Glenn Young, have been towers of strength throughout. I would like also to say what a pleasure it has been to be able to count on the support and encouragement of Ted Chapin, Bert Fink, Mike Dvorchak, Robin Walton, and Flora Griggs of the Rodgers and Hammerstein Organization. Each and every one of them has made important contributions to this book.

In the foreword to the 1978 edition, I said that what I was trying to do was recapture some of the excitement of that era, when nobody knew whether the show they were working on would be a hit or a flop, the days when it all went well and the days when nothing went right, as told by the people who were there at the time. Twenty-five years on, I'm still trying.

x

Frederick Nolan
Chalfont St. Giles, England
January, 2002

# AWAY WE Go!

*On Broadway they all know we're stagestruck.*

—Oscar Hammerstein

On July 23, 1942, *The New York Times* ran a brief report to the effect that the Theatre Guild was planning to produce a musical adaptation of Lynn Riggs's 1931 play *Green Grow the Lilacs*, with a book by Oscar Hammerstein II and music and lyrics by Richard Rodgers and Lorenz Hart. This confident announcement omitted two very important items of information. The first was that the Theatre Guild, with Lawrence Langner and Theresa Helburn as its directors, was teetering on the brink of insolvency. The second was that Richard Rodgers's song-writing partner of 25 years no longer had the will or desire to work — especially not on this project.

The idea of making a musical from Riggs's play had originated in the fertile brain of Theresa Helburn, who had always had a soft spot for it ever since its — failed — original production in 1931. A revival of the play ten years later at the Westport Country Playhouse lightened the piece by adding folk songs and a square dance choreographed by Gene Kelly, who had recently soared to stardom as the charming heel of Rodgers and Hart's musical *Pal Joey.* Noting how the audience warmed to the music, Helburn began to wonder how the play might go with a complete musical score. From there it was only a step to asking her Westport neighbor, Richard Rodgers, to come up and have a look. He saw the possibilities immediately, but — the *New York Times* announcement notwithstanding —

**Dick Rodgers and Larry Hart at a rehearsal of *By Jupiter*, 1942. The stressed-looking man in the background is producer Dwight Deere Wiman.** Theatre Collection, Museum of the City of New York.

his partner Lorenz Hart did not. According to Arthur Schwartz, Hart told Rodgers that the play was corny, that it wasn't their style, and that it wouldn't be any good. Moreover, he didn't want to do another show so soon after their latest hit, *By Jupiter*. In fact, Larry Hart did not want to work at all. He wanted to go to Mexico on vacation with his sinister friend and agent, Milton "Doc" Bender.

From the very beginning Larry Hart had been a difficult partner for Dick Rodgers: "A partner, a best friend and a constant source of irritation," as the composer had once put it. Unquestionably the most brilliant lyric writer of his own or, indeed, any succeeding generation, Hart, a homosexual trying to solve his problems at the bottom of a bottle, had become unstable, erratic, and, at best, a fitful worker. As a result, Rodgers found himself all too frequently in the unenviable position of being not only Hart's collaborator but also his guardian and nurse. Indeed, had Rodgers not spent an increasing amount of his time finding Hart and then persuading him to work, easing him through as many hours of creativity as were possible before his craving for the bottle became too intense, it is highly unlikely that any of their last few shows together would ever have been written.

Rodgers had already reached out for help a year or so earlier when he wrote to Oscar Hammerstein inviting him to collaborate on the book of a musical version of Edna Ferber's novel *Saratoga Trunk* which he and Larry Hart were then working on; the project fell through, but the door that had been opened remained ajar. A few months later, while in Philadelphia for the tryouts of *Best Foot Forward,* which he co-produced, Rodgers used the opportunity to visit the Hammerstein farm near Doylestown and talk through his problems with Oscar.

> *Much as I regretted it, there was nothing I could do about it.*
> *I couldn't stop working myself just because Larry couldn't be worked*
> *with. I had tremendous faith in Oscar. Oscar had had a bad time of it*
> *for many years, but I knew beyond argument about his enormous talent,*
> *and felt that if something did happen to Larry, this was the logical*
> *direction for me to move in. I was in Philadelphia with a show that*
> *George Abbott and I produced together called* Best Foot Forward. *Just*
> *to give you an idea how far this thing had progressed with Larry,*
> *I wouldn't put my name on the show as co-producer because things were*
> *so sensitive. I didn't want to call attention to the fact that I was*
> *working away from Larry because I thought that would be harmful.*

3

Hammerstein listened without speaking as Rodgers unburdened himself of his fears concerning Larry Hart and the future of their partnership, then advised Rodgers to go on working with Hart as long as Hart was able to work: he felt that if Dick walked away it would be the end of Larry. "If the time ever comes that he can't work, call me," Oscar said. "I'll even go a step further. If you and Larry are in the middle of a job and he can't finish it, I'll finish it for him and no one but the two of us need ever know."

Relieved, but perhaps still unsure, Rodgers returned to New York. Hammerstein was everything everyone said he was, and more, but the inescapable fact remained that Hammerstein had been associated with nothing but flops for a decade. Samuel Marx related that Rodgers then talked to Ira Gershwin, who had just returned to the Broadway stage with *Lady In The Dark.*

> *Ira told me about Dick calling him up to have dinner. It was a dinner*
> *set up by Louis Dreyfus, Max Dreyfus's son. Dick talked about the*
> *problems he was having with Larry and sort of hinted that he had to*
> *make a change. He never asked point blank but always sort*
> *of talked around it. And Ira, who was committing a slow suicide after*
> *the death of George ... turned him down.*

*By Jupiter* had been a traumatic experience for Rodgers, who produced the show in conjunction with Dwight Deere (as in tractors) Wiman. Not only did he have his usual problems finding Larry, whose drinking and unannounced disappearances were increasing to an alarming degree, but he now had to contend with a co-producer almost equally adept at vanishing, albeit for totally different reasons. Wiman was a man much more devoted to extra-theatrical activities than to his duties as a producer. He once kept the almost-maniacally punctual Rodgers and a prospective backer waiting for more than an hour, a breach of manners which, in a producer, Rodgers described as "roughly akin to self-immolation."

Rodgers had initially hoped that Larry Hart's enthusiasm for *By Jupiter* — a musical based on the play *The Warrior's Husband* by Julian F. Thompson and starring Ray Bolger, Constance Moore, Benay Venuta, and Vera-Ellen — would keep him relatively sober, if only temporarily. In fact, Hart was less dependable than ever before. After finding him lying in his apartment in a semi-coma, Rodgers had Larry admitted to Doctor's Hospital, and they completed the score there. However, as soon as Larry hit the street, he started hitting the bottle again. He disappeared for three days during the Boston tryouts and, all in all, made life hell for his partner. Joshua Logan, who directed the play, recalled Rodgers's reactions.

> *Just before I went overseas he came to me and he said, "I'm going to have*
> *to try without Larry, I can't go through this anymore. I just haven't got it*
> *in me." He told me that he and Larry had been offered* Green Grow the
> Lilacs *but Larry didn't want to do it. He had talked to Larry, and I think*
> *Larry must have felt, must have known how Dick felt. And I said to him,*
> *"Have you thought of anyone to take his place, who will you get?" And he*
> *said, "What would you think if I got together with Oscar Hammerstein?"*
> *And I said, "Oh, my God, marvelous, it would be wonderful."*

Cold-blooded, perhaps, but pragmatic. Insiders like Logan might view the possible break up of the songwriting team of Rodgers and Hart as unfortunate, even sad, but ultimately inevitable. As Larry's sister-in-law Dorothy Hart observed, the remarkable thing was not that Rodgers and Hart finally split up, it was that they had stayed together for so long in a business not noted for long and exclusive partnerships. Even so, Rodgers was still reluctant to call it a day; he arranged to meet Larry at the office of their music publisher, Chappell & Co., presided over by the elderly Max Dreyfus. But it was a waste of time. Larry did not want to do *Green Grow The Lilacs,* he wanted to go to Mexico and have fun.

Forced to play his last card, Rodgers told him, "If you walk out on me now, I'm going to do the show with someone else." "Do you have someone in mind?" Hart asked. Rodgers told him he had: Oscar Hammerstein. Without ever looking him in the eyes, Hart told Rodgers he couldn't have picked a better man. "I don't know why you've put up with me all these years," he said. "The best thing for you is to forget about me."

With that, he got up and left. Rodgers simply did not know what to do. He had worked with Larry Hart exclusively for more than 25 years. He did not know if he could work successfully with Oscar Hammerstein, or anyone else for that matter. All he could think of was that a long and wonderful partnership had just walked out of the door. He got up to go and tell Max Dreyfus, but before he even reached the door, he was crying like a baby.

Hart went off to Mexico to "have fun" with his inseparable companion (and, everyone believed, procurer) "Doc" Bender; the kind of "fun" it was may be deduced from the fact that Larry had to be brought home on a stretcher. His departure for Taxco left the composer no choice. Rodgers went to the directors of the Theatre Guild and told them he would like to invite Oscar Hammerstein to write the show with him. They agreed — not that they were in any position to do much else.

Rodgers called Hammerstein, and they arranged to meet at the Barberry Room, a place redolent of literary and theatrical history. It had begun

**Victoria Schools, June Allyson, and Nancy Walker singing "The Three Bs" (Barrelhouse, Boogie-woogie, and Blues) in 1942's *Best Foot Forward*. Allyson and Walker made their screen debuts in the movie the following year; Ms. Schools seems to have taken another road.**

Theatre Collection, Museum of the City of New York.

5

life as the restaurant of the Berkshire Hotel, just across the street from the CBS Building on 52$^{nd}$ Street. The owner, George Backer, made it a private club at the request of critic and columnist Alexander Woollcott, bringing in Norman Bel Geddes to design the room. It was long and narrow, with a very high ceiling from which stars appeared to twinkle. The largest mirror in the world was constructed to cover one wall and compensate for the lack of width. This enormous blue mirror and the plush armchairs gave the place an unforgettable ambiance. When he first saw it, Harold Ross, editor of the *New Yorker*, remarked that it would make a terrific swimming pool once they put the water in. The club, which Woollcott dubbed The Elbow Room, did not last six months. A man named Moriarty took over and turned it into a public restaurant, the Barberry Room.

Rodgers came straight to the point. The Theatre Guild wanted to do a musical based on *Green Grow The Lilacs*, and he wondered whether Oscar would like to work on it with him. Hammerstein must have smiled. Unbeknownst to Rodgers, he had tried to interest Jerome Kern in musicalizing the very same play, but Kern had been disinclined to try to make a successful show out of one that had been a complete failure. Hammerstein told Rodgers he not only knew the play but that he was crazy about it. And there and then they agreed to work together.

6      Both men were aware that difficulties of all kinds lay ahead. The musical they were about to embark upon was just about the Guild's last chance, and the odds stacked against it were formidable indeed. To begin with, the show was budgeted at $83,000, of which the Guild had not a penny. In addition, as far as either of them knew, they might

**A scene from the 1931 Theatre Guild production of *Green Grow the Lilacs*.** Theatre Collection, Museum of the City of New York.

never earn a dollar more than the nominal hundreds which the Theatre Guild had advanced them upon signing the contract. Nevertheless they decided to go ahead. Nobody they knew agreed with them. One or two came right out and said they were crazy to do a cowboy show, as Rodgers recalled.

> *There wasn't anything enormously attractive about the idea. And then on top of that Oscar and I were working together for the first time. Who knew whether this combination would work or not? They were sure in my case that it wouldn't, because I'd had all those years with Hart and suddenly came the split. They knew that I had to fail.*

In the summer of 1942, Dick and Dorothy Rodgers had bought a new home in Fairfield, Connecticut, a fifteen-room, five-bath Colonial house on a six-acre plot, one of the most attractive features of which was a massive oak tree with a ninety-foot spread. It was beneath this tree that Rodgers and Hammerstein began to work on the show which would eventually become *Oklahoma!* There were to be many, many such sessions until they were completely familiar with each other's ideas and outlook as well as with the formal content of the show itself.

7

> *What happened between Oscar and me was almost chemical. Put the right components together and an explosion takes place. Oscar and I hit it off from the day we started discussing the show. For one thing, I needed a little calm in my life after twenty-three hectic years. When Oscar would say "I'll meet you at two-thirty," he was there at two-thirty. That had never happened to me before.*

A further advantage to both men was the fact that each could now work in his preferred method. Rodgers had nearly always composed his melodies first, adapting himself to the wayward ways of Larry Hart. Larry had to have something to work on, and the music provided that, although Rodgers would have preferred to set finished lyrics to music. Oscar's experience was the very opposite. His inclination had always been to write the lyrics first, but when working with such composers as Rudolf Friml, Herbert Stothart, Vincent Youmans, and Jerome Kern, he had sublimated that preference. The reversion to preferred methods within this new partnership brought about several important changes, both in the songs and in how they fit into the show.

Almost from the beginning of his career, Oscar Hammerstein had been dedicated to the idea of bringing seriousness to the musical stage. He was impassioned by the thought of finding something which was neither operetta nor escapism, something which had purpose and coherence, something that was unmistakably American, rather than European, in tradition. He had done his share of shoddy shows which were no more than nitwitted plots upon which to hang a random collection of songs and novelty numbers. He had made a giant step towards realizing his dream when he and Jerome Kern collaborated on *Show Boat*. He had lost his shirt on a few experiments of his own. He brought all that experience, all that passion, to his discussions with Dick Rodgers, and, as Rodgers said, the result was almost chemical.

One of their first decisions was that in this show, the play would dictate the technique and not vice versa. They agreed that the only risky thing to do in the theater was not to take risks. They decided that the integration of music and text should be paramount, and that the lyrics could and should determine the form of the song. They discussed moods, textures, construction. And breaking rules.

Tradition dictated that the curtain on every musical should rise on a big, star-spangled production number, a crowded stage full of color, dancing, and song. Yet *Green Grow the Lilacs* was a simple, unpretentious story which defied them to open with extravaganza. There was no precedent, and so they did the only possible thing: they decided to set one. Which, in turn, led to other problems. Musical comedy demanded, nay, insisted on, a chorus line. Yet the play offered no opportunity for a chorus until half way through the first act, an unheard-of delay in "bringing on the girls." Musical comedy had never tolerated so villainous a character as Jeeter (who became Jud Fry), or a murder. Yet Riggs's play contained both, and both must stay, Hammerstein said.

> We both realized that such a course was experimental, amounting
> almost to a breach of an implied contract with a musical comedy
> audience. I cannot say truthfully that we were worried by the risk.
> Once we had made the decisions, everything seemed to work right and
> we had the inner confidence people feel when they have adopted the
> direct and honest approach to a problem.

Rodgers agreed; and Oscar set to work. The first task was to write a song with which to open the show, one which would set the tone and ambiance for everything that followed. For inspiration, he went back to Lynn Riggs's stage directions. He recalled reading them and thinking what a pity it was that the audience could not do so, for if they could, they would slip easily into the mood of the story. Riggs had described a radiant summer morning, "the kind of morning which, enveloping the shapes of earth, men, cattle in the meadow, blades of the young corn, makes them seem to exist now for the first time, their images giving off a visible golden emanation." From there it was but a short step to the decision to embody that description in the lyric. The bright golden haze, the meadow, the corn were already there. Hammerstein translated them into the simple phraseology of the cowboy, Curly, who would sing them, even going so far as to write at first that the corn was as high as a cow-pony's eye. For the second verse, a flash of inspiration he had experienced while relaxing at his farm came back to him.

> *I remember sitting on the porch one summer's day, watching a herd of*
> *cows standing on a hillside about half a mile away. It was very hot and*
> *there was no motion in the world. I suddenly found myself doing what I*
> *had never done before and have never done since. I was thinking up*
> *lines for a poem to describe what I saw.*

This was the simple quatrain he composed then but did not write down:                    9

> The breeze steps aside
> To let the day pass.
> The cows on the hill
> Are as still as the grass.

And there were his cattle, "standin' like statues."

There's a legend that it took him three weeks to write "Oh, What a Beautiful Morning," one whole week of which was spent agonizing over whether to start the first two lines with the word "Oh." In fact, it was written in only two days. Only!

He and Rodgers had long since agreed that in all the songs they would try to capture the essential character or mood of the singer or the scene. Oscar's intention was, to use his own words, "to sock the audience where it lives." He used simple words because he believed a song was not the place to demonstrate his erudition — a viewpoint profoundly dissimilar to that of Lorenz Hart — and that each line in a lyric should either be the continuation of the one before or the introduction of a new thought. "To stay in character,"

**The movie *Oklahoma!*— Gordon MacRae tells Shirley Jones what it will be like to ride in "The Surrey With The Fringe On Top."** British Film Institute.

he said, "the lyric must never let go of the listener for a single instant. It's like fishing. A little slack in the line and they're off the hook."

So, three weeks later, he went out to Fairfield, handed his completed lyric to Rodgers, and was astounded when the composer completed his melody in ten minutes. "When Oscar handed me the lyric and I read it for the first time, I was a little sick with joy because it was so lovely and so right," Rodgers said. "It took nothing to write it. I was so elated that the music came almost as quickly as the time elapsed in writing it down."

Quite a remarkable reaction from a man who unashamedly disliked poetry — and Oscar's lyric is undoubtedly that. Yet stories about how fast he could write a melody like this one, although perfectly true, were often a source of irritation to Rodgers. Although it might appear amazing that he wrote "Oh, What a Beautiful Morning" in ten minutes, it is not when one remembers that Rodgers was first and foremost a craftsman of the theatrical song and the theatrical song alone. Unlike most of his peers, he had hardly ever written a song that was unrelated to a specific stage or screenplay. He looked upon his songs as the given musical solution to a specific dramatic problem. As he once said:

*No melodies are running around in my head. A song almost never occurs to me spontaneously. What I have to say is essentially musical, but it isn't simply melody for melody's sake. My big involvement is with the characters. I must know how they feel and then I can give them a song to express it. A friend once asked me how long it took to compose the whole score of* Oklahoma! *I said, "What do you mean, flying time or elapsed time?" Counting everything: overture, ballet music, all the songs, the most I could make it come to was five hours flying time. But the total elapsed time covered months of discussion and planning, starting with the overall conception and then getting down to specific questions like how to bring the chorus onstage and whether to end this or that scene with dialogue or music. So, before you can say "Oh, What a Beautiful Morning" was written in ten minutes, you have to know a little about semantics. By the time Oscar gave me the lyrics and I sat down to the actual business of writing the notes ... these things had all been decided. I have to do an awful lot of thinking ... before I even dream of doing actual notes. I think that the moment of creation should be a spontaneous one, though. I think possibly the results are better if it comes in a rush.*

11

Perhaps an even better example of how closely, and yet how differently, Oscar worked with Lynn Riggs's text is the song "The Surrey with the Fringe on Top," an example of what is known in the trade as a "charm" song. Almost as difficult to create as a comedy number, charm songs are used to establish motive and, as importantly, to make the audience love the characters singing them. In the original *Green Grow the Lilacs*, Riggs's dialogue went as follows:

CURLY:

A bran' new surrey with a fringe on the top four inches long — and *yeller!* And two white horses a-rarin' an' faunchin' to go! You'd shore ride like a queen settin' up in *that* carriage! Feel like you had a gold crown set on yer head 'th diamonds in it as big as goose eggs.

LAUREY:

Look out, you'll be astin' me in a minute!

CURLY:

> I ain't astin' you, I'm *tellin'* you! An' thisyere rig has got four fine side
> curtains, case of rain. And isinglass winders to look out of! And a red
> and green lamp set on the dashboard winkin' like a lightnin' bug!

And then later:

CURLY:

> Don't you wish they *was* such a rig, though? Nen you could go to the
> party and do a hoedown till mornin' if you was a mind to. Nen drive
> home 'th the sun a-peekin' at you over the ridge, purty and fine.

The raw material is already there; but it needed Hammerstein's lyrical and theatrical genius to turn it into a lyric, and then Rodgers's perfect melody, suggesting the clip-clop of the horses' hoofs, the chicks and ducks and geese scurrying. There are the isinglass windows you can roll right down in case of a change in the weather, the two bright sidelights winking and blinking, and the sun swimming on the rim of the hill. Deceptively simple, but actually anything but.

What was, and is, remarkable about the score of *Oklahoma!* is that with perhaps one exception, the principal song "People Will Say We're in Love," none of the melodies bears even a slight family resemblance to the songs Rodgers wrote with Larry Hart. "Many a New Day" with its rippling opening triplets, "Out of My Dreams," "I Cain't Say No," and the disturbing, dramatic "Lonely Room" (which occasioned Lynn Riggs to remark, upon hearing it for the first time, that it would probably scare the hell out of the audience) are totally different from anything which preceded them in Rodgers's catalog. For all that, they are indisputably Rodgers's songs. It was often put to him that the change in lyricists had made a profound change in his writing, to which he invariably answered — with some impatience — that it had not. "There was no change in my music, none at all," he would say. "There was a difference because of the way Oscar wrote, the subjects we became involved in — they required a different kind of music. And I had been brought up that way, to make my music fit the text, for a show or a movie or whatever."

Before long, Hammerstein had a working outline, and Rodgers had written enough songs for the Guild to begin trying to interest prospective backers. It was still, of course, just a rough sketch: a cue for a song entitled "I'll Be at Your Elbow," another for Aunt Eller called "She Likes You Quite a Lot." Jud Fry was to sing "That's All I Want," Ali

12

Hakim a lament called "Peddler's Pack" and — a long, long way away from its final form — the first act finale was centered on a song called "How Would It Be?" It does not appear that any of these were actually written; there are only two other full lyrics: the cakewalk "When Ah Goes Out Walkin' with My Baby" (later replaced by "Kansas City"), Curly and Laurey's duet "Boys and Girls Like You and Me," and this one, intended as the first love song in the show, and apparently written for Curly:

> Someone will teach you and clearly explain
> Why you are the cream of the crowd.
> Someone will teach you to walk down a lane
> As if you were ridin' a cloud.
> Someone will kiss you and tell you you're wonderful.
> You'll think you're wonderful, too.
> Fer somehow the right one can make you believe
> They's no one on earth like you.

Oscar's first choice of title, *Oklahoma*, was discarded lest backers assume the show was about "Okies" in the Depression. *Cherokee Strip*, an alternative suggestion from Lawrence Langner's wife, Armina Marshall, was likewise abandoned for fear people would think it was a burlesque show. So, although no one really liked it (most of the participants preferred to call it *Green Grow*), the safer *Away We Go!* — borrowed from square dancing lingo — became the working title. The first-draft script adhered to the folksy spirit of the original, retaining all the main characters (although Jeeter's name was changed to Jud to avoid confusion with the character of the same name in *Tobacco Road*) and building up others, notably Ado Annie, the shy, fat wallflower of Riggs's play who becomes the "girl who cain't say no." Although it used many lines from the original play, Oscar's treatment compressed the time scale — particularly in the second act — and added the subplot featuring Will Parker (who was called "Bud" to begin with) and the Persian peddler, Ali Hakim.

At first, the Guild's lack of funds did not worry the composers; they had a half-century of experience between them, a string of great successes behind them. The money would come. But no matter how industriously Helburn tried, the major producers would not touch the show with a ten-foot pole, and it was not difficult to see why. Apart from Rodgers, none of the principals involved had much to commend them to investors. Hammerstein hadn't written anything successful for a decade. Langner and Helburn

13

14    **Joseph Buloff (Ali Hakim) and Celeste Holm (Ado Annie) in *Oklahoma!* He invites her to come upstairs with him at the hotel. "Upstairs," he says, "is Paradise!" "Oh, " says Annie, "I thought they was just bedrooms!"**
**Theatre Collection, Museum of the City of New York.**

could hardly dispute the fact that the Theatre Guild was unable to finance its own production. The director was to be Rouben Mamoulian; Josh Logan, the Guild's first choice, had been inducted into the Army, and Elia Kazan had turned them down. Face it, Mamoulian had not done a Broadway show for seven years and even that show, *Porgy and Bess*, had been a critical rather than a financial success. Choreographer Agnes de Mille, a niece of the film director Cecil B. de Mille, had choreographed only two shows in the past half-decade, neither successful. Nothing there to attract the money men.

Feeling that established stars might encourage investment, Terry Helburn had suggested Shirley Temple for the role of Laurey and Groucho Marx for the part of the leering peddler, Ali Hakim. Rodgers and Hammerstein, backed by Mamoulian, held out for singers and actors who would be right for the parts, regardless whether their names had box-office appeal. Innovative, perhaps, and courageous, certainly, but not the stuff to attract an $83,000 investment. Do another show with Larry Hart, Rodgers was urged. Give us another *By Jupiter*, another *Boys from Syracuse*, but not, for God's sake, a musical about two cowboys competing to take a farmer's daughter to a box social.

These reactions forced Rodgers and Hammerstein into what must have been one of the most humiliating experiences of their lives. With half a century of hits behind them, a formidable record of writing successfully for both stage and screen, they were reduced to working the "penthouse circuit" cap in hand, trying to raise money for the show. It was no fun, as Hammerstein recalled. "It was hard to finance, all right. We didn't have any stars, and those who were putting up money for plays felt you had to have stars. Dick and I would go from penthouse to penthouse giving auditions. Terry Helburn would narrate the story. Dick would play and I would sing 'Pore Jud Is Dead.' We weren't hugely successful."

Casting began in the autumn of 1942. Oscar wanted comedienne Charlotte Greenwood to play Aunt Eller, but she was unavailable; the part would go to Guild stalwart Betty Garde (Greenwood eventually played it in the movie). Alfred Drake, who won the part of the cowboy hero, Curly, had been a Rodgers and Hart discovery in *Babes in Arms* in 1938. Since then, he had appeared in shows as diverse as Shakespeare's *As You Like It* and revues like *One for the Money and Two for the Show*, but he wasn't a headliner. Neither was Celeste Holm, then appearing in *The Damask Cheek*, a "highly literate" play starring Flora Robson and directed by John van Druten. Her audition began badly when she fell down three steps onto the stage, scattering her music everywhere.

"That was pretty funny," someone said from the auditorium. "Could you do it again?"

15

The speaker was Dick Rodgers, and his friendly manner immediately put her at ease. He asked her what she would like to sing, and she said, "Who Is Sylvia?" "That's good," Rodgers said. "I haven't heard that this year."

Never having auditioned for a musical, Holm didn't realize then how heartfelt the words were. After she sang, Rodgers said, "My God, you have a trained voice. Let me ask you this: Could you sing as if you never had a lesson in your life?" Nonplussed for a moment, Holm then said brightly, "I c'n call a hog." "I dare you," he said, and she went "Sooooo-*eeeeeeeeeeeeeeeeeeeeeeeeeeeeeeeeeeeeeeeeeeeee!*" And that's how she got the part of Ado Annie.

Hammerstein also tried to persuade Mary Martin, a bright newcomer to the Broadway scene who had stopped the Cole Porter show *Let's Face It* with her wide-eyed *faux-naïf* interpretation of "My Heart Belongs to Daddy," to take on the role of Laurey, but she was already committed to a new show with a Vernon Duke-Howard Dietz score, *Dancing in the Streets*. The part went to a young singer who had been in one of Oscar's disasters, a 1941 show with music by Sigmund Romberg called *Sunny River* which had foundered after six weeks. Her name was Joan Roberts, and in her autobiography, *Never Alone*, she recalled that when she auditioned, Dick was withdrawn, as though deeply preoccupied. Oscar, on the other hand, was pleasantly talkative and gave the impression of not having problems of any kind.

They had problems, however, and plenty of them. Even when they augmented their penthouse performances with the singers, the process of raising money remained totally unreliable and painfully slow. Often, they would provide an evening of music and story for the beautiful people in their glittering palaces — and raise not a penny.

Rehearsals began in February, 1943, at the Guild Theatre. During one of these, Celeste Holm recalled, "civilians" arrived, greatly disconcerting the actors, who were still struggling with their lines and places. "Terry," she asked Helburn, "Why are these strangers here?" "Now, now, dear, don't be nervous," Helburn told her. "Just carry on." They carried on, but now Howard da Silva, playing Jud, pretended to be stinking drunk. The worse he got, the more the kibitzers hated him, and the more they hated him, the drunker he acted. Finally, they left in disgust. Only later did the cast learn that the "civilians" had been brought to see the show in the hope that some of them might invest money in it.

One of the biggest obstacles to raising money was the inability to offer the lure of potential movie profits — MGM already had acquired the dramatic rights to the original play years earlier. Helburn tried to persuade the studio to invest $69,000 in return for 50 percent of the show's profits and a further $75,000 for film rights. If the show was a hit, they would get their $69,000 back, and if it failed, they wouldn't have to buy the movie rights. The studio turned her down.

Louis B. Mayer, the head of MGM Studios, made a counteroffer — the Theatre Guild and Rodgers and Hammerstein could have an option on the movie rights, to be exercised within thirty days of the New York opening, for $40,000. (They exercised it in thirty hours.) Still Helburn didn't give up. Through producer Max Gordon, the Guild approached the forceful, leather-tongued Harry Cohn, head of Columbia Pictures, and got him to attend an audition at Steinway Hall. Cohn loved what he saw and promised to put up the money MGM had refused. For a few days, everyone thought their troubles were over, but then Columbia Pictures's board of directors disagreed with Cohn. The offer was withdrawn, although Cohn did invest $15,000 of his own money. Seeing the hard-headed Cohn put that kind of money into the show persuaded Max Gordon also to invest.

Agnes de Mille related how the last of the money was raised. Terry Helburn went to see S. N. Behrman, a playwright who had won great acclaim with plays produced by the Guild. "Sam," she said, "you've got to take $20,000 of this, because the Guild has done so much for you." And he said, "But, Terry, that's blackmail." "Yes," she said. "It is."

*Away We Go!* had at last become a viable theatrical project, and just in time. Oscar Hammerstein had been tempted to withdraw from the show by the offer of a juicy two-year Hollywood contract dangled in front of his eyes by Arthur Freed at MGM. Even Rodgers nursed the secret hope that an Air Force commission might take the problems of the show out of his hands.

More problems? Yes, even more. As rehearsals continued, Rouben Mamoulian began interpreting his contract, which gave him "a free hand," to the literal letter. Temperament — and tempers, ran high. By the time rehearsals were over, Mamoulian had become the villain of the piece. Nobody would talk to him, not even Oscar, who had been the one who most seemed to understand what Mamoulian was trying to achieve. Agnes de Mille and the director were at daggers drawn. According to de Mille, Mamoulian had tantrums when he learned that Dick and Oscar had seen the costume and set designs before he had. His version was that when he told her she was choreographing as if for ballet, and there would be no room for the kind of ballet she was devising on the stage, she screamed that he was ruining her and took her grievances to Dick Rodgers, calling Mamoulian a sour bitch and an even greater tyrant than her uncle.

**Rodgers and Hammerstein rehearsing *Away We Go!* and looking a lot more relaxed than they had any right to.**
Used by permission of the Rodgers and Hammerstein Organization.

Intense and immensely talented, de Mille became a major factor in the success of the show, but not everyone admired her disputatious manner and short temper. She began as she meant to continue, issuing an edict to Hammerstein that there would be no one in the chorus of whom she did not approve. "Oscar," she said,

> *was sorry to hear I was going to take that attitude — there was his regular girl, and Lawrence Langner had two, and Dick Rodgers always counted on some. For one beat, I took him literally, there being no trace of anything except earnestness in his face, and then I relaxed on that score for the rest of my life.*

Although Broadway tradition decreed that casting for talent was bad for business, de Mille believed blazingly in talent. When Rouben Mamoulian objected to the hiring of Bambi Linn, a brilliant dancer, but — with her small head, long legs, and braces on her teeth — by no stretch of the imagination a chorus girl, de Mille erupted. "If she goes, then I go!" she yelled, and hurled her purse against the back wall to emphasize her strong feelings. Linn not only stayed, she stopped the show.

18 Describing how de Mille worked, Celeste Holm said she would tell an auditioning dancer to "just walk" across the stage; de Mille said many dancers could dance beautifully but walked badly. If they passed the first test, she would give them a step and tell them what she wanted it to mean. If they interpreted it well, she would hire them. If not, loudly and emphatically not.

The first of three tryouts of *Away We Go!* was scheduled for the Shubert Theatre in New Haven, Connecticut, on March 11, 1943, and, as usual, interested theater people from New York — agents, angels, friends, Cassandras, the people Oscar called "grave-diggers" — came up to see it (or rather, to see half of it, because they had to catch the late train back to Manhattan), all eager to offer criticism, comments, and unsolicited advice.

Max Gordon told them they ought to bring the girls on sooner in Act One. Someone else said it needed more comedy. Composer Kurt Weill told them flatly that he did not like it at all; another well-wisher suggested they drop "People Will Say We're in Love." After seeing what was little more than a hastily patched-up version of what the final show would look like, the "grave diggers" went back to Manhattan to spread the savage *bon mot* which, according to Rodgers, was "No legs, no jokes, no tits, no chance." The fact that the verdict ignored the encouraging reaction of the New Haven audience was irrelevant. As La Rochefoucald observed, the misfortune of one's best friends is not always displeasing.

## ST. JAMES THEATRE
**44th ST. W. of BROADWAY** **MATINEES THURS. & SAT.**

The poster for the New York opening of *Oklahoma!* Not exactly informative. Theatre Collection, Museum of the City of New York.

*Oklahoma!* **The principals: Lee Dixon (Will Parker) left in checked jacket; Celeste Holm (Ado Annie);**
**Alfred Drake (Curly) and Joan Roberts (Laurey) in the surrey; Joseph Buloff (Ali Hakim) kneeling;**
**and Betty Garde (Aunt Eller) arms folded, right.** Used by permission of the Rodgers and Hammerstein Organization.

Hardly surprising, then, that at the end of the first performance of "Helburn's Folly," another of the less-than-kind sobriquets given to the show, everyone was convinced it was going to be a disastrous flop. Mamoulian recalled that there was a postmortem at two in the morning and that the general consensus was that the whole ragbag would have to be completely restaged. The director held out for the version they had, and finally convinced them that he was right. He did so by swearing that if he was wrong, he would never ever direct a stage production again.

Dick and Oscar were far too much men of the theater to disregard an affirmation of such faith and strength. They plunged into frantic sessions of rewriting as the show moved to Boston's Colonial Theatre for the second stage of its tryouts. More humor and action were written in, for both were sorely needed. They were also having trouble with the song "Boys and Girls Like You and Me" which Curley and Laurey sang together, ending with a kiss. Then the entire cast came on singing the song and each boy kissed his girl. It just didn't work. "I know the theeng weel feex thees," Mamoulian said. "Pigeons! They weel go across the stage *whoosh-whoosh-whoosh!*"

And the next evening, in the middle of the song, *whoosh-whoosh-whoosh!* the pigeons were released into the auditorium. As they circled and soared between the lights and the stage, throwing huge shadows, everyone froze. The orchestra stopped playing, the cast stopped singing — all except for Alfred Drake who soldiered resolutely on — and there was chaos. The number was cut that night.

One other hugely important change was made. Terry Helburn had expressed regret that there was no song about the land itself in the show, and her idle remark, made while sharing a taxi with Oscar Hammerstein, had stuck in the lyricist's mind. From it burgeoned the song which finally gave the show its name. Whether or not Oscar was aware of or daunted by the fact that well over a hundred songs with the same title had already been written is not recorded, but "Oklahoma" became a catalyst. Originally sung to Laurey by Curly to show he has accepted the change from cowboy to farmer, it was too "big" for the moment. A full cast version with a tap-dance interlude worked even less well. Then "Mamoo" (Mamoulian) came up with a stroke of genius. He marshaled the whole cast together in one long chorus line stretching from stage left to stage right. They threw the song out to the audience, culminating in a rousing, mounting crescendo —

21

Oklahoma,
O - K - L - A
H - O- M - A
Oklaho-o-o-o-o-mah!
"Yeeeoww!!!!"

Yeeeowww!!!! indeed. The show was "in," and they knew it. Based on the extraordinary effect of that finale, the decision was made to rechristen the show *Oklahoma*, but since all the programs for Boston had already been printed, they decided to save the new title for New York. Still called *Away We Go!*, the show opened on March 15 in Boston.

The Boston experience was so rewarding to both Rodgers and Hammerstein that thereafter they made it a point to stage all the pre-Broadway tryouts of their plays in that city. They found the constructive and sympathetic attitude of the critics — Elinor Hughes of the *Times Herald*, Cyrus Durgin of the *Globe,* and, most notably, Elliot Norton of the *Post* — invaluable. They fell in love with the Ritz Hotel and with the city itself. So much so, in fact, that Rodgers was later quoted as saying he wouldn't open anything, not even a can of tomatoes, anywhere else but in Boston.

*Oklahoma!* **The dance in the Skidmore barn — "Territory folks should stick together."**
Theatre Collection, Museum of the City of New York.

The Boston critics predictably found fault with the length of the show; over-running is common with new shows in tryout, and *Away We Go!* was no exception. But the music, the lyrics, and the dancing drew rave notices. The backstage disasters — lead dancer Marc Platt sprained two toes in one of the dances, another girl sprained her arm, and several of the cast actually appeared wearing heavy applications of greasepaint to disguise the fact that they had German measles — weren't even noticed.

Even so, *Away We Go!* was not quite a roaring success. There was competition from a new Vernon Duke musical, *Dancing in the Streets*, starring Mary Martin. Business was brisk, but by no means brisk enough to ensure a sellout for the New York opening. Everyone was still nervous: Was it good enough? Rodgers was like a rock: Yes, it was. Helburn still wanted to fuss and fiddle, de Mille still threatened to blow a fuse, Mamoulian still sought to polish here, refine there, but Dick would have none of it. "Do you know what's wrong with this show?" he asked them, closing down yet another inquest. "*Nothing.* So everybody pipe down and let's go to bed."

*Oklahoma!*, with the exclamation point added at Oscar's suggestion, opened in New York on March 31, 1943, at the St. James Theatre. The curtain went up on an uncluttered stage to reveal a woman churning butter on the porch of a farm. Offstage, a young man's voice sang, in waltz-time, of the bright golden haze on the meadow and the corn as high as an elephant's eye. The first-night audience was stunned, amazed, seduced. From those first few bars of music, it was quite clear the show was a hit. Both Rodgers, standing in the back of the theater with Agnes de Mille, and Hammerstein, sitting in the fifth row with his wife, knew it. "The audience responded to everything," Rodgers said. "Not only could I see it and hear it, I could feel it." Hammerstein agreed. "The glow was like the light from a thousand lanterns," he said. "You could *feel* the glow, it was that bright."

The curtain came down to a thunderous ovation. Up in the box he had reserved for himself and his mother, Larry Hart cheered and stamped and shouted "Bravo!" It must have been heartbreaking for him to realize, as he surely must have, that his partner had finally achieved, without him, everything they had been working toward for so long; but Larry Hart was not capable of envy or malice. He was proud of Rodgers, and he pushed his way through the crowd at the after-show party in Sardi's restaurant and threw his arms around his ex-partner, grinning from ear to ear. He told Rodgers he had never had a better evening at the theater in his life. "This thing will run longer than *Blossom Time*," he predicted, and he was right. Significantly, he did not stay. This was Rodgers's and Hammerstein's success, not his.

There was a party for the members of the cast and production at the elegant Fifth Avenue apartment of Jules Glaenzer, the president of Cartier, and a legendary host to the brightest stars of Broadway. There, they awaited the reviews of the New York critics, for New York newspapers, then as now, came out in the early hours of the morning. The reviews all confirmed Larry Hart's opinion. There was not a single holdout. *The New York Times*'s Lewis Nichols, substituting for Brooks Atkinson, who was still in the service, wrote "Wonderful is the nearest adjective." Burns Mantle of the *Daily News* called *Oklahoma!* "the most thoroughly attractive American musical since *Show Boat*." Wolcott Gibbs of the *New Yorker* confessed he had "nothing but the greatest affection for everyone in it," and that his gratitude was "practically boundless." Every review praised the show in the most glowing terms, and as they came in, Glaenzer rushed across to congratulate Rodgers and to press a celebratory drink on him. Rodgers had no difficulty in refusing. "I want to remember every second of this night," he said. "I'm not going to touch a drop!"

How sweet success was! Soothing balm indeed for those humiliating nights on the penthouse circuit, those ghastly weeks of raising the backing dollars by painful hundreds, those months when he, Oscar, and Rouben Mamoulian alone had kept up the morale of

23

the entire company. He was a steadfast believer that luck plays only a small part in success, but not even Rodgers or his partner could have foreseen how big a success *Oklahoma!* would become. They had a hit, they knew. What they did not yet know was that they had a phenomenon.

It has often been said that one of the important elements in the success of *Oklahoma!* was that it appeared in 1943, a grim period during World War II when both the United States and Britain were reeling as Germany and Japan battered them into retreat after retreat. Certainly that might explain the warmth with which its lyrical escapism was greeted at the premiere; but the appeal of *Oklahoma!* transcended every and any musical show which had been written up to that time. It ran for five years and nine weeks, an astonishing 2,212 performances. No musical had ever approached that figure and none would for another fifteen years.

The story did not end with the New York run, either. Two days after the show closed, touring companies took it on the road, visiting 70 cities over the following year. The national company, formed in 1943, played the show for 10 years, appearing in more than 250 cities and in every one of the (then) 48 states before more than eight million people. Other companies took *Oklahoma!* to Germany, to South Africa, to Denmark, to Sweden, and to Australia. And it is still going strong, with over 600 productions worldwide every year.

At London's Drury Lane Theatre, after what Lawrence Langner described as "the most exciting opening I have ever attended" — the encores went on for well over half an hour — the show went on to break the 287-year-old record for longest run at that establishment, achieving the second-longest run in London's theatrical history: three-and-a-half years. During that time, it was seen by almost three million people. It then withdrew (*Carousel* took its place) to the Stoll Theatre, where it ran for a further six months. And eight years after that remarkable premiere, it was still touring the provinces of England.

In its first decade, *Oklahoma!* produced profits of more than five million dollars for its original backers. The reluctant Sam Behrman's $20,000 eventually produced a return of $6,500,000. Richard Rodgers and Oscar Hammerstein became millionaires. The Theatre Guild pocketed $4,000,000. A one percent investment costing $1000 back in the dark days of New Haven was now worth $50,000. To this astonishing record must be added the honors heaped upon the show. In 1944, *Oklahoma!* received a special citation from the Pulitzer Prize Committee. The show also helped inaugurate a practice which has since become standard in the recording industry, the "original cast" album. Jack Kapp of Decca approached the partners and proposed that the actual cast, conductor, and theater orchestra perform the songs exactly as they did onstage for a Decca recording. "It was the most exciting concept we'd ever heard of," Rodgers said. "Naturally, we consented."

The record set of *Oklahoma!* sold more than a million copies, and this was *before* the advent of the long-playing record, in 1948. The show would also become a launching pad for the careers of a large number of actors and actresses, many of whom were unknown when they first appeared in it. Among them were Celeste Holm, Alfred Drake, Shelley Winters, Howard Keel, Florence Henderson, Isabel Bigley, Iva Withers, and Howard da Silva.

Over the six decades since its creation, *Oklahoma!* has been revived repeatedly, and always successfully. Both Rodgers and Hammerstein were immensely proud of its having achieved the status of an American classic. It needs little imagination to guess how they must have felt when they met for lunch the day after the premiere. On their way, they decided to stroll around to the St. James Theatre and see how business was going, following the rave reviews. To their astonishment, they encountered bedlam. Crowds were pushing and fighting to get to the box office. There was even a policeman trying to keep order, Rodgers recalled. He turned to Oscar and asked whether he would like to go someplace quiet and talk, or whether he'd prefer to go to Sardi's and show off. "Hell, let's go to Sardi's and show off," Oscar said. And they did.

# Oscar

*His work tended to make people think of him as an unsophisticated, platitudinous hick, when in fact he was a highly intelligent, strongly principled, and philosophical man.* — Stephen Sondheim

The accepted perception of Oscar Hammerstein II is that he didn't have a mean bone in his body, was universally loved and admired, and wrote some of the best musicals ever brought to the Broadway stage. Yet always behind the image of the benign, esteemed, and sensationally successful lyrist-librettist (Oscar himself preferred the correct "lyrist" to the more usual "lyricist") lurks a darker half, a person who could be cruel to his children and insensitive to his colleagues; a secretive and even unkind man who preferred to pretend trouble did not exist rather than face it head on, and who certainly contributed his own quota of anomalies to his partnership with Richard Rodgers. Was he really the Pollyanna of the Great White Way that many writers have tried to make him? "No, he was not," his son William once said. "But he tried to be."

His peers seem to have liked and admired him, even Josh Logan, who had every reason not to. "He was a very sensitive, very poetic, very dreamy man," Logan said, "who had many dreams of beautiful things he wanted to do. He had a doggedness, too. He was a delight. He had the most marvelous judgment." "To meet Oscar was to love him," said

Jan Clayton, Oscar's first Julie Jordan. "He wasn't obvious, not a man for small talk. And he had a great sense of humor." "He was so warm and so enthusiastic," costume designer Lucinda Ballard said. "He was a big, tall man, with a big head and wide shoulders; he had a look that my mother always used to call philoprogenitive. Some people say his songs were too sweet. They're not if you knew Oscar. Oscar was like that. His warmth and kindness were genuine. He'd never put on airs like some people do." "Oscar was able to write about dreams and grass and stars because he believed in them," Stephen Sondheim observed. Richard Rodgers agreed. "He always wrote about the things which affected him deeply. What was truly remarkable about him was his never-failing ability to find new ways to reveal how he felt about nature and music and love."

He studied law originally, but there was never much more than a pious hope that he would become a lawyer. His father, William, was the manager of the Victoria Theatre, his uncle, Arthur, was a Broadway producer. His grandfather, after whom he was named, was

a former cigar maker turned flamboyant opera impresario. Small wonder, then, that Oscar Greeley Clendenning Hammerstein became an ardent lover of the theater and remained one all his life. He said he never really knew his paternal grandfather well. That top-hatted, Prince Albert-coated, striped-trousered figure with the goatee and the big cigar was always too busy to spend much time with his grandson. Oscar always said that the longest time he spent with the old boy was a visit to his deathbed, but then, Oscar had a mordant sense of humor.

It was in 1906, when Oscar was eleven years old, that Oscar Hammerstein I decided to challenge the supremacy of the aristocratic Metropolitan Opera by building his own Opera House on West 34th Street and presenting there such modern

27

Oscar Hammerstein I. He was once asked if there was a lot of money in opera. "Yes," he said. "Mine." Author's Collection.

Oscar Greeley Clendenning Hammerstein — "Ock" to his friends — as a young man, "far south of Beau Brummel and nearer Ichabod Crane." Theatre Collection, Museum of the City of New York.

operas as *Louise, Thaïs,* and *Le Jongleur de Notre Dame,* works hitherto excluded from the rigidly classical repertoire of the Met. He imported such talents as Mary Garden, Tetrazzini, Dalmores, Bonci, and Renaud, all of whom had been unable to get a hearing at the Met. Fired by his success, Oscar built another Opera House, this time in Philadelphia, waging war upon the Met's supremacy with a gusto that forced both that organization and his own into heavy losses. Finally, the Metropolitan Opera removed or eliminated Hammerstein's competition by paying him $1,000,000 not to produce opera in the city for a decade. He was once asked if there was a lot of money in the opera business. "Yes," he said. "Mine."

Oscar Hammerstein II — he preferred the suffix to the cumbersome middle names with which he had been burdened — was born in an apartment on 135<sup>th</sup> Street in New York on July 12, 1895. He had a complex and unconventional childhood. He saw little of his father who, although an astute and successful theatrical manager — *The New York Times* called him "the Barnum of vaudeville" — was not a demonstrative man. Oscar's only contact with him was to kiss him goodbye every morning and hello when he came home in the evening. Perhaps not unnaturally, then, he adored his mother, Alice, known to the family as Allie.

Allie Hammerstein was a restless, forceful woman who — perhaps frustrated by her circumscribed middle-class life — made a career out of moving house. In his first fifteen years, Oscar would live in nine different homes in upper Manhattan. When he was five and his brother Reggie — whose inability to say his brother's name bestowed upon Oscar the lifelong nickname of "Ockie" — was three, the family decided to move down to 112<sup>th</sup> Street so that Oscar's mother, always in delicate health, could live in the apartment directly above that of her father, James Nimmo, and his wife Janet. The arrival of Oscar's infant brother had placed such heavy demands on the frail Allie that it was decided Oscar would move downstairs and stay with his grandparents, sleeping in the same bed as his grandmother, an arrangement which lasted for three years.

Although Oscar continued to share meals with his family, his maternal grandfather became his friend and confidant. Nimmo and his wife lived together but, because of an old dalliance Janet Nimmo had learned about and never forgiven, not as man and wife. Every morning, James would make his grandson a punch of eggs and milk laced with whiskey and they would walk first to the candy store and then across to nearby Mount Morris Park (now Marcus Garvey Park), where the old man would sketch — his specialty was foliage. At the top of the hill in the park — the same park, incidentally, where young Dick Rodgers would play a few years later — stood a bell tower. Daily, an elderly man climbed the spiral staircase and tolled the bell by hand. James Nimmo told his grandson that the bell ringer was the Devil, and Oscar believed him so implicitly that he was never again afraid of the Devil — he'd seen him and knew he was a harmless old coot who rang the bell in the park.

At home, Oscar was encouraged to believe he was bright and talented. "Oscar's the genius, Reggie's the clown," his mother would tell people, perhaps even then unknowingly shaping their personalities: Reggie would grow up to be charming but unsuccessful, Oscar successful but not always charming. Soon, he was fired with the ambition to become an actor. He recalled that one of the most vivid memories of his life was a visit as a four-year-old to the Victoria Theatre, the cathedral of vaudeville on 42<sup>nd</sup> Street and 7<sup>th</sup> Avenue built by grandfather Oscar in his pre-opera days and now managed by Oscar's father. Watching the show from a box, the boy was so affected by the lights and the colors and the music (and especially Frank Fogarty singing "You Can't Bunko Me") that he broke out in a cold sweat and felt faint. When he got home, he was feverish and had to be put to bed. But it was the sickness of excitement, an excitement which was to remain with him as long as he lived. "The fact is," he was to say many times, "that I am almost foolishly in love with the stage. The mere sight of a bare stage sends pains up and down my back."

After attending P.S.9 in Manhattan (he had the report cards which confirmed he was "A Good Boy" framed, and kept them all his life), in 1908, at 13, he was sent to the

29

Hamilton Institute, a private school with a partially military curriculum on Central Park West. His first story, *The Adventures of a Penny*, was published in that school's magazine when he was 12. He also edited the magazine at Weingart's Institute, his summer camp in Highmount, New York. There, he made many lifelong friends, among them Lorenz Hart, David and Myron Selznick, Harold Hyman (later Oscar's doctor), and Leighton Brill, who would be Oscar's assistant for more than 20 years.

Oscar's father (his mother had died in the late summer of 1910 and Willie had married Allie's sister, Anna, nicknamed "Mousie") did not encourage his son's artistic inclinations the way his mother had. He insisted the stage was far too uncertain a profession — indeed, made Oscar promise on his word of honor that he would never do anything so foolish as to consider making the theater his living — and enrolled Oscar in the law school at Columbia University. It was just about the worst thing he could possibly have done if he wanted to deflect his son from the theatrical life. For, from the turn of the century to the beginning of the First World War, Columbia University and the area around it, known as Morningside Heights, was one of the most astonishing seedbeds of literary talent in America.

Oscar's classmates and fellow students included Morris Ryskind, among whose later credits would be the libretto of the George and Ira Gershwin show *Of Thee I Sing*, the first musical ever to win a Pulitzer Prize. There was Bennett Cerf, raconteur, writer, and wit, who would be a founder of the publishing empire Random House. There was Herman Mankiewicz, who would create many notable motion picture scenarios, including *Citizen Kane*, and his brother Joe, a future writer and director of such films as *All About Eve, The Barefoot Contessa,* and *Suddenly Last Summer*. There was Howard Dietz, a freckle-faced youngster with a shock of red hair who would somehow successfully marry the tasks of being MGM's publicity supremo and writing lyrics to the music of Arthur Schwartz. There was gnomish Larry Hart, his partnership with Rodgers still a few years ahead, profiting from his fluent German by translating foreign plays. There were Richard L. Simon and Max Lincoln Schuster, publishers in the making, and Mortimer Rodgers, older brother of the tyro composer, who would become a distinguished doctor. There was Herman Axelrod, father of playwright George. Other friends included the three children of Lew Fields, the former renowned comedian who had turned producer: Herbert, Dorothy, and Joseph would all make a not-inconsiderable mark in the theatrical world.

Many of this exalted gaggle of talents spent their spare time — and, one suspects, a lot of time not "spare" at all — writing poetry, lyrics, sketches, plays, columns, newspa-

30

per items, or short articles. The thing was to get your name in print and the most "in" of all "in" things was to have something accepted by "The Conning Tower," a column (or "colyum," as its originator called it) which appeared regularly opposite the editorial pages in the *New York World*, signed simply "FPA." Insiders knew "FPA" was Franklin P. Adams, who specialized in light verse and quips much appreciated by the intelligentsia. His standards were very high, and contributors strove for the honor of being in his column, especially at the top of the "tower" of type. Adams himself spent most of his days playing pool at the Players' Club in Gramercy Park, donating a watch once a year to the contributor whom he considered had sent in the best piece. Not a bad way to run a "colyum" at that; perhaps his use of the word "conning" was ahead of its time. At any rate he attracted some rare talents, each using the convention of a pseudonym. Morris Ryskind was "Morrie," Deems Taylor was "Smeed," and Herman Mankiewicz "Mank." Howard Dietz acknowledged his own "Freckles." Oscar was in heady company indeed, and soon plunged into writing himself.

One of the first things he had done when school started was to join the Columbia University Players. When his Uncle Arthur reminded him somberly of his promise to his father (who had died the preceding summer), Oscar assured him it was just a fun thing, that he still intended to enter law school. And he then went right ahead and appeared in the 1915 Varsity Show *On Your Way* (the same show in which Larry Hart did a befrocked take-off of Mary Pickford, "skipping and bouncing like an electrified gnome") as a long-haired poet à la Bunthorne who, according to the critic of New York's *Evening World,* "danced like Al Jolson and had some original steps and faces of his own. Oscar is a comedian and as a fun-maker he was à la carte, meaning all to the mustard."

After the show, his faculty adviser, Carl Van Doren (who in 1939 would win a Pulitzer Prize for his biography of Benjamin Franklin), called Oscar into his office and asked him what he planned to do after graduation. Oscar told him he was going to be a lawyer, which seemed to disappoint Van Doren. When Oscar asked him what was wrong, Van Doren said, "Oh, nothing, except that I thought you were going to be a writer;" which was precisely what Oscar had been hoping to hear. "I left his office in Hamilton Hall," he said later, "and floated down Morningside Heights filled with an ambition that now seemed more possible than I had ever believed it to be."

The following year, Oscar wrote an additional scene for *The Peace Pirates*, a skit on Henry Ford's World War I peace expedition for which Herman Mankiewicz wrote both book and lyrics. He also did a blackface routine and a comedy dance in a leopard skin, which Lorenz Hart, drama critic for the college newspaper, found "thoroughly original and distinctly funny." It was following this performance that Oscar met Dick Rodgers for the first time. As he later wrote:

> *After the Saturday matinee of this same Varsity Show, while the*
> *ballroom of the Hotel Astor was being cleared for the dancing that*
> *followed ... Morty Rodgers came up to me. He had in tow a boy about*
> *twelve years old, a smaller and darker version of himself, his kid brother,*
> *Dick. As we were being introduced I noted, with satisfaction, young*
> *Richard's respectful awe in the presence of a college junior whom he had*
> *just seen playing one of the chief parts in the Varsity Show. I, too, was*
> *conscious of my current glory, and realizing what a treat it must be for*
> *the child to meet me, I was my most gracious and courteous self —*
> *a man about nineteen trying to be a man about town. Whenever I*
> *made this effort, I always finished far south of Beau Brummel and*
> *much nearer Ichabod Crane.*
>
> *I saw Dick a few more times that year. Morty brought him up to our*
> *fraternity house and I heard him play our bruised and beaten piano. We*
> *all liked him — a cute kid. In my memory of him during this period,*
> *he wore short pants. He tells me now that by that time he had already*
> *put on long pants. All right, but in my memory he wore short pants.*
> *This impression or illusion is never quite absent from my conception*
> *of him. Behind the sometimes too serious face of an extraordinarily*
> *talented composer and a sensationally successful theatrical producer, I see*
> *a dark-eyed little boy in short pants. The frequent overlapping of*
> *these two pictures is an element in what I consider to be my sound*
> *understanding of Dick and my affection for him.*

Rodgers's recollection of Oscar was of a "very tall, skinny fellow with a sweet smile, clear blue eyes, and an unfortunately mottled complexion. He accepted my awkward praise with unaffected graciousness and made me feel my approval was the greatest compliment he could receive." He also recalled that no immortal phrases were uttered, and insists that he was indeed wearing long pants.

In 1917, after transferring to law school, Oscar helped write that year's Varsity Show, *Home James*, and appeared in one scene as a French waiter with the likely name of Dubonnet. The rest of the text was by Herman Axelrod, and the composer was Robert

Lippman, neither of whom pursued a career in theater: Axelrod went into real estate, Lippman became a successful orthopedist. And for a while, at least, it looked like Oscar would become a lawyer. He contacted the firm of Blumenstiel & Blumenstiel, who handled some of his family's legal business, and was taken on as a clerk at five dollars a week, which would have made things tough had he not also had 50 dollars a week coming in from securities given to him by his father. Promoted to the job of process server, he failed miserably and was shifted back to indoor work.

When the United States entered the war, Oscar was quick to volunteer, but he was turned down (underweight) as was Lorenz Hart (undersized). Disappointed that the Army didn't want him, unhappy at the thought of continuing to work for a pittance at Blumenstiel & Blumenstiel, Oscar joined some friends at a house party in Deal Beach, New Jersey. One of the guests there was a tiny, twenty-year-old brunette named Myra Finn who Oscar knew casually (she was a distant cousin of Richard Rodgers). After he got to kiss her hand during a game of spin-the-bottle, Oscar was immediately smitten and decided to ask her father for her hand in marriage. When they met for the first time, Willy Finn looked Oscar up and down and asked him if he was a virgin. When Oscar replied he was, Finn said, "You mean you're going to practice on my daughter?"

Problem: Oscar wasn't earning anything like enough to get married on, so he asked his employers for a raise; they refused. He always felt that if they had not done so, he might very well have stayed on and become a lawyer. As it was, he went to see his Uncle Arthur and asked him for a job — any job. Arthur Hammerstein was big time now: in 1910, after years of managing his father's operatic affairs, he had produced his first Broadway show, Victor Herbert's *Naughty Marietta*. He commissioned Herbert to write another, but when the temperamental Herbert reneged on his contract, Arthur hired the then-unknown Rudolf Friml. The show for which Friml wrote the score became *The Firefly*, one of the most successful of all American operettas.

Once again invoking the promise Oscar had made to his father, Arthur said two generations of Hammersteins in show business were enough. But, why not another? Oscar pleaded: he was not looking for a stopgap job. He wanted to be a Broadway playwright, starting here, starting now. Arthur weakened and finally surrendered, giving Oscar 20 dollars a week in return for his services as assistant stage manager for the Broadway show *You're in Love*. With a book by Otto Harbach and Ed Clark, and music by Rudolf Friml, the show opened on February 6, 1916 and ran for 167 performances. Oscar shifted scenery, helped with the lighting, cued the actors, and did odd jobs, loving every moment of it.

33

On August 22, 1917, he married his sweetheart in her parents' apartment on West End Avenue. Although there would be two children, William, born October 26, 1918, and Alice, born May 17, 1921, it was not to be a successful marriage. Although to begin with, "Mike," as Myra was called, helped Oscar by typing his scripts, his total concentration on his work soon made her feel excluded and she turned to her own social circle. Lively and witty at times, moody and unpredictable at others, Myra could also be stubborn, selfish, and contrary. One friend described her as a woman who, if a window was open, would demand it be shut, and if it was shut, want it open. Oscar reacted to all this unpleasant reality typically: he pretended it did not exist.

After a short honeymoon, Oscar plunged into the four or five productions Arthur Hammerstein was readying for Broadway. "I was an office boy and playreader by day, stage manager by night, and an eager kibitzer at the rehearsals of new shows," he said. Arthur promoted him to full stage manager on another Rudolf Friml musical, this one to star Ed Wynn ("the perfect fool") and Mae West, called *Sometime*. Although the score was largely forgettable, the production clocked up a very respectable 283 performances. One night during the show's run, Mae, who had taken a fancy to him, took Oscar to one side and advised him to quit the theater and go back to the law while he still had the chance, saying "The theater ain't for you, kid. You've got too much class."

No matter how much class the highest-paid woman in America thought he had, Oscar had no intention of returning to the drudgery of the law. Arthur Hammerstein had read a story about a girl whose escape from her tyrannical family leads her to get engaged to a man she doesn't love, then to work in a gambling joint, until she is eventually reunited with her own true love. He asked Oscar if he would like to try making a play out of it. "I would have liked the telephone book if it would get me a production," Oscar said, and in short order completed a four-act tragedy about small-town girls which he called *The Light*. It failed after its fourth performance during its New Haven tryouts before an audience of perhaps 20 people, and is remembered today chiefly for the memorable (if unscripted) scene in that final performance where the ingenue bemoaned the fact that everything was falling down around her at precisely the same moment as her underwear slid down around her ankles.

Realizing he was involved with a total failure, Oscar fled the theater and sought refuge on a bench in a little park nearby. Cursing luck, fate, and ingenues with slack elastic, he suddenly thought of an idea for another show. In what would become his almost automatic response to failure, he began writing it then and there. In the movies, such determined optimism would have been met with instant success, but in real life it was to be two long years before the play Oscar started that day actually opened on Broadway. So it was back to stage managing, still keeping in touch with the Columbia Varsity Shows.

In 1917, Oscar and Myra had set up house in a small apartment on West 121$^{st}$ Street. The following year they moved to a larger place on 122$^{nd}$ Street and West End Avenue, where their first son, William, was born on October 26. A second child, Alice, was born on May 17, 1921. In between those two major events in Oscar's personal life there was another: the death on August 1, 1919, of Oscar Hammerstein I. The funeral service was held at Temple Emanu-El, which was filled to capacity. The pallbearers were the major theatrical figures of the day: David Belasco; George M. Cohan; Sam Harris; the two Shubert brothers; Klaw and Erlanger; Al Woods; Morris Gest; and Percy Williams. World-famous tenor John McCormack sang — fittingly, perhaps — "The Lost Chord." It was an acknowledgment that the Hammersteins were show business royalty, and it would have been all too easy for young Oscar to play his name and connections for all they were worth. Instead, he set out to seriously study his craft.

He had already written the book and lyrics for the 1918 Varsity "War Show" *Ten for Five*, which he also directed. He was on the committee which selected, as the next year's offering, a show by a new team, Richard Rodgers and Lorenz Hart. Rodgers had entered Columbia in the Fall of 1919, and the committee of the Players' Club (Richard Conrad, son of the Metropolitan Opera impresario, Ray Perkins, and Oscar Hammerstein) liked the Rodgers and Hart songs but preferred someone else's libretto. The show, a satire on Bolshevism, had been written by Milton Kroop. Dick and Larry adapted their songs accordingly and somehow — he professed not to know how, unless his membership of the committee had something to do with it — a couple of Hammerstein's lyrics with Rodgers's music were incorporated into the show, *Fly With Me*.

In fact, these songs had been written when Rodgers did his second amateur show, *Up Stage and Down,* for an organization called the Infants' Relief Society. For that show, Morty Rodgers had dragooned both a patient of his father's, named Benjamin Kaye, and Oscar into doing some lyrics. Kaye wrote "Can It" while Oscar contributed "Weaknesses" and "There's Always Room for One More."

On January 5, 1920, Arthur Hammerstein presented *Always You* at the Central Theatre. The score was by Herbert Stothart, book and lyrics by Oscar, its star the delightful Helen Ford (soon to have a stunning success in the first Rodgers and Hart musical, *Dearest Enemy*). The plot, which Oscar readily conceded owed more than a little to *Madame Butterfly*, concerned an American soldier who falls in love with a French girl while serving on the European front, comes home and gets engaged to his former

35

American sweetheart, but returns to France to find true love. Its first title *Joan of Arkansaw* offended the clergy, so it became *Toinette*, in turn discarded because someone thought it was too close to "toilet."

The show's run of 65 performances was somewhat short of sensational, but a six-month tour brightened the picture enough to convince Arthur Hammerstein that all Oscar needed was experience and guidance. To help him gain it, he introduced his nephew to the prolific and highly successful lyricist-librettist Otto Harbach, whose catalog included some big hit songs: "Cuddle Up a Little Closer, Lovey Mine" and "Every Little Movement Has a Meaning of its Own," as well as the lyrics for Rudolf Friml's *The Firefly*, which included the sensational "Sympathy."

36    Otto Harbach was a collaborator, librettist, or lyricist on such supremely American shows as *No, No, Nanette!*, *Sunny Roberta*, and *The Desert Song*. He died in 1963 at the fine old age of 89. Author's Collection.

Born Otto Hauerbach in Salt Lake City, Utah, on August 1, 1873, he graduated from Knox College and taught English and public speaking. He came to New York intending to study for a doctorate at Columbia University. At the age of 29 he went to work for a newspaper and then an advertising agency before breaking into the theater with a show called *Three Twins*, which opened on June 15, 1908 (the traditional date for separating theatrical seasons), and was an immediate success, closing after a run of 288 performances.

Although he was 22 years Oscar's senior, Harbach was more than willing to work with Arthur's nephew (as, in later years, Oscar would work with and encourage a young lyricist-composer named Stephen Sondheim). He suggested they bring in Frank Mandel, a nervy, intense redhead who was an expert in situation comedy. Arthur Hammerstein teamed the writers with composer Herbert Stothart and the result was *Tickle Me*, a vehicle for vaudeville comedian Frank Tinney, whose task was pretty much to play Frank

Tinney all evening. The tryouts in Long Branch, New Jersey were a disaster: when a very special "special effect'" refused to function, Tinney stepped before the footlights and told the audience "This next scene won't work, so you won't see it. I just wanted you to know the boy and girl do get together. So now you can go home."

After some frenzied reworking, which included a whole new second act written in 24 hours, *Tickle Me* opened at the Selwyn Theatre on August 17, 1920. Its plot was a nonsense about a movie company on location in Tibet. Sumptuous set-pieces such as "The Ceremony of the Sacred Bath" and an abundance of highly unlikely characters were apparently exactly the right ingredients. In 1920, no one went to see a musical expecting an intellectual evening, and *Tickle Me* went some distance out of its way to avoid providing one. It ran for a very lucrative seven months, with an additional profitable road tour.

Flushed with success and bursting with enthusiasm, Oscar sat down and wrote four straight flops in a row. The first was *Jimmie,* which ran for 71 performances. A collaboration with Mandel called *Pop* died out of town. ("I loved it," Oscar said. "Nobody else did.") *Daffy Dill,* another Frank Tinney extravaganza, duplicated the dismal record of *Jimmie,* and 1922's *Queen o' Hearts,* a vehicle for Nora Bayes (with interpolations of her own songs), managed — even with Norma Terris and Harry Richman, both protégés of the star, in the cast — to do even worse: 39 performances. Not that the failures were entirely Oscar's. His collaborators on *Jimmie* were Harbach and Frank Mandel, on *Daffy Dill,* the deft and usually reliable Guy Bolton, and, on the third show, Mandel again. Even so, this two-year cycle of failure impressed upon Oscar a truth he never forgot, a maxim of his grandfather Oscar's that there was no limit to the number of people who would stay away from a bad show.

It was beginning to look as though Arthur Hammerstein's faith in his nephew had been misplaced. Out of five shows written by Oscar, only one had been successful — and only mildly successful at that. The other four had achieved a combined run of only 213 performances, just six more than *Tickle Me.* The following year, however, his luck changed. He and Harbach put together something Oscar called, "a timid attempt to bring back operetta, but still keeping enough of Cinderella and her dancing chorus to compromise with the public who demanded those elements." The plot, which dealt with an Italian heiress who will inherit millions provided she does not lose her temper for six months, was hardly likely to strain anyone's brain, but that was what sold tickets in 1922. The name they gave the show was *Wildflower.*

Herbert Stothart was again on hand to provide songs, but this time there was an important addition to the musical side of the collaboration, a talented newcomer to the Broadway theater named Vincent Youmans. A shy young genius whose constant illnesses gave him the undeserved reputation of being cold and distant, he was just 25 when he began to work on *Wildflower*. He had served in the Navy during the recent war, and then worked his way into the theater via a well-trodden path: song-plugger for T. B. Harms, the music publishers, and rehearsal pianist — mostly for Victor Herbert operettas — until he was befriended by George Gershwin, who was exactly one day younger than himself. Gershwin persuaded producer Alex Aarons to take a chance on the newcomer, much as he had a year earlier on Gershwin himself. Aarons brought in Fred Jackson, who had written George's first show, *La La Lucille!*, to write another, *Two Little Girls in Blue*, and hired Youmans as co-composer with Paul Lannin. The lyrics were by Arthur Francis (George's brother Ira was still too shy to yet come out from behind this pseudonym). The show was a hit, and Youmans was on his way.

Badly in need of a hit, Arthur Hammerstein had first invited Rudolf Friml to write the score, but Friml did not wish to collaborate. Max Dreyfus, the influential owner of T. B. Harms, recommended Youmans, and it worked: his uncluttered musical ear and youth are discernible throughout the score. With its Italian setting, with dark-haired, wide-eyed beauty Edith Day as its star, and with the title song and a catchy, rhythmic ballad called "La Bambalina," which became very popular, the show was a 15-month, 477-performance success and its young authors were wealthily on their way.

**Rudolf Friml. Famous for "The Donkey Serenade," he got his start in the theater when Victor Herbert refused to have anything further to do with a tempermental actress in one of Arthur Hammerstein's shows.** American Society of Composers, Authors, and Publishers.

Youth was flooding into the musical theater, bringing to it a sparkle, gaiety, and freshness which would soon sweep away the old "Viennese" operetta traditions that had been slowly smothering it with sweetness. These young men were audacious and proud of that audacity. Twenty-year-old George Gershwin had led the way in 1919 with *La La Lucille!* Oscar was just 24 when he wrote his first musical, *Always You*. Youmans was 21, and Ira Gershwin, 24, when they collaborated on *Two Little Girls in Blue*. Howard Dietz was 28 when he wrote all the lyrics for Jerome Kern's *Dear Sir* in 1924. Two years later, his partner-to-be, Arthur Schwartz, encouraged by the 29-year-old Lorenz Hart, contributed songs to *The Grand Street Follies*. Hart himself was only 25, and Richard Rodgers the baby of them all at 18, when they were represented for the first time on Broadway in 1920's *Poor Little Ritz Girl*.

For all its success (it actually ran longer than *No, No, Nanette!*) and the financial independence that it gave him, Oscar looked upon *Wildflower* as just a starting point. He minded not at all that he was reaping a healthy reward from a tradition that he was trying to break away from — he saw himself as a craftsman using whatever materials came his way. But he was already becoming convinced that the day of

Vincent Youmans, who wrote *Wildflower* with Oscar Hammerstein II, but is best remembered for *No, No, Nanette!* and *Hit the Deck*. He died April 5, 1946, aged 47, the same age as Larry Hart and just as tragic a loss to the musical theater. He left behind over 175 unpublished songs. American Society of Composers, Authors, and Publishers.

the Viennese-style operetta was almost over, and began thinking about ways to create an *American* show that would have depth and realism in its story, while remaining engaging and melodically fertile. But, Oscar's theories aside, the truth was that what producers wanted was more of the same, and then more of the same. So when Arthur Hammerstein proposed a reunion of the *Wildflower* team, it was back to the Cinderella storyline for another show with Youmans called *Mary Jane McKane*, with Stothart once more providing additional music and William Cary Duncan (who would later help create the Youmans smash *Great Day*) collaborating on book and lyrics. Originally called *Plain Jane* and drastically rewritten on the road, the show produced no hits. Indeed, it is remembered more now for the songs from its score that reappeared in other guises: "Come On and Pet Me," dropped before the Christmas Day, 1923, New York opening, took on a whole new life a year or two later as "Sometimes I'm Happy." Another number, "My Boy and I," got a new Harbach lyric and became the title song for the 1925 hit *No, No, Nanette!*

Oscar missed the premiere of *Mary Jane McKane* because he was in Springfield, MA, polishing up *Gypsy Jim*, a non-musical play he had written with a Columbia classmate,

Milton Gropper. It was about an eccentric millionaire who spends his time restoring people's faith in themselves, and lasted only 39 performances. Hard on its heels, *New Toys*, another Gropper-Hammerstein play which boasted the subtitle "A Comic Tragedy of Married Life after the Baby Arrives," suffered a like fate. Apart from its "immaturity, technical inexperience, and general unintelligence" (Percy Hammond, *Tribune*), the real fault with the play was "that with all its surface pretense of realism, it is plain buncome (sic) through and through." (John Corbin, *The New York Times*). It tottered along for three weeks and then died, in the process putting an end to Oscar's playwriting ambitions for a while, although, paradoxically, it became the first work of his to be made into a motion picture.

It had been a year of intense effort; one major hit, *Wildflower*, and one minor — *Mary Jane McKane* ran for a respectable 151 performances. There were further triumphs ahead, but there were tensions, too. Although the Hammersteins had a beautiful new home in Great Neck, Long Island, there was a growing alienation between Oscar and his wife; they quarreled a lot and held widely differing views on life. It is hard not to conclude that he used his work as a hiding place, somewhere he did not need to face these realities. Billy Hammerstein, then five years old, recalled that at this time his father often slept on the spare bed in his room. "He wasn't there every night but it was always with eagerness that I'd wake up in the morning to see if he was in the bed so I could play with him."

Early in 1924, Arthur Hammerstein — who loved spectacular stage effects and had aspirations towards the glittering Ziegfeld style — heard that the city of Quebec held an annual ice carnival whose climax was the melting of a huge ice palace. What an idea for a musical! What a finale! Despite the fact that he had not the remotest idea of how such a spectacle might be effected on stage, or into what kind of story it might be incorporated, Arthur dispatched Oscar to Quebec with instructions to check out the carnival. Oscar dutifully plodded up to the Canadian city, and sadly reported that there was not and never had been any such event in Quebec (or anyplace else) within living memory. Arthur told him not to worry, but to write some other story set in Canada now that he'd been up there and seen it. The result of this inspired command was *Rose Marie*.

The story was a major departure from the usual musical comedy fluff — Oscar often recalled how people laughed at him when he said he was going to try to write a musical with a murder in it — and, although far from perfect, contained elements rarely found in a 1920s musical show. Heroine (Rose Marie La Flamme) loves Hero (rough and ready trapper and miner Jim Kenyon), but is desired by Villain (city slicker Edward Hawley).

40

Jim is (falsely) accused of murder. Rose Marie strikes a bargain: if her brother Emile promises not to give Kenyon up to the Mounties, she will do as he wishes and marry Hawley. There are many more complications until the wedding is stopped by a dramatic last-minute confession by the Indian maiden, Wanda, that she committed the murder to protect the man she loves — Hawley. And how's this for a finale? Disconsolate Jim, sitting alone in the mountains of Kootenay, singing the plaintive "Indian Love Call," when, from far, far below, Rose Marie's voice replies.

Harbach reported that it took a long time to get the story on its feet and you can see how it might have. While he and Oscar were working on the book, Rudolf Friml begged Arthur to let him write the score. Arthur agreed, but only on condition that Friml agree to work with Herbert Stothart. This time Friml agreed. As the score was put together, Arthur set out to coax opera star Mary Ellis — who had but recently quit the Met for a dramatic career, and made no bones about the fact that she was through with singing — on to the musical stage. She recalled that she was appearing with Katherine Cornell and Lowell Sherman in *Casanova* when Arthur asked her to come and see him (although perhaps, since that play opened in September 1923 and ran only 78 performances, it is more likely to have been the equally unsuccessful 1924 Grace George and Laura Hope Crews comedy *Fantastics*).

"I was very highbrow, very young, and very ambitious," she said, "and I didn't want at all to go into what I thought was then the lesser musical world." At Hammerstein's office, where she met Oscar for the first time, she observed, "a very tall, thin young man who jumped out of the chair and looked at me with the most wonderful eyes I have ever seen — gentle, kind, the inner radiance just poured out of his eyes, which I think was the thing that people remember most about Oscar." Oscar outlined the story and his enthusiasm caught her up in it. "We were very serious about it," Ellis remembered. "Every lyric, every idea. We worked like Trojans."

Spectacularly staged and magnificently sung, *Rose Marie* opened at the Imperial Theatre on September 2, 1924, and became an instantaneous, enormous success. It ran for more than a year — 557 performances — in New York, four touring companies played it across the United States, and the show was even more successful in London, running for two years at the Drury Lane Theatre. It remained London's most successful Broadway show until *Oklahoma!* twenty years later (by another remarkable coincidence, both shows cost exactly the same to finance). In Paris, *Rose Marie* became a long-running phenomenon with 1250 performances. It would be revived endlessly, filmed three times by MGM (although none of the movie versions bore much resemblance to the original),

41

Jerome David Kern (1885–1945). He inspired Gershwin and Rodgers to become composers.
Sharp-tongued and quick-humored, he "played the piano with no particular flair. In fact, what he did to his
own tunes was sheer murder, " said Arthur Schwartz. American Society of Composers, Authors, and Publishers.

and eventually grossed millions in royalties for Oscar.

*Rose Marie* was different in many ways from the usual musical. With Dennis King and
William Kent in the leads, and with Ellis looking stunningly beautiful — "the peer of any
musical show star in this country," said critic Arthur Hornblow — the show marked a
major breakaway from standard Broadway fare. As well as pioneering a storyline involving murder, *Rose Marie* attempted the innovative form of integrating the dialogue, lyrics,
and music so that they became indivisible. This was not, as anyone who has seen the show
knows, completely successful — for one thing, there were too many "specialty" interpolations marring its flow. Nevertheless, its authors felt it worthwhile to insert a program note
that the musical numbers were so integral to the action that they would not be listed

separately. This marked a clear indication of the direction in which Oscar Hammerstein wanted to go, as was something he wrote at the end of an article in *Theatre Magazine* the following year. "Is there," he asked, "a form of musical play tucked away somewhere... which could attain the rights of grand opera and still keep sufficiently human to be entertaining?"

There was; but it would be a little while longer before he found it. On May 24, 1924, the godfather of the operetta tradition, Victor Herbert of "Kiss Me Again," "I'm Falling in Love With Someone," and "A Kiss in the Dark," died at age 65. One of his more enduring legacies to music was his part in founding the American Society of Composers, Authors, and Publishers (ASCAP) in 1914 to ensure that its members would receive whatever royalties were due them. Herbert had brought a case against a New York restaurant called Shanley's, which had played one of his songs, "Sweethearts (Can Live on Love Alone)," without permission. The case went all the way to the Supreme Court, which finally decided in Herbert's favor, thus establishing ASCAP's power.

Oscar Hammerstein I had produced Victor Herbert's musical *Naughty Marietta* ("Ah, Sweet Mystery of Life"), and his namesake grandson attended Herbert's funeral, where he was introduced to Jerome Kern. Then 39, Kern was justly revered by every other songwriter in the business, and was at the height of his fame and success as composer of the famous Princess Theatre musicals, which began in the following way.

In 1914 it was the "big" shows in the big theaters that were attracting all the ticket buyers, and F. Ray Comstock, owner of the tiny (299-seat) Princess Theatre, was having trouble finding suitable attractions for it. He mentioned his problem to a literary agent named Elizabeth "Bessie" Marbury, who suggested trying musicals. Comstock agreed and hired Marbury as his co-producer, acceding to her suggestion that they employ Guy Bolton and Jerome Kern to do book, lyrics, and music.

Kern, a tireless innovator, had been waiting for just such an opportunity. He wanted to do musicals with modern stories, with comic but believable situations, and without spectacular casts and scenery. None of your *Chocolate Soldiers* and *Merry Widows* with their casts of hundreds — he wanted the Princess musicals to have a maximum of 30 in the cast, with only 11 instruments in the orchestra. Not that there was much choice anyway, given the tiny stage and orchestra pit. By using only two sets they could cut costs even further, making the musicals profitable. Far more important to Kern, however, was that, for the first time, he would have a hand in putting together libretti which would introduce his songs logically into the action, instead of hanging them on the plot like socks on a washing line. It is not hard to see why he and Hammerstein hit it off.

The first Kern-Bolton collaboration was *Nobody Home*, which opened at the Princess on April 20, 1915. The reviews were distinctly encouraging, as was the show's four-month run. The second show, *Very Good Eddie*, which opened on December 23, became a substantial success, running for 341 performances. At the opening night, Kern ran into an old London friend, author Pelham Granville Wodehouse, or "Plum," as everyone called him. Plum had provided a couple of lyrics for songs Kern had written for a London show, *The Beauty of Bath*. They celebrated their reunion by forming a partnership to write musicals with Bolton and lost no time in getting to work.

In 1917 alone they wrote four: *Have a Heart, Oh, Boy!, Leave it to Jane*, and *Miss 1917*. *Have a Heart* was supposed to have followed *Very Good Eddie* into the Princess, but due to a mix-up it had to be given to another producer, Colonel Henry W. Savage. He must have lived up to his name when Bolton, Wodehouse, and Kern put *Oh, Boy!* into the Princess, where it racked up a terrific run of 463 performances and produced the big Kern hit "Till the Clouds Roll By," while *Have a Heart* staggered out of Savage's Liberty Theatre after only 76 performances.

*Love O' Mike*, running simultaneously at the Shubert Theatre, hit a total of 192 performances. On August 26, the trio unveiled *Leave It To Jane,* which managed a respectable 167 performances. Their next, *Miss 1917*, was a flop, despite a cast which included Lew Fields, Andrew Tombes, and the ravishing Vivienne Segal. On February 1, 1918, the triumvirate opened the final Princess Theatre show, *Oh, Lady, Lady!*, which again starred Vivienne Segal. They had seldom written anything better. During the tryouts, a torch song called "Along came Bill" written for Segal had to be dropped; it would prove, when its lyric was reworked by Oscar some years later, one of the most enduring of all Kern's songs.

The Princess Theatre shows were the first real step towards a truly American musical theater, even if two of its midwives were English. The three men were celebrated in a well-known poem written by an unknown admirer, said to have been B. G. "Buddy" de Sylva.

This is the trio of musical fame:
Bolton and Wodehouse and Kern.
Better than anyone else you can name:
Bolton and Wodehouse and Kern.
Nobody knows what on earth they've been bitten by.
All I can say is I mean to get lit an' buy
Orchestra seats for the next one that's written by
Bolton and Wodehouse and Kern.

There was something eminently fitting — and eminently timely — in Kern's meeting Oscar Hammerstein at the grave of Victor Herbert. Not only did both of them have a great deal in common, but both were, in a way, at a crossroads in their careers. Kern had just had a big success with *Sally*, a Ziegfeld show starring Marilyn Miller and whose score included "Look For the Silver Lining," and had also scored a trio of shows for producer Charles Dillingham: *Good Morning, Dearie* (347 performances), *The Bunch and Judy* (63), and *Stepping Stones* (241), none of which had produced a hit song. *Sitting Pretty*, his latest effort with Bolton and Wodehouse, a vehicle originally intended for a popular vaudeville act called the Duncan Sisters, had opened on April 8 and was not doing well. Kern was discovering that, in spite of his success with the Princess musicals, producers like Dillingham, Ziegfeld, and Colonel Savage cared little for his ideas of how musicals should be constructed. They wanted comedy songs, novelty songs, or love songs. Most of all, what they wanted were "hit" songs that would bring people to see the shows, and Kern had to go along with them or not work.

Early in 1925, Oscar had gone to London to supervise the English production of *Rose Marie*, then to Paris, where he began work on a new book. When he got back to New York, however, he discovered that producer Charles Dillingham wanted another ornate vehicle for Marilyn Miller which would capitalize on (and hopefully eclipse) her success in Ziegfeld's *Sally*. He had signed Miller, Jack Donahue, Clifton Webb, and Cliff "Ukelele Ike" Edwards, and he gave the job of writing the book and lyrics to Harbach and Hammerstein, with Jerome Kern to supply the music. Shelving Oscar's unfinished project, the trio set to work immediately on the new show.

Considering some of the obstacles the authors had to overcome, the collaboration turned out to be much more successful than it might have been. One day, for instance, Dillingham called Oscar into his office and asked him to outline the plot for Miller. Oscar explained the whole thing, acting out scenes, dialogue, specimen lyrics, comedy routines, the works. Sunny (Miller) is a circus rider who is in love with American Tom (Paul Frawley). When Tom has to return to the States, Sunny doesn't have enough money to follow him. Her ex-husband suggests a way: they can remarry, go to New York together, and then divorce again. Mistrusting him, Sunny stows away on a ship, is caught, and has to marry Tom's best friend Jim Deming (Jack Donahue) to avoid being put in the brig. Of course it all works out happily in the end.

Throughout this performance Miller sat silent. Then a gleam of something approaching intelligence lit her eye. "Mr. Hammerstein," she said, "when do I do my tap specialty?" Before Oscar could reply, Dillingham stepped in. "No problem, Marilyn," he said,

"Oscar will work it into the book." As indeed, later, he did; not to mention Ukelele Ike's specialty numbers (both of them interpolations), which had to be performed precisely between ten o'clock and ten-fifteen so Edwards could catch the last train home. It's hardly any wonder that, despite its success, neither Hammerstein nor Kern ever really liked the show.

*Sunny* had a shorter run than *Sally*, but in many ways a better score. It is possible, in the lyrics of this show, to see Oscar Hammerstein blossoming for the first time as a lyrist, notably in the stirring "Who? (Stole My Heart Away)" — try to think of another word that could fill that long, long first note. (And ask yourself: Could it have been Oscar, rather than Dick Rodgers, who had the idea of making the first note of "Oklahoma!" exactly the same length?) Also typical are the charming "answer" song "D'ye Love Me?," which manages to transcend its repetitiousness (all those "oo" endings), and his lyric for Kern's rushing title song, a further example of his growing assurance. Nevertheless, when Oscar finally got around to publishing a book of his lyrics in 1949, he punctiliously avoided including any of the songs from *Sunny* — indeed, anything earlier than *Show Boat* — because everything prior had been written in collaboration with Otto Harbach, "the kindest, most tolerant, and wisest man I have ever met."

46 Dillingham hired Kern again to do *The City Chap,* this time with a book by James Montgomery and lyrics by Anne Caldwell, but the show was a flop. Oscar and Harbach, meanwhile, teamed up again with Herbert Stothart to do the story Oscar had been working on in Paris. Produced by Arthur Hammerstein, with music by Stothart and George Gershwin (replacing Rudolf Friml, who had again balked at Arthur's contractual demands), the very "Rooshian" *Song of the Flame* ran foul of Oscar's fatal home-run/strike-out record (otherwise known as "Hammerstein's Disease"), and lasted less than six months, although a successful 1930 film from First National starring Bernice Claire and Alexander Gray saved the team's financial bacon. The idea of a further Gershwin-Hammerstein collaboration seems never to have been seriously examined — George was already working with his brother Ira on the musical *Tip-Toes* — but it remains a fascinating historical might-have-been.

The hit-or-miss cycle continued. In the latter half of 1926, Oscar Hammerstein and Otto Harbach wrote two shows almost back to back — so much so, in fact, that although they agreed to share the credit on both, Otto worked almost exclusively on the first, *The Wild Rose,* a Ruritanian romance produced by Arthur Hammerstein at the Martin Beck Theatre on October 20, 1926, while Oscar concentrated his efforts on the second, known at this stage as *Lady Fair*. Despite a score by Rudolf Friml, handsome Joseph

Urban sets, and dances by a bright new choreographer named Busby Berkeley, *The Wild Rose* was a 61-performance flop. The second show, however, unveiled at the Casino just 29 days after *The Wild Rose*, was an instantaneous, roaring success. It was now called *The Desert Song*.

In writing his book, Oscar had taken topicality to the extreme. The revolt of the Riffs, under the leadership of the Berber Abd-el Krim, against the French protectorate in Morocco, had been making headlines for years and still was. Then, while Oscar was writing the book, Rudolf Valentino, world-famous for his portrayal of the title role in *The Sheik*, died. Oscar added the romantic elements of that film and others from the popular 1920 Douglas Fairbanks film *The Mark of Zorro* and its 1925 sequel *Son of Zorro*. The plot of *The Desert Song* concerned

Sigmund Romberg — "Rommie" — wrote hit shows for more than four decades: they included *Blossom Time, The Desert Song, The New Moon* and *Up in Central Park.* He was also famous for the way he massacred the English language. He once told a difficult actress, "The trouble with you, Miss, is you haven't got enough shows behind your belt!" He died in 1951 at the age of sixty-nine.

American Society of Composers, Authors, and Publishers.

47

the romance between Pierre Birabeau (Robert Halliday), the son of a governor of a French Moroccan province, and Margaret Bonvalet (Vivienne Segal), who scorns his amiable foppishness until she discovers he is also the legendary Red Shadow, freedom fighter and leader of the Riffs. The usual complications ensue, but true love conquers all again.

Working with Sigmund Romberg was an important step forward for Oscar, but not an easy one; the task required him to work harder and hone his skills finer than he had ever done before. The first day that he brought the composer a finished lyric, Romberg — who had a seemingly inexhaustible supply of melodies — led him to another room, gave him paper and pencil, and told him to write another. Reluctant to appear unable to deliver, he did as he was bidden and finished another song that afternoon. Romberg played the melody and nodded approvingly on his first hearing of the words. "It fits," he said. Disappointed at first at such limited approval, Oscar "learned later that what he meant was not merely that the words fitted the notes, but that they matched the spirit of his music and that he thought they were fine."

***Show Boat*** (1927): The show within the show on board *The Cotton Blossom.*
Cap'n Andy Hawks (Charles Winninger) is seated, left. Magnolia (Norma Terris) and Raveenal
(Howard Marsh) are onstage in "The Parson's Bride," giving it their all. Author's Collection.

Born in Hungary in 1887, Romberg had studied the violin as a young boy, then gave up music at the behest of his parents for a career as an engineer. While studying in Vienna he moonlighted as assistant manager at the Theater-an-der-Wien, the city's leading venue for operetta. He moved to London and then to New York, where he worked as a pianist and then a "gypsy" orchestra leader in Bustanoby's restaurant for 15 dollars a week and all the goulash he could eat. His first show was a 1914 Shubert Winter Garden extravaganza called *The Whirl of the World*, but he hit his not-inconsiderable stride with *Maytime* in 1919, the hugely successful *Blossom Time* in 1921, and perennially successful *The Student Prince* three years later.

A vastly sentimental man with an uncertain command of the English language that resulted in what were known in the trade as "Rommyisms" (he once told Jerry Kern, who was wearing a loud, checked suit, that he looked like a race course trout), Romberg was sometimes less than respectful of the art of the lyricist. One of Oscar's favorite stories about him concerned an evening when Romberg and Kern were partners in a bridge game and, knowing one trump was still out, Kern tried to hint how Rommy should play his hand by humming "One Alone." Romberg didn't get it, and they lost the game. Vastly annoyed — he took his cards seriously — Kern leaned over the table and said, "You dumb Dutchman, what did you think I was humming?" "One of my songs," Romberg replied. "Yes, but *which* song?" Romberg shrugged. "Who knows from lyrics?"

Surprisingly, in view of its subsequent success, *The Desert Song* met with a very mixed critical reception on its first appearance, and it was a full month before it really caught on. Indeed, one critic began his review by saying that the question of how simpleminded the book of a musical comedy could be had been debated (in *The Desert Song*) and that the answer was "No end!" There was some justice in this: to contemporary eyes and ears the plot creaks, the dialogue is corny, the comedy both unfunny and obtrusive. But the songs, those florid, sweeping, grandiose Romberg melodies were, and remain, irresistible.

*The Desert Song* made a fortune for everyone involved in it. It ran for well over a year in New York, and succeeded *Rose Marie* at London's Drury Lane where it clocked up a run of 432 performances. It has been revived time and again, filmed three times, and remains a firm favorite of amateur dramatic societies the world over, a sure-fire guarantee of full houses. Wealthy, successful, and with a brand-new $145,000 home on exclusive Shore Drive in Great Neck, Oscar Hammerstein must have felt that he had finally arrived. So it was probably just as well he didn't know what lay ahead.

In the autumn of 1926, Doubleday published Edna Ferber's novel, *Show Boat*, to ecstatic reviews. Reading it, Jerome Kern was fired by its possibilities as a musical. Here was what he had been looking for, something different, solid, adult, and new. He and Oscar Hammerstein had already agreed that if the right vehicle came along they would collaborate again. He called Hammerstein. "Oscar," he said, "I want us to do a show from a book I haven't even finished reading. It's by Edna Ferber and it has a million-dollar title." Oscar read the book and was as enthusiastic about *Show Boat* as the composer, so Kern sat right down and wrote a letter to Edna Ferber saying he would like to turn her novel into a musical. Ferber, who had just won the Pulitzer Prize for her earlier novel *So Big*, refused point blank.

Undaunted, persistent, impatient, Kern pursued his dream. At the opening of his newest show, *Criss-Cross* on October 12, he spotted critic and columnist Alexander Woollcott, a friend of Ferber's and, like her, a member of the chintzy "Round Table Club" at the Algonquin Hotel on West 44th Street. Ignoring the woman Woollcott was talking to, he grabbed Woollcott's arm and implored him to find a way of introducing him to Ferber.

Woollcott — a ham from the top of his head to the soles of his feet — pursed his lips and pretended to think about it for a few moments before condescending that it might

49

**Florenz Ziegfeld: He sued grandfather Oscar for "uncalled-for humiliation" (nothing personal — he sued everyone). And died owing more than a million dollars.** Author's Collection.

— just might — be arranged. As Kern blurted his thanks, Woollcott, waggishly savoring his moment, turned to the woman with whom he had been talking and said with a flourish, "Ferber, this is Jerome Kern. Jerry, this is Edna Ferber."

Peering owlishly at her over his spectacles and talking very fast, Kern, with Woollcott's assistance, managed to talk her into meeting him the next day to more fully discuss musicalizing *Show Boat*. Within an hour of that meeting he and Oscar had Ferber's agreement and on November 17, Ferber signed a contract giving Kern and Hammerstein "dramatico-musical rights" to *Show Boat*, the play to be "ready for delivery to the Producer on or about January 1, 1927."

Enter Florenz Ziegfeld. He deserves a better book than those which have been written about him, but this cannot be it. Tyrannical, impossible, extravagant, probably the most flamboyant and outrageous theatrical producer of them all, he lived in the manner of a Renaissance prince, spending money he often did not have on lavish, spectacular shows "glorifying the American girl" which were, with some accuracy, called "Follies." Driving, ruthless, yet utterly charming when he wanted to be, Ziegfeld was an insatiable womanizer whose private life was a disaster. His rivalries were bitter and his revenges cruel.

Notoriously bad at handling people, especially songwriters, the preceding year he had outraged the highly successful team of Rodgers and Hart by interpolating an Irving Berlin song into their score for a show called *Betsy*, and leaving them to find out on opening night that he had done so. They never forgave him. There is also a story that when Irving Berlin had finished his score for one of the early *Ziegfeld Follies*, Ziegfeld insisted that there wasn't a hit in the score and he wanted one, *right now*. Berlin pleaded that he was written out and hadn't got another melody in him. Whereupon Ziegfeld locked him in a room and wouldn't let him out until he came up with a hit song. Berlin obliged with "A Pretty Girl is Like a Melody," which became the anthem of the *Ziegfeld Follies*.

This was the man to whom Kern and Hammerstein had brought *Show Boat* and, in true Ziegfeld fashion, he dealt from the bottom of the pack. "Boys," he said, "I want this show to open my new theater in February, so you're going to have to work fast." This was a substantial inducement; everyone knew the new Ziegfeld Theatre, designed by Joseph Urban, was going to be the finest musical auditorium in the country and the first show into it was almost guaranteed success. But what Ziegfeld *didn't* tell them was that he had said exactly the same words to Guy Bolton and Fred Thompson, who were writing the book, and Harry Tierney and Joe McCarthy, who were writing the score, of a show called *Rio Rita*.

If Ziegfeld felt any shame, he gave no sign of it. Without bothering to check with the writers, he announced that rehearsals of *Show Boat* would commence in the spring with Elizabeth Hines playing Magnolia, Guy Robertson as Ravenal, and Paul Robeson as Joe. Although they had already written some songs and an outline libretto, Kern and Hammerstein managed to convince him the work was simply not ready for production and the performers were released (although Hines would instigate a spiteful breach of contract suit against Ziegfeld which he defended vigorously — and won). *Rio Rita* — which had always been Ziegfeld's first choice to open his new theater — was completed long before *Show Boat* and when it opened to rave reviews on February 2, 1927, Ziggy opted for a Florida vacation and told Hammerstein and Kern to put their show on hold. It was high-handed and they were "damn sore," but there it was.

51

But then, stories of Ziegfeld's high-handedness are legion, and his relationship with Oscar was at best uncertain. He had no great admiration for the Hammersteins. Early in his career, he had entered into a bitter and costly rivalry with grandfather Oscar Hammerstein over the professional services of Ziegfeld's discovery (and mistress) Anna Held, a rivalry which culminated in a lawsuit. Both men ultimately abandoned the suit, since neither could afford to pursue it, but Ziegfeld was like the Bourbon courtiers, he forgot nothing and learned nothing. As a result, sketches ridiculing old Oscar frequently found their way into Ziegfeld shows.

On vacation or not, Ziegfeld always took care of business. In March 1927, while at Palm Beach, he sent a long cable to Kern which expressed his reservations about Oscar. He liked Kern's music for *Show Boat*, but he was unhappy with the book, which he felt was sprawling and disappointing.

I FEEL HAMMERSTEIN NOT KEEN ON MY DOING
SHOW BOAT. I AM VERY KEEN ON DOING IT ON
ACCOUNT OF YOUR MUSIC BUT HAMMERSTEIN BOOK
IN PRESENT SHAPE HAS NOT GOT A CHANCE EXCEPT
WITH CRITICS BUT THE PUBLIC NO AND I HAVE
STOPPED PRODUCING FOR CRITICS AND EMPTY
HOUSES. I DON'T WANT BOLTON OR ANYONE ELSE IF
HAMMERSTEIN CAN AND WILL DO THE WORK.
IF NOT THEN FOR ALL CONCERNED WE SHOULD HAVE
SOMEONE HELP. HOW ABOUT DOROTHY DONNELLY
OR ANYONE YOU SUGGEST OR HAMMERSTEIN
SUGGESTS. I AM TOLD HAMMERSTEIN NEVER DID
ANYTHING ALONE. HIS PRESENT LAYOUT TOO SERIOUS
NOT ENOUGH COMEDY. AFTER MARRIAGE REMEMBER
YOUR LOVE INTEREST IS ELIMINATED. NO ONE ON
EARTH JERRY KNOWS MUSICAL COMEDY BETTER THAN
YOU DO AND YOU YOURSELF TOLD ME YOU WOULD
NOT RISK A DOLLAR ON IT. IF HAMMERSTEIN WILL FIX
THE BOOK I WANT TO DO IT. IF HE REFUSES TO
CHANGE IT OR ALLOW ANYONE ELSE TO BE CALLED IN
IF NECESSARY HE AND YOU RETURN THE ADVANCES AS
YOU YOURSELF SUGGESTED YOU WOULD AND LET

SOMEONE ELSE DO IT. IF HAMMERSTEIN IS READY
TO WORK WITH ME TO GET IT RIGHT AND YOU AND
HE WILL EXTEND THE TIME TO OCTOBER FIRST
LETS DO IT TOGETHER. I REALLY WANT TO IF OH IS
REASONABLE. ALL WE WANT IS SUCCESS. ANSWER.

Whether Kern had the opportunity to discuss this with his collaborator is not clear: to put the fallow time occasioned by Ziegfeld's postponement to good use, Oscar had decided to go to London to supervise the Drury Lane opening of *The Desert Song*. His plans were further complicated by a couple of sprained ankles and a wrenched back that necessitated canceling his berth on the *Berengaria* with the cast and crew of the show and traveling alone to London on the next boat, the *Olympic*, which sailed on March 2.

Just before the boat sailed, Oscar's friend and attorney, Howard Reinheimer, who was seeing him off, introduced him to diamond merchant Henry Jacobson and his Australian-born wife, the former Dorothy Blanchard. They said the usual polite things and went their way, but the next morning, after a casual meeting on deck, Oscar asked if he might sit next to Dorothy and — in her own words — "That was it! It was like the rivers rushing down to the sea!" It was the same for Oscar: love at first sight. The fact that they were both married, that he had two children and she a son, no longer seemed important. They spent most of the Atlantic crossing together and continued to meet in London.

Dorothy Blanchard had been born in Launceston, Tasmania on June 7, 1899 and grew up to be a tall, athletic, strikingly beautiful young woman with auburn hair and ice-blue eyes. When she was 22 she decided to go to London, where she modeled and even got a bit part in a silent movie, but felt she was getting nowhere and impulsively booked passage for New York, telling her agent to get work for her there. He sent her picture to Ziegfeld who immediately offered her a job in his *Follies*. Her parents begged her not to become a "Follies girl" (with all the term implied) and she agreed to turn Ziegfeld down. To stay in New York, however, she needed a job. She auditioned for *André Charlot's Revue of 1924*, which was to star Jack Buchanan, Gertrude Lawrence, and Beatrice Lillie, and won a part as Lillie's understudy and showgirl. Caught up in the gay life of New York, she met and blithely married the attractive and wealthy Jacobson. Not until she met Oscar did she realize what a mistake that had been.

After their return to New York, Oscar and Dorothy continued to see each other, but Oscar, as usual, avoided the growing tensions of the situation by immersing himself in work on *Show Boat*. Unhappy about what he saw as his wife's infatuation with Oscar,

53

Henry Jacobson tried to force the issue by renting a house near the Hammersteins and even engaging in an affair with another woman, but it was no use; in the late summer of 1927, Dorothy asked him for a divorce. This acceleration of his problems had the usual effect on Oscar, who, by upbringing and indeed, very nature, found the idea of divorce repugnant and continued to procrastinate.

Now Ziegfeld began using delaying tactics, too. Weeks went by without Hammerstein and Kern hearing a word from him. When they did talk, he would tell them *Rio Rita* was playing to full houses and he was in no hurry to take it off. Or that he'd offered the lead to Gertie Lawrence but they'd have to wait until she was available. Or that *Show Boat* wasn't turning out the way he had expected; there was no chorus line, no spectacle, no star interpolations. Although, of course, he did not reveal this concern to Kern and Hammerstein, another reason for the delays was that Ziegfeld was worried he might not be able to finance *Show Boat*.

Kern, who was pretty wise to the ways of producers in general and Ziegfeld in particular, hazarded a guess that Ziggy didn't have the money to do the show, and he and Oscar seriously discussed taking it to another producer — Arthur Hammerstein had expressed keen interest. But when Arthur became involved with another of Oscar's musicals, *Golden Dawn*, they decided to string along with Ziegfeld after all. Just the same, they wondered how they could find out for sure if he had the money to put the show on. "Well," said Kern, a man who would fight a *Tyrannosaurus Rex* on a point of principle, "Let's go and ask him!"

When they got to Ziegfeld's palatial mansion in Hastings-on-Hudson, Ziggy's butler, Sydney (who looked more like a bank president than a butler, according to Oscar), ushered them into the drawing room. Then a maid in a costume right out of the *Follies* took them through Ziegfeld's bedroom with its priceless four-poster and beautiful *objets d'art*, and into an immense bathroom where the producer was being shaved by his personal barber, a man with a long, white beard who reminded Oscar of King Leopold of Belgium. Shaven and dressed in a silk brocade dressing gown, Ziegfeld offered them a snack — "pot luck," as he called it — which consisted of cocktails, roast beef, champagne, and turtles specially brought up from Florida. There was a footman behind every chair, and everything exuded wealth. Ziegfeld told them about the sensational business *Rio Rita* was doing in Boston. The talk was pleasant, the food excellent, and at about four in the afternoon Jerry and Oscar waddled out in what Oscar described as "a kind of misty contentment" and headed back to town. Neither of them had dared ask Ziegfeld whether he had the money to do *Show Boat*. How could you ask a man who lived like that if he was broke?

54

For one reason or another it would be another exhausting nine months before the show opened. The unusually long gestation of the play enabled Oscar to graduate from being a clever and adept musical comedy librettist to becoming an outstanding one. He remained philosophical about Ziegfeld's dislike of his work. He realized that Ziggy had never done a play with a story before and that the producer expected that by the time the show opened, all that "story stuff" would have been cut out, leaving the pretty costumes, the songs, the dances, and the comedy. But he and Kern were determined that this would not be another Ziegfeld girlie show, but a strongly delineated musical play with songs that grew out of the plot, spectacle and dance that only occurred when appropriate to the story, and characters who developed as the play unfolded — in other words, a musical like no other musical Broadway had ever seen.

Kern's enthusiasm for the project was dynamic. Every week, he visited Edna Ferber at her apartment, bringing the latest songs and singing them for her. "Make Believe" and "Life upon the Wicked Stage" and then, at last, the sweeping, sonorous "Ol' Man River." In her memoir, *A Peculiar Treasure*, Edna Ferber recalled her reactions on hearing "Ol' Man River" for the first time. "The music mounted, mounted, and I give you my word my hair stood on end, the tears came to my eyes. I breathed like the heroine in a melodrama. That was music that would outlast Jerome Kern's day and mine. I have never heard it since without the emotional surge."

55

Finally, Ziegfeld capitulated and set rehearsals for September 8, 1927. They actually began on September 13 and were "held in a large room high up in the Ziegfeld Theatre" according to Norma Terris, who had been in Oscar's *Queen o' Hearts* and was cast as Magnolia in *Show Boat*. Charles Winninger would play Captain Andy Hawks and Edna May Oliver would play his wife. Howard Marsh, who had played the tenor leads in both *Blossom Time* and *The Student Prince*, was Gaylord Ravenal; Jules Bledsoe Joe. The only part they had a problem filling was the complex one of Julie LaVerne.

There's a showbiz legend that Jerry Kern recalled seeing a waiflike dot of a girl with huge, sad eyes sitting on top of a piano singing "Nobody Wants Me" in the revue *Americana* earlier in the season and said "*That's* our Julie!" Her name was Helen Morgan and they signed her up as soon as she got back from a London engagement, two days before rehearsals began. Perhaps an even better — and truer — story is that Helen, a former comptometer operator, cookie packer, beer garden singer, and beauty contest winner, had been an obscure, last-row chorus girl in Kern's *Sally*. And the song that she made famous, sitting on the piano in the second act of *Show Boat,* was one that had been dropped from that score because Marilyn Miller's voice was too slight for it — "Bill."

Kern and Hammerstein — who was directing — worked tirelessly throughout rehearsals. Over here you might see Kern, explaining to Norma Terris that he saw Magnolia and Ravenal as Romeo and Juliet, that she should play Magnolia as "a genuine little girl — not coy, not a flirt;" and instructing her to keep her eyes on Ravenal throughout their first meeting. Over there you would see Oscar, nursing Helen Morgan into her role by playing the part of Steve opposite her. Because no one had told her who this big, polite man with the craggy face was, she took Kern to one side and suggested — since the guy obviously knew and understood the part — that maybe they ought to give him a break. Oscar, in turn, watched her growing command with surprise and pleasure. Though she had never appeared in a musical and had no acting technique worth the name, everything she did as Julie was, he said, "exactly right. Her instincts were sure. Nobody had to tell her how to move, gesture, or put over a song. She behaved like a veteran."

*Show Boat* is set on a Mississippi riverboat called the *Cotton Blossom,* and its characters are real, three-dimensional human beings. They include the boat's captain, Andy Hawks, and his wife Parthy Ann (pun intended), whose daughter, Magnolia, falls in love with the dashing, but shallow, riverboat gambler Gaylord Ravenal. The leading lady aboard the show boat is Julie Laverne, who is cast out because of the taint of Negro blood. There is also the black riverboat worker, Joe, who had been a minor figure in the original novel, but became in Oscar's version a sort of black Greek chorus commenting on the changing scenes onstage.

After several grueling weeks of rehearsal, *Show Boat* moved to Washington's National Theatre. The first performance, on November 15, 1927, ran for four-and-a-quarter hours. Sitting on the balcony stairs, Ziegfeld was convinced it was a disaster. The big numbers did not draw much applause and Ziegfeld was distraught, cursing the audience for not liking the show. Intermission was no better and the finale worse. When the audience left the theater they seemed almost in a trance (it appears not to have occurred to anyone that they had been stunned into silence by what they had seen and heard). In gloomy despondency, the authors awaited the verdict of the critics. They might have the largest advance ticket sale of any show to that time, but that wouldn't mean a thing if they were panned. Needless to say, the critics raved. Next day, there were lines around the block to buy tickets for what its creators called "The All-American Musical Comedy."

That first night, however, all they knew was that the show was running an hour and 40 minutes overtime and cuts had to be made. Working all night in their suite at the Willard Hotel, Kern and Hammerstein reshaped and rewrote, taking 50 minutes out of the play. The next day Ziegfeld called a rehearsal for eleven o'clock, made some more cuts, watched the matinée (which ran till six), made them do another rehearsal, and then sent the cast on for the evening performance without their even having eaten. From Washington, still cutting, still reshaping, still reinventing, they moved to Pittsburgh for five days, then to Cleveland, and from Cleveland to Philadelphia on December 5 for a final 19-day shakeout. The critical and box-office response was splendid in every city they played, even though every performance was a completely different show.

Oscar had terrible trouble getting the book down to manageable length; no matter what he did the curtain rarely fell before eleven-thirty. Some wonderful material was discarded: a soaringly beautiful waltz duet in which Magnolia first tells Julie she is in love; a fine lament called "Mis'ry's Comin' Around;" one of Ravenal's songs; and a couple of minor numbers. Some equally fine substitutions were made. In Pittsburgh, for instance, Jerry and Oscar felt they needed another song for Magnolia and Ravenal. Jerry produced a charmingly simple melody with which Oscar retired to his suite. Knowing Kern's almost unreasoning hatred of corny lyrics featuring Cupid and his arrows, he concocted one to fit the tune and took it in to Kern, who propped it on the piano and began to sing:

> Cupid knows the way.
> He's the naked boy
> Who can make you prey
> To love's own joy.
> When he shoots his little arrow
> He can thrill you to the marrow...

Slamming his hands down on the keyboard, Kern gave a yowl of horror, but when he saw Oscar's smile, he got the joke. Then Oscar handed him the true lyric for the song "Why Do I Love You?" Kern had the "Cupid" version framed and kept it on his piano for the rest of his life.

Bit by bit, the show took shape. By the time they completed the Philadelphia engagement, three scenes and eight songs had been excised and the show was finally of manageable length. On the night and day before the New York opening, with Oscar acting as co-director (without credit) to Zeke Colvan, everyone worked 18 hours straight as more scenes were changed, dialogue altered, sequences shuffled. Finally, on December 27, 1927, a complete year after its inception, the show opened in New York's Ziegfeld Theatre.

57

It was still perhaps half an hour too long, but if that bothered any of the first-night audience it certainly did not show in their enthusiastic reaction. When the curtain came down there was an almost stunned five-second silence, followed by thunderous applause. That night, Arthur Hammerstein proudly told a friend he had just seen the perfect show. And best of all, he said, it was by his nephew. "My decision to take Oscar into show business has been justified," he said. "Tonight I knew that I did right by Willie after all, even though I broke my word. I'm a happy man!"

*Show Boat* was an unqualified critical and commercial success. The original production ran for 572 performances, almost two years, averaging a weekly gross of $50,000. An equally successful tour began in Boston in May 1929 and ended a year later. In 1932, the original company — with Paul Robeson taking over the role of Joe and Dennis King playing Ravenal — returned to New York for a further six-month run of 180 performances, followed by a 13-city tour. The London production at Drury Lane began in May, 1928 and ran for nearly a year. In 1929, a part-talking picture with synchronised soundtrack featured Joseph Schildkraut and Laura La Plante, but it would be the 1936 version, directed by James Whale and starring Allan Jones and Irene Dunne, and for which Kern

***Show Boat:*** **The 1936 Universal movie starred Paul Robeson, Irene Dunne, Helen Morgan, and Hattie MacDaniels, here cheering on Magnolia (Dunne) as she sings "Can't Help Lovin' Dat Man."** Author's Collection.

and Hammerstein wrote three new songs, that best captured the charm and romance of the original.

It remains Jerome Kern's most impressive work, as vivid and colorful today as it was 75 years ago. In it, for the first time, all the elements of story, setting, lyrics, and music were fused. From the shock of the opening chorus (the very first words the audience heard were "Niggers all work on the Mississippi") *Show Boat* was — and remains to this day — a stunning musical feast, every song establishing mood and character. With a cast of nearly a hundred that amply demonstrated Ziegfeld's commitment to style and spectacle — 36 white chorus girls, 16 white chorus boys, 16 black girl singers and 12 black girl dancers — the ensemble numbers were truly spectacular.

Everything worked: Ravenal and Magnolia's duet "Make Believe" and the later "You Are Love" underscored the change in their emotions. Julie's wistful "Can't Help Lovin' dat Man" is echoed by Joe's wife, Queenie, but for different reasons. The dancers Frank and Ellie, played by the team of Eva Puck and Sammy White (who had made their mark on the Broadway stage a year ealier in Rodgers and Hart's *The Girl Friend*), had a bright duet called "I Might Fall Back on You," and Ellie a mock lament about the disappointments of "Life upon the Wicked Stage" (inspired, it's said, by a chance remark of Dorothy Blanchard's, who told Oscar that backstage life had been nothing like as wicked as she had supposed). Crucially, Hammerstein helped Plum Wodehouse rework the original lyric from "Along came Bill /Who's quite the opposite /Of all the men in story books" to the vastly different "Bill" that everyone knows. And of course, dominating the entire score was the sweeping, sonorous "Ol' Man River."

Never a man to rest on his laurels, Oscar had accepted two assignments from Uncle Arthur during Ziegfeld's procrastinations. By the time *Show Boat* opened, the first of these, a Hammerstein-Harbach quasi-opera with music by Stothart and Emmerich Kalman called *Golden Dawn* — in which a European girl is forced to become the taboo wife of an African tribal god, but is saved by an English army officer — was playing at Arthur's new neo-Gothic Hammerstein's Theatre (built with the profits from *Rose Marie*). Drubbed by the critics, *Golden Dawn* ran a respectable 184 performances (thanks largely to Arthur Hammerstein's ballyhoo), did a seven-city tour, was made into a truly awful film and would by now be totally forgotten except for one reason — it featured the Broadway debut of a young British actor and ex-Coney Island stiltwalker (he had one line of dialogue and played — are you ready for this? — in blackface) named Archie Leach. Yes, *that* Archie Leach.

The second of Oscar's two shows for Uncle Arthur was back in the full-blooded operetta tradition (books like *Show Boat* did not come along every season) and it opened

59

for tryouts in Philadelphia the day before the first New York performance of *Show Boat*. It was called *The New Moon* and it was a calamity. It is impossible not to conclude that the reason for this was that Oscar had been concentrating so completely upon *Show Boat* that his work on *The New Moon* was, quite simply, unstageable. With the rapturous reception of *Show Boat* still ringing in his ears he rushed to Philadelphia where, after a week of drastic revisions and cast replacements, Oscar (who had put up 25 percent of the money for the show) persuaded his co-producers Frank Mandel and Laurence Schwab to close *The New Moon* "for revisions" — which usually means for good.

His private life looked equally bleak. Dorothy Jacobson told him she was giving her marriage another try: she was pregnant and did not wish to see him again. Whether this eased the tension between Oscar and Myra is debatable, but they sailed together to England with Jerry and Eva Kern to supervise the London production of *Show Boat*, which opened at Drury Lane on May 3, 1928. Even with Paul Robeson as a commanding Joe, Cedric Hardwicke as Captain Andy, Edith Day as Magnolia, and Marie Burke as Julie, the critics were by no means kind, but the public ignored them and the show settled in for a ten-month run.

While enjoying London, Oscar, ever the workaholic, began rethinking the book of *The New Moon*. When he returned to New York he got together with Frank Mandel and they began a complete rewrite which involved cutting nine of the original songs and building the storyline into something that might enthuse Romberg, who was still grieving over the death late in 1927 of his dear friend and longtime collaborator Dorothy Donnelly. What they came up with was the story (based on his autobiography) of Robert Misson, an 18th century French nobleman who is wanted for murder and flees Paris for New Orleans, where he becomes a bondservant. Captured and sent back to France on the ship *The New Moon*, whose passenger list includes his beloved, Marianne Beaunoir, Robert is rescued by his followers and, with Marianne, establishes a colony of free men on a West Indian island.

The next task was to get Romberg to write. So saddened was the composer still that Oscar had to virtually mollycoddle him to the piano, even writing some lyrics first — early drafts of "Lover Come Back to Me" indicate this song was one such song — to encourage Romberg's usually prolific musical imagination. By the time tryouts began at Cleveland's Hanna Theatre on September 19, they had come up with a clutch of lushly romantic songs which included "Stouthearted Men," "Wanting You," and "Softly, as in a Morning Sunrise." Despite the protests of unromantic souls who asked what other kind of sunrise there was, the show — as unquestionably old hat as a revival of *Naughty*

**Oscar Hammerstein and Dorothy Blanchard Hammerstein in the late 1920s.**
Used by permission of the Rodgers and Hammerstein Organization.

*Marietta* (which it strongly resembled) — was enormously popular, as were all its songs, even "One Kiss," for all its startling resemblance to Vincent Youmans's "No, No, Nanette." *The New Moon* racked up a thundering 509 performances, and not only spawned two movie versions but even rode out the stock market crash of 1929.

Simultaneously with all this, Oscar was also deeply involved in yet another show, with Uncle Arthur again producing and brother Reginald directing. His collaborators on this were the ever-ready Harbach, and Henry Myers, a close friend of Larry Hart's. It was mainly a vehicle for comic Eddie Buzzell with a book that was cornier than Kansas in August and short scenes reminiscent of vaudeville sketches. The score by Harry Ruby and Bert Kalmar included "I Wanna Be Loved by You," performed by the "Boop-boop-a-doop Girl," Helen Kane, with additional Identikit songs by Herbert Stothart, and dances again by young Buzz Berkeley. In spite of all these apparent strikes against it, *Good Boy* totted up a very satisfactory 253-performance run.

One of Oscar's reasons for doing the show was that he was trying to mend his fences with Otto Harbach, who had been suffering from a conspicuous lack of success and who felt — perhaps with good reason — that Oscar had ungratefully jettisoned him after *The Desert Song* and excluded him from participation in *Show Boat*. Although *Good Boy* was a reasonable success, it would be a long time until Hammerstein and Harbach worked together again.

With two major shows still running on Broadway, one might have thought Oscar could lean back and relax a little, but instead he became involved in yet another show, *Rainbow,* for which he not only collaborated on the book with Laurence Stallings (co-author with Maxwell Anderson of the revolutionary 1924 war drama *What Price Glory?*) but also wrote the lyrics and directed the play. The show was beset by difficulties from the outset. Although it was intended to be very much in the *Show Boat* tradition, the story — a scout kills an Army officer in self-defense, escapes from prison, and heads west on a California-bound wagon train, where he woos and wins his true love — obviously failed to inspire Vincent Youmans. While it was still in rehearsal Oscar was admitted to a sanatorium suffering from a nervous breakdown.

His private life was in chaos. Dorothy Jacobson's second child, Susan, had been born in March, but the arrival of another child did nothing to mend her marriage. By summer she and Oscar were seeing each other again, which added to his mental anguish. He was rarely at home, spending his time in the Manhattan apartment of his old college chum Leighton "Goofy" Brill, who, one night during the tryouts of *The New Moon,* found Oscar crying in his hotel room. A Cleveland journalist who thought he was just doing a backstage piece painted a picture of him as Brill must have seen him: a nervy, strung-out wreck who looked "more like a battle-scarred halfback than a writer" and "jumped if you looked at him." Oscar, usually a tower of backstage strength, was twanging like a guitar. He was too ill to attend the September premiere of the Romberg show. Buried in work, trapped by his own emotions, desperate to find a way to be with Dorothy in spite of Myra's flat refusal to even consider divorce, he snapped.

He was admitted to a sanitarium, where for two weeks he was wrapped in sheets and given cold baths to calm him before being taken back to his room, shaking and crying. He had no other treatment, physical or psychiatric, nor did he discuss his feelings with anyone. But over and over like a mantra he repeated the words "It's not going to lick me." Within two more weeks he was back on the street, well enough to help out on the casting of *Rainbow,* supporting Youmans in the proposition that Francetta Malloy be replaced by Libby Holman and then writing a new number for Holman called "I Want a Man." Considering what a disaster the opening night was — a mule urinating copiously during a romantic scene, the crosstown El that ran behind the theater shaking the scenery, a scene change that didn't work and held up the show for almost half an hour — the critics were largely kind, but the public was indifferent to what the show was trying for and it closed after 29 performances.

1929 was much better — one might ask, how could it have been worse? Myra finally agreed, on her own, extremely severe terms, to a divorce and Oscar went through the hotel bedroom farce that her condition that he be the co-respondent required. Dorothy Jacobson went to Reno for the statutory period until her own divorce became final, and Oscar waited it out with Jerry and Eva Kern on their yacht, where they worked on a new musical commissioned by Arthur Hammerstein to star Helen Morgan — with whom Oscar's brother Reggie was having a passionate affair.

The yacht was a dream Kern had decided to realize some time earlier. For many years an avid collector of first editions — almost entirely English classics such as Johnson, Goldsmith, Shelley, Thackeray, Lamb, Dickens, Conrad, and Hardy — he decided sometime in 1928 to send his collection to auction. The sale, which totaled 1488 lots, was held in two sessions, the first (A-J) on four days and evenings, January 7-10, and the second (J-Z) on four days and evenings, January 21-24, 1929, at the Anderson Galleries on Park Avenue at 59th Street. The sale yielded a total of $1,729,462.50, the highest amount ever brought by a collection anywhere in the world. The yacht — called *Show Boat* of course — was a direct result.

On Tuesday, May 14 of that same year, Oscar and his Dorothy were married in the Belvedere Hotel in Baltimore (his best man and attorney, Howard Reinheimer, had recommended holding the ceremony in a state other than New York because of legal complications arising out of Oscar's divorce), then left for a Paris honeymoon on the *Olympic,* by happy coincidence the same boat on which they had first met. When they got back, Oscar settled down to work with Kern on the new show, which began life with the title *Just the Other Day,* and much of which was written as the Kerns and the

Hammersteins cruised Long Island Sound. When one day Jerry played Oscar a new melody he had just written, Oscar — notoriously a slow worker — came up almost immediately with "Don't Ever Leave Me," which he dedicated to Dorothy.

The show, renamed *Sweet Adeline*, was first performed in Atlantic City on August 19, 1929. It was, everyone recalled, a "happy" show; Helen Morgan described the backstage atmosphere as "cheerful harmony." Its plot had been inspired by stories Helen told the composers about her days as a singing waitress in a beer garden called Adeline's. Oscar had an idea for a story about the sacrifices made by one sister for another, Jerry wanted to set it in the Gay Nineties (a favorite period of his). Out of all this came the story of Addie Schmidt, singing daughter of a beer garden owner, who loves ship's first mate Tom Martin but loses him to her younger sister Nellie. She becomes a Broadway star and falls in love with James Day, the backer of her show. When his socially prominent family disapproves, she runs away, but finally finds true love in the arms of Sid Barnett, the songwriter to whom she owes her stardom.

The New York critics loved *Sweet Adeline* with its bright, catchy opening "Play Us a Polka Dot" (Dot was a piccolo player) and its beautifully-captured *fin de siècle* atmosphere. They liked the folkish "'Twas Not So Long Ago," they admired "Don't Ever Leave Me," but most especially they loved tiny, sad-eyed Helen Morgan — come on, wasn't the whole plot based on her life, anyway? Wasn't one of the major characters a caricature of her pushy mother? — sitting on her piano at the end of the first act singing "Why Was I Born?" The only reason critic Burns Mantle could think of was "to sing this kind of song."

For two months, *Sweet Adeline* was the hottest ticket on Broadway, but just a few weeks after its opening the New York stock market crash changed everything overnight. The show lasted until the following March, by which time the deepening Depression was forcing closures everywhere: musical theater had always been for the elite, and the elite no longer had any money. And as the grim realities became steadily grimmer, the big producers — Ziegfeld, Dillingham, Arthur Hammerstein, even the Shuberts — went under one by one. With no one to work for on Broadway, there was only one place writers like Oscar Hammerstein could find work: Hollywood.

At the end of 1929, Oscar signed a lucrative contract with Warner Brothers-First National (Sigmund Romberg signed an identical one at the same time) to write four Romberg-Hammerstein musicals over a two-year period at $100,000 per film against 25 percent of the profits, with final approval of each film. The future looked bright indeed as he, Dorothy, and her daughter Susan boarded the 20th Century Limited early in December.

Oscar loved the movies, loved the possibilities they presented for musical drama, and plunged into learning everything he could about them. His first film, *Viennese Nights*, which starred Vivienne Segal (an Austrian shoemaker's daughter), Walter Pidgeon (the nobleman her father insists she marries), and Alexander Gray (the penniless composer who loves her), was a three-generational love story pitched somewhere between *Blossom Time* and *Show Boat*, set first in Vienna, then New York, then Vienna again. After it was completed (filming took exactly 24 days), Oscar and his new wife set off for Australia to visit Dorothy's family for a month. He worked on the storyline for the second film, *Children of Dreams*, on-board ship, radioing segments to Romberg so the composer could work on some melodies. This was another romance about a couple of impoverished youngsters, Molly (Margaret Schilling) and Tommy (Paul Gregory), who fall in love while picking apples. At the behest of a wealthy socialite, Molly goes to Rome becomes a successful opera singer. When Tommy hears her at the New York Met, he believes she is now too far above him and leaves the theater, but the lovers are reunited by the family doctor (Charles Winninger).

The problem was the studios had vastly overestimated the public appetite for musicals, producing 57 full-scale musical films, plus 40 more with songs, in 1929 alone. Well over 70 new musicals were released the following year. During 1930 alone, apart from lavish spectaculars like *Paramount on Parade* and *The King of Jazz*, moviegoers could have seen the screen versions of more than a dozen Broadway hits — *No, No, Nanette!*; *Hit The Deck; Sunny; The Vagabond King; Sally; Spring Is Here; Hold Everything; Top Speed; Good News; Whoopee; Follow Through; Big Boy; Leathernecking*, originally a Rodgers & Hart show called *Present Arms;* and another of theirs, *Heads Up* — not to mention five films based on Broadway shows by Oscar: *Song of the West* (formerly *Rainbow*), *The Song of the Flame, Golden Dawn, New Moon*, and *Sunny*. Hardly surprising then, that when *Viennese Nights* was released November 11, 1930, nobody much cared.

The California "gold rush" of 1929-30 that had attracted the cream of Broadway talent to Hollywood ended as quickly as it had begun. As movie houses tried to attract customers by putting out signs that promised there was "No music in this movie," the big studios retrenched. Expensive musical projects were dropped from production schedules and their creators, to use Oscar's own words, "fled the Brown Derby and rushed back to the sour-cream arms of Lindy's." Oscar and Romberg were among them; when studio head Jack Warner offered them $100,000 each to forget the two other pictures on their contract, they took the money and ran.

Arthur Hammerstein, who also had been lured to Hollywood by big-money offers to produce operettas for United Artists that had evaporated the same way as all the others, needed money to prop up his ailing empire and signed Oscar to write four shows: the first for W. C. Fields, with a score by Lewis Alter; the next a musical for Helen Morgan based on *Camille,* with a score by Jerome Kern; another to be written by Oscar's pal "Goofy" Brill; and the last a drama by Oscar. All of it, except the Fields show, was pie in the sky, because *Ballyhoo,* which opened on December 22, 1930, was a two-week disaster that its producer could no longer support. Early in 1931, Arthur Hammerstein filed for bankruptcy, citing debts of $1,500,000, assets of $53,083, and $5.77 in cash.

Good times, bad times, it made no difference: Oscar had to work. The big house in Great Neck was standing empty, a constant expense; meanwhile he was paying Myra alimony and child support, as well as costly rent bills for the apartment at the Dorset Hotel his ex-wife occupied with their two children and the one he and Dorothy were living in at 1067 Fifth Avenue. In addition, Dorothy was pregnant; their son James would be born on March 23. So, taking whatever he could get, Oscar got involved in trying to salvage a show written by Morrie Ryskind and Lewis Gensler called *The Gang's All Here.* A mishmash of vaudeville routines and ensemble numbers — it even featured the Tilly Losch Ballet and a comedian, Ted Healy, who was convinced his own material was superior to anything the writers could offer — it lasted exactly 23 performances. No matter what Oscar's contribution to it may or may not have been, it was a turkey, and on its New York opening one critic famously snarled, in reply to the title, "Who the hell cares?"

Reading four or five books a day trying to find a vehicle, under constant pressure from Ziegfeld to come up with another *Show Boat* (they seriously discussed a sequel featuring Magnolia's daughter Kim and Paul Robeson as Joe's son), Oscar was also wheeling and dealing with Laurence Schwab and Frank Mandel to take a two-year lease on Arthur's former theater (Oscar as a silent partner investing $100,000) and produce their own shows, which he would write exclusively for the partnership (except for one show a year for Arthur). The first flowering of the triumvirate was *Free For All*, with Oscar writing book and lyrics for Richard Whiting's score and also directing the play, which had to do with a group of socialistic students who set up a commune in a mining camp. The plot was a downer: the hero doesn't make good, there was no "romance" and hardly much more in the way of singing and dancing. Even with the Benny Goodman band on board, the slow pace and the over-serious theme robbed it of life and it slipped silently away after only 25 performances.

Within a couple of weeks, the trio took another show to Pittsburgh, this time with a score by Sigmund Romberg. A "trunk" show Oscar had written some time earlier with Frank Mandel, *East Wind* told the story of Claudette, a convent-raised girl who is loved by two brothers, René and Paul. She marries René and goes to live with him in Saigon. There, he falls for a hoochy-cooch dancer, and the disillusioned Claudette is reunited with her true love, Paul, when he saves her life in a waterfront dive. It was another stinker, with "as dreary a libretto as ever dejected a musical play," according to critic Percy Hammond. It had "no inspiration and no sense," said Burns Mantle, and was "about as unexciting as an operetta can be," added John Mason Brown. With reviews like that, *East Wind* lasted only a week longer than *Free For All.*

That was four flops in a row for Oscar, which was pretty heavy punishment even for a writer well used to not succeeding. He reacted as he always did: he "took a deep breath and started all over again," but this time he gave himself some breathing space, taking almost a whole year to lovingly fashion the book for a new show with Jerome Kern. Originally planning to do a story about life in a music publisher's office, Oscar acceded to Kern's suggestion that they set the story as far away from Tin Pan Alley as possible, deciding instead upon Munich and the mountains of southern Germany. They planned to take it to Ziegfeld, who had just staged a hugely successful revival of *Show Boat*, but Ziegfeld's sudden death just a couple of months later removed that possibility. Into the breach stepped picture palace mogul A. C. Blumenthal, coincidentally married to a Ziegfeld showgirl, Peggy Fears, who agreed to put up $100,000 to finance the show with two provisos: one, his wife got the producing credit and two, they changed the title.

What they ended up with was pretty much a retread of *The Cat and the Fiddle*, a show Kern had written with Otto Harbach the preceding year. *Karl and Sieglinde*, as it was first called, concerned the old music teacher of Edendorf, Dr. Lessing (played by Al Shean of the vaudeville team Gallagher and Shean) and the young schoolmaster, Karl (Walter Slezak), who write a hit song together and go to the big city. There, Sieglinde, the teacher's daughter and the schoolmaster's sweetheart, falls for suave librettist Bruno, while his mistress, Frieda, a prima donna, makes eyes at Karl. When Frieda gets jealous and refuses to appear in Bruno's new opera, Sieglinde takes over the part, but proves to be hopeless onstage. Frieda returns to Bruno and the Edendorf trio return home, sadder but wiser.

For the "hit" song — which they knew had to be a real-life hit, too — Kern turned to a motif he had jotted down listening to a Cape Cod sparrow singing outside his bedroom window one morning. To it, Oscar first crafted a lyric about a "Bright Bird" sitting in a tree, but was unhappy with it. Revising his melody slightly, and adding notes where Oscar needed them, Kern gave him the melody which became "I've Told Ev'ry Little Star," and they knew they had their hit. A couple more solid show tunes followed, notably "The Song Is You," which, although it featured one of Hammerstein's most romantic lyrics, was sung in cynical counterpoint. Other gems included "In Egern on the Tegernsee," "And Love Was Born," and a delightful waltz, "One More Dance/Night Flies By."

The show, now called *Music in the Air*, opened on November 8, 1932, the same day Franklin Delano Roosevelt became President of the United States in a Democratic land-slide. The show was an immediate, enormous success, running for almost a year. With two big hits at a time when one would have been a miracle, Oscar no doubt felt he was back where he belonged, at the top of the Broadway tree. In fact, it would be more than a decade before he again had a success of any kind.

In March, 1933, he took his family to England, where he supervised the London pro-duction of *Music in the Air* for producer Charles Cochran and, at the behest of Max Dreyfus's brother Louis, director of the music publishing firm Chappell & Co., set to work preparing some musicals for the Drury Lane Theatre, of which Louis was also a director. The first of these was based on a German play (which bore a striking resem-blance to *Die Fledermaus*) by Alfred Grünwald and Fritz Löhner-Beda which Oscar adapted, writing lyrics to melodies written by Paul Abraham. The finished result had, one critic said, "not a line of wit from beginning to end." The public seemed largely to agree, and *Ball At the Savoy* lasted only three months.

When Jerry Kern came over to England, he and Oscar talked again about a project they had discussed a number of times in the past, a musical based on the Donn Byrne novel *Messer Marco Polo*, for which they went so far as to write a libretto and several songs before setting it aside. Another idea about a theatrical family, *Fluffy Ruffles*, was likewise discarded. They also talked with the Theatre Guild about a musical based on DuBose Heyward's *Porgy* with Al Jolson as its star (can you imagine *Porgy and Bess* with Jolson in it?), but after considerable heart-searching the author chose to work with George and Ira Gershwin instead.

What they finally decided upon — both of them were mad about going to the races and had been enraptured by the fairground atmosphere and excitement surrounding the Derby — was a slight thing about three sisters, one of whom loves an aristocrat, another a policeman, and the third a busker (first, second, and third class, you see). Oscar tried hard to interest Otto Harbach in collaborating with him on the book, but Harbach was already committed to another show.

*Three Sisters* had a good cast — Charlotte Greenwood, Adele Dixon, Albert Burdon as the busker, and Stanley Holloway as the policeman. It had a decent enough score that included a winsome duet, "Lonely Feet," and an early version (before Dorothy Fields electrified it for Fred and Ginger in the film *Roberta*) of "I Won't Dance." It had an adequate book and all the expertise Kern and Hammerstein could put into it, but it was a mess, and on opening night it ran for three-and-a-half hours. Although the critics were not too harsh, the public stayed away, and *Three Sisters* closed after a month. "So," Oscar said to Kern, "what now?" And Kern said: "Hollywood. For good."

Taking him at his word, Oscar signed a one-year contract with MGM at $2500 a week — a sumptuously generous salary in the darkest days of the Depression — and moved his family to Beverly Hills. He was not alone; many of the leading Broadway composers and librettists headed out to the land of milk and honey as the studios again embraced musicals. For some of them, Hollywood was a frustrating and unhappy experience; others ate it up with a spoon. Richard Rodgers, for example, hated the place. The Gershwins loved it and settled there. Some writers loathed the producers, who barred them from the sets where their work was being filmed, and the management, who banished them to drafty little cubbyholes and told them to get busy writing masterpieces. Others, like Harry Warren and Irving Berlin, ignored the difficulties and churned out the hits that were all the studios wanted.

**Oscar Hammerstein and Jerome Kern rehearsing *Music In the Air* (1932).** Author's Collection.

Oscar's first assignment at MGM was a Sigmund Romberg musical for Evelyn Laye and Ramon Novarro called *The Night is Young*. Based on a Vicki Baum story set in darkest Ruritania, one critic called it "a preposteroperetta," and that just about sums it up. The only notable things about it were the title song and "When I Grow Too Old to Dream," a beautiful waltz whose lyric makes absolutely no sense whatsoever, and yet manages to remain disarmingly wistful. The next MGM project was a proposed Nelson Eddy-Jeanette MacDonald ("la Jeanette," as Jerry called her) film, *Champagne and Orchids,* for which Kern was to provide the music. Although both score and script were completed, it never reached the screen. They also wrote a plangent title song for a Jean Harlow movie, *Reckless,* and around Christmas, 1935, collaborated on five new songs for the movie version of *Show Boat.*

As well as all this, Oscar had returned east to work on a new Romberg musical, *May Wine.* Frank Mandel's book, based on the Wallace Smith novel *The Happy Alienist,* began with a Viennese psychiatrist telling the police that he has killed his wife; then in flashbacks revealed the events and reasons leading up to the "murder" — the "victim" turns out to have been a dummy and the psychiatrist and his wife are happily reunited. Perhaps unsurprisingly the story seems not to have inspired the composer to tap his most melodic vein, but even so, *May Wine* stayed on for a seven-month run, considered very satisfactory in a season when Cole Porter's *Jubilee* failed and Gershwin's *Porgy and Bess* lasted only 121 performances.

With no further offers on the table, Oscar moved to Paramount, where he worked on four pictures: a projected remake of *The Count of Luxembourg,* which was shelved; *Give Us This Night,* a film for opera stars Gladys Swarthout and Jan Kiepura with music by Erich Korngold; then *Swing High, Swing Low,* a musical version starring Carole Lombard and Fred MacMurray of the 1927 stage play *Burlesque,* which had rocketed Barbara Stanwyck to stardom. Finally, reuniting with Kern, Oscar wrote the original story, screenplay, and lyrics for *High, Wide, and Handsome,* an Irene Dunne-Randolph Scott starrer directed by Rouben Mamoulian and set in the Pennsylvania oil fields. The score included "Can I Forget You?" and "The Folks Who Live on the Hill" (that rhyme "Our veranda / will command a..." always bothered Oscar); but both songs are perfect examples of the increasingly simple, uncluttered style which would become his trademark.

Picturesque and folksy, *High, Wide, and Handsome* prompted studio head Adolph Zukor to pump Oscar's hand warmly after the sneak preview and tell him it was the greatest picture the studio had ever made. A few months later, however, when the movie was released and it became clear that box-office receipts would fall below break-even level, Zukor walked straight past Oscar in a restaurant without even acknowledging that he knew him. His stint at Paramount at an end, Oscar found a berth at Columbia Pictures (its Gower Street address was known as Poverty Gulch), where in eight months he seems to have created only one lyric, albeit a great one, for a Ben Oakland melody that became the title song for Grace Moore's movie *I'll Take Romance.*

Then it was back to MGM to put lyrics to Johann Strauss's music in *The Great Waltz.* One Strauss melody in particular again brought out Oscar's best and simplest style in the song called "One Day When We Were Young." But the offers of work were drying up; apart from a script for RKO tailored to the talents of Fred Astaire and Ginger Rogers — Oscar's title was *Castles in the Air,* but it was eventually released (two years later) as *The Story of Vernon and Irene Castle* — Oscar was pretty much through with Hollywood. The big studios didn't want to listen to his ideas; he didn't want to do what they were prepared to offer him. Despite his hits, he was considered a has-been. "He's a dear friend," someone said, "but he can't write his hat." Finally, Dorothy Hammerstein laid it on the line. "You know, Ockie," she told him, "it's better to wear out than to rust out — and we're rusting out."

"Do you mean that?" he said, like a man who couldn't believe his luck. She said she certainly did and, as soon as they could, they moved back east. Throughout his Hollywood hegira, Oscar's heart had always remained on Broadway, and he had kept in touch with his New York collaborators, meeting Kern or Harbach or Romberg, swapping ideas, looking for new projects. Now he plunged back into work, signing up to produce two shows with Laurence Schwab, two more of his own, and another with Harbach and Kern. "I'm coming back to the Broadway stage in a big way," he told Louis Dreyfus.

The Kern show was the first, a pageant-like musical commissioned by the Municipal Theater Association of St. Louis to celebrate its 20th anniversary and scheduled to run from June 3-12, 1938 at its open-air theater in that city. *Gentleman Unafraid* was a story about the heart-searchings of a group of Southern West Point cadets torn between their loyalties to the South and their duty to the North. Producer Max Gordon announced his intention of bringing it to New York in due course, but that never happened. Although Harbach would tinker with it for the rest of his life, and although it had a couple of beautiful Kern melodies (one, "Your Dream Is the Same as My Dream," turned up in *One Night in the Tropics,* the 1940 movie that introduced Abbott & Costello to the screen), *Gentleman Unafraid* lived only that one week.

Next came *Knights of Song,* a punnishly-titled play by Glendon Aldive which examined the not-too-astonishing fact that, offstage, Gilbert and Sullivan didn't get along well.

The idea seems to have been to interpolate "best bits" of the G&S operettas into a completely invented story about Sullivan's romance with an American girl, but it didn't work, and the show lasted only two weeks. Shrugging off its failure, Oscar was already working on two more shows scheduled to open within weeks of each other the following month. *Where Do We Go From Here?* was "an amiable frolic" about fraternity boys trying to save their fraternity house, but even the presence of such future luminaries as Don DeFore, Ralph Holmes, and budding songwriter Hugh Martin couldn't keep it going more than 15 performances. As it closed on November 27, the curtain rose at the Mansfield Theatre on Oscar's third offering of the season, *Glorious Morning,* a play to which he had acquired American rights after seeing Jessica Tandy perform it in London. Roughly based on the story of Joan of Arc, set in a mythical country ruled by a dictator, it was anti-Nazi, pro-freedom of religion, passionate, and preachy. In its first week it grossed precisely $355 at the box office and closed after nine performances.

Producer Oscar Hammerstein's track record was looking distinctly shabby: to the roster of undistinguished movies could now be added one play that never made it to New York and three that totted up a pathetic total of 30 performances between them. So once again he did what he always did when failure stared him in the face: he began writing another show. And another. He worked some more on the Marco Polo idea with Kern. He experimented on a project with Alice Duer Miller, and another set in Cuba with a Sigmund Romberg score. None of these ideas got much further than some preliminary writing. Finally, when Max Gordon put up the money, he elected to do a Princess Theatre-type show with Jerry Kern and went out to California to work on it with him.

The result of their endeavors was *Very Warm For May* (yes, a principal character was called May) whose story, based very loosely on the career of Bessie Marbury of the Princess Theatre, concerned a summer stock company in New England that is nearly wrecked by the ineptitude of an artsy-fartsy impresario (Oscar hated amateurs and dilettantes). The show tried out in Wilmington, Washington, Philadelphia, and Boston, where audiences responded very positively to the show's screwball charm, a talented cast that included Jack Whiting, Grace MacDonald, Richard Quine, Eve Arden, Vera-Ellen, and June Allyson, and a score that included "All the Things You Are."

It has been the convention to blame producer Max Gordon for the show's failure, to say he became convinced the show had to be rewritten, fired Vincente Minnelli and brought in Hassard Short to make it "commercially successful." In fact, the book needed all the help it could get, but the help it got was not the kind it needed. The verve and humor it had contained, such as the preposterous impresario who had got so many laughs on the road, were excised. What was left was a mess. The "new, improved" *Very Warm For May* opened at the Alvin Theatre in New York on November 17, 1939, and died. Oscar, who said the reviews ("labored," "exasperating," even "stupid") were the worst he'd ever gotten in his life, pleaded with Gordon to close the show but he refused; after 59 performances the producer had no choice.

Down but still not out — "All The Things You Are," No. 1 in the Hit Parade for many weeks, boosted Oscar's ASCAP royalties to around $25,000 a year — he wrote a screen treatment of the life of his grandfather, Oscar Hammerstein I, which he sent to MGM stipulating that he would not sell it unless he was signed to write the screenplay. The studio bought the property but no movie was ever made. In February, 1940, after Rodgers & Hart took a pass, he signed with John Krimsky of the World's Fair Corporation to write an extravaganza with music supplied by Arthur Schwartz that featured important occasions and characters in American history — the inauguration of George Washington, Lincoln at Gettysburg, Barnum and Jenny Lind, Teddy Roosevelt and his Rough Riders, Diamond Jim Brady, and Lillian Russell — culminating in a massive fireworks display to the accompaniment of the national anthem. Despite driving rain which drowned the opening performance, the show was a success, running for nearly five months at Flushing Meadows.

At last he found time to get together with Sigmund Romberg again, this time on a story called *New Orleans*. While he was working on the book in the summer of 1940, Paris fell to the German army. So moved was Oscar by this event that he did something he had rarely ever done; he wrote a poignant poem about the city he loved and felt he had lost. A week or two later when he was in Beverly Hills to attend an ASCAP dinner honoring Rudolf Friml, Oscar asked Jerry Kern to put a melody to his words. Kern did just that in almost a single sitting, and "The Last Time I Saw Paris" became the only Kern-Hammerstein song to exist outside a musical or screenplay. The following year it was sung by Ann Sothern in the movie *Lady Be Good!* (ironically, based on the hit Gershwin show) and won an Academy Award for best song of the year in 1941.

In the summer, Oscar received an approach from an unexpected quarter: Richard Rodgers, who was considering a musical based on an Edna Ferber novel, *Saratoga Trunk*, but was uncertain whether his longtime partner Lorenz Hart was in good enough physical and mental condition to write a libretto, suggested Ferber ask Hammerstein if he would be interested. The next day, Rodgers added his own encouragement by cable. LARRY AND I SIT WITH EVERYTHING CROSSED HOPING THAT YOU WILL DO SARATOGA TRUNK WITH US.

73

Oscar was indeed interested — Rodgers & Hart were just about the hottest team on Broadway, and working with them might well provide the jump-start his career needed. As it turned out, the project never got off the ground, but it had opened a door, as Rodgers's reply indicates.

> *I can say this, however, I was delighted and warmed by several things in*
> *your letter. Even if nothing further comes of this difficult matter, it will*
> *at least have allowed us to approach each other professionally.*
> *Specifically, you feel that I should have a book of "substance" to write to.*
> *Will you think seriously about doing such a book?*

There was nothing casual about this; it was a direct invitation toward eventual partnership and Oscar knew it. But other projects crowded the proposition out of his mind. *New Orleans* had now become *Sunny River*, an operetta about separated lovers in the New Orleans of the early 1800s. After the usual tribulations during its summer tryouts (in the same St. Louis open-air theater where *Gentleman Unafraid* had been performed) plus a couple of days in New Haven to tighten ship, Max Gordon announced December 4, 1941, as the show's opening night (at the same St. James Theatre at which Oscar would shortly triumph with *Oklahoma!*). It ran for 36 performances.

"I feel sure that you did everything that was humanly possible to give the show its chance to find a public, and it didn't," Oscar later wrote Max Gordon. "I don't believe there is one — certainly not in New York. Operetta is a dead pigeon and if it ever is revived it won't be by me. I have no plans at the moment and don't feel like making any."

It's not hard to see why he felt that way. He was 46 years of age. Thirty of those years had been spent in or around the theater. He had collaborated with every major theatrical composer in the business — except one. And he was washed up. So, with nobody wanting to hire him, nobody wanting to work with him, he decided he would return to a "dream" project he had long cherished and write (or more properly, rewrite) a show with a dead composer — Georges Bizet. Once, way back in his early Hollywood days, he had put forward the idea of a movie based on Bizet's opera *Carmen*, but transposed to a present-day setting. The more he thought about it, the more enthusiastic he became.

Carmen became Carmen Jones, the Seville cigarette factory in which she works a parachute factory in South Carolina during the war (which had begun when the Japanese bombed Pearl Harbor just two days after the opening of *Sunny River*). Don José became a GI corporal named Joe who is seduced and persuaded to desert by Carmen. Micaela becomes a sweet kid called Cindy Lou and the bullfighter who becomes Don José's rival was transformed from Escamillo to "Husky" Miller, a prizefighter. Oscar was, he said (although many years later he admitted that he only kept going through inner conceit), "portraying two human beings in terrible trouble, two confused souls moving toward their destruction with every note they sing."

*Carmen Jones* took shape quickly. The songs worked beautifully, the plot had form and reason, and Oscar believed it was good work. But he also believed, at this lowest of low points in his life, that with his track record he had about as much chance of finding a producer as the pot of gold

Oscar Hammerstein in Hollywood, c.1935. That's MGM's Music Department, where at one time or another, the greatest songwriters in the world worked. Used by permission of the Rodgers and Hammerstein Organization.

75

at the end of the rainbow. The funny thing was, he found both when, the following year, he teamed with Dick Rodgers to write *Oklahoma!* Its success was so big, its impact so enormous, he might have been forgiven if he became enamored with the idea of his own genius. But not Oscar. Shortly after the opening of *Oklahoma!* he bought an Easter weekend ad in *Variety* which listed every one of his recent failures: *Very Warm for May* (seven weeks), *Ball at the Savoy* (five weeks), *Three Sisters* (six weeks), *Free for All* (three weeks), *The Gang's All Here* (three weeks), *East Wind* (three weeks), and *Gentlemen Unafraid* (three weeks). In typical Hammerstein style, the headline read: I'VE DONE IT BEFORE — AND I CAN DO IT AGAIN!!

# CHAPTER THREE

# Dick AND Larry

*When asked what the difference was between working with Larry Hart and working with Oscar Hammerstein, Dick Rodgers said: "When I worked with Larry Hart they used to say, 'There goes the little guy with that sonofabitch.' When I started to work with Oscar they said, 'There goes the big guy with that sonofabitch.'"*

Richard Rodgers was a phenomenon: no other word will do. In a career spanning more than six decades, he wrote an astonishing succession of 40 Broadway shows, some of which dramatically altered the traditions of the musical stage. He received countless honors and awards: Pulitzers, Oscars, Tonys, Emmys, and Grammys — there is even a Broadway theater named after him. Throughout his life Rodgers was a driving perfectionist, a constantly restless innovator, and a tough man to do business with. Yet for all his melodic fertility, his brilliance as a theatrical producer, and his enormous contribution to every aspect of the musical, as an individual he was and remains an enigma.

He came to the partnership with Oscar Hammerstein, as we have seen, after almost 25 years of collaboration with Larry Hart, begun before Rodgers himself was out of school. In their last — and many think finest — decade together, Rodgers and Hart had become renowned for constantly breaking new ground. Their 1936 show *On Your Toes* was the first to make extended use of both ballet and a musical interlude, the famous "Slaughter on Tenth Avenue" sequence. In the following year's *Babes in Arms* they prefigured the demise of the traditional line of chorus girls by replacing it with a cast of exuberant 16-year-olds. In 1940's *Pal Joey* they broke every rule in the book by having a leading man who was not only a dancer rather than a singer, but a cheap knave rather than a hero. Successful as they were, however, it was not until Rodgers's flair for seeing the dramatic and truly new was finally mated with Oscar Hammerstein's enormous range of theatrical experience that the pieces fell into place perfectly. Even so, no understanding of their achievements is possible without first examining Rodgers's collaboration with febrile, tragic Larry Hart.

Richard Charles Rodgers was the second son of William and Mamie Rodgers, who were married in New York in 1896. He was born in a summer house rented by Mamie's parents on Brandreth Avenue at Hammels Station, near Arverne, Long Island, on June 28, 1902. Some years before Dick was born, his parents had moved into the Lexington Avenue home of Mamie Rodgers's parents, Jacob and Rachel (Lewine) Levy; his brother Mortimer was born there January 13, 1898. The following year the Levys sold their town house and moved to a five-story brownstone at 3 West 120th Street in Harlem. Dr William Rodgers — the family name was originally Rogazinsky — conducted his medical practice on the ground floor. On the second floor were the dining quarters and a spacious living room with a Steinway grand piano.

It was not a happy household; there was constant conflict between Dr. Rodgers and his domineering mother-in-law, and he often would not speak to her for weeks on end. In later years, her grandson would call Rachel Levy a "know-it-all" and relate how the constant bickering, the stony silences, and the way his grandmother mocked her husband's Orthodox beliefs and inability to lose his Russian accent had instilled deep feelings of tension and insecurity in him. These were probably exacerbated by the fact that his mother, a shy and hypochondriacal woman, found it difficult to openly display affection, a trait that would mark her son's relationship with his own children. Offsetting that, however, was the warm bond between Richard and his father, who would throughout his

The Hart family home at 59 West 119th Street, Manhattan. This was where Dick met Larry in 1919.
Author's Collection.

lifetime devotedly assemble scrapbook after comprehensive scrapbook of his son's achievements.

Mortimer seems to have wanted to become a doctor from the start; he eventually became director of gynecology at Lenox Hill Hospital. His brother took an almost equally direct line towards his chosen career: music. Dick's parents were inveterate theatergoers, their taste running to musicals and operettas. In those days, the complete score of the show was always sold in the theater foyer, and Dr Rodgers invariably purchased one. Back home, Mamie would seat herself at the Steinway and play, while her husband sang the songs from *Mademoiselle Modiste* or *The Chocolate Soldier* until little Richard, with his infallible musical ear, would know them by heart. Whereupon he would clamber up on the piano stool and try to play them himself. Formal piano lessons were unsuccessful. By the time he was a toddler, he was picking out fragments of melodies on the piano, and, at six, playing fluently — if by ear — with both hands. By this time the Rodgers family had moved to a large fifth-floor apartment at 161 West 86th Street. Again, the ground floor became the consulting room, waiting room, and office of Dr. Rodgers's successful upper-class practice; among his patients was the movie star Constance Talmadge.

The first show Dick saw was probably Victor Herbert's 1908 musical *Little Nemo*, remembered today chiefly because it featured a mythical creature called a Whiffenpoof, which so captivated a group of Yale students who saw the show that they named their glee club after it. At his first school, P.S. 166, he recalled, there was a music teacher by the name of Elsa Katz who let him play for assemblies. "I could play the hymns and 'Star Spangled Banner' and the march for the kids to come in with and go out with, and she had some sort of influence on me because I was given the position and it made me a little different from the other kids and I enjoyed that because it was different in a good way." In 1955, his biographer, David Ewen, set out to find Miss Katz and did. "Well, that's amazing," Rodgers remarked. "What did she have to say?" And Ewen said, "She doesn't remember you."

At age 12, Dick was spending hours daily at the keyboard; his friend Samuel Marx recalled that at summer camp Dick would be indoors playing the piano for hours when all the other kids were out swimming or playing games. When he was 14, Dick composed a song called "Campfire Days" which celebrated the joys of Camp Wigwam in Harrison, Maine. He spent his allowance on seats for Saturday matinees, especially the Princess Theatre shows by Bolton, Wodehouse, and Jerome Kern, who was his idol. "I remember sitting in the balcony at a show of Kern's called *Love O' Mike*. It was a failure but I listened to the score and I said to myself, 'I have to be able to write like this.' It was very important to me. I know Kern was the impetus for the whole thing, it was what got me going."

In that same year, the year he met Oscar Hammerstein, Dick's first song, a novelty number with a lyric by James Dyrenforth called "Auto Show Girl," was copyrighted. That fall he wrote his first complete score, the Akron Club's *One Minute, Please* (presented, during a howling blizzard, at the Plaza Hotel on December 29, 1917); and a second, *Up Stage and Down*, which played the night of March 8, 1918, in the ballroom of the Waldorf-Astoria. With the success of this show and another in the offing, the members of the Akron Club — a group of gregarious kids who put on shows to pay for their basketball, baseball, and football equipment, baiting the ticket hook by donating a portion of the proceeds to charity — realized what they and Rodgers needed was a regular lyricist. Philip Leavitt, the son of a paint manufacturer and a classmate of Morty's at Columbia, took the matter in hand.

> We realized Dick needed someone who could write lyrics that
> approached [the quality of] his music, and I suggested … that he do a
> tie-up with Larry because Larry had been doing some translations from
> the [Max] Reinhardt shows abroad and I suggested he meet Larry.
> Larry had a habit of sitting in front of an old Victor phonograph and
> listening to the Kern, Wodehouse, and Bolton operettas, and he loved the
> lyricisms that were in there, and he developed a style all of his own …
> He had a very quick and accurate mind [and] he had a different
> objective in what he saw and heard in both music and lyrics.

So, one Sunday afternoon in the spring of 1919, Leavitt took 16-year-old Rodgers to the Hart house at 59 West 119th Street. Although the Harts had servants, Larry answered the door himself. He was dressed, Rodgers recalled, in tuxedo trousers, carpet slippers, and some kind of shirt. He needed a shave ("Larry always needed a shave," Rodgers added). And he was one of the shortest men Rodgers had ever seen, barely five feet tall, with hands and feet like those of a child. His head was too large for the small body, which gave him a gnomelike appearance. Leavitt remembered:

> *It was all so simple. Dick sat down at the piano, and Larry said, "What have you written?" and Dick played some of his music and it was really love at first sight. All that had to be done was [for me to] sit, listen, and let nature take its course.*

Rodgers and Hart hit it off immediately. They talked and talked and talked. Rodgers discovered that, although Hart was a man with a vast cultural background and worldly airs, he had no job. He was eking out a living translating the lyrics of German operettas for Gustave Amberg, a friend of his father's whose United Plays company had a first-sight arrangement with the Shuberts, the theatrical producing firm. Amberg would pick up German plays that might lend themselves to adaptation and give them to Hart to translate — for a flat $50 a week, no royalties, no percentage — and then show them to the Shuberts. If the Shuberts liked the play, they might take it on. If not, it cost them nothing to look.

**Lorenz Milton Hart at the age of twenty-three. He had just produced his first play *The Blond Beast* by Henry Myers. It flopped.** Author's Collection.

Rodgers soon discovered that Larry Hart had deeply felt and forcefully expressed opinions about the musical theater. "His feeling for the basic ideas of musical shows were different from anyone else's," Rodgers remembered. "He felt they ought to tackle subjects that at that time hadn't been touched at all. He talked about interior rhyming schemes and female endings, things I knew nothing at all about. He attacked writers who would not take advantage of the chances there were in the theater to explore hitherto unexplored territory. I played him some of my songs and he liked them as much as I liked his ideas."

They agreed to collaborate, and throughout the late spring and summer of that year, wrote song after song together. The story goes that an enthusiastic Phil Leavitt paved the way for them to see a producer,

80

the famous Lew Fields. At one time half of the celebrated vaudeville comedy team, Weber and Fields, Fields had turned to producing his own shows and often starring in them. An appointment was made, and when Rodgers arrived at the Fields's summer place, he found the entire Fields clan awaiting him: Joseph, the eldest son; Herbert, whom Dick already knew slightly; the willowy, dark-eyed Dorothy; and Frances. Rodgers played some of the songs he and Larry had written and was gratified — not to say stunned — when Lew Fields said he liked one, "Any Old Place with You," so much that he would like to buy it and put it into his current show, *A Lonely Romeo.*

**Richard Charles Rodgers at age sixteen, about the time he met Larry Hart.**
Author's Collection.

That's one version. The other comes from Herb Fields himself, who said he, Dick, and Larry kept "serenading Pop Fields with 'Any Old Place with You' nightly outside his dressing room until in disgust, to keep us quiet, he put it in a show." Whichever tale is true (and maybe both are), the song was in, and shortly after theaters reopened following the August 1919 actors' strike, Eve Lynn and Alan Hale (later to be Errol Flynn's sidekick in many a Warner Bros. swashbuckler) launched the professional career of Rodgers and Hart. It was a jaunty enough little number (originally performed in a Camp Paradox show where it was known as "The Geography Song"), all about honeymooning in such diverse places as Syria and Siberia, or Virginia and Abyssinia, with fairly outrageous wind-ups in which the ardent Hale vowed "I'm goin' to corner ya /in California," "I'd go to hell for ya /or Philadelphia," or even

81

> Clothes won't encumber ya
> Down in Colombia.
> Chile's saucy, too.
> Let's get pneumonia
> In Macedonia —
> Any old place with you!

Thus Richard Rodgers became the first (and probably the last) 17-year-old to land a song in a full-fledged Broadway show. In December, "Any Old Place with You" was copyrighted and published. The partnership of Rodgers and Hart was up and running. What could stand in their way now?

Like Rodgers's, Larry Hart's family was middle class, but their fortunes were much more erratic, and their lifestyle the diametric opposite of the disciplined, almost severe household in which Rodgers grew up. Larry's parents, Max and Frieda (Eisenberg) Hart, had come to America from Hamburg, and both spoke English with thick German intonations. In addition, the rotund — he is said to have weighed well over 230 pounds in his prime — and diminutive Hart senior had a lisp. He called himself a "promoter;" many of his commercial ventures were on the dubious side of the street. His wife, Frieda, was a tiny, doll-like woman, well under five feet in height.

Their first child, James, was born in 1892 but died in infancy. Lorenz Milton Hart was born on May 2, 1895 in the Hart apartment at 173 111<sup>th</sup> Street. Two years later, a second son, Theodore Van Wyck, always called Teddy, arrived. In 1904 the Harts acquired a brownstone just a couple of blocks south of the Harlem Courthouse at 59 West 119<sup>th</sup> Street, where Max ran a lavish and open house to which he invited business partners, political cronies, and show-business people — tonight Lillian Russell and "Diamond Jim" Brady, tomorrow Gustave Amberg or Willie Hammerstein. The Harts often went to bed and left the parties roaring along down below, for when Max Hart was "flush" only the best would do. There were other times when Frieda Hart would have to pawn her jewelry to keep up the menage, which consisted of a chauffeur, a footman, two housemaids, and Rosie the cook. It was hardly surprising, in view of all this, that Larry Hart grew up without any real respect for money or respectability.

The Hart side of the family claimed to be descended from the German poet Heinrich Heine, although Larry's sister-in-law, Dorothy Hart, insisted that Larry "couldn't have cared less about all that stuff." Nevertheless, it was only in Larry that genius flowered, and it is hard to see how the genius came from either his father — a crude, coarse, vulgarly loud-mouthed man seemingly impervious to culture, even if he had trained himself in business and the law — or from his genteel, tiny, strict mother. Precocious from the very beginning, Larry began writing verse at the age of eight or nine. Max Hart would frequently get the boy out of bed to recite his poetry for visitors. He also encouraged the youngster to drink, so that by the time he was in his late teens, Larry already had an unhealthy appetite for alcohol; it would become a lifelong addiction.

He attended the prestigious De Witt Clinton High School on 59<sup>th</sup> Street, Weingart's Institute on 120<sup>th</sup> Street (and its summer camp extension, where they called him "Shakespeare" Hart, because of his penchant for packing his clothing trunk with books instead of sweaters and shirts and sneakers, and "Dirty-neck" Hart for more obvious reasons), and later, Columbia Grammar School, where he dashed off all kinds of prose and poetry for the school newspaper. He entered Columbia University in 1915 after a European holiday with his family, transferring to the School of Journalism after a year, although he had no intention of becoming a newspaperman. He soon became a member of the group which contributed verse and vignettes to Franklin P. Adams's "The Conning Tower" column, but his main ambition — as he himself put it — was to major in Varsity Shows.

In 1916, having heard Larry recite some of his poems at the Hart house, producer Gustave Amberg was impressed enough to introduce him to a man named Stefan Rachmann, who produced knockabout German-language shows at the Deutsches Theater in the East Side area of Manhattan known as Yorkville. Rachmann needed someone to translate the song lyrics for a "vivacious musical comedy" by Pordes Milo and Hermann Frey called *Die Tolle Dolly*, and Larry got the job. The songs that have survived suggest the show was even cornier than the lyrics, but that wouldn't have bothered Larry; what was important was the credit "English Lyrics by Lorenz M. Hart" on the sheet music.

In September 1919, Dick Rodgers entered Columbia University as a freshman. He and Larry collaborated on their first show together, with Larry's new chum Milton "Doc" Bender, a dentistry student with a yen for show business, providing book and direction for "An Atrocious Musical Comedy" (their own subtitle) called *You'd Be Surprised*. The musical director was Lew Fields, and the cast included his daughter Dorothy and also Phil Leavitt. Among the songs was one about "poor bisected, disconnected Mary, Queen of Scots" with a lyric by Herb Fields, and a cute one by Dick and Larry called "Don't Love Me Like Othello (I'm Much Too Young to Die)." Oscar Hammerstein was represented as well, with a Rodgers melody to his song "That Boy of Mine."

The show was again for the benefit of the Akron Club, and again played a one-night engagement in the ballroom of the Plaza Hotel on March 6, 1920. Eighteen days later, the Columbia University Players presented *Fly With Me*, the 1920 Varsity Show, for which three songs with Oscar Hammerstein lyrics (including "There's Always Room for One More") were lifted from the score of *Twinkling Eyes*, and Rodgers and Hart re-used "Don't Love Me Like Othello." Most important of all in that year, however, was the fact that Lew Fields found himself with a problem.

He had hired two songwriters to do a score for a new show he was producing, *Poor Little Ritz Girl*, and he was desperately unhappy with their work. He came to the Columbia Varsity Show and, since he already knew Rodgers and Hart, suggested that he might use some of their songs in his show, and some new ones if they would write them.

83

Rodgers was stunned, Hart overjoyed. They didn't yet know that Fields was in a bind; they honestly believed he was hiring them because he thought they were terrific. *Poor Little Ritz Girl* was due to begin its Boston tryouts on May 28. Fields told the boys he could not pay them as high a fee as "known" names, neglecting to add that the real reason was that he had to pay off the other team as well. It didn't matter; Dick and Larry would probably have written the score for nothing.

They set to work eagerly, providing songs for the slender story of an unsophisticated Southern girl who comes to New York to dance in the chorus of a show, and rents the apartment of a wealthy young bachelor, with appropriately embarrassing results when he returns to town unexpectedly. Dick and Larry provided 15 songs for the show, among them a rewritten version of "Don't Love Me Like Othello" called "You Can't Fool Your Dreams" — an early foray by Larry Hart into that unexplored territory he had been talking about, with Freudian undertones like, "You tell me what you're dreaming, I'll tell you whom you love."

Their work, as they thought, completed, the boys went off to be counselors at summer camp, Larry to Brant Lake, Dick with Herb Fields to Camp Paradox, where Herb supplied lyrics to Rodgers's melodies for such camp show songs as "We Want You to Feel at Home," "My Tent in Paradox," "The Melting Pot," and the rousing "Paradox Victory Song." Meanwhile, Pop Fields had come down with a bad case of cold feet. He was ready to take *Poor Little Ritz Girl* to New York, but the show was anything but ready, so he decided to make some changes. He fired the leading man and lady, rewrote the book, and hired a new musical director, Charles Previn. Worst of all for Rodgers and Hart, Fields cut their score to bits to make room for eight numbers by Sigmund Romberg and Alex Gerber.

The boys came down from the Adirondacks for the show's opening on July 27, 1920 to discover that more than half of their score had been discarded and that the recast, rewritten show bore hardly any resemblance to the one they remembered. Rodgers never forgot the misery with which he watched it, the disappointment of being what he called "a badly-bruised conquering hero." Nevertheless, the reviews were surprisingly good; the show ran for three months, which was considered very satisfactory at a time when a six-month run was a resounding hit.

It was even more satisfactory considering the competition it had. There was a Kern musical, *Night Boat*, and Fanny Brice and W. C. Fields in the latest *Ziegfeld Follies*. The Gershwins had contributed a score to *George White's Scandals*, the second of that ilk. There was also the Hammerstein-Harbach-Stothart show *Tickle Me* and the vastly successful *Irene*, with its huge hit "Alice Blue Gown." On the face of it, therefore, Rodgers

84

and Hart could have been said to have started with a success. What faced them now — and would for the next five years — was a desert of amateur shows, unsuccessful auditions, and complete failure.

The following year, after writing another Akron Club show, *Say Mama,* and the 1921 Columbia Varsity Show *You'll Never Know* (with Oscar Hammerstein helping to stage the book, dances by Herb Fields, and lyrics by Larry Hart), Rodgers quit the college and enrolled at the Institute of Musical Art at 122$^{nd}$ Street and Claremont Avenue, now the renowned Juilliard School. The next three years were the happiest ones of Rodgers's student life. "At the IMA," he said, with his usual penchant for understatement, "I started to learn for the first time what it was I had been doing right."

To reinforce that knowledge, the following year young Rodgers obtained a leave of absence from the IMA and spent a season on the road conducting the orchestra for one of what were known as "Shubert Units," complete touring shows mounted by the Shubert organization, who were challenging the domination of the Keith-Albee vaudeville circuit. The first half of each show consisted of a series of vaudeville acts and the second a tabloid or "tab" musical comedy, in this case a Lew Fields production starring Fields and Nora Bayes called *Blackbirds of 1922.*

In addition, Dick — with some lyrics by Larry and a few by others — wrote the music for one year-end show for each of his years at IMA: *Say it with Jazz* in 1921, *Jazz à la Carte* the following year, and *A Danish Yankee in King Tut's Court,* the latter having its genesis in Mark Twain and the recent discovery of the Egyptian Pharaoh's tomb. It was an idea to which he, Larry, and Herb Fields would return a few years later with infinitely more success. Another idea they all worked very hard on was a show called *Winkle Town,* in which an inventor comes up with an electronic system that renders electric wiring obsolete, but they could not get the book right. They went — "almost on a dare," Rodgers said — to an old friend, Oscar Hammerstein, then enjoying the enormous success of *Wildflower.* To their surprise, Oscar offered to collaborate with them because he so liked the book and the score, one of whose songs was a pretty little schottische praising the delights of "Manhattan."

As things turned out, Hammerstein never found time to work on the book, so Rodgers took the whole thing to Laurence Schwab, a new producer who was teaming up with writer Frank Mandel to do a musical. Schwab confessed to not knowing enough about music to be able to make a decent judgment, and asked Rodgers to play them for his friend, the powerful Max Dreyfus, head of the premier music publishing house of T. B. Harms, Inc.

85

**Arthur Schwartz, in his Schwartz and Dietz days. He also wrote "Tennessee Fish Fry" with Oscar Hammerstein and "I Know My Girl By Her Perfume" with Larry Hart.**

American Society of Composers, Authors, and Publishers.

86

Rodgers was understandably elated by the chance to audition for Dreyfus, who was Jerome Kern's publisher, but even when he played "Manhattan," Dreyfus shook his head. He told Schwab the score had nothing of value in it and suggested he listen instead to the work of another composer on the Dreyfus books, Vincent Youmans. Rodgers slunk out; he was beginning to get downhearted at being told that his songs were "too collegiate" and that he had better change his style or quit the business. As it turned out, Vincent Youmans didn't get the Schwab-Mandel assignment, either; it went to George and Ira Gershwin, already establishing themselves as a top song-writing team.

Rodgers was vastly disappointed by this experience, and found it enormously depressing to be again relegated to the grind of the amateur circuit; perhaps Hart felt the same way. It is hard not to wonder whether at this time the partnership faltered a little. Larry, for example, had become deeply involved in producing a play by another friend, Henry Myers, called *The First Fifty Years*, persuading Livingston Platt to direct and Tom Powers and Clare Eames to star in the two-hander. He invited all the top-string critics to the March 13, 1922, opening — that it was at the Princess Theatre, once the home of the Kern-Bolton-Wodehouse musicals, must have given him especial pleasure — but although the majority of them liked it, the customers didn't, and the play folded after 46 performances. Nearly 30 years later, Jan de Hartog would use the same basic premise for the Jessica Tandy-Hume Cronyn hit *The Fourposter.*

Not only was Larry producing plays with Henry Myers, he was writing songs with his pals Mel Shauer and Morrie Ryskind, with Herb Fields, and for an abortive reunion of the comedy team of Weber & Fields, "Chloe, Cling to Me," a cute piece of nonsense by a 28-year-old Wall Street broker named Joe Trounstine. The following year, he wrote a lyric to a melody by another composer destined to later make a mark in the movie world, L. Franke Harling. The song, "Moonlight Lane" was interpolated into *Helen of Troy, New York,* a 1923 show starring Helen Ford, one of Troy, New York's most famous exports. Meanwhile, Dick Rodgers was working with other lyricists on two amateur shows, one for the Benjamin School for Girls and the other for the IMA. Even if there were no hiccups in the partnership, all this would appear to effectively dispose, once and for all, of the myth — propagated throughout his life by Rodgers — that once they met, Rodgers and Hart never worked with anyone else.

It was around this time that a young lawyer named Arthur Schwartz (who really wanted to be a songwriter) heard Larry's pal Doc Bender play some of the early Rodgers and Hart songs and liked the lyrics so much he got a job at Brant Lake just so he could have the chance to work with Larry. Together they wrote a show called *Dream Boy*, a slight fable about a boy who didn't much care for the athletic life. It was one of the first things Schwartz had written, and Larry came up with a lyric which went:

> I love to lie awake in bed
> Right after taps I pull the flaps above my head.
> I let the moon shine on my pillow.
> 0, what a light those moonbeams shed.
> I feel so happy I could cry
> And tears are born within the corner of my eye.
> To be at home with Ma was never like this.
> I could live forever like this.
> I love to lie awake awhile
> And go to sleep with a smile.

Many years later, Arthur Schwartz would dig that tune out of his trunk for Clifton Webb to sing in *The Little Show of 1929*. With a new lyric by Larry's classmate Howard Dietz, it became "I Guess I'll Have to Change My Plan."

At the time when they worked together at Brant Lake, Arthur Schwartz was hopeful that he and Larry Hart could strike up a permanent collaboration, but Larry explained that he already had a partner, Dick Rodgers. Schwartz even went so far as to set up an audition for himself and Larry to play a few of the Rodgers and Hart songs to Elliott Shapiro of the music publishing firm Shapiro, Bernstein, and Von Tilzer, whose nephew was one of the camp kids. Shapiro — Schwartz described him as "the grimmest-faced man you could ever play a song for" — listened, predictably grim-faced. When they were finished, he said "It's too collegiate. You fellows will never get anywhere unless you change your style. I have to tell you the truth fellows. Change your style or give up."

No chance. Larry was confident his big break was just around the corner. That he already had a reputation as a writer is confirmed by the fact that Billy Rose, himself a jobbing songwriter who was keen to branch out into the impresario business, would come up to the camp to work with Larry. "Their system was to go out in a boat at ten or eleven o'clock in the morning," Arthur Schwartz said, "take sandwiches with them, and Billy Rose and Larry Hart would go over the melodies Billy was working on, and at the end of the day Larry would show me a hundred dollar bill — every day. He never got any royalty, he never got any credit. This went on for three weeks, and I'm sure it went on in New York before Larry became established himself."

Undaunted by the failure of *The First Fifty Years*, Larry plunged into producing another of Henry Myers's two-handers, this time "A Modern Comedy" called *The Blond Beast*. Larry had concocted another daring scheme, this time inviting all the leading theatrical producers to a special matinee performance on March 2, 1923. And it worked: every one of them either attended or sent a representative. Unfortunately, just before the curtain, word arrived at the Plymouth Theatre that there might be another actors' strike and every single one of the producers present left to attend an emergency meeting in David Belasco's nearby office. Like its predecessor, *The Blond Beast* rolled over and died.

88

**Dorothy Fields (with "beard") and fellow Benjamin School for Girls pupil Miriam Rosenwasser in Rodgers and Hart's 1923 amateur show *If I Were King*.** Author's Collection.

After a couple more amateur shows — *If I Were King*, based on the life of François Villon, and an adaptation of the Anthony Hope novel *The Prisoner of Zenda* for the Benjamin School for Girls (the male leads in both played by Dorothy Fields) — the boys decided to collaborate on a straight play, using the unlikely nom-de-plume of Herbert Richard Lorenz, and persuaded Lew Fields to produce it. First called *The Jazz King* and then *Henky*, it was toured through half-a-dozen states before it eventually got into the Ritz Theatre in New York on May 13, 1924, as *The Melody Man*. After a couple of weeks it transferred to the 49$^{th}$ Street Theatre, where it staggered along for another month before Pop Fields, who also starred, pulled the plug after exactly 56 performances. Notable for two rather good "bad" Tin Pan Alley-type songs, "I'd Like to Poison Ivy" and "Moonlight Mama," the play's only other theatrical distinction was in giving a young actor named Fred Bickel, who was easily persuaded to change his name to the more mellifluous Fredric March, his first Broadway part.

Walking down Lexington Avenue one day, Larry Hart spotted a sculpted frieze on the wall of a house which had once belonged to Robert Murray, for whom the district below and east of Grand Central Station was named. Larry became intrigued by the plaque beneath it, which commemorated a little-known event of the Revolutionary War:

MRS MURRAY RECEIVING THE BRITISH OFFICERS
FROM THE PAINTING BY
JENNIS BROWNSCOMBE

HOWE, WITH CLINTON, TRYON AND A FEW OTHERS, WENT
TO THE HOUSE OF ROBERT MURRAY, ON MURRAY HILL, FOR
REFRESHMENT AND REST. WITH PLEASANT CONVERSATIONS
AND A PROFUSION OF CAKE AND WINE, THE GOOD WHIG LADY
DETAINED THE GALLANT BRITONS ALMOST TWO HOURS,
QUITE LONG ENOUGH FOR THE BULK OF PUTNAM'S DIVISION
OF FOUR THOUSAND MEN TO LEAVE THE CITY AND ESCAPE TO THE
HEIGHTS OF HARLEM BY THE BLOOMINGDALE ROAD,
WITH THE LOSS OF ONLY A FEW SOLDIERS.

FLIGHT OF THE AMERICANS ON THE LANDING OF
THE BRITISH, SEPTEMBER 13$^{TH}$, 1776

Larry's theatrical mind immediately recognized this as the raw material for a "bicycle" —
a fertile piece of ground in which to plant a musical — and turned the idea over to Herb
Fields, who added a subplot about a romance between Mrs. Murray's niece, a pretty
colleen named Betsy Burke, and a British officer, Sir John Copeland. The trio dubbed it
*Sweet Rebel* and took the idea to Pop Fields, who promptly turned it down. Other producers were equally discouraging — who wanted a musical about the Revolutionary War,
for godsakes? — so the trio resorted to other dodges. Herb ambushed actress Helen Ford
in the lobby of the Algonquin Hotel; her husband George was a producer, maybe if she
liked it he would raise the money to do the show. Helen, who had just had a big success
in *The Gingham Girl*, liked what there was of the book — they had no second act yet —
very much. She promised to try and interest her husband and also John Murray
Anderson, the director, whom she knew.

"I stuck with it for two reasons," she said. "The first was that I didn't have a job. The
second was that I knew this would make a star of me, I knew this instinctively. Up to
that time I'd been playing these leads in shows where the comedian was probably the
most important character and ... well, I just wanted a good part. You know what sold it
to me? The entrance. We were going through a period when they were sneaking the leading lady on, so she'd come on with the chorus and they wouldn't see her ... So when I
read the book, I saw this marvelous entrance, I made the entrance in a barrel. At that
time, that was shocking, you know?"

*Sweet Rebel* would indeed make a star of Helen, but not just yet. Broadway was
bursting at the seams with hit musicals that year: Friml's *Rose Marie*, Romberg's *The
Student Prince*, Irving Berlin's fourth successful *Music Box Revue*; there was another
*Ziegfeld Follies*, another Gershwin hit — and a big one — called *Lady Be Good!*, starring
Fred and Adele Astaire; and Vincent Youmans's *No, No, Nanette!*, trying out in Chicago,
was said to be sure to become the hottest ticket in town. "I spent almost a solid year with
them," Helen Ford said, "doing auditions for anybody. At the drop of a hat we did it,
man, woman, or child, anywhere, all over town, on Seventh Avenue for the cloak-and-
suiters, even some men who I think were gangsters. They were putting money into shows
in those days, although usually they had a cutie they wanted to put in, too. Would you
believe it, we did about 50 auditions?"

And no one was interested. The falter became a limp. Rodgers later confessed that this
was one of the worst periods in his life. He knew that Larry Hart was beginning to lose
hope; Herb Fields also. He decided that he had better give some thought to the advice
producers had so freely given him and get out of the music business altogether. "Don't

forget I'd reached the age of 22," he said, "and I wasn't earning any money, and I had to make my mind up whether I wanted to go along with another amateur show or ... well, I had been offered a job in the commercial line, babies' underwear, as a matter of fact." A friend had introduced him to a Mr. Marvin, who was looking for a young man to take the weight of his one-man baby-clothes business off his shoulders. He offered Rodgers $50 a week to start, which was exactly $50 a week more than Rodgers was earning. Dick went home, promising to think it over.

That very night, however, he got a call from Benjamin Kaye, a patient of his father's who had written a couple of lyrics for Akron Club shows which Dick had scored. Kaye ("an enchanting old gent," according to Edith Meiser) was working with the understudies of the Theatre Guild, putting on a show to raise money for tapestries to hang in the Guild's new theater. Would Dick be interested in writing the music? If so, he would ask two members of the cast and committee, Romney Brent and Edith Meiser, to come and talk it over with him. Rodgers agreed; as it turned out, the date they selected conflicted with Brent's previously arranged date with the lovely Asian movie star, Anna May Wong. Brent wasn't about to pass that up in order to talk to an unknown musician, so Edith Meiser went to see Rodgers alone. "I walked into this very elegant apartment and it had an enormous foyer with an enormous grand piano. Dick was there, and he said, "Well,

**Charles Purcell and Helen Ford (center) in Rodgers and Hart's 1925 "baby grand opera"**
***Dearest Enemy.*** Used by permission of the Rodgers and Hammerstein Organization.

**Sheet music for *Dearest Enemy* featuring Helen Ford.**
Author's Collection.

92

I'll play you a few things I've done for the Varsity Shows up at Columbia," and I wasn't terribly impressed, to tell you the truth. Then he played "Manhattan" — and I *flipped!* "

Edith Meiser excitedly told her committee that she had found their composer, fully expecting to write the lyrics to the songs herself. When they began working, however, Rodgers diffidently said that he usually worked with Larry Hart, and wondered whether they would mind if Larry tried a few ideas. Miffed, Meiser agreed, and Rodgers broached the idea to Larry, who turned him down flat. The strange coincidence of Theatre Guild, enthusiastic Rodgers, and reluctant Hart is almost bizarre, but there is no question that Larry was absolutely against doing the show. To begin with, it was a revue, not a book show; second, it would play only two performances, and those on a Sunday; third, the budget was at best inadequate; and in the fourth place, he was sick and tired of the amateur grind that put no money in the bank in the first place. Rodgers talked him around, however, and Edith Meiser remembered how, when the first lyrics began to take shape, she had the good sense to know that she was "outclassed — but *way* out! When those lyrics began to float in, you know, to all these ideas we had, they were so absolutely sensational! I can remember Larry Hart coming into the Garrick Theatre, this little bit of an almost-dwarf man. I've always said he was the American Toulouse-Lautrec, really. He was that kind of personality. Of course, we *adored* him. I mean, Dick we were terribly fond of, but Larry was *adored.*"

The cast were young, irreverent, enthusiastic, and bright, the pets of the theater world: many of them would become well-known names in the years ahead, among them Sterling Holloway, Romney Brent, Lee Strasberg, Betty Starbuck, Libby Holman, Alvah Bessie, and Harold Clurman. They called their revue *The Garrick Gaieties*, and the two performances were scheduled for the afternoon and evening of May 17, 1925. Orchestra seats were $2.20, balcony $1.65 or $1.10. The program notes proclaimed that the revue's progenitors had neither principals nor principles and proceeded to prove it by lampooning everything in sight — Michael Arlen's novel *The Green Hat* became *The Green Derby*, Sidney Howard's hit play *They Knew What They Wanted* became *They Didn't Know What They Were Getting*, and so on. A song performed by Betty Starbuck, Libby Holman, and June Cochrane, "Ladies of the Box Office," neatly skewered such skewerable types as *Follies* showgirl Mary Pickford, and Sadie Thompson, heroine of the 1922 Jeanne Eagels hit, *Rain*. Right after this frolic, Sterling Holloway and June Cochrane did Rodgers's favorite song from the ill-fated *Winkle Town* "in one" — that is to say, before an unadorned curtain behind which the scenery was being moved. The audience responded with delight to Larry Hart's felicitous ode to the joys of Manhattan, the Bronx, and Staten Island too, of going to Coney and eating boloney, or to Yonkers where true love conquers.

> We'll go to Brighton
> The fish you'll frighten
> When you're in.
> Your bathing suit so thin
> Will make the shellfish grin
> Fin to fin.
> Our future babies
> We'll send to *Abie's*
> *Irish Rose*
> Perhaps we'll live to see it close.
> The great big city's a wondrous toy
> Just made for a girl and boy.
> We'll turn Manhattan into an isle of joy!

93

The matinee audience loved it; they gave Holloway and Cochrane a standing ovation. Rodgers remembered Larry Hart running backstage shouting "It's gonna run a year, this show's gonna run a year!" The evening performance was greeted just as enthusiastically — there were a dozen encores of "Manhattan" and the audience just wouldn't let the performers leave the stage. The verdict of the critics was nothing short of delirious. Rodgers and Hart had a hit, but one that had already closed before it really got started.

There was only one thing to do and Rodgers did it. He talked to Terry Helburn, and she agreed to let them do matinees for another week; they played to standing room only at every performance. "Now I was feeling really cocky," Rodgers wrote. "Again I spoke to Terry, this time proposing that our show be allowed to play the Garrick for a regular run." And what, pray, should they do with the Alfred Lunt and Lynn Fontanne play *The Guardsman* which was the Garrick's current attraction? Helburn asked. Close it, Rodgers said.

His *chutzpa* paid off. *The Guardsman* was closed and, on June 8, *The Garrick Gaieties* began a regular theatrical run. Some sketches were dropped, and a new song, "Sentimental Me (and Poor Romantic You)," was added. With the song "Manhattan" front page news all over the country, recording managers of the big phonograph companies were competing to put records of the new song on the market. For the first time, Dick and Larry were actually earning money regularly from their work. Gone were Larry's thoughts of returning to the translation of more blasted operettas, gone forever Dick's career in the baby clothes business.

With the success of *The Garrick Gaieties,* things began to happen with the Revolutionary War musical *Sweet Rebel,* now retitled *Dearest Enemy.* Helen Ford, still doggedly pursuing support for the play, came up with what they called "a butter and egg man" named Robert Jackson, a former classmate of her husband George at Dartmouth. Jackson had just made a million selling out his chain of stores in Canada and was easily persuaded to invest in the show. While he took Dick, Larry, Herb, and Helen on a mad whirl of the Manhattan night spots, Helen's husband, Shakespearean stock-theater company manager George Ford, the show's producer, arranged for them to try out the show at the Colonial Theatre in Akron, Ohio. Scion of an old theatrical family, Ford had connections throughout the country; his uncle had been the Harry Ford in whose Washington theater President Abraham Lincoln was assassinated in 1865.

With George Ford's brother directing, and the cast provided by the Colonial Theatre's resident stock company, they rehearsed for a week. Encouraged by the audience response to their one-night performance on July 20, the triumvirate brought the show back to New York, where John Murray Anderson, free now of the commitment which had prevented his directing earlier (and perhaps encouraged by the fact that the show had backers), agreed to direct it. They tried out in Baltimore; Helen Ford recalled it was so hot that the beautiful Revolutionary War costumes were soaking wet with perspiration, and her husband noted glumly that the burlesque house across the street was attracting a lot more customers than they were. *Dearest Enemy* opened at the Knickerbocker Theatre in New York on September 18.

Show, star, and songs won plenty of praise. Helen Ford — "our little flowerpot," as Herb called her — was proved right; *Dearest Enemy* made her a star, due in part to her then-outrageous entry, apparently clad only in a barrel. Thanks to Anderson, the settings were visually charming and apposite. The songs were neat, witty, and just naughty enough to charm, as in "War Is War," when the young ladies at Mrs. Murray's establishment, who have been bemoaning the absence of their American suitors, are warned by Mrs. Murray that the British are coming:

> Mrs. Murray:    Ev'ry soldier is a frightful brute who
> Snatches little ladies for his loot…
> Girls:    Hoo-
> -ray, we're going to be compromised!
> Hooray, we're going to be compromised!
> War is war!

The undoubted hit of the score was "Here In My Arms," which by clever alternation of the lyrics was at one stage a duet for Betsy and her British lover ("Here in my arms, it's adorable"), and then a solo lament when she mistakenly believes he has betrayed her ("It's deplorable you never will be there"). After many misunderstandings between the handsome British officer and the feisty Irish colleen, there was a rousing patriotic finale (devised by George and Harry Ford) in which George Washington appeared and the lovers were reunited.

*Dearest Enemy* settled down for a run of nearly a year at the Knickerbocker, a success indeed for the newcomers. There was also a moment of sweet satisfaction for Rodgers. He received a call from Max Dreyfus of T. B. Harms, complaining peevishly about Dick's having taken the music of *The Garrick Gaieties* to one of Dreyfus's competitors, and inviting him to join Harms with the score of *Dearest Enemy* and all his and Larry's future work, at a royalty of three cents a copy. It would have taken a saint to refrain from reminding Dreyfus that he had dismissed most of the songs in *The Garrick Gaieties*, including "Manhattan," as of no value at that traumatic interview. Dick Rodgers might have been a lot of things, but a saint he wasn't. He and Dreyfus became good friends anyway.

*Dearest Enemy* opened during one of the most scintillating weeks in the history of American musical theater. Two nights earlier, *No, No, Nanette!* had opened, an immediate smash hit. Three days after *Dearest Enemy* opened, Rudolf Friml's *The Vagabond King* made Dennis King a star overnight. The following evening, the curtain of Ziegfeld's New Amsterdam Theatre rose on *Sunny*, the first collaboration of Jerome Kern, Oscar Hammerstein II, and Otto Harbach, starring Marilyn Miller. Every single one of them

95

was a major hit.

Rodgers and Hart had picked *exactly* the right moment to "come good." Between 1924 and 1929 no less than 26 theaters would open in New York, bringing the total to 90, which would house an *average* of 225 new shows a year for the decade. In that decade, Dick and Larry would write a minimum of two shows a year, often more. It was a dream come true for both of them, and Rodgers plunged into work as though it were water, pushing Larry Hart to produce song after song after song lyric to match his abundant outpouring of melody. By 1926, Rodgers and Hart had five musicals playing on Broadway and another in London; as if this were not enough, they also wrote songs for a short-lived Billy Rose revue called *The Fifth Avenue Follies*, staged in a mansion converted into a theater-restaurant. The opening number from that forgotten score provides a perfect example of how different Rodgers and Hart songs were from anything else being heard.

> Kind auditors, you see in us a most unholy Trinity!
> Compared to us, Boccaccio's a doctor of divinity!
> Our sins, if laid from end to end, would stretch into infinity
> We earn an honest living while we rob you of your sleep.
> Our manager has warned us it's the height of asininity
> If we'd offend the morals of this sacrosanct vicinity
> Our show must please both movie stars
> And ladies of virginity!

Perhaps only half the audience — if that — got that wicked little punchline, so very typical of the Larry Hart style. Nobody had ever written lyrics like these for the stage before. Audiences of that year were more used to songs that were really jingles: "Tea for two /and two for tea /and me for you /and you for me" or "Your eyes of blue /your kisses too /I never knew /what they could do" or "When the red, red robin comes bob, bob, bobbin' along." Producers weren't ready for the kind of wit and sophistication that Dick and Larry Hart were determined to bring to the Broadway stage, and as a result, during this first decade of their collaboration, they had to handle their share of shows with nitwitted plots, well-signaled song spots, and familiar comic routines. Such a one was their next show, *The Girl Friend*.

Produced by Lew Fields and centering on the then-topical theme of six-day bicycle races, *The Girl Friend*, which opened in New York on March 17, 1926, had about as much plot as a fortune cookie. Even so, the score was another gem that contained not only the title song and a rousing ditty called "The Damsel Who Done All the Dirt," but also the durable, lilting "Blue Room," which composer and musicologist Alec Wilder called "the first identifiable Rodgers song." Although *The Girl Friend* faltered in its opening weeks (leading Dick and Larry to waive their royalties until it got through the sticky patch), it soon caught on with the public and ran until the end of the year, reinforcing the claim of Rodgers and Hart to being the brightest, freshest songwriting talents on Broadway. Robert Benchley, writing in *Life* magazine (not the picture magazine, but an earlier one best remembered because Benchley was its critic), remarked that Hart's lyrics showed unmistakable signs of the writer's having given personal thought to them. "Considerably more," said Abel Green in *Variety*, "is anticipated from Rodgers and Hart."

The boys did their best not to disappoint. Two months later they unveiled a second edition of *The Garrick Gaieties*, their score again studded with charming songs. "Sleepyhead" (cut from the score of *The Girl Friend* — and cut again a few days after the opening) and "What's The Use of Talking?" are little sung these days, but "Mountain Greenery" is as fresh and popular now as it was nearly 80 years ago. Their show-within-a-show, *The Rose of Arizona*, sailed into pretty well everything Broadway had to offer, roasting *Rose-Marie* and *The Vagabond King*, even guying Rodgers's hero Jerome Kern's "Till the Clouds Roll By" in a cutely arch number that began "It may rain when the sun stops shining."

Next, they were approached by English actor Jack Hulbert, who was planning to produce a play called *Lido Lady* in London starring himself and his wife, Cicely Courtneidge. He wanted songs in it: Rodgers and Hart songs. It took the partners little time to decide that since the show was to be set in Venice, they ought to take a trip to Europe to do some research before heading for London to rehearse the show in the autumn. They sailed on an Italian ship, the *Conte Biancamano*, whose name Larry Hart kept rolling around his tongue, pretending he was speaking Italian. They went to Naples and Sorrento. In Venice they met Noel Coward and an immensely rich young fellow with delicate features and large, soft eyes named Cole Porter who lived with his equally wealthy wife Linda in the palazzo where Robert Browning had died. Porter had already done a couple of unsuccessful Broadway scores, but nothing had come of them, so he composed mainly for the entertainment of his friends.

From Venice the partners went by train to Paris and on to London, where they added songs to the already written libretto, one of them being "Here in My Arms." The show was successful, if undistinguished; the songwriters more than a little disenchanted with their producer. Hulbert treated them distantly — he referred to them in his autobiogra-

97

phy as "our American college boys" — so they set sail for home as soon as the score was complete. Back in New York they were soon deeply enmeshed in two new productions. One of these was Herb Fields's newest idea, a show built around the dream fantasies of its heroine, *Peggy-Ann*. Since the theme was (to say the least) unusual for a musical, the boys decided to go the whole hog. There was no opening chorus as such — in fact, for the first 15 minutes there was no singing or dancing at all. The finale was not a rousing medley of the show's songs but a slow comedy dance in the dark, nearer ballet than the usual "routine," and indicative of the direction in which Dick and Larry were pointing.

The songs were as unusual as the show, which, after two weeks in Philadelphia, opened on December 27 at the Vanderbilt, home of many of the great Rodgers and Hart shows. "A Tree in the Park" was the hit at the time, although "Where's That Rainbow?" has weathered the years better. It was a "family" show, produced by Lew Fields with Helen Ford in the leading role and some other familiar names aboard: Edith Meiser, Betty Starbuck, and Lulu McConnell, the original *Poor Little Ritz Girl. Peggy-Ann* became one of the big successes of a season in which no fewer than 47 new musicals and revues opened, clocking up a ten-month run on Broadway followed by a four-month tour.

Not so the second production, which sounds to have been cursed from its inception. It had begun with a call from Florenz Ziegfeld, the master showman and great glorifier of the American girl whose *Follies* were the Broadway benchmark for quality, opulence, style, and success. He was building a show around Belle Baker, a tiny woman with a big voice he had "discovered" — although she was already an established vaudeville artiste — when she performed during a transatlantic crossing. He already had writers Irving Caesar and David Freedman working on a book and had begun lining up a supporting cast. What he wanted now was a score by Rodgers and Hart — but it had to be ready before the show went into rehearsal.

Rodgers claimed he protested they couldn't possibly have a score ready in a few weeks because they were already working on a show for Lew Fields. "I know all about that," Ziegfeld replied. "But you two are the whiz kids of Broadway. I'm sure you can do it. Besides, I wouldn't think of doing it with anyone else but you." Rodgers's inference is that they were flattered into writing the show, but since the contract they both signed is dated November 3, 1926, it would appear they went into the deal with their eyes open.

The plot, if you could call it that, revolved around the antics of the six Kitzel children — three boys, three girls — as they desperately try to marry off their sister Betsy because Mama Kitzel won't let any of them marry until Betsy finds a husband. It is clear from the record that the show — it started out as *Buy Buy Betty*, then became *Betty Kitzel,* and, finally, *Betsy* — was in trouble from the start. "Larry and I seldom saw Freedman or Caesar," Rodgers wrote, "and there was hardly any effort at genuine collaboration. I don't think we had more than one meeting with La Belle Baker. Ziegfeld, whose function should have been that of a coordinator, rarely paid any attention to us. There was nothing else for us to do but go on our not-very-merry way trying to write songs that might fit a story for which we had been given little more than a rough outline."

Another problem was that it was a big show — dozens of scenes, a large cast, and of course, the Ziegfeld specialty, lines and lines of showgirls — that really needed months to whip into shape, instead of the one-week tryout Ziegfeld had scheduled in Washington. By the time it got there, everybody was screaming at everybody. "The book, if you can call it that, is terrible," Rodgers wrote his wife, "and the score has been such a source of extreme annoyance that I am anxious only to have done with it."

To add insult to injury, the night before the show opened — without informing either Rodgers or Hart — Belle Baker or Ziegfeld (or, more probably, both) prevailed upon Irving Berlin to write her a "hit." Working all night, Berlin came up with "Blue Skies," and when Belle stepped forward in Act Two and belted it out, it stopped the show. Unbelievably, she did 27 encores. When she blew her lines on the 28th, Ziegfeld had them put the spotlight on Irving Berlin, who fed her the lyric while Dick and Larry goggled in astonishment. Certainly nothing of theirs was anything like as notable, except perhaps "This Funny World," a darkly pessimistic song revealing the other side of Hart's mercurial character. Good score, bad score, indifferent score, it wouldn't have made any difference; the critics ripped the show to ribbons and the public stayed away in droves. *Betsy* lasted only five weeks, putting a very large dent in Ziegfeld's bank account.

99

Between May of 1925 and December of 1926, Rodgers and Hart had turned out an astonishing six

**Helen Ford, Patrick Rafferty, and Lulu McConnell in one of the dream sequences in *Peggy-Ann*, 1926.** Author's Collection.

**Belle Baker, whose performance of Irving Berlin's "Blue Skies" in *Betsy* won her a standing ovation from everyone in the theater — except Dick and Larry.**
Author's Collection.

Broadway musicals, one revue, and a London show. Yet for the first time in their ten-year partnership, they didn't have a new show to write. Surprised to hear from London that *Lido Lady* — which they had walked away from before it opened — was playing to capacity audiences, Dick suggested they take the *Aquitania* over and see why for themselves. Needless to say, Larry needed no persuading to embark upon a first-class-all-the-way trip with no work attached, and they sailed for Europe on January 26, 1927.

*Lido Lady* was undoubtedly a hit. "The show has broken all records for the Gaiety Theatre," Rodgers wrote to Dorothy Feiner. "No one can tell us whether it or *Sunny* is the biggest hit in London." But he and Larry agreed it still wasn't much of a show. The book was infantile, the jokes corny, the leading lady considerably past her prime, the antics of Jack Hulbert and Cicely Courtneidge graceless and unfunny — yet the audience clearly loved every minute of it. Go figure.

If *Lido Lady's* producers, Jack Hulbert and Paul Murray, felt any gratitude to their "college boys" for their success, they managed to keep it very successfully concealed, so for the rest of their time, apart from a couple of business meetings, Dick and Larry had little to do except go to parties and see all the new plays — but what fun! Rodgers met the cream of London society: the Prince of Wales, the d'Erlangers, the Guinnesses, "royalty" of the Mayfair set. Larry Hart had different predilections and rarely attended the sort of parties the d'Erlangers threw. He had "his own group," Rodgers said.

Then, in mid-February, London impresario Charles B. Cochran invited them to provide the songs for a revue called *One Dam Thing after Another* (the final "n" in "damn" was dropped to mollify the British censor) that he was mounting at the London Pavilion in May. They said yes on the spot, but since there was no book for them to write to yet, they decided to take another European trip before going to work.

It was during their stay in Paris that the most famous — or should that be "most apocryphal?" — near-collision in songwriting history took place. Dick and Larry were seeing the sights with two girls, Rita Hayden and Ruth Warner, whom they knew from New York. Suddenly, a car came out of a side street and missed their taxi by inches. As Rodgers recalled:

> *"One of the girls said, 'Oh, my heart stood still!' and Larry said, 'Say, that'd make a great title for a song.' I called him a dirty name for thinking about work instead of the fact that we'd been almost killed. And the next thing I knew, we were in London working on a show and I found in my little black notebook the words 'My heart stood still.' Finally I placed the words and remembered the incident. I knew that he'd been right, there was a good title there, and I wrote a tune for it. Larry came into the room and I said, 'I've got a tune for your lyric' and he said, 'What lyric is that?' I said, 'My heart stood still.' 'Never heard it before in my life,' he said. I said, 'They're your words, it's my tune, and I think we've got a song.' And sure enough, we did."*

101

As well as providing an example of Rodgers's penchant for understatement, the story of how "My Heart Stood Still" was written (it's also said, by the way, that he used to groan and leave the room if it was repeated in his presence) gives an insight into how Dick and Larry worked. The songs usually began with Rodgers improvising a melody, or working with a couple of lines or an idea for a title which Larry had given him. By now Rodgers had learned that "work" with Larry meant starting towards midday, because until then Larry would still be getting over the night before; and ending towards late afternoon, by which time Larry would have had enough — he would want to go lay a bet, call a pal, have a few drinks. And once he got into that frame of mind, further work was impossible.

"The difference in Larry when he was drunk and when he wasn't drunk was fantastic," Rodgers said. "It was a real Jekyll and Hyde difference. He was nice in both conditions. He was kind, never got rough, never got mean about anything, but he simply didn't function, and all you had to do was take one look at him and you knew what condition he was in. It showed in his face and his eyes, and the way he talked and the way his mind functioned … He was not obstreperous, not belligerent; he just fell apart when he drank. One could never be angry with him."

On top of that, Larry hated work. He was, Rodgers said, "a maddeningly careless craftsman who would settle for anything." Maddening also in that if there was an obscene rhyme for a given word, Larry would use it. Any objection would be met with a sulky, "What's wrong with it? It rhymes, doesn't it?" And if Dick remonstrated that there were some things you just couldn't say on the Broadway stage, Larry would dismiss his objection with an airy, "Why not? Just because nobody has ever done it?" Whereupon Rodgers would try again and — to quote him — along with "a good deal of incidental screaming," the two of them would work out the lyric together. It was a pattern which would remain constant throughout their partnership.

*One Dam Thing after Another* starred Jessie Matthews and Sonny Hale, soon to be the cynosure of the tabloid press because of their rules-be-damned romance. Hale was married to the actress Evelyn Laye, who sued for divorce amid banner headlines a year or so later. Also featured were former vaudeville dancer Edythe Baker, who now performed popular songs on a white grand piano, goofy comedian Max Wall, and comedians Douglas Byng and Morris Harvey. The show was only moderately successful at first, but when the papers ran a story about how the Prince of Wales had "taught" society bandleader Teddy Wilson to play "My Heart Stood Still," sales of the song — and tickets for the show — soared. *One Dam Thing after Another* eventually ran for 237 performances, in the process making Jessie Matthews a star.

Back in New York, Larry of necessity immersed himself in family matters; his 61-year-old father was suffering from heart trouble and could no longer negotiate the three flights of stairs in the 119th Street house. With considerable reluctance Larry arranged for its sale and moved the Hart household, Max, Frieda, Teddy, and the family housekeeper, Mary Campbell — a buxom Jamaican woman everyone called Big Mary who ran things *her* way and was renowned for her sharp tongue — to a penthouse apartment at the Beresford on Central Park West.

As soon as they were able, Dick and Larry kicked ideas around with Herb Fields, turning finally to one they had shelved five or six years earlier, when they had approached Charles Tressler Lark, executor of the Mark Twain estate, for permission to turn Twain's novel *A Connecticut Yankee in King Arthur's Court* into a musical. Lark had given them the rights free, but they'd never got the show together, not even in the amateur production called *A Danish Yankee in King Tut's Court*. Their option had lapsed and now when they went back to the lawyer, things had changed. Rodgers, Hart, and Fields were not unknowns anymore. They were being spoken of as the natural successors to Bolton, Wodehouse, and Kern, and lawyer Lark — no fool he — made sure that the Twain estate got a healthy royalty.

Herb tried to get his father interested in producing, but Pop Fields turned him down, saying it would not make a good musical. The trio persisted, and when they completed the book in which the Yankee, "Sir Boss," comes to modernize Camelot on a percentage basis, Fields changed his mind. *A Connecticut Yankee* went into rehearsal in the summer of 1927, and the boys had lots of fun with the plot, which has Sir Boss introducing King Arthur to such inventions as telephone, radio, efficiency experts, and other "benefits" of the 20th century. The King gradually begins to talk like President Coolidge; and Merlin like Damon Runyon, his speech a mixture of Olde English and Broadway slang ("Methinks yon damsel is a lovely broad"). The knights are reduced to carrying sandwich boards, "a hell of a job for a knight," with advertising slogans proclaiming "I would fain walk a furlong for a Camel" or the merits of a show called *Ye Hibernian Rose of Abie.*

To beef up the score, Rodgers decided to add "My Heart Stood Still," now a big hit in London. Several other producers, notably Ziegfeld and Dillingham, had already heard of it and were anxious to buy it for one of their shows — in fact, *Variety* reported that Ziegfeld (who denied it) had already offered Cochran $10,000 for the song, which Cochran refused. However, when Rodgers and Hart approached Cochran, he didn't let sentiment get in the way of business. In the deal that was struck, Rodgers and Hart paid Cochran $5000 for the song and, "as a consideration," agreed to a reduction of their royalties on the revue it had appeared in. Even though, in the end, they probably paid something like $15,000 to get the song back, it was probably still the best bargain struck for a song since Ed Christy of Christy's Minstrels paid Stephen Foster $50 for the rights to "The Old Folks At Home."

*A Connecticut Yankee* opened at the Vanderbilt (replacing *Peggy-Ann*) on November 3, 1927. It was another happy show; indeed, Rodgers had had only one disagreement with his producer during the whole thing. During rehearsals at the Walnut Street Theatre in Philadelphia, numerous songs were dropped. Rodgers shrugged off the idea that it was tough to let go of something good. "I'm not married to my tunes," he said. "I never was. And Larry wasn't married to his words. There were plenty more where those came from. We were interested in making the show work. If a song didn't fit or if the audience reaction told us it was wrong, out it came." However, when Lew Fields wanted to cut "Thou Swell" because he was afraid the audience wasn't warming to Hart's cute Olde-English/American slang lyrics, Rodgers put his foot down, insisting on keeping it. But if it didn't fit or it was wrong, why? "Ah," he grinned, "that was different. I was stupid. I liked it."

*A Connecticut Yankee* was a resounding success; only one other Rodgers and Hart show would run longer in Larry Hart's lifetime. "Thou Swell" was only one of its many delights. Larry had concocted lyrics that made everything else on Broadway look infantile, and even if the book wasn't everything it could have been — Herb Fields tended to rely far too often on well-tried "routines" and situations from his father's enormous files — the score was a miracle of originality. It included a cute tongue-in-cheek love song called "I Feel at Home with You," in which Sir Galahad serenaded his lady by telling her that he felt that way because neither of them was too bright. In "On a Desert Island with Thee," Hart went as far as to rhyme

> Let the foolish people quarrel
> We'll forget them for the nonce
> If they think our love immoral
> *Honi soit qui mal y pense*

— erudition heretofore unheard-of in a Broadway show. Add "My Heart Stood Still," and it's easy to see why the show was a thundering hit — 418 performances (almost a year) on Broadway and a year and four months on the road. (It failed, however, to survive the Atlantic crossing.)

Despite their having kept a hit song from him, Charles Dillingham still wanted Dick and Larry to score his new show, a revue to star Beatrice Lillie, Jack Whiting, Clifton Webb, and Irene Dunne. The book, by Guy Bolton and the songwriting team of Kalmar and Ruby, who also wrote libretti (including the successful *Lido Lady* in London), was at best so-so, a frail thing about a young man (Whiting) who wants to put on a show starring his girlfriend (Dunne) but to do so must convince his backers that he is a married man with a child, and persuades his maid (Lillie) to play the part. Alexander Woollcott called it "dreary rubbish" and he had a point; some of the lines, as Bea Lillie remarked in her autobiography, had obviously been imported at great expense from the British Museum.

**Lew Fields rehearsing *A Connecticut Yankee* at the Vanderbilt Theatre, 1927.** Theatre Collection, Museum of the City of New York.

*She's My Baby,* which ushered in

104

the New Year of 1928 (January 3, at the Globe), took such a terrible beating from the critics ("a wonderwork of inanity," "wretched," "ludicrous," "so stale that it is musty") that it folded after 71 performances. It produced nothing of note for the Rodgers and Hart songbook, perhaps because many of the songs were retreads from earlier productions, perhaps — more likely, even — because Rodgers's mind was on other things. His relationship with Dorothy Feiner was on the rocks and he clearly didn't know how to handle it. Dick had known Dorothy all her life. Their romance (or "the trouble," as he smilingly called it) had begun in 1926, when she was 17 and he 24. He and Larry had just finished *Lido Lady* and were coming home on the *Majestic*. On board were the Feiner family, and Dick and Dorothy "got to sitting up nights on the boat deck." Arriving home, Dorothy returned to her studies at Wellesley, but after a year and a half Dick persuaded her to return to New York, and they saw each other regularly — although in his case, by no means exclusively; indeed, both her father and her brother told Dorothy she'd just have to get over Dick the way all the other girls did. But somehow or other, then and for a lifetime to follow she hung — the word "grimly" is not inapposite — on.

Thinking a trip to Europe might cure his blues, Dick found that instead of enjoying Paris with his parents, he was suffering from "an active and intense feeling of depression which [was] absolutely impossible to shake off." It was not improved much when, soon after his return to New York to write a new Lew Fields show, his grandfather Jacob Levy had a stroke while Dick was working at the piano in another room, and died shortly after. Dick learned early how to cope with trauma by telling himself that what happened, happened, and then "getting past it."

The new show was pretty much another retread — in these early years of their collaboration Dick and Larry seem to have been happy to accept anything they were offered, rarely expressing any opinion of the book to which they were expected to write. Herb Fields had just had a big success with a show about the Navy called *Hit the Deck!* (with Vincent Youmans's music). What could be more natural (for Herb) than to do another about the Marines, call it *Present Arms*, and put it on in Pop Fields's newly-acquired Mansfield Theatre? Although it broke no records, the show ran for five satisfactory months and contributed yet another standard to the Rodgers and Hart songbook: "You Took Advantage of Me."

As soon as *Present Arms* opened, Rodgers decided to get away from it all — the death of his grandfather, the relationship with Dorothy that was still on fragile hold — for a vacation at the Broadmoor Hotel in Colorado Springs. From there he wrote to "Dot" to tell her it was "going to take all summer to figure out one or two problems, but there'll be a difference." It's difficult to imagine what the young woman made of that.

Dick was still in Colorado when Herb and Dorothy Fields, on their way back east from Hollywood, dropped in to tell him excitedly about a new project Larry had come up with, a musical based on a novel by Charles Petit called *The Son of the Grand Eunuch*. Rodgers read it and told them they were crazy; the plot concerned the efforts of Chee-Chee, the devoted wife of Li-Pi-Tchou, the eponymous son, to prevent his succeeding to his father's position in fact as well as in name. It would be a one-joke show, and that joke in extremely bad taste.

But Pop Fields had already agreed to produce it, they protested, with Alex Leftwich directing. Helen Ford, under contract to the producer, would play Chee-Chee. And it was a great idea: there were colorful scenes involving Tartars, a kidnap, a happy ending. Finally, not wishing to be the sole holdout, Rodgers went along with the idea. Maybe it would give them the chance to do something more original — he had been stung by the fact that not a few critics had remarked on the debt of *Present Arms* to *Hit The Deck*.

Halfway through the writing, Dick began to believe that maybe *Chee-Chee* was going to be something special, but there were other problems that would not go away. The first of these was Helen Ford. "I read the novel," she said, "and I thought they were absolutely crazy. I cabled Herbie [from Paris] and told him there was no part in that for me ... [but when I got back] in spite of what I'd told Herbie, they were all ready to start on the show. The costumes were being made, the chorus was in rehearsal, it was a foregone conclusion that I'd do it. Then ... I couldn't get hold of a script. It wasn't until the Saturday before we went into rehearsal that they gave me one."

The following Monday, Helen told the boys she was not going to do the show, that her husband George had read the script and said it was awful. "But they steered me into a restaurant on Broadway, and they all started talking at me: 'Helen, we've already sunk so many thousand dollars into it, you've got to do it,' and I said, 'But I just told you, I don't want to do it.' And they, Dick I think it was, said, 'Just open with us, just until we can get somebody else.' So I finally — stupidly — agreed..."

At first things went well at the tryouts in the Forrest Theatre in Philadelphia. "We are doing away with the ordinary idea of the musical comedy dance routines and chorus number stencil," Larry Hart told a local newspaper. "Here we dare to write musical dialogue not as *opera bouffe* with recitative, but with little songs, some of them not a minute long, [and a] heroine who dares to be a sophisticated and even naughty little baggage."

It was no good: further problems arose when, to use Rodgers's typically understated phrases, musical director Roy Webb "sort of fell apart on us" and Helen Ford, just a few

Dick and Larry posing for a newspaper shot with Flora LeBreton, Charles King, and Joyce Barbour as they "phone through" the songs from *Present Arms* to English producer Jack Buchanan in 1928. Author's Collection.

years earlier Rodgers's lover, "became a bitch of the first water" and hurled a hairbrush at him because (she said) he changed the keys of her songs without consulting her. Small wonder, really; by now she hated the show and hated herself for being in it. "I could hardly rehearse it, I was so unhappy in it. Even the cast was dumb," she said.

When they brought *Chee Chee* to New York the critics were bored or pained or disgusted by the story, and although the staging was beautiful, the absence of dance routines and the almost experimental nature of the score — some of the pieces were just a few lines, a minute or two of music — were not enough overcome the obstacle. As a result, several attractive songs, including "Dear, Oh Dear," "Moon Of My Delight," and "I Must Love You" (a reworking of which would appear as "Send For Me" in 1930's *Simple Simon*), failed to catch the fancy of the public and *Chee Chee* turned out to be the biggest failure any of them had ever experienced, lasting only 31 performances.

Rodgers knew how to take failure as well as success; neither changed his positive attitude toward life. He was 27, a good-looking, stockily-built young man with center-parted hair who looked, according to one newspaper reporter, like an amalgam of Noel Coward and George Raft. He dressed then, as always, like a conservative banker. He had a terrace apartment at the Lombardy Hotel on East 56th Street, where his next-door neighbor was Edna Ferber. He was earning about a thousand dollars a week; he had plenty of time for pretty girls (and almost to the end of his life he enthusiastically embraced the opportunities that his profession offered of getting to know more of them) and his new automobile, a red La Salle coupe. His biggest problem — apart from coping with his own success, which he seems always to have done with aplomb — was, as usual, the effervescent, irrational little man who wrote his lyrics.

Dick loved Larry, and Larry loved Dick, but there were times when their differences resulted in flaring arguments and bitter words. Rodgers was methodical, systematic, organized. Hart was everything else. Only one thing remained constant in his approach to his work — he hated doing it, and loved it when it was done. To get Larry to work, Rodgers had to bully, plead, order, or trick him into it. But once Dick got him moving in the right direction — that is to say, away from the scatological — Larry wrote quickly and fluently, the most intricate, clever lines falling off the point of his pencil seemingly without effort. Rodgers told a story about seeing him write lyrics for *The Girl Friend* in a noisy rehearsal hall, with the dancers thundering away on the stage and the principals shouting out their lines. "In half an hour, he fashioned something with so many interior rhymes, so many tricky phrases, and so many healthy chuckles in it that I just couldn't believe he'd written it that evening." George Abbott concurred, "He would go into another room and come back with a lyric in no time."

The problems arose when rewrites or extra material were needed. While his partner fumed and fretted, Larry would be off somewhere "having fun" — his euphemism for getting crocked. He'd done his lyrics; that was that. Rodgers, however, had to remain with the show and take the stick when revisions were needed, new choruses had to be added, songs cut and new ones substituted. Then it was always "Where's Larry?" And it was his job to find him, a task which became increasingly difficult as the years went by.

Larry Hart's haunts were not the ritzy clubs like "21" or the Stork Club, but the Eighth Avenue bars around West 44th and 45th Streets, where the young actors hung out. His constant companion was his old college chum Milton "Doc" Bender, who had abandoned dentistry and become a showbiz groupie. Because he turned up with a gaggle of chorus boys or young actors hoping to be noticed every time Larry threw one of his impromptu parties — and that was fairly frequently — everyone said he was Larry's procurer. The man was universally detested, but if you wanted Larry, you had to take Bender as well. And since Larry was the easiest touch on Broadway, everyone wanted him. Dorothy Hart recalled an occasion when he walked into a barbershop and, as he left, grandly announced that he was going to pay for everyone else's haircut and shaves, too. Another time he told the astonished diners in a Hollywood restaurant he was paying for all their meals. Money was for burning. An actor he knew borrowed $500 from him "to buy the option on a play" but actually used the money to get his girlfriend an abortion. Larry hooted with glee when he found out how he'd been conned. He thought it was a great trick.

"I think of him always as skipping and bouncing," Oscar Hammerstein said. "In all the time I knew him, I never saw him walk slowly. I never saw his face in repose. I never heard him chuckle quietly. He laughed loudly and easily at other people's jokes and his own too. His large eyes danced, and his head would wag. He was alert and dynamic and fun to be with." But not so much fun to work with, Rodgers pointed out. "When the immovable object of his unwillingness to change came up against the irresistible force of my own drive for perfection, the noise could be heard all over the city. Our fights over words were furious, blasphemous, and frequent, but we both knew that we were arguing academically, and not personally."

Larry had a terrible temper, the scream and shout variety, especially when he was defending his lyrics. Rodgers's was more the "slow burn" variety, but when it concerned his music he was implacable. It's not hard to see where the conflict would arise. As Joshua Logan pointed out, Dick was not only a sensational editor of Larry's words, but also brilliant at surrounding them with exactly the right melodic invention. As a result, whatever tribulations both of them underwent in the creation, the results were superb.

1928 ended up being a pretty miserable year for Larry Hart, too. His father, Max, who had been suffering with heart problems for a decade or more and had been pretty much of an invalid since the family moved to the Beresford, was felled on October 9 by a fatal heart attack. According to Larry, who was with him when he died, the old reprobate's last words were, "I haven't missed a thing!" The death of Max's brother Harry two weeks later cast further gloom over the Hart household, but a more optimistic note was sounded just before Christmas when Larry and Dick were hired by producers Alex Aarons and Vinton Freedley to do the score for a musical based on a story by Owen Davis called *Loving Ann.*

They wrote a dozen songs for the show, a couple of which were dropped out of town. *Spring Is Here*, as the show was called, reached Broadway on March 11, 1929, and audiences at the new Alvin Theatre, built in 1927 by the producers and named for the first syllables of their Christian names, found they were in for another of those Long Island "anyone for tennis?" stories in which Betty thinks she loves Stacey but then realizes it's

109

actually Terry she was meant for, which is bad news for her sister Mary Jane who also loves Terry; but in the end unrequited love again gets itself requited.

*Spring is Here* was notable for one of Rodgers and Hart's most famous creations: "With a Song in My Heart," the soaring melody of which, Rodgers said, came to him during the elation he felt in the hours following his first trip in an airplane. The show also featured a clever lyric and verse for a song titled "Yours Sincerely" which solved two problems simultaneously: it connected the three sides of the eternal triangle in the plot, and — since he could not sing — it could be recited by the leading man. Soaring melody or clever lyrics notwithstanding, the opening performance ended with what Rodgers called at the time "a noiseless bang," and the show ran only three months.

At some point around this time — the manuscript material is not dated — Rodgers and Hart also flirted with the idea of a musical adaptation of Ferenc Molnár's 1926 hit, *The Play's the Thing.* Whether they had Molnár's approval (unlikely) or whether they had a producer interested (equally unlikely, since they seem to have completed only a couple of songs and 30 or so pages of script), it was yet another idea that died a-borning, and they moved on to more profitable endeavors. Their next show, *Heads Up!*, another Aarons and Freedley production, opened at the Alvin on November 11, two weeks after

110

**Inez Courtney sings "Baby's Awake Now" from the 1929 show *Spring Is Here*.** Author's Collection.

the great stock market crash, and managed even in those circumstances to run until the following February. It was a sprightly enough little thing, but apple-pie ordinary, and produced nothing of their usual musical excellence.

They followed this with *Simple Simon*, starring the great Ed Wynn and produced by Florenz Ziegfeld. But why, after their mortifying experiences with Ziggy, did the songwriters elect to work for him again? There was one very simple reason: as the effects of the Wall Street crash had begun to bite, money, to put it mildly, was nervous. For another, if any more were needed, Rodgers, having finally put his uncertainties to one side, was marrying his Dorothy. The ceremony took place on March 5,

1930, at the Feiner apartment, 270 Park Avenue. Larry Hart and Herb Fields were ushers; Morty Rodgers, Dick's best man. The bride and groom honeymooned in Europe, dined with the Mountbattens in London, and lived in a borrowed house at 10 York Terrace. Later, Larry Hart joined them to work with Dick on the score of a new Cochran show (again starring Jessie Matthews) called *Ever Green*. They all went to the first night of their friend Noel Coward's *Private Lives*. They met the Duke of Kent. They heard that "Ten Cents a Dance," a last-minute addition to the score of *Simple Simon*, was a hit in New York.

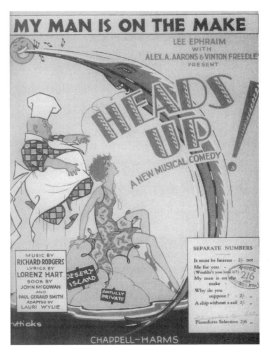

Sheet music for the 1929 Rodgers and Hart show *Heads Up*, in which the song "My Man Is On The Make" was sung by the "Boop-boop-a-doop girl," Helen Kane. Author's Collection.

It had come about in a curious manner. During the Boston tryouts Ed Wynn came up with an idea for a scene in which he would accompany featured singer Lee Morse on a piano that he could ride like a bicycle with her sitting on top. All they needed now was a song to go with the scene. Ziegfeld, who had already cut several songs, including "Dancing on the Ceiling" which he seemed to especially dislike, told Dick and Larry that he didn't want any more of their clever-clever stuff. "Everything you fellows write is fancy," he said. "I want you to write me an ordinary song. You hear? Just an ordinary song." So Rodgers and Hart went back to the Ritz-Carlton and, in one afternoon, wrote a song that began life as the tale of a manicurist whose customers maul her, and ended up as the lament of a dance-hall hostess whose company you can buy for "Ten Cents a Dance."

The next night, Wynn's bicycle-piano entrance got a big hand, but unfortunately, Lee Morse had been hitting the bottle and couldn't remember the song. A furious Ziegfeld fired her on the spot and replaced her with a young singer who had been making a name for herself in a show called *The 9.15 Revue*. Her name was Ruth Etting; she joined the cast and learned her part the night before they closed in Boston, and when the show came to New York her rendition of "Ten Cents a Dance" stopped it cold every night.

*Simple Simon* opened at the Ziegfeld Theatre on February 18, 1930, but in spite of numerous changes and the addition of a couple of new songs, lasted only for 135 performances, which put another dent into Ziegfeld's bank balance at a time when a dent in the bank balance was something the worried and ailing producer could have well done without. Convincing himself Rodgers and Hart hadn't been as committed to the show as they should have been — hadn't they taken time out in February to write four songs (all but one of which were dropped) for the Paramount movie based on the Broadway hit *Follow Thru* — Ziegfeld refused to pay them any royalties. Rodgers later claimed he made Ziegfeld pay up by threatening him with action by the Dramatist's Guild, but bearing in mind Ziggy's financial situation at this time, not to mention his well-known preference for getting sued — and getting more publicity thereby — it would seem at least likely Rodgers and Hart never got paid for writing the show.

Something else was in the air: the movie musical. By 1930, a couple of Rodgers and Hart shows had already reached the screen in one truncated form or another, but the demand for good songs stimulated in 1928 by the enormous success of the all-talking, all-singing *Broadway Melody* was insatiable. Shortly before Dick's marriage, he, Larry, and Herb Fields had signed a three-picture contract with First National, and as soon as they could, they headed west on the Super Chief, hugely enthusiastic about the prospects ahead of them. Indeed, Rodgers went out of his way to toss garlands at his new employers, the brothers Warner. In a long interview with the magazine *Cinema*, he explained not only his own feelings, but the ideas he, Larry, and Herb had for writing movie musicals.

> *We had all sorts of ominous warnings before we came out here. All the routine fables about stars who ate peas with their knives and producers who couldn't read or write. We were good and scared. Herb and Larry got here first. When they saw how wrong the advance reports had been, they had Jack Warner frame me. The first day in, I went to the studio to meet Mr. Warner. He was just like the producers in the funny stories. He sprawled over the table and said, "Well, now you're here, you got to get to work. And I don't vant none of your highbrow songmaking. Musik vit guts ve got to have — songs vit real sentiment like 'Stein song' and 'Vit tears in my eyes I'm dencing.'" It turned out the whole thing had been a put-up joke arranged by Jack Warner with the others...My God,*

*offices with Oriental rugs and studio cars at your disposal, and people to carry your papers so you won't strain yourself...Our supervisor never interferes and we have almost carte blanche. They gave us the cast we wanted; they've put every facility at our disposal, given us intelligent co-operation. These gags about Hollywood slavedrivers must be myths.*

They weren't, as Rodgers and Hart would all too shortly discover, for their love affair with Hollywood would be but a brief one. Nevertheless, fired by their first project, a Herb Field screenplay called *The Hot Heiress* which was to star Marilyn Miller, Rodgers outlined the way they planned to write for it.

*In the theater, musical comedy is framed in footlights and its honest artificiality is charming in itself. But the screen is too personal for that. There are no footlights, nothing between the audience and the people talking intimately on the screen. On the stage no one is jarred if the ingenue suddenly goes into a tap dance. But on the screen her earlier actions have been too believable to allow for this. The dialogue, the action, and the story progression are kept in quick tempo. As for the songs, the point is not that they be logically "planted." The very planting of the number is false. The heroine kidnapped by Arabs and in the middle of the desert singing an aria to the accompaniment of a fifty-piece orchestra is ridiculous. Most important in songs for the screen is their relevance. We are not making them numerous. They are seldom reprised. And they are all definitely connected with the story, pertinent to the actors and the action. We ease into them in the dialogue, so that before you know it, the characters are speaking lyrics and their gradual entry into the song appears very logical.*

113

All this was pretty much overkill; the release print of *The Hot Heiress* featured only three songs (one other, "He Looks So Good to Me," a reworking of one of the better songs dropped from *Simple Simon* before its New York opening, was discarded). The film itself — Marilyn Miller was replaced by Ona Munson, with Ben Lyon and Walter Pidgeon as the rivals for her affection — was a fragile thing not helped much by numbers like "Nobody Loves a Riveter" or the positively arch "You're the Cats," which was so unlike Larry and Dick as to stir doubts that they actually wrote it. Their work on the movie completed, they recrossed the continent and the Atlantic to do some extra work on Cochran's show *Ever Green*, which was due to begin its out-of-town engagement at the Kings Theatre, Glasgow.

Difficult though it is to envision either of them transplanted from sunny California to Glasgow in the truly miserable sort of weather that dour city can produce in October, Larry and Dick were there, worried sick by the late arrival of a huge revolving stage which Larry had suggested would facilitate the many scene changes in the show. The turntable arrived three days before the show was due to open — and didn't work.

Panic. Half the cast had colds or bronchitis. Finally, they got things working, with much revision and — according to the show's star, Jessie Matthews — much bullying by Rodgers. "It's strange," she said. "He didn't seem to understand artistes at all." (It should be added that she seems to have been one of the very few artistes ever to have found that to be the case.) Anyway, they got *Ever Green* to London and opened it on December 3 and, perhaps to their surprise, drew extremely good notices. No doubt they took special pleasure in the fact that much mention was made of "Dancing on the Ceiling," the song Ziegfeld had ditched during the tryouts of *Simple Simon* because it was "too fancy."

Dick and Larry were not able to stay in London to savor their success, comforting though it must have been after the failure of their first movie. They were already committed to a new show for producers Schwab and Mandel — the same Laurence Schwab to whom Rodgers had once taken *Winkle Town*, the same Frank Mandel who had once collaborated with Oscar Hammerstein — which utilized some of their Hollywood experiences. Staged by Monty Woolley, a chum of Cole Porter's, *America's Sweetheart* starred a pert newcomer named Harriette Lake, making her Broadway debut. Talking to Samuel Marx many years later, the little girl from Valley City, North Dakota, who was to be offered a movie contract on the strength of her performance in *America's Sweetheart* and change her name to Ann Sothern, remembered that Rodgers was very stern and scared her half to death. He didn't want her in the play; she remained only at the insistence of Schwab, who was crazy about her. Harriette, whom one critic described as "a lovely synthesis, one part Ginger Rogers, one part Ethel Merman," was a big success.

Although not a huge hit, the show did at least run out the season, and added two more gems to the growing list of Rodgers and Hart standards, "I've Got Five Dollars" and "We'll Be the Same." It had one other distinction: it was the last full collaboration between Herb Fields and Rodgers and Hart. Rodgers always insisted that there was no falling out between them; yet it seems considerably more than likely the parting came about because he and Larry had realized that the weakest part of their collaboration was Herb's "books."

He was a formula writer who tended to rely on the tried-and-true routines of the early musical, whereas Dick and Larry were beginning to see that formulae must be avoided at all costs, something they demonstrated with panache in their next project.

Warners had bought off their contract after *The Hot Heiress* flopped, but the following year Paramount offered Dick and Larry a contract to write a score for a new musical movie to star Jeanette MacDonald and Maurice Chevalier. They arrived back in Tinseltown in November, 1931. At first Larry stayed with the Rodgers family, but that didn't work out too well. "He decided," Dorothy Rodgers said, "since it was our house and we were running it, that his contribution would be the liquor. If we were having guests for dinner, he would make the cocktails...so when our guests arrived Larry would go out into the pantry and there'd be one for him and one for the cook, and there'd be one for him and one for the cook, and pretty soon...no dinner!"

Eventually, when Frieda Hart and Big Mary and Kiki the chow dog came out to California, Larry rented a rather special house at 920 North Bedford Drive, Beverly Hills. The property of silent movie star Norman Kerry, it had been built in what was called the Craftsman style with handcrafted floors, doors, and windows as well as Tiffany glass. It was not the echoing mausoleum depicted in the 1948 biopic *Words and Music*, although it did have an Olympic-sized swimming pool. This was actually the main reason Larry rented the place: he was a passionate swimmer. His Sunday lunches around the pool at "Squeaky Hollow" became legendary; during the 1932 Olympics in Los Angeles, he invited the entire U.S. Olympic swimming team, including its "star," Eleanor Holm (later Mrs. Billy Rose).

The film they had come out to work on was called *Love Me Tonight*, and was originally to have been directed by George Cukor, but he was dropped without explanation and replaced by Rouben Mamoulian. Larry Hart wrote about their experience on the movie some years later in *The New York Times*, one of his rare declarations on the subject of his craft.

> *The first thing we did was to study pictures, not on the sound set but in the cutting room. Then, with Chevalier and Rouben Mamoulian, we developed for the first time dialogue with a sort of phony little half rhyme, with a little music under it cut to the situation. We also put a portable soundtrack in an open field with an orchestra. We had a doctor coming to Jeanette MacDonald's room and the sing-song conversation went something like this:*

The production team of *The Hot Heiress* (1931) including, from l. to r., cameraman Sol Polito, featured player Tom Dugan (in dressing gown), Larry Hart (on someone's knee), director Clarence Badger (in dark suit), Herb Fields (in sweater), and a very natty **Dick Rodgers.** New York Public Library at Lincoln Center.

116

> *Now, my dear, remove your dress.*
> *My what?*
> *Your dress.*
> *Is it necessary?*
> *Very.*

*It isn't rhyme, it isn't anything like it; but it's screen talk and it isn't difficult if you know the medium. I'm a great believer in conversational rhythm. I think in terms of rhythmic dialogue. It's so easy, you can talk naturally. It's like peas rolling off a knife. Take the great screen actors and actresses, Bette Davis, Eddie Robinson, Jimmy Cagney, Spencer Tracy. They all talk in rhythm. And rhythm and movement are the life of the screen.*

*Love Me Tonight* was unquestionably the best movie score written by Rodgers and Hart and is still regarded as one of the best musicals of its decade. Its songs were fresh and lilting, the music and lyrics beautifully interwoven into the dialogue and action. In the opening sequence of the film, for instance, Maurice sings "Isn't It Romantic?" in his tailor's shop, performing it as a jaunty, optimistic tune which is picked up by one of his customers, then a taxi driver, then a man on a train, then some soldiers riding through the countryside (they thunder it out as a rousing march), and finally, via a troupe of gypsy musicians, to Jeanette, dreaming of love in her chateau. Since Chevalier was famed for his "Louise" and "Valentina," they wrote him another "girl" love song to sing called "Mimi" — although in the movie he sings it to Jeanette. There were typically cheeky Hart puns in the swaying waltz which Jeanette sang as she drove her carriage recklessly through the forest, at one moment serenading her "lover" and in the next admonishing her horses. "Like two children playing in the … *hey!*" or "Leaving far behind me all my … *whoa!*"

Light-years ahead of its time, *Love Me Tonight* clearly demonstrates Rouben Mamoulian's early dedication to the integration of song, lyric, and dialogue, and indicates how much of the technique — which he would use some years later when he directed Gershwin's *Porgy and Bess* — he brought to *Oklahoma!* when the time came (and how little credit he has been given for it).

Paramount picked up Dick and Larry's option, and assigned them to *The Phantom President*, a starring vehicle (his first) for the original Yankee Doodle Dandy, George M. Cohan. It turned out to be an unhappy experience for everyone. Cohan, who had written many successful shows and such hit songs as "Mary's a Grand Old Name" and the World War I anthem, "Over There," thought Dick and Larry upstarts. At age 53, he was pretty much over the hill; as a former director, writer, composer, and producer he felt he ought to have been not only writing the songs but running the show and didn't take it kindly when he was not too gently told he was not. He hated the place and everyone in it, and it was mutual. When he left Hollywood, Cohan told an interviewer, "If I had to choose between Hollywood and Atlanta, I'd take Leavenworth."

*The Phantom President* shows Dick and Larry again trying for integration, for the kind of interweaving of dialogue and music that had been so successful in *Love Me Tonight*, but director Norman Taurog was no Mamoulian, and there wasn't a spark of chemistry, sexual or otherwise, between Cohan and his costar Claudette Colbert. Although the critics liked it, the movie, released September 23, 1932, was not a success, and the few songs retained did nothing at all for the reputations of Rodgers and Hart.

They returned east, partly because Paramount did not renew their contract, partly because shortly after the movie was completed Dorothy Rodgers, pregnant for a second time, had lost the child she had been carrying. They soon discovered there was no work in New York, either; on July 8, an era had ended with the death of Flo Ziegfeld. So, leaving Dorothy with her family, Dick and Larry reluctantly returned to Hollywood, where they were offered a job by United Artists, this time to score a new Al Jolson film.

117

Jolson had been the star of the first talking picture, *The Jazz Singer*, but his career was on the wane (although, like Cohan, Jolson was not about to face up to that unpleasant fact). Larry Hart was excited and awed to be working with Jolson, who had always been one of his idols (his sister-in-law Dorothy Hart said he did a passable imitation of the Singing Fool). Rodgers was more impressed by the fact that the authors of the screenplay were Ben Hecht and Sam Behrman, two very highly-paid writers (Behrman, of course, was the playwright who some years on would be dragooned into reluctantly backing *Oklahoma!* ). Ex-journalist turned Oscar-winning scriptwriter Ben Hecht is remembered as the one who, when a disgruntled writer complained that the moguls of Hollywood had no taste and that working for them was hell, replied, "Yeah, and all they give us for it is a lousy fortune."

Originally *The New Yorker*, then *Happy Go Lucky*, then *Heart of New York*, then *The Optimist, Hallelujah, I'm a Bum!* (genteelly altered to *Hallelujah, I'm a Tramp!* or even *Lazy Bones* for British consumption) was a flimsy tale about unemployed men, victims of the Depression, living in a Central Park shantytown in New York. The movie was nothing but trouble from the outset. Originally, Irving Caesar was hired to write the songs, Lewis Milestone slated to direct, and Roland Young to star as the Mayor. Milestone was still tied up on another picture so another director was brought in. Production was begun and abandoned on the first day of shooting, July 7. With yet another replacement director, the film recommenced shooting on July 21. It was another month before Caesar was fired and Dick and Larry brought in.

Working flat-out against the clock, they went the whole way with their rhythmic dialogue, working so closely with the writers that it is almost impossible to separate the "talking dialogue" from the "singing dialogue": only five individual melodies emerge from the entire soundtrack. Many of the "songs" are almost recitative, nearer perhaps to Gluck than movie music.

More trouble: Roland Young left the picture and his scenes had to be reshot with a new Mayor, Frank Morgan. Then someone pointed out that a lot of the slang used in the script wouldn't mean a thing to audiences outside the U.S., and further reshooting was scheduled. The final cost was a staggering $1.2 million, an immense sum in those days, and there was no way the movie could recoup it. Both Dick and Larry played minuscule parts in the film, as a photographer and bank teller respectively. It was their second appearance on screen. In 1929 they had taken part in a two-reeler called *Makers of Melody* in which they "acted out" the writing of such songs as "Manhattan," "The Girl Friend," "The Blue Room," and "Here in My Arms." Movie stars they were not; Rodgers later referred to the experience as "embarrassing."

Much as they enjoyed working on *Hallelujah, I'm a Bum!*, this Rodgers and Hart experiment did not set off any fireworks at the box office, and so their agent Phil Berg negotiated a new contract for them with Metro-Goldwyn-Mayer (MGM), where the last tycoon, Irving Thalberg, was head of production. Thalberg had been very impressed by *Love Me Tonight* and offered Dick and Larry a choice of assignments. One was a musical version of a Thorne Smith novel. The other was a fantasy, a Hungarian play about a man who marries an angel. They chose the play and set to work with a young writer named Moss Hart (fresh from his successful collaboration with George S. Kaufman on the hit 1930 play *Once in a Lifetime*, later to crown his career by becoming the director of *My Fair Lady*). "An intense, Mephistophelean fellow, fairly bursting with ideas," according to Rodgers, Moss was not related to Larry Hart (except, as one newspaper noted, "by mutual consternation").

Louis B. Mayer, head of MGM, had envisaged *I Married an Angel* as a starring vehicle for Jeanette MacDonald, and had lured the Iron Butterfly away from Paramount for just that purpose. With the screenplay and the score still uncompleted, although seven or eight songs — including the title song — were written, Mayer, who had taken over all production when Irving Thalberg was felled by a heart attack, cancelled the project. It seemed someone had told him that the Catholic church would object to the idea of someone going to bed with an angel.                                                    119

Next, Dick and Larry were assigned to a movie which MGM's publicity chief, Howard Dietz —who composed lyrics for Arthur Schwartz songs in his "spare time"—

**Dick Rodgers and Maurice Chevalier during the filming of *Love Me Tonight*.** Author's Collection.

**Rodgers and Hart pretending to write "Manhattan" in the 1929 Paramount two-reeler *Makers of Melody*.**
Used by permission of the Rodgers and Hammerstein Organization.

and producer Harry Rapf had dreamed up. It was going to be called *Hollywood Party* and its *raison d'etre* was that it would star every comedian and comedienne on the MGM lot with lots of "guest" spots for the studio's big names, one of whom would be Jean Harlow, another Joan Crawford. For Crawford they wrote a song called "Black Diamond" (unbelievably, she was scheduled to appear in blackface) and for Harlow (who had a vocal range of maybe three notes) they came up with a "Ten Cents a Dance"-style plaint called "Prayer" in which Harlow, playing a stenographer who wants to get into the movies, would wail: "Oh, Lord, I know how busy you are /If I'm not going too far /Be nice and make me a star."

*Hollywood Party* turned into an even worse nightmare than *Hallelujah, I'm a Bum!* Neither Harlow nor Crawford ever came near it, the song "Prayer" was dropped — along with 16 others — and before the movie was completed it featured interpolations by Nacio Herb Brown and Arthur Freed, Walter Donaldson, Gus Kahn, and Dietz himself. Rodgers and Hart moved on. They wrote some songs for *Meet the Baron*, a stinker featuring radio comic Jack Pearl, and in addition to the title song for the Joan Crawford-Clark Gable movie *Dancing Lady*, they contributed "That's the Rhythm of the Day," sung by Nelson

Eddy as if his very life depended upon it, which, at that stage of his career, it may very well have.

Another song, "That's Love," was sung by Anna Sten in Samuel Goldwyn's film of Emil Zola's *Nana*. They supplied a couple of songs for a Marion Davies movie, *Peg o' My Heart*, that were never used, and Larry rewrote the Jean Harlow number as "The Bad in Ev'ry Man," to be sung by a sepia-stained Shirley Ross in a nightclub scene in the Clark Gable-Myrna Loy-William Powell starrer *Manhattan Melodrama* (chiefly remembered today as the movie Public Enemy Number One John Dillinger watched just before he was shot down by G-Men in Chicago on July 22, 1934).

Then, one day, Jack Robbins, MGM's music publisher, met Dick and Larry, and as Arthur Schwartz recalled, the conversation went something like this:

> *[Robbins] heard the melody and the lyric and said the tune is great but that lyric of course is not commercial, you ought to write a commercial lyric for it. And Larry was offended by this, because he wrote his songs to fit the scenes in which they were called for, and he said. "What do you mean, commercial, what do you mean? It should be something like 'Blue Moon' I suppose you think?" And Robbins said, "Yeah, 'Blue Moon!"*

121

Larry dutifully provided yet another lyric. According to Rodgers, when Larry showed it to Robbins, the publisher made some changes to the last three lines of the chorus, which may explain why Hart is said never to have liked the song. Nevertheless, in its third incarnation, "Blue Moon" went on to become a huge success, one of the very few songs they ever wrote outside a score. As the *Hollywood Reporter* noted on January 17, 1935, "That 'Blue Moon' number of Rodgers and Hart — the stenographer's prayer that was so unceremoniously thrown out of *Hollywood Party* — is the first quick hit song the boys have ever had." According to ASCAP, it is still the most performed of all Richard Rodgers's songs.

All this was little consolation to Rodgers. He felt disconnected from his work. He was playing tennis and wasting time, living what he later referred to as the life of a retired banker. He began to loathe Hollywood, loathe the conditions in which they worked. Samuel Marx, who was MGM's story editor then, remembered their office: "They had a little cubbyhole that was just big enough for a small, a very small, grand piano. At least the company was prepared to go that far and gave them a grand and not a battered upright. So they had a grand piano and they had a piano stool. There may have been a chair. They had nothing else."

Totally disenchanted, Dick and Larry felt they had only one course of action left open to them, as this item from the *Hollywood Reporter* of December 10, 1933 (the day Mary Pickford filed for divorce from Douglas Fairbanks), indicates:

> *Richard Rodgers and Lorenz Hart ironed out their MGM difficulties and withdrew the resignation they handed in just before they hopped off on two weeks' vacation. The songwriting team was dissatisfied with the assignments they had been receiving and felt they could not do themselves or the studio justice with them. The team will write the musical score and additional music for the Lehar operetta* Merry Widow *on their return.*

If that was a victory, you begin to wonder what defeat would have been like. *The Merry Widow* turned out to be yet another unhappy experience. Rodgers found there was no "additional music" for him to write, and he had no clear idea of how he could be expected to improve on Lehar anyway. So the assignment ended with Larry (with some assistance from Gus Kahn) writing new and appropriately syrupy lyrics for some of the old songs, notably "Paris in the Spring," "Vilia," and the title waltz. In February of 1934, after what the *Reporter* described as "plenty of arguments and bickering one way and another," MGM set Jeanette MacDonald to play the widow opposite Maurice Chevalier, a choice which that worthy opposed noisily, saying he would fight to the last ditch. Called in to the front office, however, he "had to bow to the logic of the situation as was outlined by both Irving Thalberg and Ernst Lubitsch." As someone or other said, when he saw the last ditch it looked too much like a grave.

*The Merry Widow* is charming to watch, sumptuously mounted, and utterly vapid — MacDonald, never the most expressive of actresses, is beautiful but empty; Chevalier's Gallic charm is laid on with a very large trowel; and it is impossible to care about what happens to either of them. Hart's lyrics are — as might be expected — apt and original, but there is little trace of his impish charm in any of them except the jolly opening march "Girls, Girls, Girls." It was during the production of this film that the egos of Rodgers and Hart were dealt a further blow by an item in O. O. McIntyre's *Los Angeles Examiner* column that asked, rhetorically, "What ever happened to Rodgers and Hart?"

It was a good question and there was only one way to respond to it, so in April, 1934, they gave up on Hollywood and headed back to God's country. But the Great White Way they returned to was no longer the bustling theatrical mainstream they had left four years earlier. Now, luxurious movie palaces like the Roxy and Radio City Music Hall offered patrons not only a movie, but a stage show as well, for less than the price of a balcony seat in a legitimate theater. For $1.50 at the Broadway, you got dinner and a floor show featuring Rudy Vallee and his Connecticut Yankees, singer Alice Faye, and a 50-girl chorus line. Why spend twice that on a show and still be hungry?

The Broadway musical was in a parlous state; there was one Kern show, a revue at the Music Box called *As Thousands Cheer* written by Moss Hart with songs by Irving Berlin, and the last of the *Ziegfeld Follies*. (Ziegfeld had died on July 22, 1932, and this ersatz production was the work of the Shuberts, who had bought the title from Ziggy's widow, Billie Burke). Lew Fields was no longer producing; Mandel and Schwab had split up; so had Aarons and Freedley. The Theatre Guild was tied up with *Porgy and Bess*. Between March and June of that year, not one musical opened on Broadway.

So after their brief look at the Broadway scene, Dick and Larry were happy when they got a call inviting them to return to their velvet-lined rut, this time to work on a Paramount musical called *Mississippi*. Intended as a vehicle for the studio's singing discovery Lanny Ross, it was an adaptation of an old Booth Tarkington novel, *The Fighting Coward*, adapted as a play, *Magnolia*, by the novelist and further adapted for the screen

123

**Jeanette MacDonald in *The Merry Widow* (1933). She and Chevalier got along about as well as Jekyll and Hyde.**
British Film Institute.

by none other than Herb Fields. The love interest would be supplied by Joan Bennett and the comedy by W. C. Fields.

They completed the score by the end of August. Reading that RKO was looking for a vehicle for Fred Astaire, they put together a two-page outline and two or three songs about a vaudeville hoofer who gets mixed up with the ballet world — and a temperamental ballerina — before returning to the sweet kid he really loves. They took the idea to Pandro Berman, head of the studio, and he liked it, but when he showed it to his board of directors they turned it down because they felt the part wouldn't fit Astaire's top hat and tails image. So that left Rodgers and Hart with nothing to do but go back to New York again and see if they could find work. They had no sooner got there than word came from California that there had been a palace revolution at Paramount and the new president, Barney Balaban, had fired Lanny Ross from *Mississippi* and replaced him with sure-fire box-office winner Bing Crosby.

Dick and Larry were excited at the idea of Crosby performing their songs: everything he sang became a hit. So they were flattened when they got word that Der Bingle didn't like their songs and wanted producer Arthur Hornblow to hire a new songwriting team. When Hornblow flatly refused, Crosby offered a compromise; the Rodgers and Hart score could stay if they would write another ballad (in short order, they came up with "It's Easy To Remember"), and he would interpolate "The Old Folks at Home," an old Stephen Foster song that had not been successfully recorded for nearly 20 years. Despite furious opposition from Dick and Larry, the song stayed in the film (with typical obtuseness, Paramount credited it to Rodgers and Hart), but they had to admit that the Crosby renditions of "It's Easy To Remember," "Soon," and "Down by the River" were considerably more successful than anything else they had done latterly. The movie was a major box office success.

*Mississippi* was Rodgers and Hart's Hollywood swan song; they went back only twice after that, and then on their own terms. Rodgers's dislike of the place grew stronger as the years went by until, by the time he worked with Oscar Hammerstein, he would not deign to go near it. "[Larry and I] were enormously unhappy there," he said in later years. "They didn't understand us, and we didn't understand them. There was no meeting of minds at all."

Things were beginning to slowly get better on Broadway, but they were still far from bright. For a year after they got back, Dick and Larry had a lean time of it. They managed to arrange to audition for Lee Shubert the story they had dreamed up in Hollywood for Fred Astaire and Ginger Rogers, now called *On Your Toes*. They went up to Shubert's apartment (his office was too small to hold a piano) and Rodgers began to play the score while Larry Hart, who had no voice at all ("low, but disagreeable" was how he described

**How Hollywood prefers to see its songwriters: a still from *Words and Music,* a purported movie biography of Rodgers and Hart. Marshall Thompson (Herb Fields) looks uneasy, Tom Drake (Rodgers) tries hard for the expression Dick often wore, and Mickey Rooney (Hart) is chewing up the scenery the way he always did.** British Film Institute.

it) began to sing. By the third number Hart was doing his best to bellow and Rodgers had the loud pedal on the floor, all to no avail: Lee Shubert had fallen fast asleep.

Although he later took an option on the show, Shubert made no immediate move to go into production and kept Dick and Larry dangling. By now, Rodgers was anxious to get back to work — even Larry was. Their Hollywood money had disappeared, and Dick now had a second daughter, Linda, who had arrived on March 5, 1935, coincidentally her parents' fifth wedding anniversary. The problem was their own reputation, their own prestige; they couldn't hang around producers' offices as they'd done in their early days, they were used to producers coming to them. So they waited it out: 19 long and workless months, at the end of which Dick was $34,000 in debt. How deep Larry's hole was — his expenses that Christmas of 1934 included a Caribbean cruise on the *Monarch of Bermuda*, with Doc Bender freeloading as usual — can only be guessed.

With still no word from Lee Shubert about a start date for *On Your Toes,* they got a call from Billy Rose, Larry's old lyric-writing friend, now aiming to be a Broadway producer. Had they heard, he asked, that he had hired Ben Hecht and Charlie MacArthur

126    **Larry Hart and Dick Rodgers in Hollywood, 1933, photographed by Clarence Sinclair Bull.** Author's Collection.

**Show poster for *On Your Toes*.** Author's Collection.

**Show poster for *Jumbo*.** Author's Collection.

to write the libretto for what was going to be "the biggest musical extravaganza in the history of the world?" Of course they had — everyone had. According to Broadway rumor, millionaire John Hay "Jock" Whitney was putting up a quarter of a million to finance it. Part circus, part musical, Rose intended to stage it in New York's biggest theater, the Hippodrome on 44<sup>th</sup> Street and 6<sup>th</sup> Avenue. He had gutted the interior of the theater and turned it, almost literally, into a three-ring circus.

Why, when he could have anyone, someone asked him, did he want a score by Rodgers and Hart after they had been absent from the stage for so long? "They were tops in their field," Rose replied. "So I got 'em. I wouldn't have cared if they hadn't had a show in ten years." Handing over to George Abbott (with some relief, one senses) the job of tweaking the book for *On Your Toes*, Dick and Larry set to work.

*Jumbo*, as the show was called, rehearsed all through the summer of 1935. Huge signs were erected on the Sixth Avenue frontage of the theater: SHHHH! JUMBO IS REHEARSING! Rose's press agent Dick Maney churned out stories about Billy scouring Africa for animals larger than elephants (because the Hippodrome stage was so big they would be using elephants to simulate dog acts), while the impresario himself raided the circuses of the world for talent and costs mounted ever higher. He had hired Jimmy Durante, Paul Whiteman and his orchestra, and actress Ella Logan (later replaced by Gloria Grafton). "This show will either break Jock Whitney," Rose said, "or make me."

Meanwhile, everybody and his aunt dropped in on the rehearsals, so many of them that the Broadway joke had it that Billy was not going to open the show until everyone in New York had seen it. However, after many vicissitudes, *Jumbo* opened on November 16, 1935. What Hecht and MacArthur had come up with was a variation on the Romeo and Juliet theme, with the children of rival circus owners feuding until they won each others' hearts. If it wasn't as sophisticated a plot as Rodgers and Hart might have wished, that didn't stop them from coming up with a hatful of fine songs, including "Little Girl Blue," "The Most Beautiful Girl in the World," and a rousing waltz, "Over and Over Again." In "My Romance" — arguably one of the best songs they ever wrote — Rodgers hit a new vein of melody and Hart his best, simplest bittersweet style.

Although *Jumbo* was far too ponderous an investment ever to make money, it ran well into 1936, and two further months at the Texas Centennial in Fort Worth, by which time Dick and Larry had not only taken time out to write the songs for a CBS radio show called *Let's Have Fun*, but also transferred the lapsed option of *On Your Toes* from the Shuberts to Dwight Deere Wiman, a producer with whom they were to share a string of memorable hit shows. Marilyn Miller was set to star. George Abbott, who had worked

127

with them on *Jumbo* to get experience in staging a musical, and rewritten the libretto of the new show, was brought in as director. In a 57$^{th}$ Street rehearsal loft, Larry Hart met the former principal choreographer of the *Ballets Russes*, George Balanchine, who had come to America a few years earlier, and persuaded him to choreograph the show. Jo Mielziner was signed to design the sets and Irene Sharaff would do the costumes.

There were a few glitches, of course; there always are. Marilyn Miller withdrew from the show — Rodgers and Hart didn't seem to have much luck with her — and the book was again rewritten to accommodate the authentic balletic abilities of Tamara Geva, opening the way to much more ambitious dancing than might have been the case had Miller stayed on board. Ray Bolger, the "jazz Nijinsky" as one critic called him, played Junior Dolan, the son of vaudevillians who gets involved with the upper classes, represented by Luella Gear and Monty Woolley, and almost loses his true love, Frankie.

*On Your Toes,* which marked the beginning of a creative renaissance and a tremendously productive time for the two men, opened on April 11, 1936 at the Imperial Theater in New York and ran for 315 performances. If the book wasn't Tolstoy, the score was distilled Rodgers and Hart. The big hits were "There's a Small Hotel" (an "escapee" — as Rodgers called recycled tunes — from *Jumbo*), and the perennially popular "Glad To Be Unhappy," often thought to be Larry Hart's most autobiographical lyric. "Too Good for the Average Man" poked wicked fun at the fads and fancies of the wealthy: psychoanalysis, birth control, caviar, and, even more daringly, abortion ("the *modus operandi*"). Hart's outrageous rhymes — matching "stick to" with "*in flagrante delictu,*" for example — were pure delight, and Rodgers produced melodies that sparkled. "It's Got To Be Love," "Quiet Night," and the title song are vintage, if now somewhat neglected, Rodgers and Hart.

*On Your Toes* was remarkable in several other aspects. It was the first time Rodgers and Hart had a hand in fashioning the book. It was their first show to run over 300 performances and their first to make the Transatlantic crossing. And for the very first time, ballet was used in a musical comedy both as spectacle and to advance the story itself. The music Rodgers wrote for this scene, the finale of the show, has become a near-classic. It was, of course, "Slaughter On Tenth Avenue."

Rodgers and Hart had never rested on their laurels, and never would. After completing a Hollywood assignment to write the songs for a virtually forgotten movie called *The Dancing Pirate*, they signed with Dwight Deere Wiman to do another show. There seem to have been difficulties, in all probability financial ones, and instead of opening around the end of 1936, as originally planned, it was delayed until April of the following year. The wait was worth it; the show was *Babes in Arms*.

Bing Crosby and Joan Bennett in *Mississippi* (1935). Author's Collection.

129

Once again, Rodgers and Hart threw away the rulebook. The cast was led by real youngsters — the lead girl singers were 17 and 15 — and were all relatively unknown. The traditional chorus line was tossed out. Scenery and props and costumes were far from elaborate (the whole budget was $70,000), and the story was just a wisp of a thing about the children of vaudeville troupers who put on a show to avoid being sent to a work farm.

**A rehearsal of *Babes in Arms* (1937). Singer Mitzi Green gazes adoringly at Dick Rodgers, who is explaining a musical point to pianist Edgar Fairchild (in hat). George Balanchine is seated behind Fairchild, and that's Larry Hart's head you can see the back of. Standing far right is producer Dwight Deere Wiman.** Author's Collection.

The score for *Babes in Arms* includes so many great songs that one can only marvel at it: a wistful hymn to déja vu called "Where or When" and "The Lady Is a Tramp," "My Funny Valentine," and "I Wish I Were In Love Again" (note that subjunctive!); a number called "Johnny One Note" that took a knowing swipe at Allan Jones's famous sustained note in Rudolf Friml's "Donkey Serenade" not to mention that wicked lampoon upon the current craze for cowboy songs, "Way Out West," where, according to Larry Hart, "seldom is heard an intelligent word." Although most of the reviews were ecstatic, ticket sales for *Babes in Arms* didn't take off, perhaps because *Variety* complained (uncannily presaging a remark that would be pinned to the first Rodgers and Hammerstein show) "No nudity, no showgirls, no plush or gold plate may mean no sale." When there was no improvement after two months, Wiman cut seat prices by 50 percent but it was not until, quite coincidentally, every other musical on Broadway closed that *Babes in Arms* became a solid hit, notching up 289 performances at the Shubert Theatre.

Once again Rodgers and Hart had a hit; once again they began looking for another vehicle which satisfied their credo: Don't have a formula and don't repeat it. So when they were approached by George S. Kaufman and the same Moss Hart with whom they had worked in Hollywood on the aborted *I Married an Angel* to do a musical in which Franklin D. Roosevelt, the President of the United States, would be played by Charles Winninger, and all the members of his Cabinet would appear on stage, they hesitated not at all. Kaufman and Hart were the hottest playwrights on Broadway, with the smash hits *Once in a Lifetime* and *You Can't Take It with You* (which had just won a Pulitzer Prize) to their credit. Where could you get a better book than that?

Before they embarked upon the new show, however, Dick and Larry spent a couple of months in beautiful downtown Burbank, writing the score for *Fools for Scandal*, a "film operetta" written by their old pal Herb Fields and his brother Joe which was to be directed by Mervyn LeRoy and star Carole Lombard, Ethel Merman, and Fernand Gravet, with appearances by Fanny Brice and Kenny Baker. They wrote half-a-dozen songs, but by the time they turned them in, Merman and Baker had been replaced by non-singing actors and Brice had been dropped. On release, the "operetta" had become a half-baked shot at wacky Lombard comedy that didn't work, and most of the music was never used.

Rodgers and Hart returned to New York in August ready to go to work on the Kaufman and Hart project, only to discover to their intense dismay that Charles Winninger had turned the part down, and, without consulting them, Kaufman and Hart had signed George M. Cohan. Needless to say, Dick and Larry were appalled and made their feelings known. Somehow — he really must have been the "dazzler" his biographer named him — Moss Hart schmoozed them into believing that Cohan had always had the highest regard for them and that it had been Paramount and not them he was mad at when they worked on *The Phantom President*. Or maybe they just chose to believe it; the fact of the matter was the contracts were signed.

Predictably, the association with Cohan turned out to be as unpleasant as before. At the first play-through of the score in Sam Harris's office, Cohan listened expressionlessly until the end, then walked out, patting Rodgers on the shoulder and saying, "Don't take any wooden nickels, kid," by way of farewell. During rehearsals when they brought in a new number, he said, "Tell Gilbert and Sullivan to run over to the hotel and write a better song." He even went so far during the tryouts as to interpolate some lyrics of his own — it turned out that he actually loathed Roosevelt both personally and politically — which, he told the audience, would probably get him fired. But he knew damned well it wouldn't: Cohan was the show, the show was Cohan.

The news of Cohan's involvement and whom he would play caused a tremendous furor, which in turn resulted in *I'd Rather Be Right* having an almost unprecedented advance sale. In fact, it was a pretty harmless spoof whose action all takes place on one Fourth of July in Central Park. Dick and Larry were reported to have written the entire score in three weeks ("I don't know if it's true," Rodgers said, "but I do know it's possible"), and a lot of the time it feels like it. Apart from "Have You Met Miss Jones?" none of its songs is ever heard these days, not because there was anything particularly wrong with them — in fact, one or two were very funny indeed — but primarily because they were so closely integrated with the story that they don't come to life away from it. But — it also has to be said — most of them are unmemorable.

Perhaps it's not altogether surprising. Dick and Larry were working with both hands tied behind their backs, pilloried by Cohan, who hated them, and bullied by Kaufman, whose idea of a musical was something starring the Marx Brothers. Stuck with a book that had no character but that of the star, they were reduced to trying to put life and warmth and tenderness into two characters — Peggy and Phil — who were virtual ciphers. They actually managed to do it with the original opening of Act Two, in which Peggy finds Phil asleep and sings the lovely "Everybody Loves You," but Kaufman, who mistrusted tenderness, would have none of it, and out went the scene — and the song.

In addition to all this, Dick Rodgers was dissatisfied with a financial arrangement which gave Kaufman and Hart eight percent of the weekly gross while he and Larry got only five. During the tryouts at Ford's Theatre in Baltimore, they were asked to replace one of the songs, "A Treaty, My Sweetie, with You." The new number, "Have You Met Miss Jones?", stopped the show, and Rodgers was delighted. "Now maybe we can have an encore," he said during a run-through, "and someone may even remember a couple of bars!" Kaufman was not amused; he did not believe that any show — especially one written by him — depended for its success on music, for which he had no ear and less regard. He and Rodgers argued, and the argument boiled over with all the other frustrations Dick was suffering — Cohan's cavalier attitude to himself, Larry, and their songs; Kaufman's indifference; the unfair royalty split; and so on. They stood on the pavement outside the theater and yelled at each other loudly and at length. In the end, Kaufman had his way. "He was bigger, richer, and older," Rodgers said, not admiringly.

One critic called the glitzy, star-studded New York premiere of *I'd Rather Be Right* "the biggest opening since the Grand Canyon." Everyone who was anyone was there, and the huge after-show party at the Hotel Carlyle was undoubtedly, Lucius Beebe said, "the season's most illustrious gathering of professional celebrities." The reviews confirmed what the glitterati had already decided: the show was a smash hit and would eventually run for nine months. In two short years, Rodgers and Hart had re-established themselves as the kings of the musical theater.

The next Rodgers and Hart show was a much happier affair — in fact, they announced they already had half of it written at the first night party for the Cohan show. On May 11, 1938, they brought *I Married an Angel* into the Shubert, a new show based on the Janos Vaszary play they had worked on at MGM back in 1933, the rights for which Rodgers had urged Wiman to buy from the studio. A brilliant young director named Joshua Logan joined the "regulars" — producer Wiman, choreographer Balanchine, designer Mielziner, musical director Gene Salzer, and orchestrator Hans Spialek.

The star of the show was Vera Zorina, a lovely ballerina who had brilliantly danced the "Slaughter on Tenth Avenue" ballet in the London production of *On Your Toes*. There was a special part for Vivienne Segal, one they had promised to write for her ever since they had seen her playing light comedy in California. Larry Hart wanted the French singer Jean Sablon for the part of the banker who marries the angel, but Dennis King was signed. Walter Slezak, Charles Walters, and Audrey Christie were the other stalwarts who performed such delights as that hilarious send-up of Radio City, "At the Roxy Music Hall," "Did You Ever Get Stung (Where the Doctor Can't Help You)?," and the sweetly cynical advice Vivienne Segal offers the angel, that a woman can get away with almost anything...providing it's done with "A Twinkle in Your Eye."

"Musical comedy has met its masters!" shouted Brooks Atkinson in *The New York Times*, sending *I Married An Angel* off on its 338-performance run with the kind of rousing critical acclaim producers pray for. The show was bought for filming soon after the opening by — yes, of course — MGM, and compounding the irony, to star Jeanette MacDonald. It was the only instance, Rodgers said, where they ever got paid three times for the same material.

Long before MGM had swallowed its pride, however, he and Larry were hard at work on yet another show. The idea for it had come to them while they were en route to Atlantic City to polish off some songs for *Angel* and Larry remarked that no one had ever adapted a Shakespeare play for the musical theater. Great notion, Dick said, but which play? Then Larry had a brainwave. His brother Teddy was always being mistaken for another comic actor, Jimmy Savo. How about casting them as the Dromio twins in an adaptation of *The Comedy of Errors*?

It took them only a couple of days to block the idea out but then they had to lay it aside while they finished *Angel*. As soon as that was done, they called in George Abbott

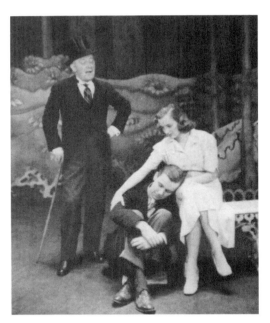

*I'd Rather Be Right:* George M. Cohan as Franklin D. Roosevelt meets Peggy Jones (Joy Hodges) and Phil Barker (Austin Marshall) in Central Park and promises to balance the budget so they can get married. Author's Collection.

and went to work on the new idea, and by November, 1938, the boys from Morningside Heights were ready to present *The Boys from Syracuse.* It was, it still is, vintage Rodgers and Hart champagne.

George Abbott's complex story of the two sets of twins — the finished script contained but one line of Shakespeare — encouraged Larry Hart to come up with eruditely complex lyrics to match Rodgers's witty and eminently singable melodies, among them the bittersweet "Falling in Love with Love," the slightly punch-drunk "This Can't Be Love," or the comedy number extolling the pleasures of being in jail where, in good conscience, "You're privileged to miss a row /Of diatribes by Cicero." In fact, the audience was left in no doubt about what to expect from the moment the curtain rose. "This," it was announced, "is a drama of ancient Greece. If it's good enough for Shakespeare, it's good enough for us!"

The critics loved it as much as the audience did. Richard Watts, Jr., writing in the *New York Herald Tribune,* said, "If you have been wondering all these years what was wrong with *The Comedy of Errors* it is now possible to tell you. It has been waiting for a score by Rodgers and Hart and direction by George Abbott." The show's success was doubly satisfying for Larry, for his brother Teddy made a big hit in it.

Once again a smash hit. Once again a long-running show — seven months, this time — and a film sale immediately following the opening. Six really big successes in precisely half that many years made Rodgers and Hart big news, and on September 26, 1938, just a few weeks before *The Boys from Syracuse* began its tryouts in New Haven, they received the ultimate American accolade: their picture on the cover of *Time* magazine. (The only other American songwriter who had ever appeared there up to that time was George Gershwin.)

*Time*'s essay made full use of the colorful habits of Larry Hart, describing him as "a tiny, swarthy, cigar-chewing bachelor who at forty-three is getting bald and...lives with his mother, whom he describes as 'a sweet, menacing old lady'." Rodgers, said *Time*, took the world in his stride; his partner was ever tempted to fume, deprecate, explain, protest, and meet a question with a wisecrack rather than an answer. Rodgers and Hart told the world they didn't think much of the new "swing" music that was all the rage, and preferred their songs played at the tempo in which they had been written — a topic they would turn into song in their next show. *Time* estimated their income at $100,000 a year, a very great deal of money indeed in 1938, the lowest point of the Depression. And very bad news for someone as profligate — and careless with money — as Larry Hart. "Larry was always a sweet and lovely guy," his friend Irving Pincus said. "But by the time he was doing *The Boys From Syracuse*, he was sweet, lovely, and screwed up."

Rodgers, too, was deeply concerned about his partner's alcohol problem. "For one thing," George Abbott said, "he saw his collaborator gradually deteriorating; secondly, he knew from experience that when a show got on the road, it needed a lyric writer ready for emergencies." Dick's worst fears were realized. While the show was in Boston, Larry was admitted to Mount Sinai Hospital in New York suffering from pneumonia. For the first time in his life, he missed his own opening night.

After Christmas, Rodgers, Hart, and George Abbott headed for Miami to work on "a trio of ideas" — a proposed Shubert show starring Al Jolson, a Dwight Deere Wiman show to feature Zorina, and a college football musical based on a screenplay by George Marion, Jr., who had worked with Dick and Larry on *Love Me Tonight*. In April, still undecided, they conferred with Claire Booth Luce about a musical of her play *The Wedding Day*, loosely based on the Romeo and Juliet story; Max Gordon had been sufficiently impressed by it to send it to them, but they declined and the project died.

By late summer, they had settled on the football story which proved easy to adapt to the stage. Full of fresh-faced kids once again, *Too Many Girls* was a college story unlikely to have strained anyone's intellect. Among its discoveries were Desi Arnaz, Eddie Bracken, and Van Johnson. Bracken became a most unlikely wartime star out at Paramount, Van Johnson a teenage idol at MGM. Desi Arnaz, too, was snapped up by the movies, and went out to RKO to film *Too Many Girls*, in which he was teamed with a vivacious redhead named Lucille Ball. So it's fair to say that had Larry Hart and his pal Doc Bender not literally shoveled Desi into the cast of the show (Arnaz didn't even know who Rodgers and Hart were), a couple of zillion television viewers might never have sampled the wacky delights of *I Love Lucy*.

*Too Many Girls* was merry, melodious, mindless, and successful. As well as its best-known song, "I Didn't Know What Time it Was," it included a sardonic elbow-in-the-eye for Manhattan called "Give It Back to the Indians" and another which bewailed the fate of songwriters in the swing era. Men like Gene Krupa played the drums like thunder, "but the melody is six feet under," averred "I Like to Recognize the Tune." However, a couple of the songs in the show — "Heroes in the Fall" is one — are entirely the work of Richard Rodgers, music and lyrics, because Larry Hart was simply not there to write them. The same problems were to arise with their next show, *Higher and Higher*, which had more than enough problems of its own.

Written by Joshua Logan and Gladys Hurlbut "based on an idea by Irving Pincus," it was a sort of *Pygmalion* story about the maidservant of a suddenly-bankrupt millionaire being trained by her peers to marry a rich playboy, and arose out of Dwight Deere Wiman's — and Rodgers and Hart's — not unnatural desire to write another starring vehicle for the lovely Vera Zorina, who had been such a hit in *I Married An Angel*. Wiman hired Jack Haley, Shirley Ross, and Robert Rounseville as leads, Joshua Logan to direct, Jo Mielziner to design the sets, and Lucinda Ballard to do costumes. But Zorina, filming *On Your Toes* in Hollywood (where they removed all the songs), couldn't get away; the substi-

**Eddie Bracken, left, and Hal LeRoy, right, protect a somewhat the worse for wear Desi Arnaz from Marcie Westcott's scorn in *Too Many Girls*, 1939.** Author's Collection.

**Jack Haley gives the servants a golf lesson in *Higher and Higher*. That's Shirley Ross wearing the neat suit in the background.** Author's Collection.

tute was Marta Eggerth, a Budapest-born operetta singer, which meant the script had to be completely revamped to fit her totally different abilities. *Higher and Higher* doggedly refused to come together. Logan and Hurlbut couldn't do a hell of a lot with the book. Larry didn't like it and retreated to the bottle as *Higher and Higher* sank lower and lower.

    As if all that were not trouble enough, writer Hurlbut had discovered a performing seal at an animal fair held for the local library in Woodstock, NY, and persuaded Logan — *persuaded?* — that the animal would be a valuable addition to the show. His name was Sharkey, and he was a graduate of Huling's Sea College at Kingston-on-the-Hudson, where all the well-trained seals came from. His specialty was nipping people's rumps. The fact everyone went along with this indicates all too clearly how much trouble they were in. *Higher and Higher* was never exactly a flop, but 108 performances — fine in 1926 for *The Girl Friend*, but no good at all in much more expensive 1940 — was a long way short of success. As Rodgers said later, "When a trained seal steals the show, you know how bad it is." Even so, there were some fine songs in the score, including one of Rodgers's prettiest waltzes, "Nothing But You," and the wistful "It Never Entered My Mind." The problem, as Logan said, was that "although the songs were perfectly good, they didn't come out of anything that interested you. So when Shirley Ross sang 'It Never Entered My Mind' about a man you just didn't care about, it just didn't have any impact."

    Dick and Larry realized that perhaps their change of pace had been a mistake, but they

137

were not in the habit of holding inquests. They were already preparing another show that had grown out of an idea put to Rodgers by the novelist John O'Hara while they were trying out *Too Many Girls* in Boston the preceding year. O'Hara thought that a series of stories he had been writing for *The New Yorker* about a brass-faced master of ceremonies in a cheap night club who gets mixed up with "Mrs. Chicago Society" and a couple of even cheaper blackmailers, might be made into a show. Yes, yes, and yes again, said Rodgers and Hart, and John O'Hara started work on a libretto for what would become *Pal Joey*.

They needed someone special to play the lead, a dancer rather than a singer, someone who could make the audience like the hero even though they knew they ought to despise him. They found him playing a small part in a show called *The Time of Your Life*. His name was Gene Kelly. For the part of Joey's sex-hungry patroness, John O'Hara had someone like Marlene Dietrich in mind, but Rodgers and Hart — especially Larry — preferred Vivienne Segal, who "could sing scabrous lyrics like a lady." When he saw her, O'Hara liked her, too, and even changed the name of the character to Vera Simpson, matching Segal's initials.

With George Abbott directing, they brought *Pal Joey* into the Ethel Barrymore Theater on Christmas Day, 1940, with not a few misgivings. How would the audience react to the idea of a heel as a hero, a society lady who pays for her boyfriends as his patron, and a not-too-bright dancer as his girlfriend? Vivienne Segal, who played the society lady, remembered that Rodgers was nervous about some of Larry's more risqué lyrics and wanted her to change them; Larry as adamantly refused to allow it. Abbott was nervous, not at all sure that the show wouldn't flop. *Pal Joey* was radical and different, and — probably — ahead of its time.

In many ways it was the apotheosis of the Rodgers and Hart partnership, unquestionably the most biting, daring thing they wrote together; as good to watch today as it was nearly 40 years ago. (It bears practically no resemblance whatsoever to the politely-laundered movie version, by the way.) With Leila Ernst as the not-too-bright Linda and Vivienne Segal perfect as the cynical woman who buys her boys and discards them when they become tiresome, *Pal Joey* was something totally new to the Broadway stage. Hard-edged and brittle, it lived in a world Larry Hart knew like the palm of his hand, and everything he wrote for it was sharp, hip, and sardonic. Rodgers matched his partner note for word, even achieving the remarkably difficult feat of writing wonderfully good "bad" tunes like "Chicago," "That Terrific Rainbow," and "The Flower Garden of My Heart" for the deliberately tacky nightclub sequences.

Larry loved to get his naughty lyrics past Mrs. Grundy. In the song "Bewitched, Bothered and Bewildered," for instance, Vivienne Segal sings about losing her heart and not caring. Joey is a laugh, she says, but "I love it because the laugh's on me." Innocuous enough; until you know how Larry Hart chortled with delight when he read those lines over the phone to Joshua Logan and explained with glee that they meant Joey was actually *on top of* her.

Critical reaction to *Pal Joey* was mixed, but mostly good, although Larry was badly wounded by the adverse comments of Brooks Atkinson who liked the concept better than the realization. "Although it is expertly done," Atkinson wrote, "can you draw sweet water from a foul well?" Gene Kelly recalled that when the review was read over the phone to him, Hart broke down and cried. Raves from Richard Watts, Jr. ("brilliant, sardonic, and strikingly original"), Wolcott Gibbs ("musical comedy took a long step towards maturity"), and others were no consolation. Strangely enough, the legend has sprung up that *Pal Joey* was not a success, which is far from the truth.

Although, as Gene Kelly says, the flower-hatted matinee audience stayed away from it in their thousands, *Pal Joey* ran for eleven months, with a three-month tour afterwards. It was and it remains a landmark. It demonstrated that a musical could be set in a world completely removed from operetta-land and be about people who were not all peaches and cream. Who else but they would have written as pretty a love song as "I Could Write a Book" and have it sung so cynically, for effect, by the hero-heel? Who else could have created "Zip," the lament of the intellectual stripper who thinks about Schopenhauer while taking off her clothes?

Rodgers was supremely happy, basking in the glow of success, recognition, and the wealth that was beginning to come now that he and Larry were sharing in the financial rewards of producing as well as writing their shows. He was doing work he loved to do, he had a beautiful wife, two delightful daughters, friends galore. Hart remained what he had always been, only more so. Success couldn't change Larry, because Larry couldn't change. He had always drunk too much, but now he drank more. He had always stayed out all night, but now he began staying out for two or three nights, or disappearing without explanation. He had always been late for meetings, but now he often did not show up at all, or, if he did, Rodgers would take one look at him and know that Larry could no more work than fly. Rodgers had always tried to protect Larry from himself, but now Larry was going around with a pretty pernicious crowd, dreary stupid people who were happy to let Larry pick up the bills for their fun, and vacuous blond boys brought along by his pal, his gofer, his procurer Doc Bender.

The gulf between Dick and Larry had reached irreparable proportions. Drinking far too much, shadowed everywhere by Bender, Larry became so disheveled and careless of

139

**Dick and Larry working on *Pal Joey* (1940). Compare with Hollywood's version.** Author's Collection.

his own appearance that former acquaintances would cross the street to avoid him. "He became increasingly neurotic until he could hardly sit still for even a few minutes," wrote Harold Clurman, who had known Larry since the days of *Garrick Gaieties*. "He paced and paced and paced, a large, thick cigar always in his mouth. He drank heavily, despairing all the while of his drinking. He was horrified by his homosexuality; he had been brought up in a stereotypical Jewish family where such things were 'unheard of.' He felt thoroughly disgraced and acted as if he were determined to punish himself for his anomaly."

Was this unhappy, maudlin, reeling wreck the same man who, between 1935 and 1942, had written the words for such imperishable ballads as "Glad To Be Unhappy," "It's Got To Be Love," "There's a Small Hotel," "Have You Met Miss Jones?," "Spring Is Here," "The Shortest Day of the Year," "Who Are You?," "You're Nearer," "I Didn't Know What Time It Was," "My Romance," "The Most Beautiful Girl in the World," "It Never Entered My Mind," "On Your Toes," "I Could Write a Book," and "Bewitched"? It was, all too sadly, it was.

As we have seen, most of *By Jupiter*, the last completely new Rodgers and Hart show, was finished while Larry was "drying out" at Doctor's Hospital in New York. It was ironically to be their biggest hit, although the irony must have twisted the knife in Larry Hart's soul, for it was still running when *Oklahoma!* opened at the St. James Theatre and made such shows as *By Jupiter* obsolete.

On the Easter Sunday after *Oklahoma!* opened, Frieda Hart died, and with her went Larry Hart's last tenuous link with any kind of normal life. He quit the huge duplex apartment at 320 Central Park West, once the scene of loud, never-ending parties where nobody knew how many people would arrive, and moved to a small penthouse above Delmonico's Hotel on Park Avenue. He talked about projects in which he had no real intention of becoming involved; a musical version of a novel called *The Snark Was a Boojum*, a show called *Miss Underground* with a book by Paul Gallico and music by Emmerich Kalman. There were rumors that he was going to work with Kern now that Hammerstein was partnering Rodgers, but nothing came of that, either, nor of a reported offer from Arthur Freed to team with him on an MGM musical called *Royal Wedding* (which was eventually written by Burton Lane and Alan Jay Lerner).

His sister-in-law, Dorothy Hart, who spent a great deal of time with Larry during this low period of his life, averred that Larry felt "he and Dick had reached a point where they had done everything together that they could. All partners sooner or later split up. The remarkable thing was not that they split up but that they ever stayed together for so long. Dick had lost his patience with Larry. I don't blame him, I can't. Larry didn't want to write any more. He didn't know what to do with his life or himself. The break didn't mean anything; he wanted the break. His life had come to an end long before he died."

Everyone who knew Larry was saddened by his sudden, drastic decline. Everyone wanted to help but nobody knew what to do. Herbert Fields went to see Dick Rodgers and they came up with the idea of reviving one of Larry's favorite shows, *A Connecticut Yankee*. A revival, they felt, would be better than a completely new show, for Larry would balk at that. If they added a fatter, meatier role for Vivienne Segal, whom Larry adored, they might just get him interested. Delicately,

**Gene Kelly, Leila Ernst, and Vivienne Segal, as Joey, Linda, and Vera in *Pal Joey*.**
Theatre Collection, Museum of the City of New York.

141

they broached the idea to Larry, and to their joy and relief, he agreed. He brightened up, as if reassured to be working with old friends again.

He had always been especially fond of Herb, who was hitting a winning streak with his books for musicals by Cole Porter: *Du Barry was a Lady* and *Panama Hattie* (co-authored with B. G. de Sylva); and *Let's Face It* and *Something For the Boys* (which he wrote with his sister Dorothy). Herb was part of the gay scene, too, but he always maintained the fiction of straightness with a string of statuesque chorus girls for whom he bought immensely ostentatious mink coats. They began reworking the original plot of *A Connecticut Yankee* to bring it more up to date. Dick Foran, playing the Yankee, was now a lieutenant in the Navy, Alice, who is Alisande (Sandy) in the Camelot sequence became a WAC, and so on.

Dick persuaded Larry to come and work at the Rodgers's home in Connecticut, beneath the same tree under which so much of *Oklahoma!* had been conceived. Larry was docile and well-behaved: convalescent, almost. He cut out liquor completely and gave the impression of really trying hard to stay on the wagon. Keeping the best of the original songs, Dick and Larry added "The Camelot Samba" — the new dance was all the rage — and "You Always Love the Same Girl," plus a song that might very well have been an expression of Larry's deepest personal feelings at that time. The opening lines of its verse "You can count your friends on the fingers of your hand /If you're lucky you have two" set the tone, and "Can't You Do a Friend a Favor?" might well have been addressed to everyone for whom Larry felt love and affection, everyone who, he felt nonetheless, rejected him because he was mis-shapen and ugly. For him to have written such words is tragedy indeed.

Although perhaps not as bitingly witty as some of the things he had done, one of the very last songs he wrote still had the old Hart pizzazz. It was called "To Keep My Love Alive" and it stopped the show every time Vivienne Segal sang it. Once rehearsals were over, however, Larry fell off the wagon and rolled right back into the gutter. He went back to the clipjoints and the clubs, the bars and the alleys. He had always managed to lose his overcoat and hat when drinking, and now he navigated around Philadelphia during bitter winter weather in a light suit, sowing the seeds of pneumonia. He attended the opening of *A Connecticut Yankee* in New York with the illness already killing him, but nobody knew that.

The night of Wednesday, November 17, 1943 was bitterly cold, with sleet in the wind. Larry was at Delmonico's on Park Avenue, where he had taken a smaller apartment, and he telephoned Helen Ford and invited her to go with him to the premiere. She was mortified when she came down the steps into the dining room of the hotel. Larry was drunk, and his voice carried across the whole room when he announced her slurringly as the most beautiful singer in America. "It was terrible," she remembered. "Larry was with a young couple, a beautiful young man and an actress I recognized vaguely. He was falling-down drunk, and there was no food. He kept on ordering more drinks until finally we got him into a cab and went to the theater."

When they arrived at the Martin Beck Theatre, Larry disappeared, and Helen spotted Dorothy Hart. They joined the crowd milling around the ticket window and discovered that no tickets had been set aside for them. Larry, who was nowhere to be seen, had simply assumed he could turn up and ask for as many as he wanted whenever he wanted to. Helen Ford and Dorothy Hart went backstage to see if Larry was there. Instead they met Dick Rodgers. "Oh, my God!" he blurted, "is Larry here?" He sent two men out into the

143

**Gene Kelly and girls in *Pal Joey*. He never appeared in another Broadway show.**

Used by permission of the Rodgers and Hammerstein Organization.

144

Frank Sinatra, Kim Novak, and Rita Hayworth in the movie *Pal Joey* (1957). Columbia boss Harry Cohn originally intended to co-star Marlene Dietrich and Sinatra, but Frank wasn't available. Cohn suggested Jack Lemmon but Dietrich wouldn't work with "a nobody" and walked. Ah, the movies! Author's Collection.

lobby to watch for Larry, but Larry somehow eluded them. When the curtain went up and the lights went down, he was standing in his accustomed place at the back of the theater. Rather than create a scene, they let him alone.

Larry was quiet at first, but gradually grew more agitated and feverish, reciting the lyrics in an undertone that steadily grew more audible. As Vivienne Segal performed "To Keep My Love Alive" in the second scene of the first act, Larry's croaky voice could be clearly heard, loud and slurred. The two men whom Rodgers had charged with keeping Larry quiet bundled him out into the lobby, where he began kicking and yelling and creating exactly the kind of scene everyone had been so anxious to avoid.

Dorothy Hart rushed out and got Larry into a taxi, taking him to her apartment. When she had him settled down on the couch, she hurried out again to meet her husband Teddy, who was playing at the Imperial Theatre in the Mary Martin musical *One Touch of Venus*. When they got home, Larry was still asleep on the couch, breathing stertorously and perspiring heavily. They left him there, having no inkling that he was critically ill. At four in the morning, Dorothy Hart looked in on her brother-in-law, but he was gone; a check with the doorman revealed that Larry had taken a cab home to Delmonico's.

Two days later he was found there in a coma and rushed to Doctor's Hospital. There, at 9:30

**Larry Hart's grave at Mount Zion Cemetery. Not even a hint who he was.** Author's Collection.

145

P.M. on the night of November 22, 1943, as the sirens wailed "all clear" after a practice air-raid alert, the troubled spirit of Larry Hart slipped away. The doctor came out and told the little group of people, including Teddy and Dorothy Hart; Larry's business manager, William Kron; Doc Bender; and Dick and Dorothy Rodgers, that it was all over.

"It was inevitable," Dick muttered. "The way it had to be." And perhaps, unknowingly, he was right. The Rodgers and Hart era was ended; the musical theater in which they had flourished would never be the same again. The Rodgers and Hammerstein years lay ahead; inevitable, the way it had to be.

# CHAPTER FOUR

# ABOUT AS FAR AS THEY

## Can Go!

*It is not our intention to die broke*
*if we can help it.*

— Richard Rodgers and Oscar Hammerstein II

W hile his new collaborator was giving his partnership with Lorenz Hart one last try, Oscar Hammerstein had gone back to a long-cherished project he'd been tinkering with off and on — without any thought of either a deadline or first interesting a producer — long before he teamed up with Rodgers, in fact since way on back in 1934 when he had tried to interest Hollywood in the idea, a musical based on Bizet's opera *Carmen*. With *Oklahoma!* putting fire in his belly, he decided to show what he'd done to a few producers. And of all the producers in all the gin joints in all the world, Billy Rose took it on.

He was smart — it was probably some of the best work Oscar had ever done in his life. This was no "Americanization" with a few bits of business and topical allusions thrown in, it was a *translation* of Bizet's original intention into mainstream American musical theater. The first thing Oscar had done was to cut out all the recitatives added to the libretto after Bizet's death. He then set the action in the present day, just as Bizet had done in 1875. He changed the locale from a Seville cigarette factory to a South Carolina parachute-packing factory, Don José to a GI corporal named Joe, Escamillo the *torero* to "Husky" Miller, a prizefighter, necessitating — virtually stipulating — an all-black cast. Which was why

— apart from Rose — all the producers he showed it to turned him down, because at that time in that era, there were no black opera singers and precious few theatrical ones either. The show looked uncastable.

Unless you were fast, flashy Billy Rose. Ever the *macher*, Billy got hold of that premier discoverer and developer of black talent, John Hammond, Jr., and gave him the job of finding a cast for the show, now called *Carmen Jones*. And that was how a photograph developer named Muriel Smith became Carmen; how Glenn Bryant, a New York cop, became Husky Miller; and how an odd-job man named Luther Saxon got the part of Joe. Billy Rose, being Billy Rose, decided to play it big. Utilizing all the skills he'd picked up from opening nightclubs and staging such extravaganzas as *Jumbo* and "Aquacades," starring his wife Eleanor Holm (the former Olympic swimmer who'd once gone to Larry Hart's party in Hollywood), he hired a huge cast and went for spectacle all the way. And it worked like a charm.

147

**Rodgers and Hammerstein: producers, publishers, and composers, available for interviews and photocalls.**
Used by permission of the Rodgers and Hammerstein Organization.

Bizet's melodies and Oscar's "vernacular" lyrics — recapturing that naturalness he had once found in *Show Boat* and rediscovered in *Oklahoma!* — blended beautifully, indeed, improving on the original and in so doing, making the characters themselves more real. Bizet's "Toreador's March" became the prizefighter's anthem "Stan' Up an' Fight," and the "Habañera" the sinuously rueful "Dat's Love." Carmen's gypsy dance, speeded up to provide the exciting "Beat Out Dat Rhythm on the Drum," provided the basis for a spectacular dance number. *Carmen Jones* was vivid and different, and Oscar was gratified to discover that he had another big hit on his hands (the show ran over 500 performances, did two hugely successful tours, and was later filmed with Dorothy Dandridge as Carmen and Harry Belafonte as Joe). No wonder he thumbed his nose at everyone in that *Variety* ad.

By the time *Carmen Jones* opened in December, 1943, however, Rodgers and Hammerstein were already planning their next collaboration. Oscar felt the next thing they did should be as "small" as *Oklahoma!* had been "big," and one of his ideas was a musical version of Lindsay and Crouse's hit play, *Life With Father*. He had known Russell Crouse ever since Crouse's disastrous playwriting debut back in 1931, when Crouse had collaborated with Morris Ryskind and Oscar on a turkey called *The Gang's All Here!* Rodgers wasn't keen on the *Life With Father* idea, but that did not matter. Both of them knew they could — and must — proceed cautiously. They were to some degree in the position of the man who went to an agent and told him that he concluded his act by committing suicide onstage. "Oh, yeah?" said the agent, "And what do you do for an encore?" Indeed, one of Dick's old Hollywood friends made that analogy explicit:

> *I had a short dialogue with Sam Goldwyn one night. He was a very*
> *funny man and I was very fond of him. But when he saw* Oklahoma! *he*
> *phoned me at home and said, "Would you come down to the theater,*
> *I'd like to see you." This was at the end of the first act. At the end of the*
> *second act I went down to the theater and stood in the back and he came*
> *up with his wife Frances, and they were dewy-eyed. Terribly enthusiastic.*
> *And Sam said, "I have a great idea for you. You know what you ought to*
> *do next?" I said, "What, Sam?" And he said, "Shoot yourself!"*

The anecdote points up the problem perfectly. Publicly, Rodgers always professed to never being bothered by the thought of having to follow his own act. "You get into the habit of disregarding the problem," he said, "and just go ahead and try." The reality was rather different. Unlike Oscar, who seems to have taken success as readily in his stride as he accepted failure, Rodgers increasingly became nervous, tense. "People would say things like, 'You'll never write anything [else] as good as that,'" his wife said. "Well, that was a terror he had deep inside. I mean, every writer thinks he'll never be able to do anything as good as his best work." "He began to be power-driven, and very jealous of his rights," Agnes de Mille observed. "You couldn't gainsay him about anything at all."

In the months following the opening of *Oklahoma!*, Dick and Oscar began setting up a series of other business arrangements through their lawyer, Howard Reinheimer. Between them they laid the foundation for what would become within a few short years one of the most powerful and influential organizations in the American theater. Their basic intention was to put themselves in a position, vis à vis their own work, that would have turned even Ziegfeld green with envy.

They had already discussed with old Max Dreyfus the idea of becoming publishers of their own work in affiliation with his company Harms, Inc. (now called Chappell & Co.) In 1944, Williamson Music, Inc., was established (so named because both its proprietors had fathers named William) and a suite of offices was rented at 488 Madison Avenue. A London branch was established at the same time. It would later be run by Dick's close friend and, later, "minder," Jerome Whyte (the former stage manager, now R&H production manager, who had once confided to Rouben Mamoulian that he wouldn't give him ten cents for *Oklahoma!*'s chances in New York). Chappell & Co. agreed to charge Rodgers and Hammerstein a percentage for the use of their offices, staff, and distribution facilities, but Williamson Music was and would remain one hundred percent the property of the two men. It started off by publishing the music of *Oklahoma!* — not a bad start by any standard.

Their second step was to announce that Rodgers and Hammerstein would also act as producers of other writers' work. A small office in the RKO Building at Rockefeller Center was opened, dubbed Surrey Enterprises, with Morris Jacobs as its manager. On October 19, 1944, the new organization announced that its first venture was to be *I Remember Mama*, John van Druten's play based on stories from *Mama's Bank Account* by Kathryn Forbes. It was a resounding hit.

It is worth digressing for a moment to examine, if briefly, the record of Rodgers and Hammerstein as producers. Between 1944 and 1950, they presented six straight plays and two musicals — *Annie Get Your Gun* and a revival of *Show Boat*. The income from these — only two of the plays were failures — together with out-of-town presentations and Hollywood movie deals made for an extremely profitable sideline, which added even further richesse to the substantial sums the two men would reap from their own musical

149

productions. In 1951, the magazine *Business Week* estimated the income of the team as around $1,500,000 a year. By the mid-50s, the firm was grossing well over $15,000,000 a year, by which time it had also bought back The Theatre Guild's investments in the early Rodgers and Hammerstein triumphs. Dick and Oscar owned one hundred percent of everything they wrote, and a good-sized piece of everything else.

They set other rules and stuck to them. Anyone wanting motion picture rights to their work had to pay up 40 percent of the profits of the movie, and no haggling. Collaboration with Rodgers and Hammerstein meant that Rodgers and Hammerstein got 51 percent of the credit, and 51 percent of the billing, not to mention the action. The effect of this was to consolidate the Rodgers and Hammerstein interests, to make them into an empire with Rodgers (and, to a much lesser degree, Hammerstein) at its head. He was no longer a theatrical songwriter with business interests, but a chairman of the board who happened to write songs. He supervised every detail — he even signed the weekly paychecks — spending more and more time in an office above a bank on Madison Avenue that had as little charm as a dentist's waiting room, the only concession to his craft a Steinway grand he rarely played.

Always publicity-conscious, Rodgers next hired Samuel Goldwyn's publicity agent, Lynn Farnol, who was briefed not just to handle publicity for himself and Oscar (most shows employ a press agent anyway) but to actively to seek it on their behalf. Dick felt that the name of Rodgers and Hammerstein should be kept constantly in front of the public; that it would help to sell tickets. To that end, he and Oscar became the most available composer and lyricist in theatrical history. Hundreds of thousands of words were written by, for, and about them — their work, their methods, their history, their hopes, and their plans.

This in turn necessitated the creation of a recognizable and repeatable story with a beginning, middle, and foreseeable end, ironing out all the kinks, creases, frays, and tears in the material of their lives. The "factoids" about R&H thus created (to use Norman Mailer's immortal word) were presented as unassailable fact and with their repeated use, the "image" of Rodgers and Hammerstein was manufactured and firmly established. It stressed how Dick and Oscar came from strikingly similar backgrounds, how both had grown up in the same part of New York, gone to the same schools and summer camps, done Varsity Shows. Both had grandfathers who played a strong part in influencing the boys, both had fathers named William. Both had strong-willed wives named Dorothy who were interior decorators.

It didn't stop there. In the Authorized Version, both men subscribed to the Puritan Work Ethic, both had the same orderly, disciplined approach to what they did. Both had similar inclinations in their private life, neither smoking nor drinking to excess, favoring early nights rather than late ones. Like the Rodgers family, the Hammersteins maintained two homes. Dick and Dorothy Rodgers had a duplex in the East 70s, Oscar and Dorothy Hammerstein a town house on East 63$^{rd}$ Street. Rodgers had a country home in Connecticut, Hammerstein a farm in Bucks County, Pennsylvania. They had the same interests, the same circle of friends, the same ambitions. And the two men themselves added to the legend. The longer they stayed together, they claimed, the more similar their outlook became. Towards the middle of their partnership, Rodgers was to remark that he and Oscar had an almost telepathic rapport, rather like an old married couple who can almost communicate without speaking.

This rapport, this similarity of outlook was made to appear so preordained that the initial uncertainty of the partnership was soon forgotten. It is, however, a matter of record that shortly after the opening of *Oklahoma!*, Rodgers discovered to his dismay that Oscar Hammerstein was actively discussing a new project whose composer would be Jerome Kern. When Rodgers learned that the lawyer involved was his old friend Howard Reinheimer, he immediately called Reinheimer, who brought Oscar along for a meeting at which Rodgers urgently (and perhaps a shade anxiously) persuaded both of them that, after a success like *Oklahoma!*, it would be a major mistake for he and Oscar to separate.

151

In fact, there were far fewer similarities in their personalities and lifestyles than all the foregoing would suggest — and a great many major differences. The Hammersteins, while hardly the Waltons, were a big, noisy, close-knit family (her kids, his kids, their kids, and other people's kids — one of whom was Oscar's almost-adoptive son, Stephen Sondheim) who lived on a Bucks County farm far from the rarefied atmosphere of Broadway, who argued and played complicated word games and killer tennis.

The Rodgers's family life was organized, precise, and fastidious, reflecting Dorothy Rodgers's personality. They played croquet, Dorothy cooked Cordon Bleu dinners, both tried to feel what they ought to feel. Her husband's serial infidelities had over the years distressed her so much that Dorothy Rodgers became a neurotic control freak. "She was a woman of great principle," her daughter Mary said, "but she did not want unacceptable emotions." Nor to have anyone know she had experienced them; one of her last acts was to destroy the diaries she had kept all her life.

Oscar was expansive, outgoing. Dick Rodgers was a man who lived inside himself and who, over the years, found it increasingly difficult to relate to other people. The Hammersteins and the Rodgerses put on a happy face for the public occasions when they were seen together, but privately they did not socialize. Very early in their partnership,

**Dick, Oscar, and their two Dorothys arriving in London in 1960 for the opening of *Flower Drum Song.*** Author's Collection.

each realized the other's importance and gave whatever situation came along the necessary slack. "I think Dad had an exercise in patience, in a way," Oscar's son Jamie Hammerstein said. "Dick tended to express himself in absolute terms. Dad would come by sometimes and say, 'You've got to have a thick skin in this business,' and just walk on by." This emotional time bomb would tick for a very long time before it detonated.

By Christmas of 1944, Dick and Oscar were thinking seriously about their next musical. The idea for it grew out of a weekly luncheon that Dick and Oscar shared with Terry Helburn at Sardi's. They called it "The Gloat Club" (for obvious reasons), but they also used these meetings to discuss new ideas. From the very beginning, Dick and Oscar always made it a point to ask everyone they knew to come up with ideas for shows. They either already knew or had quickly learned how to listen to everyone, no matter how screwy their ideas might sound, on the off-chance that there might be a show in them. Terry Helburn's suggestion that Ferenc Molnár's play *Liliom* might be just such a vehicle certainly sounded as screwy as most.

*Liliom* had originally been produced by the Theatre Guild in 1921, with Joseph Schildkraut playing the part of Liliom, who is allowed to return to earth 16 years after his death to do a good deed. He visits his wife Julie and his daughter Louise in the guise of a beggar, but does more harm than good before he is called back to eternity. Originally produced in Budapest in 1909, *Liliom* had been twice translated. The first version was called *The Daisy* and it was never produced. There is an undying Broadway legend to the effect that the second translation was one of Larry Hart's uncredited adaptations, which Benjamin "Barney" Glazer, a Broadway boulevardier, paid him $100 for and then sold to the Theatre Guild. If the story is true (and Joseph Schildkraut swore it was), there is wry historical irony in Terry Helburn's having suggested it for a new Rodgers and Hammerstein show.

Dick and Oscar had seen the 1940 revival starring Burgess Meredith and Ingrid Bergman as Liliom and Julie, and were convinced that it was impossible to turn the play into a musical. Neither had any feel for the Hungarian locale; additionally, the play had a bitter "down" ending totally unsuitable for a musical. Helburn persisted, getting Lawrence Langner to add his weight to her pleas. It didn't have to be set in Hungary, did it? Why not New Orleans? Oscar was just as unhappy with that idea — he'd had all the New Orleans he wanted in *Sunny River*. Then there were all the other problems. It was well known that Puccini had once approached Molnár asking permission to turn *Liliom* into an opera. Molnár haughtily turned the composer down, saying that he wanted *Liliom* to be remembered as a Molnár play, and not as a Puccini opera. It was agreed,

153

however, that Molnár be approached with the proposition that Rodgers and Hammerstein adapt the work. If he turned them down, nothing was lost.

Meanwhile — perhaps "inevitably" is again the right word — Hollywood wanted a Rodgers and Hammerstein show for the screen. There was no question of a movie of *Oklahoma!* for years yet; Dick and Oscar had not the slightest intention of killing the golden goose at the St. James Theatre. But 20<sup>th</sup> Century Fox's Darryl F. Zanuck came up with a good idea. In 1933, Fox had filmed Phil Stong's charming novel *State Fair*, with Will Rogers, Lew Ayres, and Janet Gaynor. Wouldn't that make a good musical?

Rodgers and Hammerstein screened the movie and loved it. They agreed to write the score for a remake which would star Jeanne Crain, Dana Andrews, Dick Haymes, and Vivian Blaine, but with one proviso in the contract: that neither of them would have to work in Hollywood or, for that matter, even visit the place. It must have given both of them a very great deal of pleasure to insert that clause. "They were so intimidated by the fact that Oscar and I had written *Oklahoma!*" Rodgers said, "that they made the picture just the way we wrote it, and it turned out to be one of the two first-class pictures I ever had in my life."

154

**A scene from the Theatre Guild's 1921 production of *Liliom* with Joseph Schildkraut, Evelyn Chard, and Eve Le Gallienne.** Theatre Collection, Museum of the City of New York.

*State Fair*, which was set in Iowa, was written in Pennsylvania and filmed in California. Oscar's screenplay stuck fairly close to the original (Sonia Levien and Paul Green had done the 1933 adaptation), and his lyrics and Rodgers's music were quite masterful. They wrote eight songs for *State Fair* (one, called "We Will Be Together," was never used), including the martial opening chorus "Our State Fair," "That's For Me," "Isn't It Kinda Fun," a splendid waltz called "It's a Grand Night for Singing," and "It Might as Well Be Spring."

Since that winsome lament is the only Richard Rodgers song ever to have won an Academy Award, its genesis deserves recording. One day Oscar telephoned his partner. He was stuck trying to come up with a song for Maggy (Jeanne Crain, whose voice was dubbed by Luanne Hogan), who has the blues for no good reason. She feels as if she has spring fever, he told Dick, but that won't work because everyone knows State Fairs are held in the fall. How would it be if he wrote that she knows it's autumn but, feeling the way she does, it might as well be spring? "Oscar," Rodgers said, "That's exactly it."

Jeanne Crain and Dana Andrews in *State Fair* (1945). Her performance of "It Might as Well Be Spring" won Rodgers and Hammerstein their only Academy Award, but the song was really sung by Luanne Hogan.
British Film Institute.

155

*State Fair* was the same kind of homey, just-folks story as *Oklahoma!* — which, of course, was precisely why Darryl Zanuck wanted it. If, as it seemed, homey, just-folks stories were what the public wanted, then that was what they were going to get. For nearly a decade after *Oklahoma!* and *State Fair*, there was a freshet of movies that looked back nostalgically at an America that probably never existed but everybody wished had. All were sentimental and beautifully mounted: Judy Garland in MGM's *Meet Me In St Louis*; Deanna Durbin in Universal's *Can't Help Singing*, its music provided by Jerome Kern; Rita Hayworth in *My Gal Sal*; and Jeanne Crain again in *Centennial Summer* with music once more by Kern, his 109th (and sadly, final) score.

Rodgers and Hammerstein had no intention, however, of lingering in the same pastures. On October 23, 1944, the *New York Post* carried a short item with a cynical twist in its tail. "After 15 months, all the legal technicalities involved in the production of the musical version of *Liliom* were settled last week. The smallest percentage: eight-tenths of one percent go to Ferenc Molnár, who merely wrote the play." Dick and Oscar were beginning as they meant to continue.

The play was very difficult to find a way into, Rodgers recalled, and he and Oscar spent months in what he dubbed "the 'tunnel' in the story through which we could see no light at the end." They had agreed, quite suddenly, that *Carousel*, as they were going to call the show, should be set in New England and not New Orleans. Liliom — nicknamed "Lily" in the original because in Hungarian slang a "Lily" was a tough guy — would become Billy, like Lily a "barker" on a carousel at a fairground, and simple servant girl Julie, a young woman working at a nearby textile mill.

That part was easy, but Billy — cocksure and proud, but without self-esteem — was harder to "get," and Oscar was stuck until Dick remembered that they had had the same problem with Joey Evans in *Pal Joey*. Seeking a way to make him understandable to the audience, he and Larry Hart had written a sort of soliloquy called "I'm Talking to My Pal," which

**Rouben Mamoulian: true originator of the integrated musical.** Author's Collection.

Joey sang to his "one and only friend" — himself. The song had been cut before the show opened, but perhaps this was the way to explain Billy to the audience? Oscar picked up the idea and ran with it, coming back quite quickly with "My Boy Bill," the first part of which was to become the famous "Soliloquy." It gave the writers the "door in" — the opening they needed to get into the play.

After that, scene after scene suggested itself, and everything began to fall into place except the ending. It proved just as hard to find the "door out" of the play as it had been to find the "door in." Molnár's pessimistic finale, in which Liliom fails at his one chance for redemption, simply would not do for a musical; it had to end on a more upbeat note. After a couple of abortive attempts, Oscar solved the problem by replacing Molnár's ending with a graduation scene, in which just before he is led away to eternity Billy convinces Julie she can let go — "I love you, Julie. Know that I loved you" — while, simultaneously, his daughter Louise realizes that she doesn't have to be an outcast if she doesn't want to. From that scene the song "You'll Never Walk Alone" sprang almost naturally.

First auditions were scheduled for January 22, 1945. The show was already taking its final shape, even if Oscar's original opening was unsatisfactory (he had two old people, Mr. and Mrs. God, sitting in rocking chairs outside their New England cottage) and there were still great chunks of pure Molnár dialogue to be rewritten. Rouben Mamoulian was signed as director, and Agnes de Mille to choreograph. Out in California, Theresa Helburn found a beautiful, intelligent young singer named Jan Clayton who had made a couple of minor films for MGM. She brought her East to audition for the part of Julie opposite another unknown, John Raitt, who had been in a touring company of *Oklahoma!*. Once again, Rodgers and Hammerstein deliberately cast unknowns in their musical, or brought in graduates from their earlier shows. Jan Clayton recalled that only one member of the cast of *Carousel* had ever been in a New York show: Jean Casto, who had been in *Pal Joey*. Everyone commiserated with her on being plunged into her "blood bath." It wasn't, though. "We had worked so hard, and we had complete confidence in Dick and Oscar. I had no idea of the troubles they had gone through or how apprehensive they were about the show. The New Haven opening night was — I believe — about a 1:30 A.M. finish, I might be a little wrong."

Cutting and rewriting every day, they moved to Boston's Colonial Theatre, and opened there on March 27, 1945. Mr. and Mrs. God were still on their porch, but when Rodgers said he still didn't think it worked, Rouben Mamoulian came up with the much more charming and workable idea of the Starkeeper, the nebulous heavenly setting, and the stars hanging out like clothes on a line to dry. The actors and actresses had constantly to learn and relearn their parts, Jan Clayton recalled.

> Oh, those were the most fascinating times in Boston because we had three weeks there and every night we'd play the show, then go back to our hotel, beautiful marvelous Ritz, all go to our rooms, get into our pajamas and robes, meet in one big room, order the coffee and sandwiches and everything, and memorize our changes for the next day. John Raitt was absolutely phenomenal because he had more changes to begin with, he had so much more to do. He could do that better than anyone else I ever worked with in my life — and stay solid. Because every night there were changes.

157

**Rodgers runs through the score of *Carousel* with the cast.** Theatre Collection, Museum of the City of New York.

Elliot Norton, theater critic for the *Boston Post*, filed two reports which illustrate the development of *Carousel* — and its problems. The first, written on opening night:

CAROUSEL HAS FINE MUSIC BUT IT IS RUNNING HALF
AN HOUR TOO LONG AND GETS RATHER TEDIOUS.
DANCING NOT WHAT IT MIGHT BE AND A MINIMUM
OF COMEDY. I DOUBT VERY MUCH WHETHER IT WILL
EVER BECOME ANOTHER OKLAHOMA! FOLLOWS TEXT
OF LILIOM PRETTY CLOSELY FOR MUCH OF THE
EVENING BUT POLICE COURT JUDGE HAS BEEN
REPLACED BY ELDERLY MAN AND WOMAN, CO-RULERS
OF HEAVEN. JOHN RAITT AS LILIOM CHARACTER SINGS
WELL BUT LACKS ACTING SKILL. THE PLAY NEVER GETS
UNDER YOUR SKIN THE WAY LILIOM DID.

Right after that performance the whole company sat down to a two-hour conference, during which five scenes were cut; half of a ballet, two complete songs, and several of the verses in others went the same way. As stage manager John Fearnley remarked, "Now I

158

see why these people have hits. I never saw anything so brave in my life." On April 11, a scant eight days before the New York opening, Norton saw the play again in Boston. It was vastly changed, and this time his report was much briefer.

> CAROUSEL MUCH IMPROVED BY REVISIONS. FIRST
> ACT NOW EXCELLENT, SECOND ACT SEEMS TO ME
> TO DRAG. MUSIC HEARD FOR SECOND TIME SEEMS
> UNUSUALLY BEAUTIFUL. TWO ENTIRELY NEW SCENES
> IN PLAY, SEVERAL SHORT SEQUENCES, TWO NEW
> BALLET SEQUENCES.

The score, in fact, deserves closer examination than usual, for it is not always possible to isolate the songs in the way that one normally can in a musical. Rodgers had dispensed with the conventional overture, replacing it with a waltz suite he had originally written for Paul Whiteman, who never performed it. The first notes the audience hears are the fractured dissonances of a hurdy-gurdy organ warming up, changing into a sweeping waltz as the curtain rises on a colorful fairground scene that immediately brings the audience into the correct mood, time, and place. And as Billy and Julie ride on the carousel, as Carrie watches anxiously, Mrs. Mullin jealously, Mr. Bascombe disapprovingly, we are readied for the story. Simple — now. Then, breathtakingly daring.

159

The first scene — "the bench scene" — is almost pure Molnár, but Molnár so cunningly mixed with Hammerstein's lyrics, so sensitively underscored by Rodgers's music, that it is only after several viewings that the watcher realizes that the whole scene is one wonderfully inventive extended musical piece, what Stephen Sondheim correctly described as "probably the single most important moment in the revolution of contemporary musicals." It runs from Carrie Pipperidge's mildly-exasperated "You're a Queer One, Julie Jordan" and Julie's philosophical reply, "I like to watch the river meet the sea," and then moves on to Carrie's rapturous description of her new beau, "Mister Snow,"

> The first time he kissed me,
> The smell of his clothes,
> Knocked me flat on the floor of the room;
> But now that I love him,
> My heart's in my nose,
> And fish is my fav'rite perfume.

There follow short scenes between the girls and Billy, then Billy's employer Mrs. Mullin, then Julie's employer and a policeman, all constantly backgrounded by Rodgers's music, thematically underscoring what the characters onstage are saying and doing. It was Molnár, rather than Oscar, who provided the title for "If I Loved You," *Carousel*'s principal love song. In the original play, Liliom, talking to Julie, says he bets she wouldn't marry a rough fellow like him...that is, of course, if she loved him. And Julie replies: "Yes, I would Mr. Liliom...if I loved you."

There was no big chorus number until the second scene, but it was a crackerjack when it came: "June Is Bustin' Out All Over" (Oscar having again been inspired by the weather). The charming "When the Children Are Asleep," sung by Carrie and her Mr. Snow, is best known for its chorus, although its bright, irreverent verse tends to be regrettably overlooked. The "Soliloquy" had grown considerably from Oscar's original "My Boy Bill" (Billy was the name of his oldest son) to a seven-and-a-half minute narrative of unashamedly operatic dimensions. (Jan Clayton said she would never forget the look on John Raitt's face when he was presented with the manuscript: "There seemed to be miles

**The opening scene of *Carousel*: Julie (Jan Clayton) and Billy (John Raitt) on the carousel (center), watched suspiciously by Mrs. Mullins (Jean Casto, in striped skirt, right). The setting is, as always, by Jo Mielziner.**
Theatre Collection, Museum of the City of New York.

The opening sequence of the movie of *Carousel* (1956) — worth comparing with the original stage version. Frank Sinatra was cast in the Billy Bigelow part, but when he learned the film was being shot in both 35mm Cinemascope and a new 55mm wide screen process, requiring at least two takes of each scene, he said "I will not make two films for the price of one" and stormed off the set. British Film Institute.

of it.") As the father of two girls, Rodgers had come up with the suggestion that Billy ought at least to consider the fifty-fifty chance that his wife might produce a daughter, so for this segment of the soliloquy (which has eight distinct melodic themes), Oscar added the sentimental "My Little Girl." Dick put a melody to this segment of Oscar's lyric which could well stand alone as one of his best, but then, everything in *Carousel* was top drawer — melodious, moving, merry, at times even genuinely philosophical, as in the song that tells us everything about Julie: "What's The Use of Wond'rin'?"

Hammerstein always felt that this song's failure away from the play was entirely due to the single word, "talk," with which the song ends. According to Joshua Logan, Oscar knew that he was defying convention by making the ending abrupt and hard to sing. His original lines were "Anywhere he leads you /You will go," leading naturally into "You're his girl and he's your feller /That's all you need to know." Nevertheless, he had a perverse desire to do it the hard way, so he substituted "walk" for "go, and ended with "and all the rest is talk." He was never entirely happy with it.

Now as ready as they could be, the entire company had to undergo its most rigorous scrutiny. Ferenc Molnár expressed his desire to see the show. This is how Jan Clayton remembered the occasion:

> *I understood they were all very nervous about his reaction, understandably; they wanted so much for him to like it. So after it was all over, Mr. Molnár, who was a charming gentleman, I can tell you, said to the Theatre Guild, to Mr. and Mrs. Langner and Theresa, "It's a beautiful thing that you've done with my story. And Mr. Hammerstein, your words, what you've done with the book, I'm so pleased. Mr. Rodgers, your music made the whole thing." Then he turned to Rouben Mamoulian (who, in case you don't know, smokes cigars about the size of a baseball bat and doesn't use an ashtray — he uses a bucket!) ... and he said "But you, Mr. Mamoulian!" and everybody's face changed. You can just imagine — Mamoo's heart just plummetted to his feet! "But you, Mr. Mamoulian," Molnár said, "you smoke too much."*

162    When *Carousel* opened at New York's Majestic Theatre on April 19, 1945, Richard Rodgers, who had ripped a back muscle carrying his cases from train to taxi (war service had virtually stripped railroad stations of porters), watched it from a stretcher placed behind some curtains in a box at the theater. In his blurred state — he was heavily sedated — he was convinced at first that *Carousel* was laying an egg, but he was entirely wrong: it was a triumph. Indeed, after her show-stopping ballet as Louise, Billy's daughter, dancer Bambi Linn had to step out of character to take the bow the wildly applauding audience insisted upon. Mary Rodgers and Steve Sondheim caught sight of each other, both with tears streaming down their faces. Irving Berlin said later "You'll Never Walk Alone" had the same kind of impact on him as the 23rd Psalm.

*Carousel* won the hearts of all the critics, even those who compared it with its predecessor. It was at the start of a two-year run, during which it would win the New York Critics' Award as best musical and the Donaldson Awards in no less than eight categories. In London, it would pack the Drury Lane Theatre for sixteen months. Although these figures are nowhere near as impressive as those of *Oklahoma!*, it was in many ways a more daring and innovative show, and the nearest Rodgers and Hammerstein would ever come to writing an American opera. It is, for many, their best score, and Rodgers made no bones about its being his personal favorite of all his musicals. "It affects me deeply, every

The "If I Loved You" sequence from the movie *Carousel*. You have to wonder why, with authentic locations available, director Henry King chose to film the famous "bench scene" on such a phoney-looking set. British Film Institute.

time I see it," he wrote. Even so, he could still be as unsentimental as an accountant about his work. After one performance, Mel Tormé encountered Rodgers at the back of the theater and told him that the finale and the song "You'll Never Walk Alone" had made him cry. Rodgers nodded impatiently. "It's supposed to," he said.

Three months later, as Oscar celebrated his fiftieth birthday (which rather neatly coincided with the thousandth performance of *Oklahoma!*) at a lunch thrown in his honor by the Theatre Guild, *Variety* published a situation report on the R&H empire. *Carousel*, in its thirteenth week, had been a $43,000 sellout at the Majestic; *I Remember Mama* was in its tenth month, with receipts of $21,000; the gross for *Oklahoma!*, now well into its third year, was over $4 million, with a further $37,200 from its eleventh week in Philadelphia. In San Francisco, *Carmen Jones* netted $35,096 at the Curran Theatre, and a new production of *Rose Marie* in Los Angeles added $45,900, with the movie of *State Fair* still to come (it was released on August 20).

With all this, including the Donaldson awards for best musical, best lyrics, and best score, with their director Rouben Mamoulian named best director and Agnes de Mille a winner for dance direction, with John Raitt tapped as best male performer in a musical and Peter Birch as best male dancer, and *Carousel* named best musical of the year by the New York critics, it was beginning to look as if Dick and Oscar could do no wrong. Whereupon, true to their record of never doing the same thing twice, they did something quite astonishing. They gave a smash hit show to another composer.

Herbert and Dorothy Fields had known both Dick and Oscar since childhood. They had been collaborating successfully as librettists on Cole Porter musicals, and had just finished work on a show scored by Sigmund Romberg called *Up in Central Park*, which looked like it was going to be a big hit. Rodgers takes up the story: "They came into the office one day and said, 'We have an idea: How would you like to see Ethel Merman playing Annie Oakley?' And the next sentence in the dialogue was us saying to them, 'Go home and write it and we'll produce it.' We may have been involved in something else, I don't know. But I think for that particular subject we felt we could do better than have ourselves as writers."

The "something else" was obviously *Carousel*, but in retrospect the decision to write neither book nor songs seems a strange one for them to have made, unless it was occasioned by the fact that Dorothy Fields, who had written some pretty nifty lyrics herself, expected to do so with *Annie Oakley*. Producers Rodgers and Hammerstein decided immediately that the composer should be Jerome Kern, who was out in Hollywood putting the finishing touches to *Centennial Summer*.

Lyricist Leo Robin ("Thanks For The Memory," "Beyond the Blue Horizon," "Diamonds Are a Girl's Best Friend") had been assigned to work with Kern on the film and was in great awe of the composer. Every day, Kern would call him and ask him if he had anything yet, and Robin found that, far from encouraging him, the calls had exactly the opposite effect. Impatient as ever, Kern started looking for other lyricists, eventually calling in Johnny Mercer, who wrote "Two Hearts Are Better Than One;" Yip Harburg ("Cinderella Sue"); and Oscar Hammerstein ("All Through the Day"). Although he never classed them as his best work, it would be a brave musical purist who'd care to say whether Robin's lyrics for "In Love in Vain" and "Up With The Lark" were better or worse than the lyrics for the others' songs.

Oscar visited Kern in Hollywood in August (when he wrote "All Through the Day") to discuss a revival of *Show Boat*. Then, wearing his R&H hat, he asked his old friend if he would consider writing the music for *Annie Oakley*, with Herb and Dorothy Fields doing the book and Dorothy the lyrics. Kern was interested, but reluctant. "I'm too old," he said. Oscar kept after him, and finally, encouraged by a telegram from Rodgers

(IT WOULD BE ONE OF THE GREATEST HONORS OF MY LIFE IF YOU WOULD CONSENT TO WRITE THE MUSIC FOR THIS SHOW), he told them he would be happy to work on *Annie Oakley*. Could that 15-year-old boy in the balcony of the Princess Theatre have ever dreamed that one day he would be commissioning the composer he idolized to write a show for him?

Kern and his wife Eva arrived in New York on November 2, 1945, taking a suite at the St. Regis. On Monday morning, November 5, the 60-year-old composer collapsed on the corner of Park Avenue and 57th Street, just a few blocks from the Rodgers and Hammerstein offices. Suffering from a cerebral hemorrhage, he was taken to the Welfare Island charity hospital (the same institution in which Stephen Foster had died) because when he was picked up no one knew who he was.

At the hospital, an ASCAP membership card was found in his pockets, and that organization was called. They, in turn, called Oscar's office. Hammerstein got hold of his own physician, Dr. Harold Hyman, and the two men rushed to the hospital to find that Kern was in a ward filled with some 50 or 60 mental cases, drunks, and derelicts. The doctors and nurses had gathered them together and explained who the new patient was, and asked them not to make any noises or disturbance. Not one man disobeyed. The nurse on duty, Oscar recalled, extended her shift that day to 24 hours, and when Kern's wife, Eva, thanked her, said that Kern had given so much pleasure to the world, she wanted to give something to him. Two days later, Kern was moved to Doctor's Hospital, where he died on Sunday, November 11, at 1:10 in the afternoon. The following Monday, funeral services were held in the chapel of Ferncliff Crematorium in Hartsdale, New York. Oscar Hammerstein delivered the eulogy, as he had done eight years earlier for George Gershwin. This time, he was too emotionally affected to finish it. Once the shock of Kern's death had worn off, Dick and Oscar were faced with the enormous problem of how to replace him. They had told Joshua Logan, who was still in the service, that they wanted him to direct *Annie Oakley* as soon as he got out. Josh called Rodgers one day and learned that the producers had come up with another composer. Logan asked how they'd gone about it, and Dick said they had made an alphabetical list of every composer they knew. The first name on the list was Irving Berlin. Everybody said there was no point in even approaching Berlin, because if he was involved, it would have to be his show, his ideas, his money, and his songs. In that department, Irving Berlin wrote the rulebook; his control over the minutiae of his own career and output was all-embracing.

It was at this point Oscar Hammerstein said, "Wait a minute! How can a man say no until he's been asked?" So they asked him, and Irving Berlin, although "more or less awed and impressed" by being asked to do a R&H show, turned them down. He was tired, he said, and besides, he didn't like the idea of stepping into Kern's shoes. Oscar persisted, and got Berlin to read the script. Still Berlin balked. "This is hillbilly stuff, Ockie," he said. "It's not my style. I don't know the first thing about this kind of lyric." "You can do it, Irving," Oscar said. "All you need to do is drop the 'g' of words that end in 'ing'."

The conference was held on a Friday. Berlin said he would like to take the script away for the weekend to see if he could come up with anything. The following Monday morning he bounced into Rodgers's office with three songs: "Doin' What Comes Naturally," "You Can't Get a Man With a Gun," and "There's No Business Like Show Business." *Annie Get Your Gun* was on its way.

With astonishing facility, Berlin added "They Say It's Wonderful," "The Girl That I Marry," and "Who Do You Love, I Hope?" Josh Logan remembered that everyone was very enthusiastic about the latter song.

> *Now, Irving has a way of doing his songs, of looking right into your eyes, almost grabbing you by the collar as he sings, as if he wants to get your reaction to every nuance, the moment you think it. If your eyes should get out of focus or whatever, Irving will shake his head and say "No good, eh? You don't like it, right?" and he's quite likely to toss it out. Well, this day, right after he'd played "Who Do You Love, I Hope?" he played us the second chorus of "There's No Business Like Show Business." Now, I don't know what we were doing, maybe we were thinking where to put the other song, or discussing something else. Anyway, we'd all raved about how marvelous it was already, we couldn't rave again. Well, to cut a long story short, a few days later Irving was playing the score for Hugh Martin — he likes to get everyone's opinions of his songs, it's as if he really needs that reassurance that they're terrific — and I said, "Irving, you didn't play 'Show Business.'" "No," he said, "that's out, I threw it out." I said "Whaaaaaat?" "I threw it out," he said. "I could see from your faces the other day you guys didn't like it."*

And that is how the anthem of show business very nearly didn't get into *Annie Get Your Gun.* They grabbed a cab and hurried down to Berlin's office, where they spent a very tense and frantic half-hour trying to find the lead sheet, which Irving had told a secretary to put away. It was discovered beneath a phone book.

Berlin turned out the score of *Annie Get Your Gun* so fast that it was hard to keep up with him. Logan recalled that during a discussion in Oscar's living room at the East 63rd Street house, they decided they needed another song in the second act. The principals, Frank Butler and Annie Oakley, have quarreled, and Logan felt the situation called for some kind of song. "A quarrel duet, maybe?" Rodgers said. The words were hardly out of his mouth when Berlin jumped to his feet, bringing the meeting to a close by saying he had to go and write the song. Logan and his wife, Nedda, took a cab back to the St Regis Hotel, just a few blocks downtown. When they got to their room, the phone was ringing. It was Irving Berlin, who triumphantly sang them "Anything You Can Do, I Can Do Better." He had written it in the taxicab on the way back to his office.

*Annie Get Your Gun* opened at the Imperial Theatre on May 16, 1946, and ran for nearly three years, making it the second-longest running Broadway show ever, after *Oklahoma!* It took Donaldson Awards in three categories: best female performer in a musical (Ethel Merman), best director (Logan), and best score. Surprisingly — it had half a dozen big-time hits in it — some of the critics didn't think much of the latter; Brooks Atkinson actually referred to it as "undistinguished." But then, even experts have their off days; Jerome Kern had once said that the score of *Oklahoma!* was "condescending."

167

**Herbert, Dorothy, and Joseph Fields: The best thing that ever came out of Far Rockaway.** Author's Collection.

**Producer Richard Rodgers with two of the reasons why he considered** *Annie Get Your Gun* **"failure-proof" — Ethel Merman and composer** **Irving Berlin.** Used by permission of the Rodgers and Hammerstein Organization.

There was an important consequence of Dick and Oscar having been the producers of *Annie Get Your Gun*. Richard Halliday and his wife, Mary Martin, were at the New Haven opening of the show, and Halliday became convinced that Annie would be a great role for Mary. Until then, everyone thought of the girl from Weatherford, Texas, as the "cute" type, the sex-kitten who'd done a mock striptease in *Leave It to Me* singing Cole Porter's "My Heart Belongs to Daddy," the witty goddess of *One Touch of Venus*. Halliday knew better, so at the Langners' Connecticut home he had Mary prove she could belt out a song as well as La

Merman. Dick and Oscar were there, weekending with their wives. So were Terry Helburn and Ina Claire. The tradition was that after lunch everyone had to perform. Mary cut loose with "You Can't Get a Man With a Gun," and Dick and Oscar were knocked out. When the time came to open *Annie Get Your Gun* in London, they invited Mary to play Annie, but — after an unhappy experience in the Noel Coward musical *Pacific 1860* — she didn't want to stay in England. Instead she proposed that she return to America and take the show on the road.

Rodgers and Hammerstein were even more amazed. It was flying in the face of accepted wisdom for an established star to go on tour in a role someone else had made famous, but by now they were becoming accustomed to flying in the face of tradition and said yes on the spot. So Mary Martin went on the road with *Annie Get Your Gun* and made the show thoroughly her own, although in a different way from Ethel Merman. Anyone who saw both performers will tell you it is difficult to say which of the two was a better

Annie. The show began its tour in Dallas on October 3, 1947. Until it reached San Francisco the following May, Mary Martin would be out of sight but never far from Rodgers and Hammerstein's minds.

Meanwhile, they were busy, producing a play by Anita Loos called *Happy Birthday*, written for and starring her friend Helen Hayes, with Joshua Logan again directing. Logan warned Dick and Oscar he wasn't sure he could pull "this flimsy piece" off, and his gut feeling was right. "It was a Nabisco wafer of a play and I had no idea what the first audience in Boston would make of it," Logan said. Answer: they hated it. At a council of war in Oscar's suite, Logan got his first glimpse of how tough his producers were. "I expected the worst," he said, "perhaps they would close it at once. But instead, Oscar said calmly, 'Let's fix it.' And Dick added, in the same tone, 'And by Monday.'"

Fix it they did. And when it opened in New York on October 31, 1946, the play was a hit; despite very mixed reviews it eventually ran for almost a year and a half at the Broadhurst. One of its more charming moments had Helen Hayes singing an unobtrusive little song by Rodgers and Hammerstein called "I Haven't Got a Worry in the World." It must have been pretty much the way Dick and Oscar were feeling.

Their next production was the Norman Krasna play *John Loves Mary*. Krasna, a veteran Hollywood scriptwriter and playwright, is famous as the man who, while working for the foul-mouthed and tyrannical Harry Cohn, legendary boss of Columbia Pictures, dictated a codicil to his will which he then announced to the press. It stipulated that on his death Krasna be cremated and his ashes thrown in Harry Cohn's face.

*John Loves Mary* was a slight thing about a young soldier coming back from overseas with a British girl whom he has married so she can come to America with him. He is doing a favor for his friend, her true love, but the friend had thought her dead in an air raid and married someone else. The complications arising from all this and from concealing those complications from the girl's parents resulted in a happy comedy which was destined for success. It opened at the Booth Theatre on February 4, 1947. One of the cast, a little-known actor named Tom Ewell, would eventually become the star of a play (and movie) called *The Seven Year Itch* written by George Axelrod, son of the man who had written the book for the 1921 Columbia Varsity Show staged by Oscar, with songs by Rodgers and Hart. Sometimes the theater is a very small world indeed.

During the Boston tryouts, director Joshua Logan felt unhappy about the ending of the second act. Dick and Oscar came up to see the play, agreed that the ending was weak, and stayed on, trying to come up with something. The more they watched, the less successful they were; after several days, tempers began to fray. Then Logan came up with an idea: "I

169

**Dick Rodgers with the chorus at rehearsals of *Allegro* (1947).**
Used by permission of the Rodgers and Hammerstein Organization.

said, 'Listen, how would it be if we have the father and the mother see the boy out of the house, then go to bed. As soon as they've gone, he comes back in, kisses the girl, and they go into the bedroom — curtain!' Well, you'd have thought I'd suggested they make love onstage. Oscar got up out of his seat, you know, purple! He glared at me, and said 'Anybody who'd make a suggestion like *that* is a *cad!*' Afterwards, Norman said to me, 'You know, Josh, everyone always told me Oscar was as cool as a cucumber. Well, if he is, he's the most belligerent cool cucumber I've ever seen.'"

They finally solved the problem by just bringing down the curtain, ending the scene. While lightweight and far from "important," *John Loves Mary* ran for 421 performances and turned in a profit of $250,000, making it yet another success for Rodgers and Hammerstein. They were the golden boys. Nothing, it seemed, could go wrong for them. Oops.

During this time, Oscar was deeply immersed in something that it had been one of his most cherished ambitions to write ever since he could remember: a play which chronicled the life of one man, from his birth to his death. The man would be a doctor, and the play would set out to make some fairly large statements about life and love and ambition and the pursuit of happiness. Oscar put the idea to his partner, and Rodgers, a doctor's son, loved it.

Hammerstein put a great deal of himself into the play. His son William thought that Oscar tried to say in it everything he had learned about life. "Much of the first act was based on his memories of his own childhood," he said. "He had always been intrigued by it, you know; his mother died when he was twelve. I always felt his songs came out of his feelings about her."

As Rodgers and Hammerstein developed the story, which was to be called *Allegro*, they became increasingly convinced that once more they were going to be forced to defy conventional techniques. Perhaps, in their earnest desire to do something truly different and important, Dick and Oscar lost sight of their first duty, which was to entertain. As it turned out, *Allegro* was a great deal closer to a morality play than a musical, and the unorthodox techniques they used to stage it — nearly bare sets, a sort of Greek chorus which comments on the action onstage, and ghosts ("presences," as Oscar called them) of characters who have died earlier in the story — militated against a light touch.

Joshua Logan confessed later that he was "deeply grateful" when Dick and Oscar told him, apologetically, that they had promised the director's job to Agnes de Mille. He felt that the book was deeply flawed, sentimental and mawkish in parts, and that the score was not one of Rodgers's best. "I think, too," he added, "that they had had a rough time facing the smash success of Irving Berlin with *Annie Get Your Gun*. They were overanxious. They wanted to do something sensational and they tried too hard."

At Oscar's suggestion, a newcomer to the world of Broadway musicals joined the *Allegro* company as a $25-a-week gofer: Stephen Sondheim. "It was a seminal influence on my life," he said, "because it showed me a lot of smart people doing something wrong. Years later, in talking over the show with Oscar — I don't think I recognized it at the time — I realized he was trying to tell the story of his life…Oscar meant it to be a

171

The opening sequence of *Allegro*: The ensemble propose that "Joseph Taylor, Jr." might well be a possible future President of the United States, a role Oscar suggested for more than one of his stage "sons."
Used by permission of the Rodgers and Hammerstein Organization.

metaphor for what had happened to him. He had become so successful with the results of *Oklahoma!* and *Carousel* that he was suddenly in demand all over the place. What he was talking about was the trappings, not so much of success, but of losing sight of what your goal is."

Reexamined today, *Allegro*'s main fault seems to have been that it was ahead of its time, the integration of story and music far too advanced even for audiences now becoming accustomed to musicals which actually had stories (*Brigadoon* and *Finian's Rainbow* are its contemporaries). But its 40-week run was nothing like enough to recoup the huge investment that had been needed to put it on. Cole Porter had once remarked that the changes Rodgers and Hammerstein had effected in musical theater had made it that much harder for everyone else. They had also made it that much harder for themselves.

*Allegro* was to be the last association of Rodgers and Hammerstein with the Theatre Guild, who brought the show to New York on October 10, 1947. It had undergone drastic changes out of town, and suffered a few small calamities as well. At the New Haven opening, dancer Ray Harrison caught one of his taps in a curtain track and tore the ligaments in his right leg. He was carried off screaming from the stage, Sondheim recalled. Then, while William Ching, playing the father, was singing the tender "A Fellow Needs a Girl," the scenery wall started to collapse and he had to hold it up until the stagehands noticed. The performance went on, only to be stopped again when, in the second act, Lisa Kirk fell into the orchestra pit while singing "The Gentleman Is a Dope." Two of the musicians hoisted her back onto the stage, where she continued singing as if nothing had happened.

"Need I tell you, the audience was giving her an ovation the Pope has never received," Sondheim said. "Everybody pushed her back onstage and she had to take two bows. Next day in the *New York Herald Tribune*…Billy Rose, of all people, said 'A star is born.' Next night she comes back, gets to the same point in the song, and starts to fall again, and the entire audience gasps because they'd all read the *Herald Tribune*. She recovers quickly, they all sigh, and she gets another ovation. Oscar came backstage at the end and said, 'You do that a third time and you're fired.'"

There was one further drama on that dramatic opening night. In the quietest and most uplifting moment of the show, as the cast began to sing "Come Home," there was a false fire alarm. Panic was averted only when Joshua Logan, who was in the audience, got to his feet and in stentorian tones told the people scrabbling for the exit doors to sit down. When Logan gave orders at the top of his voice, people obeyed. The panic subsided and the show went on.

In New York the critics were kind, but divided. The show had been weakened by giving the job of director to a choreographer. Agnes de Mille's dances were fine, but if Sondheim is to be believed, as a director "she was a horror." That may be why she had handed the staging of the songs and dialogue over to Rodgers and Hammerstein. Neither man had ever aspired to be a Joshua Logan, and so the presentation was uninspired. The sheer size of the production and the unusual staging subtracted what little warmth there was from the story. Most of the songs were too much a part of the story to work away from it; "A Fellow Needs a Girl" and "You Are Never Away" had brief popularity, but they have not stood the test of time. Even though it had an advance sale of over $700,000 and ran for 315 performances, the enormous costs involved meant *Allegro* was a failure, although, as Rodgers said, nothing to be ashamed of — after all, it won Donaldson Awards for best book, best lyrics, and best music.

"Two things were really remarkable about *Allegro*," Stephen Sondheim said. "The experimentalism of its form and its message. *Allegro* was an attempt to use epic theater in contemporary musical theater. It used a Greek chorus and tried to tell the story of a life, not through events but through generalities. This is what would now be called a Brechtian approach. The chorus comments to the audience on how to perceive the action happening on stage. That kind of distancing had never been used before in musical theater. Usually a chorus comments on a single moment; these choruses commented on the structure of a man's life."

Dick and Oscar both retained their affection for the play. "The comments we made on the compromises demanded by success, as well as some of the satiric side issues — hypochondria, the empty cocktail party — still hold," Rodgers said later. In other interviews, both men philosophically accepted that in *Allegro* they had overestimated the ability of the audience to identify with its leading character. As Hammerstein ruefully conceded, "If the writer's aim is misread, it can only be because he hasn't written clearly enough." "Oscar wanted to tell the life story of one person, as in *Citizen Kane*," Sondheim said. "But he regretted that no one understood it. The audiences thought the message was: don't get swallowed up by the big city, go back to quiet country life. To the end of his days he wanted to rewrite the show to point up the real message."

But all that was much later. At the time, the failure of the show really got under their skin, as a young author who was to be associated with them on their next venture remembered. "They were inwardly burning because of the reception accorded to *Allegro*," said James A. Michener. "Those fellows were so mad I was fairly confident that they could make a great musical out of the Bronx telephone directory."

# CHAPTER FIVE

# THE South Pacific YEARS

*I had the same feeling about* South Pacific *as I had about* Oklahoma! *and* Annie Get Your Gun. *It was failure-proof.*

— Richard Rodgers

The outstanding hit of the 1948 theatrical season was *Mister Roberts*, starring Henry Fonda, William Harrigan, Robert Keith, and David Wayne. It was written by Thomas Heggen and Joshua Logan, and Logan directed. While he was preparing the play for Broadway, Logan dined one evening with scenic designer Jo Mielziner, and during dinner Jo's brother Kenneth McKenna joined them. He mentioned to Logan a book which had been submitted to him (he was a story editor at MGM), and which the studio, with its usual unerring judgment, had turned down. The book was called *Tales of the South Pacific*, and McKenna suggested that Logan might find it useful for background material, since *Mister Roberts* was also set in that theater of war. Oh, by the way, there are others who will tell you that in fact it was Henry Fonda who was reading the book for background, and that he, not Kenneth McKenna, drew it to Logan's attention. Take your pick.

It wasn't until Logan was on vacation in Miami prior to the opening of his play that he finally got around to reading James A. Michener's collection of stories. Michener, a Macmillan textbook editor recently returned from service in the U.S. Navy, had been stationed during the war on the island of Espiritu Santo in the New Hebrides. Over a six-month period in 1945, he had set down a series of "tales" such as might have been told by a naval officer (which Michener was) about the American servicemen and local inhabitants on an island in the South Pacific. The book, rewritten twice before he submitted it to his employers, was published in the spring of 1947 and not expected to generate much excitement — a book of short stories by an unknown author? George Brett, the head of Macmillan, went so far as to tell Michener, who had also submitted a second book, that he didn't think Michener had much future as an author and might do better to stick to editing textbooks. Michener took his second book to Random House, who signed him on the spot. Three days later, *Tales of the South Pacific* won the Pulitzer Prize.

Logan was particularly impressed with the story called "Fo' Dolla' " about a Tonkinese woman called Bloody Mary (four dollars is the price she asks for the grass skirts she hawks) who "arranges" a doomed love affair between her daughter Liat and a young American Lieutenant, Joe Cable. He also liked, although to a lesser degree, "Our Heroine," which featured Nurse Nellie Forbush from Otolousa, Arkansas, whose "hearthunger" leads her into a romance with an older man, the French planter Emile De

The principals of *South Pacific* assembled in the Rodgers and Hammerstein office to discuss the play, or at least look as if that's what they're doing. Left to right: Joshua Logan, Rodgers, Hammerstein, Mary Martin, and James A. Michener. Author's Collection.

Becque. Logan was sure this material was adaptable into a play or a musical or a movie, although at this stage he was not sure which.

Visiting Logan and his wife Nedda in Miami was Leland Hayward. Hayward was the top, top theatrical agent — "the Toscanini of the telephone," George Axelrod called him — among whose clients were Fred Astaire, Gene Kelly, Judy Garland, Helen Hayes, and Henry Fonda. Hayward and his wife, movie star Margaret Sullavan, had homes in Hollywood and New York, they owned planes and boats and cars. Hayward, who had 300 pairs of shoes and nearly as many suits, lived a reckless, disordered life. He was a sharp-eyed, crafty entrepreneur who rarely missed a trick, and while Logan was taking an afternoon nap, Hayward picked up *Tales of the South Pacific* and read it. Logan awoke to find Hayward almost exploding with excitement. "Josh," he said, "we've got to buy this sonofabitch!"

Logan agreed, even though neither he nor Hayward was exactly sure what they were going to do with the property. All they knew was that it was terrific material and that they had better grab it before someone else did. Hayward set to work to put a deal together, meanwhile swearing Logan to secrecy — an act not unlike forbidding a skylark to sing. Logan was far too excited about the book, far too much a theater man not to talk about it, and when he ran into Dick Rodgers at a cocktail party, he had to tell him. It wasn't just that he loved the book; he had felt right from the outset that Rodgers and Hammerstein would be the only people to talk to if they decided to do "Fo' Dolla' " as a musical. Rodgers methodically noted down the title of the story in his little black notebook, and as promptly forgot what it referred to.

When *Mister Roberts* tried out in Philadelphia, Oscar Hammerstein came over from nearby Doylestown to see the show, and Logan asked him to give him some pointers on anything that was wrong.

> He said, "I'll tell you all about it, give me a ring tomorrow." When I called him he read me his notes on Mister Roberts, which were very helpful, we always help each other in any way we possibly can. Then he said, "Before you hang up, have you got any ideas of anything for Dick and me to do? We can't find a property that's suitable." And I said, "Didn't he tell you about Tales of the South Pacific?" Oscar said he'd never heard of it, so I told him to call Dick and ask him whether he'd read it and what he thought of it. So he called Dick, who said, "Yes, I've read it, Oscar, and it's great, but some sonofabitch owns the rights and

*we can't get them." Now, I'd told Oscar that we already had the rights
and he said to Dick, "Is the name of that sonofabitch Logan?" And
Rodgers said, "Yes! That's the sonofabitch!"*

Now Joshua Logan had to break the news to Leland Hayward, who was "absolutely, desperately upset" with Logan for letting Rodgers and Hammerstein in on their secret,
because he had not yet finalized the deal with Michener. He angrily told Logan that
Rodgers and Hammerstein would have them over a barrel and, sure enough, Dick and
Oscar insisted that if they were going to do the show, they wanted 51 percent of the
property. "That gives them final say and us no say, Josh," Hayward said. "All this thanks
to you." He was very bitter about it.

Logan said he didn't care what they demanded — a statement he was later to regret
— because he so much wanted Dick and Oscar to do the show. Hayward capitulated,
without ever forgiving Logan for spilling the beans, and the contracts were signed. In the
light of subsequent events, it is interesting to note exactly how dominant Rodgers and
Hammerstein were, both in creative and financial matters.

Nine percent of the gross went to Dick and Oscar, with Logan taking three and the
author of the book on which the whole thing was based a mere one percent. The management's half of the takings was split two-to-one in favor of Surrey Enterprises, the producing firm owned by Rodgers and Hammerstein. Co-producers Hayward and Logan
took the remaining third, which in turn was split two-to-one between them, Logan taking the larger share. In addition, the stars of the show, Mary Martin and Ezio Pinza (both
of whom agreed to reduced salaries to help the budget), would each receive seven percent
of the gross, and designer Jo Mielziner a flat hundred dollars a week. These royalties were,
of course, over and above whatever return the participants might realize on their investment in the show's $225,000 budget. (A five percent investment in *South Pacific* would
produce a return of $25,000 at the end of its first year.)

These rewards were still, however, a long way in the future. As always with Rodgers
and Hammerstein, months were spent discussing the way the show would be mounted,
how it would look, what its tone would be. Logan and Hammerstein had some meetings
and Oscar told the director that he envisaged the story "Our Heroine" as the main theme
of the show, possibly, Logan felt, because Oscar identified more closely with the older
man in it, but also because a romance between a 40-something expatriate French planter
and a young American nurse was (then) daring stuff for a musical. Of the two, he added,
"Fo' Dolla'" had the stronger storyline. "He always said you should have a stronger sec-

**Nellie Forbush (Mary Martin) rehearsing the "Honey Bun" number for the Thanksgiving show in *South Pacific*.**
Theatre Collection, Museum of the City of New York.

ondary story, because that's the one that hasn't got all the attention on it, or the stars playing in it, so it's got to be a stronger story in itself," Logan explained.

Ezio Pinza, who was inspired (and extraordinarily lucky) casting as De Becque, came to the show almost accidentally. Edwin Lester, the Los Angeles Civic Light Opera Association's producer, had called Rodgers one day and admitted that he was in a bind. He had signed the Metropolitan Opera star with the intention of starring him in a musical, *Mr. Ambassador*. When this fell through, Lester could find no suitable alternative musical on the horizon, and his contract with the mettlesome opera singer had a penalty clause in it which Pinza would have no hesitation in applying. Lester did not want to pay Pinza $25,000 for doing nothing; had Rodgers and Hammerstein anything cooking that might be suitable?

Rodgers immediately saw the potential of the handsome, mature, swaggering Pinza in the role of the French planter, De Becque. Although they had neither script nor songs, they signed him almost immediately.

Ever since he'd seen her wearing a gingham dress in a scene from *One Touch of Venus,* Oscar had felt Mary Martin ought to play "the real Mary, a corn-fed girl from Texas" (he tried to get her to play Laurey in *Oklahoma!,* remember?) so he never had any doubt about whom he wanted for the part of the nurse, Ensign Nellie Forbush. Mary was out in California with the touring company of *Annie Get Your Gun* when Dick and Oscar called her.

> *By this time I'd practically lost my voice, it had gone down about twelve octaves because of yelling those songs, 22 songs a day on matinee days. And Dick said, "We've just bought a property called* South Pacific *and Ezio Pinza is going to be the male star. Would you come back and listen to the score? We want you to play opposite Pinza in the show, play the part of the Army nurse." And I said, "What do you want, two basses?" I couldn't conceive of playing opposite an opera star, but they said please, please, come back to New York and listen to it. So we went back east, and went over to Dick's house in Connecticut. There was Dick and Oscar Hammerstein and Joshua Logan, and they said, "Now just listen to three songs, that's all we've written. We have no book yet. But — don't give us your answer for 24 hours." So we heard "A Cockeyed Optimist," "Some Enchanted Evening," and the "Twin Soliloquies." My husband, Richard [Halliday], and I went home and we didn't say a word to each other. We sat there and looked at each other, and then he said, "Do we really have to wait for 24 hours? Can't we call them now?" And I said, "Yes, yes, yes, please, please, please!"*

179

By the time Dick and Oscar contacted Mary Martin in California, they had written some songs, but the book was not even begun. Joshua Logan went to Europe on vacation, expecting to return at the end of the summer to find Oscar's first draft completed.

> *I had heard one or two songs from the first scene before I left: "Some Enchanted Evening" and "Twin Soliloquies." I asked Dick about the book, whether I could get a copy. And suddenly the truth came out, he'd been covering up until then, he didn't have to face anybody he knew. He said, "He's stuck, he's absolutely stuck. He can't write. I don't understand it. He's got the first scene written and a little tiny bit of the next scene,*

*but they don't jell." I said, "How could that be?" He said, "Well, he*
*claims to hate the military to such a degree that he's never read*
*anything about the Army, it's always gone past him. He doesn't know*
*the difference between a lieutenant and a captain."*

Rodgers suggested that Joshua Logan go down to Doylestown and give Oscar some help. After all, Logan had been educated at Culver Military Academy, and had served in the Army Air Force during the war: he knew about the military. Logan called Oscar and got himself, his wife, and a secretary, Jim Awe, invited down to the Hammersteins's farm. He told Oscar that he would bring along a dictaphone (an early form of tape recorder), and Oscar recoiled from the idea as though it were a snake. "I'm not very comfortable around machinery," he protested, "besides, I thought we ought to start on a horse and buggy." Logan looked at the calendar. They had about six months before the show was due to begin tryouts in Boston. "I think we'd better start on a jet airplane, Oscar," he said, "or we'll never make the date."

Highland Farm was a working farm, run by Oscar's Norwegian masseur. Oscar had bought it when the masseur threatened to quit his profession to raise prize Black Angus cattle. The masseur got his farm, Oscar got his cherished daily massage and the Hammerstein brood got a country house. Logan and Oscar started work as soon as Logan got there.

*He had these marvelous ideas for solidifying the story, but he really didn't*
*know how to write about the military and he was also stuck on Southern*
*talk. He seemed to be uncertain; frightened, even. Well, we started*
*kicking ideas around and the two of us got on fire. We used to meet in*
*the afternoon. He'd write lyrics in the morning and I'd sleep. Then we'd*
*work all afternoon, dictating, and the two secretaries would type the first*
*draft, and then we'd correct it and make a second draft with six copies.*
*We found that we were using not only "Fo' Dolla'," and "Our Heroine,"*
*but also "Operation Alligator," the story of the coast-watcher, and "A*
*Boar's Tooth," which is the one with Billis in it. All of those were brought*
*into the story plus an idea that Oscar had had, that they were going to*
*give a Thanksgiving show. It went really very well, and we did finish the*
*first draft in ten days. And all through this time, when I would come to*
*bed at night, my wife would say, "But aren't you writing it? How could*

**Ezio Pinza and Mary Martin: "When I keess, I *keess!!*"** Theatre Collection, Museum of the City of New York.

*you be making all these contributions without being a coauthor?" And I
said, "Well, I am a coauthor, but I just can't ask him to let me be." She
said she didn't see why not. She said you couldn't write a man's play for
him and expect to do it for free. I said, "Well, he is embarrassed about it,
I'm sure, because he never brings it up."*

Logan hurried back to New York with the draft, and the question of coauthorship was
left unresolved. There was work to do: auditions, casting, staging. It was not for a week
or so that Logan saw Oscar again, by which time Logan was becoming convinced —
determined was his word — that the play was going to win the Pulitzer Prize. Feeling
enormously apprehensive, he told Hammerstein that he wanted a credit as coauthor.
"Oscar was silent for a moment, and then said, 'I'm sorry I didn't offer it to you myself.
Of course you can have it. We'll work out the exact details later'." They worked on the
script for a while, and Oscar left. Logan and his wife opened a bottle of champagne, but

their celebration was premature. The next day Oscar appeared again. It was clear he was uncomfortable with what he was going to say but was going to say it come hell or high water. "I'm sorry," he said, "but I can't do it. I don't think that I should be penalized for not being the author of this show. Every body expects me to be the author and giving someone else coauthor credit would be a great penalty."

"You can't look me in the face and tell me that I didn't write the major part of this story," Logan said. "No, perhaps even more than that," Oscar replied. "But Rodgers and Hammerstein cannot and will not share a copyright. It's part of our financial structure." He went on to enumerate the points that the corporation required: this size of credit for Logan as director, that size of credit for Rodgers and Hammerstein as producers. "Their word was law," Logan says. "They were that powerful. And when somebody disobeyed that law, they were punished." He told Leland Hayward about his talk with Oscar. Hayward shrugged. "You're at their mercy," he said.

> *The thing was, I wanted to do the show more than anything else in the whole world. And now the whole thing had become terribly ugly to me. All of this, of course, had been dictated by Howard Reinheimer, their lawyer, and Dick Rodgers. I don't, however, think that Oscar was completely blameless. He had a certain amount of steel in him, otherwise he wouldn't have survived the way he did. I suppose, looking back, I could have forced them to share the copyright. Lindsay and Crouse got them to do it later on* The Sound of Music.

With the libretto in working form, the cast began to take shape. Ezio Pinza and Mary Martin were set as the leads from the start. Juanita Hall, who had been in the original production of *Show Boat*, was spotted by casting director John Fearnley singing in *Talent '48*, a show put on by the Stage Manager's Club. She auditioned, and walked off with the part of Bloody Mary, Liat's mother. The role of Liat went to Betta St. John, who, as Betty Striegler, had been Bambi Linn's replacement in *Carousel*. For the part of Lieutenant Cable, they tried to get a young singer named Harold Keel who had led the English production of *Oklahoma!* Unfortunately, he had just signed a contract with MGM and changed his name to Howard Keel, so the part went to a little-known actor named William Tabbert.

Four days before rehearsals began, on February 3, 1949, *The New York Times* carried a succinct announcement. "In recognition of the extraordinary contribution made by

Joshua Logan in the preparation of the first script of *South Pacific*, Rodgers and Hammerstein announce that henceforth he will share credit for the book with Oscar Hammerstein II." It was grudging recognition of Logan's decisive part in the preparation of the musical, but it was all he was going to get.

Oscar's problems with the script were, however, only one factor among the dozens confronting the partners in staging the show. James Michener recalled the first meeting they had in New York to discuss it.

> *Everyone was there — Josh Logan, Leland Hayward, Oscar*
> *Hammerstein, Richard Rodgers, Jo Mielziner, all these great names of the*
> *theater. The meeting lasted for about two-and-a-half hours, and they laid*
> *out the complete framework for the work they were going to do. During*
> *the first two hours, Richard Rodgers did not say one word. At the end of*
> *the two hours he turned to me and said, "Michener, I'd like to ask you one*
> *question." I thought he was entitled to that. He said, "When I score this*
> *music, do I have to use a wailing guitar?" I said, "In the part of the South*
> *Pacific I was in, I never heard such an instrument." "Thank God," he*
> *said, and he said not another word that whole meeting.*

183

In a long article in the *New York Herald Tribune* of April 3, 1949, a few days before the show opened in New York, Rodgers recorded his reservations about scoring *South Pacific*.

> *An island in the South Pacific could only mean one thing musically,*
> *and that was the sound of a steel guitar or a xylophone, or perhaps a*
> *marimba struck with what is known as a soft stick. This is a particularly*
> *mushy, decayed sound, one which is entirely abhorrent to me. The idea*
> *of having to deal with it for an entire evening was far from enticing...*
> *To my amazement and joy I found that in this part of the South Pacific*
> *there was no instrumental music of any kind...This caused a complete*
> *shift in my approach to doing the score...I realized that I would be*
> *allowed to do what I'd always wanted to do by way of construction: give*
> *each character the sort of music that went with the particular character*
> *rather than the locale in which we found him...In the whole score there*
> *are only two songs that could be considered "native." These are sung*
> *by a Tonkinese woman and here I made no attempt whatsoever to be*

*authentic or realistic. The music is simply my impression of the woman and her surroundings in the same sense that a painter might give you the impression of a bowl of flowers rather than provide a photographic resemblance.*

The two "native" songs were, of course, "Bali Ha'i" and "Happy Talk." The first had been in Rodgers's mind almost from the outset when they were discussing the opening of the play. Logan and Hammerstein had told him that they wanted to do a song about the island, and gave it a working title, "Here I Am," and Oscar got started on it. It took him quite some time to find the key to the song, which came when designer Jo Mielziner was preparing his scenery sketches for the show. For the third scene of Act One, he needed a backdrop with a picture of the island. As he painted it, he became dissatisfied; the island did not have enough mystery. Dipping his brush into some water, Mielziner blurred the top of the island, making it look as if it were surrounded by mist. He called Logan. "Come on down and have a look at Bali Ha'i." When Logan saw the painting he called Oscar. Hammerstein took one look at it and the words "my head sticking up from a low-flying cloud" came to him. The lyric came very quickly after that, but not as quickly as Rodgers's melody. There's a legend (he repeats it in his autobiography) to the effect he wrote that in about ten minutes flat, reputedly over coffee at Joshua Logan's apartment. In fact, what he "got" that day was the song's striking three-note motif. "This," he told his colleagues, "is not only the beginning of the song, but the beginning of the show."

**Lt. Cable (William Tabbert) looks disapproving as Luther Billis (Myron McCormick) explains why they both might enjoy a trip across to Bali Ha'i.**

Theatre Collection, Museum of the City of New York.

It's instructive here to pause a moment and look at how Oscar Hammerstein transmuted one bit of Michener into Broadway. Here's Michener:

> *To himself, De Becque said, "This is what I have been waiting for. All the long years. Whoever thought a fresh, smiling girl like this would climb up my hill? It was worth waiting for. I wonder…"*

And here's Hammerstein in the "Twin Soliloquies":

> This is what I need.
> This is what I've longed for.
> Someone young and smiling,
> Climbing up my hill…

Pinza was hugely enthusiastic about everything they were writing for him. On one occasion when he congratulated Rodgers on a new tune, the composer's hand was too numb to write for a week. "What I have to say about you," Pinza declaimed grandly, "I would like written in the sky!"

New songs were coming thick and fast, Mary Martin remembered.

> *We were in Josh Logan's apartment in New York. Dick Rodgers had called and said, "Come on over, I have a song, I have the song for you." We went over, it was about midnight, and he was playing the piano and Oscar sang the song "I'm in Love with a Wonderful Guy" in his darling, darling voice. And I said, "Could I have it, could I have the lyrics and sing it?"' And I realized he expected me to sing 26 words on one breath. So I sat down beside Richard and he played it and I sang it. I sang it at the top of my voice, and when I finished I fell off the piano bench, because I was all in when I got to the end. And Richard Rodgers turned and looked at me on the floor and said, "That's exactly what I want. Never do it differently. We must feel you couldn't squeeze out another sound."*

"Happy Talk" was done in about twenty minutes, so the story goes. Oscar sent the lyric to Rodgers while the latter was in bed with a cold. He rang Rodgers half an hour later to check that the messenger had arrived. "I've not only got the lyric," Rodgers said.

185

"I've got the music, too!" Even so, "Happy Talk" was nearly thrown out; Oscar was convinced there was no way the song could be successfully staged. Joshua Logan said if he could have the song, he could stage it; it took him perhaps ten or fifteen minutes to create and shape the scene in which Bloody Mary sings the song and her daughter Liat expresses the words in eloquent hand-mime.

It became apparent very early in the process that the show would contain little or no conventional choreography, no dream ballets or choral groups to develop the songs. Rodgers said,

> *When we thought of backing up our principals with a ballet or a singing ensemble, we feared that sincerity would go out the nearest exit and we would be back in an artificial and unemotional form. It was easy enough to say "no groups" but it wasn't easy to find a substitute for them...*
> *It happens that the simple, direct answer is often the easiest one. We decided the only thing to do was to try to make the songs good enough, and have them sung so well that they would stand on their own and need no further development... The final resolution of our problem came from Joshua Logan, in the extraordinary way he has managed to stage the songs as though they were both book and dialogue, not unpleasant little interruptions in the scheme of the place. His extraordinary sense of balance has made it possible for the small values of the songs to create a large effect. He has been able to follow a rare, subdued technique but has never neglected showmanship or refused to allow the audience what I consider to be its greatest joy: that of being able to applaud."*

Everyone agreed: throughout the rehearsals Logan was fiery, demanding, and brilliantly inventive. He adapted and improved the cinema-style scene changes that Dick and Oscar had pioneered in *Allegro*, making them almost seamless; the actors of the next scene coming onstage while those of the preceding one were making their exit. In the third scene, he got the men pacing like caged animals, back and forth, killing time, breaking into random, rather than choreographic patterns. "Feel it in your crotch!" he yelled at the actors. "Feel it in your crotch!" In less than half an hour, singing all the time, tramping about the stage, doing every gesture, every grimace, he had the scene fixed, and the entire company gave him a standing ovation. The staging was never altered, and "There Is Nothing Like a Dame" became, and remains, one of the high points of the show.

Myron McCormick, who played Luther Billis, recalled how the famous "belly dance" originated in a conference between himself, Logan, Hayward, and John Fearnley, the company manager:

> *We started out when Logan outlined what he fancied to be very*
> *fetching pigeons facing each other across my chest. Doves, he chose to call*
> *them. We rubbed those off and drew a very nautical sketch — a gob*
> *with two mermaids, as I recall. Logan said no in the interests of civic*
> *decency ... The chest was the wrong place, everyone agreed. It was then*
> *that [Jack] Fontan (an ex-Marine retained by Logan in the dual*
> *capacity of scene painter and physical trainer for the cast) came along*
> *with the ship. He knew all about ships and how to utilize my*
> *background, as it were.*

They tried a balloon dance first, but that didn't work. "I'll never forget the briefing Josh once gave me about the technique of acting," McCormick continued. " 'Don't knock yourself out over a part,' he said. 'Sneak up on it. It's the subtle approach that does the trick, the oblique touch.' So he paints a full-rigged ship on my stomach. I suppose that contributed to the subtle approach on my part!"

Dick and Oscar had given Pinza a second-act song called "Will You Marry Me?" but it didn't fit the spot they wanted. "We'll get it, we'll get it," they told the impatient actor, who was a laboriously slow learner and who knew he hadn't much time to memorize, rehearse, and perfect a whole new number. Dick and Oscar came up with a song called "Now Is the Time," but this one made the situation even

187

**Bloody Mary (Juanita Hall) and Liat (Betta St. John) teach Lt. Cable "Happy Talk."** Theatre Collection, Museum of the City of New York.

**Nellie tells the girls "I'm Gonna Wash That Man Right Out Of My Hair" — and she did, eight times a week for three-and-a-half years! By the way, whose idea was it to call one of the nurses in the show "Ensign Lisa Minelli"?**
Theatre Collection, Museum of the City of New York.

more unbelievable. De Becque and Joe Cable were going off on a mission from which they might never return. It wasn't likely that they would stand around singing "Now! Now is the time to act, no other time will do." Everyone agreed that what was needed was a lament. Dick, Oscar, and Josh went into a huddle, out of which the title "This Nearly Was Mine" emerged, together with the decision that it would be a big, bass waltz. Despite his legendary slowness, Oscar wrote the lyric in a couple of days; it became Pinza's favorite.

More problems: because she speaks no English, how would Cable express his love to Liat after their first lovemaking experience in the little hut on Bali Ha'I? Would he sing? If so, what? Oscar went back to his notes and came up with an alternative. He was fascinated by the idea of the girl waiting for Cable's boat to come around the bend of the headland. What if Liat sang? A few days later he and Dick brought Logan a song called "My Friend" which literally appalled the director. "I was so astonished," he recalled, "that I said, 'My God, that's awful! That's the worst song I ever heard in my whole life!' " Dick and Oscar looked at Logan in shock. This was Rodgers and Hammerstein he was talking to. No one had ever said anything so damning about one of their songs before, or even spoken to them that way. But they were pros and took it on the chin. As Rodgers said, "I'm not married to my tunes. There are plenty more where they came from." Oscar was not married to his words, either, and so the deathless lines "My friend, my friend, is coming round the bend" were consigned to the limbo that they sound as though they deserved.

A few days later they came back with a lilting melody called "Suddenly Lovely." It was something Rodgers had run up for Mary Martin to rehearse the show-within-a-show until they wrote the actual song she would sing. It's one of the better Oscar Hammerstein lyrics that never made it to the stage and it deserves recording:

> Suddenly lovely,
> Suddenly my life is lovely.
> Suddenly living
> Certainly looks good to me.
> Suddenly happy,
> Suddenly my heart is happy.
> Is it a girl?
> Could be, could be.
> Suddenly lovely,
> Suddenly to be together.
> Suddenly sharing,
> Ev'rything we hear and see.
> Suddenly wond'ring,
> Suddenly I wonder whether
> Are we in love for ever and for good?
> Are we happy as we could be?
> Could be!

189

Logan vetoed this one, too. The boy and girl have just made love, he explained, drawing Oscar's (reluctant) attention to Michener's description of Cable finding "incarnadine proof that he was the first who had loved her." The song was too "up" for such a moment, and Bill Tabbert wouldn't be able to do it with true emotion. Now it was Rodgers's turn to dig in his heels. He announced that he was damned if he was going to go on writing tunes until he came up with one that Josh Logan just happened to like. "Dick, please, give me one more," Logan said. "Something slower, deeper."

Rodgers thought for a moment, and then played a melody that he had written for no particular reason some years earlier. It had been considered for *Allegro* then dropped. The rough lyric that Oscar had put to it went "You are so lovely, my wife /You are the light of my life," and when he heard the melody Logan knew it was third time lucky. Two days was all Oscar needed to come through with a great lyric: the song became "Younger Than Springtime." "Suddenly Lovely" was laid aside, to have a reincarnation two years later, when Gertrude Lawrence needed a song with the children in *The King and I*. Mary Martin, who had always hoped that one day they would rewrite it for her, reminded them of "Suddenly Lovely," and they gave it to Gertie with a new lyric. It was called "Getting To Know You."

By the time *South Pacific* opened out of town — on March 7, 1949, at the Shubert Theatre in New Haven — the word was beginning to spread that it was going to be the biggest show ever to hit Broadway. This was partially due to a rehearsal in New York held one day before the New Haven opening, to which an audience of show business people

**South Pacific: The final scene.** De Becque is back from his mission, and Nellie is waiting for him, her previous reservations about him and his half-white children dispelled. The little girl who played Ngana was Barbara Luna, who became a popular movie and TV actress. Used by permission of the Rodgers and Hammerstein Organization.

had been specially invited. The cast worked with makeshift props, old benches, anything; the lighting wasn't even set. The seasoned professionals watching gave them a standing ovation. Many of those who saw it said it was one of the best performances they ever saw in any theater anywhere. In New Haven, Mary Martin recalled meeting Mike Todd with his then wife, Joan Blondell, the same Mike Todd who had once damned *Oklahoma!* with his wisecrack about no girls and no gags. He came backstage and faced Mary Martin gravely, telling her not to take the show to New York. The actress could not believe her ears, and asked him why. "Because it's too damned good for them!" Todd said, "It's too goddamned good for them!"

**Mitzi Gaynor in love with a wonderful guy in the movie version of** *South Pacific* **(1958). Try to visualize Doris Day in the part; she very nearly got it.** British Film Institute.

191

Despite the enormous enthusiasm the show was generating, it was still far too long and there were still a number of staging problems. One was with the song that Mary Martin sang in scene seven. The idea for it had come to her one evening while she was in the shower; she realized that she had never seen anyone wash their hair onstage. She called Joshua Logan and asked him whether he had. "Wow!" said Logan and called Oscar Hammerstein. Before you could say "shampoo" there was a new scene in the show where Mary washed her hair onstage to the tune of "I'm Gonna Wash that Man Right Outa My Hair." The trouble was, audiences were so intrigued by her doing it that they were ignoring the song. Nobody could come up with another way of doing it. Then Josh Logan had the idea of Mary singing the song first and *then* washing her hair, flinging suds about as she did the dance which followed the song. That did it: Mary Martin washed her hair onstage eight times a week for three-and-a-half years and loved it every time.

A small historical footnote here. While there's no doubt whatsoever that the song came into the show just the way Mary said, Oscar Hammerstein had amazingly anticipated the same idea something like a decade and a half earlier, during an abortive collaboration with Sigmund Romberg for a 1930s show called *Cuba* which never seems to have gotten off the ground. Here is Oscar's untitled lyric:

> Wash dat man right outa yo' hair, honey,
> Wash dat man right outa yo' hair, honey,
> Wash dat man right outa yo' hair, honey,
> Soap an' water's gonna cure yo' care.
> Beat dat man right outa yo' heart, honey,
> Beat dat man right outa yo' heart, honey,
> Beat dat man right outa yo' heart, honey,
> You'll feel much better when you're miles apart.
> Blink him outa your eyes,
> Think him outa your brain,
> Wave him outa your arms,
> Kick him goodbye and don't try to explain...

Nobody involved with *South Pacific* seems ever to have known about the little trick Oscar pulled on them all. You can almost see his smile.

In Boston, Logan also had to completely restage "I'm in Love with a Wonderful Guy," as well as reluctantly cut two of the songs: Cable's "My Girl Back Home" and one of De Becque's numbers, "Loneliness of Evening." (He would reinstate them in the movie in 1958, the latter as incidental music.) Still the show was too long. Logan asked his friend Emlyn Williams, who was in Boston with a play of his own, to take a look at the script and see if he could suggest some cuts, as he had done with *Mister Roberts*. Williams's technique, according to Logan, was brilliant; he would go for the shortest form of every verb, cut all dependent clauses, all unnecessary adjectives, and all repeated phrases. Most importantly, he went for those bits of which the author says, "Oh, that's rather nice, I'm rather proud of that."

With the "Emlyn Williams Cutting" done (by way of thanks they gave him a pair of gold-plated scissors and a blue pencil, both engraved "Emlyn the Ripper"), the format tightened, and the songs restaged, *South Pacific* got ovations every night in Boston. The advance sale for the show in New York ($400,000 at pre-opening and $700,000 after the premiere) was the highest in theatrical history, and it was fast becoming a mark of the utmost social distinction to possess tickets to see it. The furor was so great that playwright George S. Kaufman, no great admirer of either Rodgers or Hammerstein, threw down his paper with its glowing reports of the show's success and complained bitterly to his friend Moss Hart that people in Boston were so excited about *South Pacific* that they were shoving money under the doors of the Shubert Theatre when it was closed on Sundays. "They don't actually want anything," he complained, disgustedly. "They just want to push money under the doors."

Also part of *South Pacific's* mystique was the persistent rumor that Pinza and Martin were having a red-hot backstage affair, this in spite of the fact that Pinza was happily married with two children and that Mary's husband Richard Halliday was fiercely possessive, picking her up each night from the theater, then permitting her just one drink when she got home, where she did needlepoint. If she remonstrated with Pinza about his lusty onstage kisses, he would defiantly boom "When I keess, I keess!" and during the performance, he would whisper "Mary, I loff you" in her ear. Mary, whose heart was as big as all outdoors, went along with it; she knew Pinza was like that with all the girls. As Rodgers told Logan, Pinza was keeping all the girls in "a pleasant state of anxiety. They just never know what end to protect."

*South Pacific* opened at the Majestic Theatre in New York on April 7, 1949, and proceeded to write another incredible chapter in the success

193

"I'll never forget Oscar's face when he brought 'Honey Bun' to me," Mary Martin said. "Those twinkling eyes in that granite face — he just loved having written something so deliberately corny. " Here's Mitzi Gaynor singing it in *South Pacific*. British Film Institute.

story of Rodgers and Hammerstein. The celebrity first-night audience repeatedly stopped the show with applause and cheers, and there was a prolonged standing ovation after the final curtain. So confident were the partners in the enterprise that they joined in throwing a gala party on the St. Regis roof for the cast, collaborators, and friends — even going so far as to order two hundred copies of *The New York Times* to hand out *before the reviews were in*. It was a risk, perhaps, but a calculated one. The reviews were in fact better than even the most optimistic had expected, hurling adjectives like bouquets at everyone involved. "South Terrific," as one critic said.

The excitement continued to mount as the show ran. Tickets became such precious commodities that columnist Leonard Lyons printed an entire column of stories about what people had paid or done to obtain a couple. "House seats" — the tickets reserved for important members of the production staff and the stars of the show — were being sold by brokers at such high premiums (two hundred dollars and more) that the attorney general's office threatened to close the show, but found it impossible to establish who was responsible for the practice, which was and still is known as "scalping."

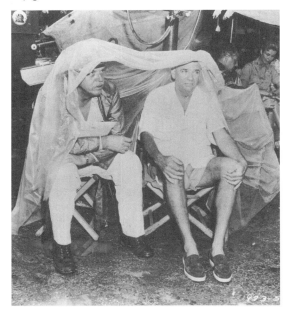

194

Joshua Logan and Oscar Hammerstein sheltering from a tropical downpour on the location set for *South Pacific*. In the background are Rossano Brazzi, who played De Becque, and Mitzi Gaynor. Not an enchanted evening, by the look of it.

British Film Institute.

Although the show would not, in fact, run as long as *Oklahoma!* (1,925 performances), it was to prove infinitely more profitable. Its gross of $2,635,000 was bigger than that of *Show Boat.* Of the $50,600 weekly gross, Rodgers and Hammerstein each took $2,227, Logan $1,518, and Michener $506. Of the approximately $10,000 weekly profits, half went to the backers (among whom, of course, were Rodgers, Hammerstein, Logan, Hayward, Reinheimer, and their wives) and the other half to the producers. Rodgers and Hammerstein took

$1,667 each of this half, Logan $1,111, Hayward $556. Weekly, remember; and the show was to run profitably for five years in New York, two-and-a-half in London.

Then there were to be the equally profitable touring companies. The national company began its tour in 1950; after one year, its gross was over $3,000,000, its profit $1,500,000. By August of 1949, the sheet music sales were in excess of a million copies; it had taken *Oklahoma!* six months to achieve in sheet music sales what *South Pacific* did in four. The backers who had put up the $225,000 budget (the show cost $163,000 to bring to Broadway) received their money back in four months. After a year, their return on investment was a thousand percent, and by the end of the run nearer five times that. By January 1957, the show's profit was close to $10,000,000. (This figure, by the way, does not include revenue from the sale, in 1956, of the motion picture rights to 20$^{th}$ Century Fox.) The long-playing record album of the score with the original cast sold more than a million copies at $4.85 — the income from this single venture alone being very probably more than that from any of the shows Dick Rodgers ever wrote with Larry Hart.

There were artistic as well as financial rewards. *South Pacific* swept the Antoinette Perry Awards ("Tonys") for best musical, best male and female performers (Pinza and Martin), best supporting male and female performers (Myron McCormick and Juanita Hall), best director, best book, and best score. The Donaldson Awards went to the same starry roster: Pinza, Martin, McCormick, Hall, Logan, Hammerstein and Logan, and Richard Rodgers. The show walked away with the New York Critics Circle Award as best musical of the season 1948-49, and in 1950 came its greatest accolade: *South Pacific* won the Pulitzer Prize in drama. Not a consolation award, such as had been given to *Oklahoma!*, but the full prize, something which had not happened to any musical since 1933, when it went to the writers of the Gershwin show *Of Thee I Sing*: George S. Kaufman, Morris Ryskind, and (as lyricist) Ira Gershwin. This time, the citation included Rodgers as composer, making him the first ever to receive the award.

Unfortunately, in making the award, the Pulitzer committee neglected to include the name of Joshua Logan. Like everyone else, they had accepted the show as Rodgers and Hammerstein's. Even though the omission was later remedied, and Logan got his Pulitzer, he was served with all the proof he needed that his part in the creation of *South Pacific* was being smothered by the legend of the other two. So strong were his feelings about what he felt to have been their shabby treatment of him that, although they offered him full coauthorship and direction of their next production, Logan turned them down. He regretted the decision all his life; the show he refused was *The King and I*.

# BROADWAY'S
# *Miracle Men*

*Too many people cling to the grief that comes
from failure and too few people cling long enough to the
thrill that comes from success.* — Oscar Hammerstein II

S *outh Pacific* was a stunning success, a marvelous achievement with which to celebrate
Rodgers's 25<sup>th</sup> anniversary on Broadway. The name of the show was licensed for cosmetics, clothing, and fashion accessories. Every single member of the cast seems to have
been interviewed about his or her role in the play: Myron McCormick, Juanita Hall, Joshua
Logan, Jo Mielziner, Betta St. John, James Michener, musical director Salvatore dell'Isola,
Mary Martin, Ezio Pinza — especially Ezio Pinza, who had become a matinee idol and was
living it up in a spectacular way — and, most of all, Rodgers and Hammerstein.

Reporters described life at the Rodgers house in Connecticut, Hammerstein's work
methods at Doylestown. *Ladies Home Journal* published a novella-length Lincoln Barnett
essay on Rodgers's life and work. Earl Wilson went up to Highlands Farm and filed a column in the *New York Post* with Oscar's remarks about his collaboration with Rodgers.
*Variety* ran banner headlines hailing *South Pacific* as the "one-year Broadway box-office
champ." *Life* magazine did a pictorial feature on them and their Pulitzer Prize. The partners themselves appeared on the Groucho Marx TV show *You Bet Your Life*. Groucho
pretended to be unimpressed with them (perhaps he was) and referred to them through-

out as Roy Rogers and Trigger. When Oscar remonstrated that his name was Hammerstein, Groucho looked at him contemptuously. "That's a funny name for a horse," he snarled, and then, almost as an afterthought, "It's a funny name for a man, come to think about it." Dick and Oscar didn't even seem to mind being told they looked like "a couple of chiropractors" — as long as they got in the plug for "Some Enchanted Evening" and "There Is Nothing Like a Dame."

Rodgers himself was formally honored in many other ways. The Theatre Guild commemorated his 25th anniversary on Broadway with a presentation and a party attended by some of the original members of the first *Garrick Gaieties* cast. He was presented by Dwight D. Eisenhower with the Hundred Years Association's award for his distinguished contributions to the American theater. *Variety* reported in July that some 15 Rodgers and Hammerstein concerts had been performed by symphony orchestras up and down the country, playing to standing-room-only audiences of 10,000 at a time. (These concerts led, the following year, to the establishment of a unit managed by Jim Davidson which toured the country for an entire season, playing a 22-number Rodgers and Hammerstein concert). On March 4, NBC Television devoted an hour to "An Evening for Richard Rodgers" featuring Mary Martin, Bing Crosby, Celeste Holm, Vivienne Segal, and Alfred Drake. On August 6, the first Rodgers and Hammerstein concert (it was to become an annual event) was held at Lewisohn Stadium in New York. Despite a ten minute downpour which threatened to wash out the performance, 9,000 people turned up and waited the storm out. The very name of Rodgers and Hammerstein was box-office. Well, almost.

Surrey Enterprises, the Rodgers and Hammerstein producing arm, decided to present a new play by Samuel Taylor based on Robert Fontaine's novel about a French-Canadian family, *The Happy Time*. Taylor was an old friend of Rodgers; he had begun his theatrical apprenticeship when the Dramatist's Guild had asked the composer to let him watch the preparation and staging of *The Boys from Syracuse*, and had kept in touch with Rodgers ever since. The play, which starred Claude Dauphin and also featured Kurt Kasznar and Eva Gabor, was presented at the Plymouth Theatre in New York on January 24, 1950. The critics and the public liked it enough to keep it there for almost 18 months, and a movie sale was clinched with Columbia Pictures (the film, directed by Richard Fleischer, and starring Charles Boyer, Louis Jourdan, and Bobby Driscoll, with Kasznar reprising his stage role, appeared the following year), making it another solid success for Rodgers and Hammerstein.

Then, in fairly rapid succession, they produced two thundering flops: *The Heart of the Matter* and *Burning Bright*. The first play was written by Graham Greene and an actor friend of his, Basil Dean, based on Greene's novel of a couple of years before. It just didn't work (the story was later filmed with equal lack of success in Britain) and there was no alternative but to close the play in Boston. This abrupt reversal of their fortunes made the partners closely re-examine their role as producers. They had several properties under their wing for possible production: a new play by John O'Hara, another by John Steinbeck, and the dramatic rights to a book by Sholom Aleichem called *Tevye's Daughters* which they thought might make a musical. (It later did, with a score by Sheldon Harnick and Jerry Bock. It was called *Fiddler on the Roof* and for a while, in those halcyon pre-*Phantom* and *Les Mis* days, it displaced *Oklahoma!*, *Hello, Dolly!*, *Annie*, *My Fair Lady*, and *Man of La Mancha* as the longest-running show (3,242 performances) in the history of the Broadway musical.)

They decided to go ahead with *Burning Bright*, the Steinbeck play, partly because the project was already well advanced, and partly out of loyalty to and friendship with the author. (His wife, Elaine, had been stage manager for *Oklahoma!*) The capable cast included Barbara Bel Geddes, Kent Smith, and Howard Da Silva, returning to Broadway after being blacklisted by the House Un-American Activities Committee (HUAC). When someone warned him the actor was a Communist, Oscar Hammerstein shrugged. "I don't care what he's called. He's perfect for the play and he has the part." Although the out-of-town critics praised it, *Burning Bright* was another failure, folding after two weeks at the Broadhurst in October, 1950.

"Perhaps our admiration for the author blinded us to its shortcomings," Rodgers said. "I couldn't agree with the New York press…but can't quarrel with them. It was obviously not right for the stage but it was certainly right for the eye in the reading if not for the ear. I think Barbara Bel Geddes is a fine actress. It was our first time with [Guthrie] McClintick as a director and one of the dividends from *Burning Bright* was getting to know that fellow. Another was getting to know Steinbeck."

By the time *Burning Bright* had died its death, however, the partners had withdrawn from the producing business, except where it concerned their own shows. They composed a long rationale called "The Pleasures of Producing" which appeared in *The New York Times* the day after they closed *The Heart of the Matter* in Boston. Their friends had been asking them for years, they said, why they functioned as a producing team when, with their own created hits and the others they had produced, they were working mostly for Uncle Sam. They pointed to the satisfactions in their producing role, not the least of which was the fact that they had been financially successful. That there was little profit in it all was outweighed by the sense of accomplishment, the knowledge that people were enjoying, and being emotionally engaged by, their plays. They said:

*It would be difficult to imagine any greater fun, than taking a little
blonde girl with one line to speak out of the cast of* South Pacific *and
putting her in the lead of the company of* Oklahoma! *which is now
touring the country. On dreary March mornings with not enough sun,
the memory of Patricia Northrop's face when she learned she had the
part of Laurey, and would eventually play it before her
parents and school chums in California, is something to turn a dull day
into a very happy one. What we are trying to explain is that, in this
sense alone, producing can be creative, perhaps almost as much as
writing itself, but there are other reasons. We are as aware as anyone
that the theater is having difficulty in maintaining itself, and it
is our deep feeling that so long as we can help to keep some of the
theaters lighted here and throughout the country and contribute towards
the employment of actors, stagehands, musicians, and hard workers in
the theater, we are in the position of having to do so, whether we
like it or not.*

These and many more hundreds of brave words on the subject notwithstanding, Surrey
Enterprises was effectively out of the producing business because of the failure of the two
plays. Hence, perhaps, Joshua Logan's dry comment, "I've always had a suspicion that
Dick was more interested in money than art."

Of course, there was another reason for their putting aside the burden of being producers — sooner or later they had to find a property to follow *South Pacfic*. Big as that
show was, neither man was the kind who can deliberately not work. So, by the summer
of 1950, the word was already out that the next Rodgers and Hammerstein show would
be a musical based on Margaret Landon's 1944 novel, *Anna and the King of Siam.*

Its genesis as a musical by Rodgers and Hammerstein is no less unusual than all the
others. If anything, it would appear the credit for the idea should go first to the William
Morris Agency, representing the author, who sent the book to Fanny Holtzman, the
shrewd theatrical attorney, suggesting it would make a wonderful vehicle for her client
Gertrude Lawrence. Holtzman, already worried that the parts Lawrence ought to have
been getting were going to the likes of Mary Martin and Ethel Merman, pounced on the
idea. She first discussed it with Cole Porter, who turned it down flat. She was about to
contact Lawrence's longtime friend and mentor, Noel Coward, when she accidentally
bumped into Dorothy Hammerstein. Bells rang and she grabbed Dorothy's arm.

*The King and I* : Yul Brynner as the strutting, swaggering King — a long way away from the robot gunfighter he later became in *Westworld.* Used by permission of the Rodgers and Hammerstein Organization.

"Listen," she said, "why don't Oscar and Dick do a show for Gertie Lawrence? If I send over a book, will you see Ockie reads it?"

Standard operational procedure — both Dorothys were trained to always say "yes" to such propositions. And later that day a messenger brought over a copy of the Landon book. As it happened, both Dorothys had read it when it first appeared in 1943, and both had enthusiastically recommended it to their husbands as possible material for a musical. Both men had as strenuously resisted. *Anna and the King of Siam* was a novel based on fact, about the English governess Anna Leonowens who went to the court of the King of Siam in the 1860s to teach the King's many children English. The form of the book was to present, chapter by chapter, vignettes of life at the court of Siam and, through the character of the King, to heighten the exotic and sometimes savage aspects of daily life there.

They still felt pretty much the same way — where was the *story?* — and continued to do so until they saw a print of the 1946 movie produced by 20th Century Fox, starring Rex Harrison as the King and Irene Dunne as Anna. The film had been a big hit (even though Fox had wanted James Mason or Robert Montgomery as the King), and after seeing it, Dick and Oscar knew at once it was a perfect vehicle for a musical, and indeed, for Gertrude Lawrence. *Here* was the story the Landon book lacked. Here were the unspoken attraction between Harrison and Dunne, the presentation of the wives and offspring that would become "The March of the Siamese Children" — even the King's broken speech patterns, the "etcetera, etcetera, etcetera."

A great idea, then. But taking on Lawrence, who had been a huge hit a couple of years back in *Lady in the Dark*, had its drawbacks. To begin with, she would be expensive (indeed, she ended up getting an unheard-of ten percent of the gross on top of five percent of the net — more than the composers, in fact). Secondly, although she had a unique stage presence — what Oscar called the "magic light" — her vocal range was, to say the least, limited, and she had a distressing tendency to sing flat. In addition, they had never set out before to write a show with a specific star in mind.

Although Lawrence neither needed nor wanted a costar, they felt a solid theatrical name would be helpful to the production. The obvious choice for the role of the King was Harrison, and they got in touch with him right away, but he was committed to doing a film called *The Long Dark Hall* and had an offer to do a play — T. S. Eliot's *The Cocktail Party* — in London. "I'd seen Alec Guinness playing it in New York and I wanted to try my hand at it, it was such a marvelous play," Harrison recalled. "I also had to do the film because I'd found a plot of land in Portofino that I wanted to build a house on, and the film was really to pay for it. It turned out to be one of the worst pictures I've ever done. I don't think that more than 20 people ever saw it. Of course, if I had done *The King and I* for five years, and then the film afterwards, I probably never would have got *My Fair Lady*."

Oscar was already at work on the libretto. He found the "door in" to the story in the novel's account of a slave writing about Abraham Lincoln, an episode which would finally grow into the delightful story-ballet "The Small House of Uncle Thomas." He altered the King's physical appearance (Landon had described him as excessively thin and of medium height) and built up the romantic subplot about the slave-girl Tuptim from a small vignette which occurs about three-quarters of the way through the book. (The man involved is a priest, and there is no amorous relationship with the girl whatsoever.) Hammerstein added the "arranged" marriage and made the priest a slave, Lun Tha. In fact, hardly any aspect of what was to become *The King and I* remains literally true to the original novel. Yet throughout, it is totally true to the spirit and intention of the book. Oscar's most radical alteration, and his most daring unorthodoxy yet in terms of the musical, was to have the King die at the end of the play. As Oscar wrote to Josh Logan:

> *I believe I have caught the quality that made the book so strangely appealing. I don't know. By its very nature, the story will not permit the pace and lustiness of a play like* South Pacific *and I am sharpening a very long knife for the first one who tells me it hasn't the qualities of* South Pacific. *It is a very strange play and must be accepted on its own terms or not at all.*

Examined in isolation and without hindsight, the show should have been a failure. There was no conventional love interest between the two principal characters — they do not even kiss (indeed, when the relationship was made more overt in the 1996 revival starring Lou Diamond Phillips and Donna Murphy, it was less rather than more convincing). There were no Americans in the story; all the characters were either British or Siamese. The setting was Bangkok (*where?*) and the period Victorian. There was precious little humor — as Oscar pointed out, he had been especially wary of jokes about harems, and of dancing girls with Oriental costumes who sang "ching-aling-aling" with cymbals on their fingers. Instead, he aimed his libretto towards the pageantry and dignity of the East, succeeding so admirably that Rodgers confessed himself "crazy about Oscar's book," which was "a wonderful job." Anyone who knew Rodgers would tell you that this was almost rhapsodic praise; when a performer or a performance especially pleased him, "adequate" or "very adequate" were his highest terms of approbation.

By Christmas, Rodgers had written six or seven songs and expected to write perhaps another dozen. Rehearsals were scheduled for January, 1951, and casting was going apace. Failing to get Rex Harrison for the King, Rodgers and Hammerstein now went after the biggest musical star on Broadway. He was, curiously enough, their own discovery: Alfred Drake, the original Curly of *Oklahoma!* Drake had just left the cast of the smash-hit Cole Porter musical *Kiss Me, Kate!*, and Dick and Oscar thought he would be ideal as the strutting King. Drake decided to play hard-to-get, however, making conditions and demands that Dick and Oscar decided were too high a price to pay.

No doubt reflecting upon the irony that had made Drake too big a star for them to hire, they finished their lunch and went back to the Majestic, where John Fearnley was still auditioning. "They told us the name of the first man and out he came with a bald head and sat cross-legged on the stage," Rodgers said. "He had a guitar and he hit this guitar one whack and gave out with this unearthly yell and sang some heathenish sort of thing, and Oscar and I looked at each other and said, 'Well, that's it!' "

Well, it was and it wasn't. Yul Brynner, who in 1979 said Rodgers's account of his audition was "very picturesque, but totally inaccurate," had made his movie debut in 1949 in *Port of New York* (which nobody anywhere seems ever to have seen). He had directed on Broadway and in television and had also appeared in *Lute Song* in 1950 with Mary Martin, who urged Oscar to sign him. "No one can play this part but Yul Brynner. Kidnap him if you have to, but get him!" Brynner, however, was hard to get: he was making a lot of money directing and acting in a CBS television variety series with his wife, Virginia Gilmore. It wasn't until she, his agent Bill Liebling, and Mary Martin

Gertrude Lawrence as "Mrs. Anna" and Yul Brynner as the King in *The King and I*. She got ten percent of the gross even if she did sing off-key. Theatre Collection, Museum of the City of New York.

ganged up on him that Brynner agreed to read the script. And once he did, he was hooked.

Knowing something about Gertrude Lawrence's temperament, Rodgers and Hammerstein had invited Noel Coward to stage and direct *The King and I* — if anyone could handle Gertie it was he. But Coward turned them down, so they approached playwright John van Druten, who agreed to stage the book although he had never before directed either a musical or a play he hadn't himself written. As things turned out, van Druten wasn't anything like tough enough to handle the often insecure and temperamental Gertrude Lawrence; but fortunately, Brynner was. When he spoke, Lawrence listened. Rodgers later confessed they would have been in a lot of trouble had Brynner not been around, and just how important Gertrude Lawrence found his strength may be gauged from the fact that just before she died, still playing the lead, she asked that Brynner be given star billing. "He's earned it," she said, and she was not just talking about acting. And as all the world knows, Brynner went on to make the part of the King,

**Yul Brynner in the movie of *The King and I* (1956) — old enough now to play the part without "aging" makeup.**
**British Film Institute.**

and over the years, the play, his own — he stepped down in June, 1985, after giving more than 4,600 performances.

*The King and I* was a lavish and expensive show. The budget was $250,000, three times that of *Oklahoma!*, with an overcall of $50,000 and a further $40,000 underwritten by the producers ("Something actually cost more than *Allegro*?" said the Broadway cynics). Six carloads of sets designed by Jo Mielziner were shipped up to New Haven for the tryouts. Irene Sharaff — recognized as the foremost costume designer in the theater — used genuine imported Thai silks and brocades for the costumes. The show was going to look, as well as sound, stunning.

The money for *The King and I* was raised in the usual Rodgers and Hammerstein manner. They were firm believers in bringing outside capital into the theater, and in their own words, sternly averse to "this procedure of peddling family jewels" to finance shows, which they deemed "violently unhealthy." The backers of *The King and I* (their investment shown in brackets following their names) were: 20th Century Fox, represented by Joseph H. Moskewitch ($40,000); theatrical attorney Howard Reinheimer ($37,500) and his wife ($7,500); Billy Rose ($15,000); Dorothy Rodgers ($10,000); Dorothy Hammerstein ($5,000); Leland Hayward ($12,500); Joshua Logan ($1000) and his wife Nedda Harrigan ($1000); theater owner Howard Cullman ($15,000); producer and theater owner Anthony Brady Farrell ($12,000); Mrs. William Hammerstein ($5,000); Reginald Hammerstein ($5,000); Oscar Hammerstein's stepdaughter, Mrs. Susan B. Fonda ($2,500), and her husband, Henry Martin Fonda ($2,500); Richard M. Blow ($10,000); bandleader Meyer Davis ($2,500); producer Sherman Ewing ($2,500); souvenir program agent Hal Greenstone ($5,000); Mary Martin ($2,500) and her husband Richard Halliday ($2,500); Nancy Hawks (Mrs. Leland Hayward) ($2,500); Theresa Helburn ($5,000); Lawrence Langner ($2,500) and his wife Armina Marshall ($2,500); designer

Jo Mielziner ($5,000); R&H general manager Morris Jacobs ($2,500); lighting techni-
cian Edward F. Cook ($2,500); former silent movie star Carmel (*Ben Hur*) Myers
($2,500); The Author's League of America ($5,000); R&H stage manager Jerome Whyte
($2,500); and ad executive Lawrence Weiner ($2,500).

Once again the financial arrangements reveal how closely Rodgers and Hammerstein
were involved with both the financing and the rewards of their work. As authors, they
took eight percent of the gross, giving one percent to the original novel's author,
Margaret Landon. As usual, they took a further two percent as managers. John van
Druten got three percent as director, and, as already noted, Gertrude Lawrence ten percent of the gross and five percent of the profits until her untimely death in 1952. Brynner
got no percentage (nor did any of the actresses who followed Lawrence), but choreographer Jerome Robbins got $350 a week, with Mielziner again drawing $100. Irene Sharaff
received $50 a week. The theater shared a flat 25 percent.

The profits of the show — by June 30, 1953, they were over $700,000 — were to be
shared 60/40 between backers and management. In taking the extra ten percent up front,
the backers waived all rights to any share in the movie rights or any foreign incomes from
the show. Even so, they would eventually draw an 117 percent profit on their total investment of $360,000. Thus attorney Reinheimer's profits, for instance, would be $43,875
at the end of the show's run on Broadway. All that, however, was some way in the future.

Tryouts began at the Shubert Theatre in New Haven on February 26, 1951. There
was still a lot of work to do, especially in trying to cure Lawrence of her insistent
propensity to sing off-key, so noticeably as to sometimes make audiences uncomfortable. Rodgers had taken as few chances with her songs as possible, keeping them all
within a relatively limited range — a note or two, no more, outside an octave. His score
was not yet complete, but he already had some delightful melodies for the huge cast to
work on, among them "I Whistle a Happy Tune," "Shall We Dance?," and "Hello,
Young Lovers."

This last song had given Oscar Hammerstein some of the most agonizing weeks of his
entire career. In trying to create a lyric to establish Anna's character and tell the ladies of
the court (and the audience) something of her past, he wrote — and threw out — seven
different songs. In one he has her "dazzled by the splendor of Calcutta and Bombay"
where "celebrities were many and the parties very gay," but it wasn't until he realized he
needed to make her *simpatico* rather than superior and understanding instead of self-
regarding, that in a "final burst of perspiration" — to use his own words — he "got" the
whole thing in 48 hours.

The banqueting hall in the King's Palace: What Hollywood can do that Broadway cannot, and why the movie won Academy Awards for best art direction (Lyle R. Wheeler and John De Cuir) and best set decoration (Walter M. Scott and Paul S. Fox). British Film Institute.

Finally, after weeks of work, he typed out the finished lyric and sent if off by messenger. He considered "Hello, Young Lovers" one of the best things he had ever written, and couldn't wait to hear what Rodgers thought of it. But Dick didn't call. He didn't call that day or the next day or the next. By this time, Oscar was practically a basket case — couldn't work, couldn't sleep. Yet something made him wait, some kind of stubborn pride kept him from calling Rodgers to ask him whether he had liked the song. Finally, on the morning of the fourth day, Dick called him about something else entirely. They talked for perhaps ten minutes about various things in the show — everything except "Hello, Young Lovers." Then, finally, Rodgers remarked that he'd received the lyric and told Oscar it was "okay." "It works just fine," he said, and hung up, leaving Hammerstein completely wrecked.

Oscar called Joshua Logan and told him what had happened. Logan tried to reassure Oscar, but Oscar was so embittered that he poured out all the hurts, all the slights, all the frustrations he had undergone in all these years of working with Dick. He had made a very conscious effort — both of them had — to avoid jeopardizing their working relationship. In doing so, although he was the older and, in many ways, more experienced half of the partnership, Oscar had accepted second billing. When the limousines came to the door, it was Dick who drove away first. If there was only one suite at the Ritz, Dick was the one who got it. Rodgers was a brilliant man, a near-genius, but, as Logan tellingly remarks, he was not a generous one. Quite simply, he took genius for granted; or maybe, because he had been surrounded by it throughout his working life, he didn't know there was anything else. So Oscar had made all the adjustments, without complaint until now, when something he considered as good, if not better, than anything he had ever done was dismissed with a casual "okay."

"Dick would never have any idea of how hard it was for Oscar to write that lyric," said Logan. "He just figured that was what Oscar could do. He had no idea of the agonies Oscar went through because Oscar would never show Dick that side of him at all. I don't think he showed it to anyone. He never talked about his work at all, with anybody, except to me that one time."

Work went apace at New Haven — in spite of mischievous children, in spite of the star's frequent health problems. Leland Hayward came up and saw the show, at the conclusion of which he astonished Rodgers by advising him to close it before it went any further. They moved on to Boston with still at least 45 minutes too much play, and maybe three or four songs that either had to be cut or replaced, somehow, somewhere. "Waiting", a trio for Anna, the King, and the Kralahome; and two laments begging Anna to stay in Siam — the Kralahome's solo "Who Would Refuse?" and Lady Thiang's "Now You Leave" — went back into the trunk, never to reemerge (left without a note to sing, the original Kralahome, Murvyn Vye, abandoned his part and was replaced by John Juliano).

Even with the substantial cuts they had made to the text, however, Dick and Oscar felt that the show still lacked a vital lightness of touch. The King was well served with a

207

number aptly expressing his bewilderment at the number of options he had to consider in his diplomatic dealings with the West, all of which he declared "A Puzzlement." Lady Thiang, his head wife (played by Dorothy Sarnoff) had a beautiful song, "Something Wonderful," which explained to "Mrs. Anna" her love for and devotion to the King. The slave Tuptim's bitterness towards the King was shown in "My Lord and Master," as was Anna's vexation in "Shall I Tell You What I Think of You? (You're Spoiled!)"

The march which accompanies the entrance of the King's children, with its dynamics increasing in proportion to their size (and with its faint echoes of the verse of a Rodgers and Hart song called "On a Desert Island with Thee"), was stunningly staged by choreographer Jerome Robbins. So, too, was Robbins's balletic *divertissement*, in which the slave Tuptim strives to explain the concept of freedom to the King by means of a free Siamese interpretation of Harriet Beecher Stowe's *Uncle Tom's Cabin*. With all this, the first act still lacked that "lift" they were all looking for.

Then, Gertrude Lawrence came up with an idea. Couldn't they give her a song to sing with the children? Something to explain that she was becoming attached to them, getting to know and like them? That was all Dick and Oscar needed. Mary Martin reminded them of the lilting *schottische* that had been used to rehearse *South Pacific*'s show-within-a-show (until it was replaced by "Honey Bun"), the song which had lived but briefly as "Suddenly Lovely." Oscar put the lyric of "Getting To Know You" to the melody, and the first act had all the lift it could use. It is one of the few Rodgers and Hammerstein songs which bears a family resemblance to a Rodgers and Hart melody: no one who hears "Getting To Know You" could doubt that it springs from the same melodic source as "Manhattan."

There were a few further changes to be made, another couple of songs to write, and then they were ready to take the show to New York. They closed in Boston on March 24 and, that day, critic Elliot Norton dashed off the following report to his paper:

THE KING AND I LEFT HERE WITH THREE NEW SONGS ALREADY INSERTED. GERTRUDE LAWRENCE HAS "GETTING TO KNOW YOU" IN ACT ONE, DOROTHY SARNOFF HAS "WESTERN PEOPLE FUNNY" OPENING ACT TWO DORETTA MORROW HAS "I HAVE DREAMED" ALSO IN ACT TWO. "WESTERN PEOPLE" NOT MUCH BUT OTHER TWO LOOK LIKE BIG HITS. UNDERSTOOD BING CROSBY AND OTHERS ALREADY RECORDING SCORE INCLUDING SINATRA.

Yul Brynner and Deborah Kerr in the movie of *The King and I*. Her voice was dubbed by Marni Nixon, who finally got her own showing as Sister Sophia, a singing nun in the movie *The Sound of Music*. British Film Institute.

Tuptim's song "I Have Dreamed" points up one of Oscar Hammerstein's own "puzzle-ments." Talking to Earl Wilson about how he wrote his lyrics, he said he usually made up a dummy tune, "usually something corny. I started going to vaudeville at three, and all those songs are still in my head. It angers me that I can't write music, that I've got no creative ability with melody. Very often I've written what I thought was a waltz, and it comes back from Dick Rodgers as a foxtrot." "I Have Dreamed" is clearly a case in point: although it exists as a "big" ballad, it reads like a waltz.

> I have **dreamed**
> That your **arms** are **love**ly.
> I have **dreamed**
> What a **joy** you'll **be**...

Elliot Norton's advance notices were good auguries indeed, and when *The King and I* opened on Broadway on March 29 — in the same theater and almost eight years to the day that *Oklahoma!* had burst upon the world — the critics tossed their hats into the air and hailed another triumph from the miracle men of Broadway. Yul Brynner became a star overnight, his swaggering, likable King a perfect foil for the fey charm of Gertrude Lawrence's Anna. The Robbins ballet was hailed as the tour-de-force it undoubtedly was (he would go on to create the sensational dances in *West Side Story*), and the words used to describe the score were "exuberant" and "radiant" and "glorious." *The King and I* was another solid-gold hit.

Gertrude Lawrence was plagued with ill health throughout the first year. She left the cast early in 1952 for an extended vacation (her replacement was Celeste Holm, the original Ado Annie of *Oklahoma!*) and returned in mid-March looking so rested and well that everyone was encouraged to hope she would be able to realize her ambition to return to London triumphantly in the part she had made her own, but it was not to be. Her voice became weaker, and her tendency to sing flat now became so embarrassing that on May 20, Dick and Oscar wrote her a letter expressing their grave concerns, pointing out that her singing had deteriorated to the point where, eight times a week, she was "losing the respect of 1500 people. This is a serious thing to be happening to one of the great women of our theater, and it would be dishonest and unfriendly of us to stand by any longer without making you aware of the tarnish you are putting on your past triumphs and your future prospects." It was brutally frank; gallantly, they never sent it. What no one knew was that Gertrude Lawrence had leukemia. She continued to play the part of Anna until three weeks before she died on September 6, 1952.

Rodgers and Hammerstein had yet another clean sweep. They were making the astonishing look normal. *The King and I* played for three years — 1246 performances — on Broadway and another 18 months on tour. Two-and-a-half years (longer than *South Pacific*) at London's Drury Lane Theatre, where Valerie Hobson played Anna to Herbert Lom's King. Antoinette Perry Awards for best musical, for Gertrude Lawrence, and for Rodgers's score. Donaldsons for Brynner, Morrow, Robbins, Mielziner, and Sharaff. A stunning movie in the works (with a $400,000 advance). It was the old story all over again. Was there anything that these men couldn't do? And more important, what would they do next?

The answer was totally unexpected: they split up.

It was not a parting, a sundering such as had occurred between Rodgers and Larry Hart, but, nevertheless, for the best part of a year Rodgers and Hammerstein worked apart. That is not to say that they did not pursue their mutual endeavors, nor is it to say that they were not actively considering another joint project — as was his wont, Oscar already had an idea for a new show by the end of 1951. All the same, either by accident or design, they were more apart in the final months of 1951 than at any time in the

210

preceding decade. If there was a serious rift between Dick and Oscar, it has never been mentioned or acknowledged. It would be presumptuous to suggest that there was one at all, were it not for the story Joshua Logan told about Oscar's deeply wounded feelings from Dick's unfeeling reception of "Hello, Young Lovers."

That each sometimes found the other hard to take is not surprising — Rodgers could be petty and spiteful; Hammerstein, sulky or evasive, and so on. Rodgers confessed after Hammerstein's death that he had no idea whether Oscar liked him or not. Hammerstein said pretty much the same thing about Rodgers. But because both men were adept at presenting a united front, never letting anyone drive a wedge between them, their differences tended to remain private rather than public. But there is no question that at this particular juncture the relationship was on hold. Around this time it was reported they had been approached by the Metropolitan Opera to write an opera based on *Moby Dick* but turned it down. Rodgers denied it ever happened. "Look," he said, "people talk...Stories get around in the columns and they have the sanctity of print. That doesn't make them any more likely to be true than gossip stories."

What did happen was that Rodgers accepted a commission from NBC to write the background score for a proposed television documentary series about the exploits of the U.S. Navy during World War II. He also involved himself enthusiastically in a revival of the 1940 Rodgers and Hart show, *Pal Joey*, which his friend Anthony Brady Farrell (one of the backers of *The King and I*) was producing in collaboration with Leonard Key and songwriter Jule Styne. There were also plans for a spectacular television salute on two consecutive Sunday evenings telling the Richard Rodgers story.

So, throughout that autumn of 1951, Dick and Oscar worked apart. It was, of course, unthinkable that they separate, and they both knew it — they had split an estimated $1.5 million in 1951, not counting royalties earned from earlier works. Perhaps it was just breathing space. Rodgers worked on music unsupported by libretto or lyric (the first time he had done anything of the kind for more than ten years) and took a nostalgic, but far from unhappy, look back at his finest collaboration with Larry Hart. Ahead of him was an eventful Silver Jubilee year. Oscar Hammerstein, however, does not seem to have been giving any interviews around this time.

211

# ONLY

# *Human*

*The audience are the only smart people in show business.*

—— Richard Rodgers

O scar Hammerstein often remarked that he was foolishly in love with the theater. There was no way he could elect to be away from it for any appreciable time and, whether he liked it or not, no way he could elect now not to be Dick Rodgers's partner. So, when at the end of his "celebration" year, Dick broached the idea of their doing a show about show business, something he'd been mulling over for a long time, Oscar concurred. Not enthusiastically; the idea didn't at all excite him and he wasn't terribly keen to write an original play (adaptations were his forté). But he went along with it, telling Rodgers he had been thinking of something along the same lines himself, something about what happens to a theatrical company during a long-running hit show. But none of that stereotyped Star, Ingenue, and Bitch stuff. It would be a many-layered story charting how a rag tag group of performers grows into a family, a community unto itself, a show-within-a-show in the truest sense of the words. They agreed to get together to work on it as soon as Rodgers was free of his commitment to NBC for *Victory at Sea*.

Once committed, Oscar warmed to the idea and began work, striding around the snowy pastures of Highlands Farm — a tall, lumbering man with crew-cut hair, gentle blue eyes, and a pockmarked face — surrounded by the people of his imagination: chorus boys, musical conductors, stage managers, understudies, electricians, and grips; their interrelated loves and hates; and the things that, as Oscar knew only too well, could happen to them.

A man who always left parties early (Jerome Kern dubbed his edgy shuffle toward the door "the Hammerstein glide"), Oscar was himself an anomaly in the upside-down world of show business, where everyone stays up until three and sleeps until midday. As he said,

> *I'm not a nighthawk. Unlike so many of my friends, I hardly ever stay up until midnight. Usually I'm in bed by around eleven, although I always take some books with me. I'm asleep in a few minutes. This allows me to get up around eight in the morning, feeling quite rested — an hour which would seem like the middle of the night to most people in show business. I have a hot bath, followed by a massage and a cold bath, then a leisurely breakfast during which I usually read through the New York morning papers. Around nine-thirty I go off to my work room. I plug away at my writing until lunch, occasionally going for a walk around the farm whenever I've struck a snag and need a change of scenery. By two o'clock or thereabouts I'm back at the job, but my wife, who is an Australian, has taught me the British custom of breaking off at about four-thirty for tea. Frankly, I look forward to it every day with a lot of pleasure. I like to walk a lot when I'm working. If it's a bad day I stay on the porch.*

213

Meanwhile, Rodgers savored his solo success. The revival of *Pal Joey* brought Vivienne Segal back in her original role as Mrs. Vera Simpson and paired her with a Joey played by Harold Lang, who had just scored in *Kiss Me, Kate!* Elaine Stritch — great casting — had the part of Melba Snyder, the girl reporter who does the wicked send-up of strip teaser Gypsy Rose Lee in "Zip," originally performed by Jean Casto. This time around, Brooks Atkinson and the rest of the critics saw *Pal Joey* clearly and hailed it as the landmark of musical theater it had always been. Alas, their well-eaten words came a little late for Larry Hart, but were highly rewarding for Richard Rodgers.

In more ways than one: not only did the Critics Circle rate the show the year's best musical (it also won a Donaldson), not only was the Columbia cast album a best-seller and "Bewitched, Bothered, and Bewildered" back in the Hit Parade, but *Pal Joey* ran for 542 performances, a record both for a revival and for a Rodgers and Hart show. All of which meant Rodgers made a lot of money. So you might have thought he would be grateful to producer Jule Styne for coming up with the idea of the revival, but it appears he wasn't in the grateful business.

**Dick and Oscar at work in the Ritz, Boston; some of the best songs in theatrical history have been written in hotel rooms or ladies' rest rooms.** Used by permission of the Rodgers and Hammerstein Organization.

A year or two later Styne got excited about the idea of a musical based on *The Rodgers and Hart Songbook*, published in 1951. He got George Axelrod to come up with a rough outline of a story called "Tinseltown," lined up nightclub troubadour Bobby Short, Evelyn Keyes, and Johnny Desmond as leads, and set up an audition for Rodgers. After they had run through "My Funny Valentine," "The Lady Is a Tramp," and "My Heart Stood Still," Rodgers shook his head. "These are not my kind of singers," he said coldly, "and I don't approve of their interpretation of my music." And that was the end of the Rodgers and Hart musical. And, need it be said, Mr. Styne's association with Mr. Rodgers.

*Pal Joey* settled down for a comfortable 15-month run which would make it the longest-running of all the Rodgers and Hart shows, in the process turning Broadway into Rodgers's personal fiefdom. *South Pacific* was still at the Majestic, *The King and I* at the St. James. Now *Pal Joey* completed a very satisfying hat trick, and nobody enjoyed it more than Rodgers himself. He would often visit one or two or all three of the theaters in the course of an evening, checking the performances, listening to the songs or — the cynics said — counting the receipts.

He was not uncharming, Richard Rodgers, but he rarely went out of his way to be lovable. Brilliant, intelligent, witty, and incredibly gifted, he seems to have chosen a persona to be, rather than to be the person he actually was. He had a strong sense of purpose, he loved his work and was perfectly happy as long as everyone around him met and continued to meet his extraordinarily high standards. When they did, no matter at what cost to themselves, he accepted that as his due. He was sparing with praise, although always supportive with advice and help. Despite his claimed aversion to it, he actually enjoyed the hurly-burly of business, and pretty much to the end of his life, when he was far from strong and it was far from necessary, he commuted regularly to his office on Madison Avenue and 57th Street, then located not-inappropriately above the Chase Manhattan Bank.

"A fantastic workman," said Jan Clayton. "Stern, you bet, but fair, courteous, and confident. Everyone who worked with him knew he expected, demanded, the very best we could give." Mary Martin agreed. Rodgers was "very exact and demanding of an artiste," she said. "But he got it back because he gave so much." She found him "terribly reserved and terribly emotional, but you'd never know it to see him or be with him." She added a story that Dorothy Rodgers once told her. Sometimes, after playing a new song for an audience for the first time, Rodgers would go into the bathroom and throw up, so tense and strung-up would he be about reactions to his work. "Very paternalistic," George Abbott said. "Maybe because he's a doctor's son, he has this bedside manner. He talks to actors and actresses at auditions in a very personal way, encouraging them even when he's turning them down."

"The only way I can define it," Robert Russell Bennett said, in a decidedly two-edged encomium, "is that deep down somewhere in that soul of his there must be a warm, beautiful thing that produces all these melodies." Dorothy Fields referred to him as a "gentle" man, but Helen Ford, who knew him a lot better than most, recalled that beneath the gentleness there was always "the steel fist in the velvet glove," the temper that would "burn, but deep down." Martha Wright, who succeeded Mary Martin as Nellie in *South Pacific*, felt the same way. "Oh, he was very nice to me and very gentle," she said, "but I knew that, underneath that, there was a tough guy, believe me."

A man who never forgot his mistakes and rarely made the same one twice, Rodgers did not seem to want to know, or, more probably, chose not to explore, the wellsprings of his talent. In 1973, I posed the following question: "Perhaps at this point I could ask you to describe your own working method by putting it thus: you have worked out where the song will appear, its mood, its motivation. The lyric arrives from Oscar. It is called 'Will You Marry Me?' and Pinza will sing it. What happens now?" He looked at me for a long moment, as if trying to decide whether I was mad. "I write the music," he said. Like, *what else?*

A man, then, of many contradictions. A theatrical songwriter who preferred to be called a composer and dressed like a banker. A hugely successful creator of melodies who, according to John Green, did not care for poetry when it was not married to music. A man who, writer George Oppenheimer said, hated homosexuality, cliques, and in-groups, yet worked for a quarter of a century with a homosexual and, all his life, in that most cliquey and in-group-ish of all professions, the Theater. A man of infinite talent and limited soul, according to Stephen Sondheim. A blessed man who led a blessed life, according to Mary Martin.

Kurt Singer, author and literary agent, liked to tell an anecdote which illustrated more clearly than most how Rodgers saw himself and his profession. New to America in 1943, Singer was invited by a friend to a dinner at the Players' Club in Gramercy Park. He knew no one there — they were all theater people — and found himself sitting next to "someone who looked like a shoe clerk." Singer asked the man what he did for a living. "I'm a musician," the man said. "That must be a difficult profession at the moment," Singer remarked, referring to wartime conditions. "Oh," said the musician off-handedly, "I'm managing." Later, Singer was told that his "shoe clerk" was Richard Rodgers, just then riding the crest of the biggest wave in the history of the musical theater, *Oklahoma!* Perhaps, then, as Joshua Logan once hypothesized, Rodgers was somehow embarrassed by the ease with which he wrote his songs, and added the hard-bitten, ruthless business-man exterior to cover it up only to discover he actually enjoyed the role.

For all that, throughout his career Rodgers was unfailingly courteous, endlessly patient, infinitely available to the hundreds and hundreds of people who felt they *had* to talk with him, offer him ideas, seek his support. In our several hours of 1973 interviews, at a time when he was suffering very badly from a diseased larynx, he never once expressed impatience or referred to his own discomfort. In our last interview, when he was learning to "talk" all over again after the removal of his larynx, he was as urbane and helpful as before.

Nevertheless, everyone seems to agree that after *South Pacific* there was a change. Success seems not to have made him blossom, but to have soured him. He became more ruthless, almost dictatorial. He flew off the handle more often. "He didn't take criticism well and he was always getting his feelings hurt," actress Billie Worth recalled. And there were other, more personal problems. His wife Dorothy underwent a hysterectomy shortly after the show opened, another internal operation a year later. He was suffering from a depression he would not admit to, and drinking heavily.

If the recent revelations of his daughters are anything to go by, Rodgers was imprisoned in a desperately unhappy marriage. Dorothy Rodgers, beautifully poised and chic in a Duchess of Windsor sort of way, was also a neurotic hypochondriac, the kind of woman whose house was so organized there were postage stamps on the envelopes in the guest-room writing desks. Perhaps as a result, or perhaps anyway, he was a vulpine womanizer. And he wasn't very subtle about it, either. Many, many years earlier Larry Hart had commented that Dick adored chorus girls. What kind? "Blonde. And very innocent-looking. Brains not essential — but they must be innocent-looking." Jamie Hammerstein said much the same thing several decades later when he remarked that Rodgers's idea of a pretty girl was Shirley Jones. It probably didn't matter if they were blonde or brunette, brainy or dumb, as long as they were available. Josh Logan probably put it as simply as it can be said. "We used to say to him, 'Dick, for God's sake don't screw the leading lady till she's signed the contract.'"

In the spring of 1952, Dick and Oscar got together in Palm Beach, where Rodgers and his convalescent wife were vacationing while Dick put the finishing touches to his melodic sketches for *Victory at Sea*. They discussed the tentative outline Oscar had written for the new show, agreeing that if they did it, the action would have to be confined to the various parts of one theater: the wings, stage, dressing rooms, and even the lobby. Rodgers suggested that they dispense with an overture, saving it for the "overture" of the show-within-the-show they had already decided upon.

By summer, Dick had completed the main musical themes for the television series and handed them over to the brilliant orchestrator and arranger Robert Russell Bennett, whose job it would be to extend, expand, and score them in line with Rodgers's basic intentions — "the dirty work," as Rodgers put it. The final score for *Victory at Sea*, if played in one piece, would run for some 13 hours, but, of course, Rodgers did not compose anything like 13 hours of music. The finished nine-movement symphonic suite, which contained such evocative subtitles as "Song of the High Seas," "Guadalcanal March," "Theme of the Fast Carriers," and "Under the Southern Cross," was — and Rodgers unashamedly admitted it — largely Bennett's work.

"Under The Southern Cross," written in the unusual (for Rodgers) tempo of the tango, became very popular when *Victory at Sea* was premiered in October, 1952. Rodgers was to receive two of the highest awards television could confer upon his work for *Victory at Sea*: the Television Academy's "Emmy" award and the George Foster

217

Peabody citation. The following year the composer would also receive the Distinguished Public Service Award of the United States Navy.

In that same summer of 1952, Dick's 50th birthday celebrations included two Sunday evening hours on CBS's *Toast of the Town* program, in which host Ed Sullivan introduced, among others, Yul Brynner, Vivienne Segal, Lisa Kirk, Jane Froman, William Gaxton, John Raitt, and Rodgers himself. One evening was devoted to Rodgers and Hart songs, the second to those of Rodgers and Hammerstein. Cementing their relationship publicly, Oscar Hammerstein filled a page in the June, 1952, issue of *Town & Country* magazine with an affectionate salute to his collaborator entitled "Happy Birthday, Dear Dick." On June 28, Rodgers's birthday, the Hammersteins hired a boat, brought aboard an orchestra, and sailed a huge party of theater people, including members of the casts of the three Rodgers shows now playing on Broadway, up the Hudson River and back again, serenading Rodgers all night with his own music.

If there had been any difference between Dick and Oscar, any sort of rift, it appeared to have been resolved. Through the summer they worked in their usual fashion, blocking out the story, talking over every aspect of the production. Not one word or one note would be written until they were finished with these preliminaries. There were one or two mechanical problems, so they called in Jo Mielziner. Was there a way they could show action onstage and backstage simultaneously? He reassured them: yes, they could play scenes on the light bridge or partly onstage and partly off. It would be expensive, but it could be done

By August Oscar had begun working on the book proper. His original idea of a show-within-a-show had been expanded and there was now a subplot interwoven into the main story which, by fall, was taking definite shape. In October Oscar told a newspaper reporter that he had done some dialogue for the first act, but no lyrics at all. "We have no title in mind yet," he said. "All I can tell you about the theme is that it's about the theater. We are going to do our utmost to avoid the usual clichés of show-business musicals." A more astute interviewer might have asked "What show business musicals?" — this was long before *A Chorus Line,* long before *42nd Street.* As usual, Rodgers and Hammerstein were breaking new ground.

With a rough script from which to work, Mielziner and his three assistants began to draw up designs for the twelve sets. At the Rodgers and Hammerstein offices, wheels started turning. Robert Alton was engaged as choreographer, Salvatore dell'Isola to conduct the orchestra (although as yet there was no music for him to conduct), and Don Walker to do orchestrations and vocal arrangements — each appointee in his own way confirming the R&H intention to do "musical comedy" and not "musical play." The Majestic Theatre was booked for May 28, 1953, which in turn necessitated the relocation of *South Pacific*, showing no signs yet of running out of steam.

Frantic revisions of theatrical schedules were made; *South Pacific* could move into the Broadway Theatre, but not until June 29, and so it was scheduled into the Opera House, Boston, for a five-week engagement from May 18 to June 27 of the following year. Cleveland (the show was too big for the Shubert in New Haven) and Boston theaters were also booked for the tryouts of the new show, and production manager Jerome Whyte began to interview stage managers, master carpenters, chief electricians, property masters, and wardrobe mistresses. Auditions were pencilled in for March 9, rehearsals to begin nine days later.

This immovable schedule was in no small part responsible for what followed. As William Hammerstein perceptively observed, "Along about April you read that Rodgers and Hammerstein had been working on a show about showbiz. Came September and they had to get the damned thing on the stage. That had a lot to do with the failure of *Me and Juliet* and, probably, with *Allegro*."

Dick and Oscar had decided by now that *Me and Juliet* (the title — it had originally been *Hercules and Juliet*, but wisely they changed it — was announced December 18) would be a "musical comedy" and not, as formerly, a "musical play." Oscar had the book pretty well in working order, and Dick began work on the songs. By the end of the year they had three of the thirteen songs finished; one of them was the tango "Under the Southern Cross," lifted from Rodgers's score for *Victory at Sea*. It became "No Other Love" and, incidentally, the only hit song in the show.

Rodgers's happiness at being involved in a new show with his partner is evident in a December 1952 newspaper interview. "It's wonderful to be writing again," he said, "to sit quietly in a room and work. It's what I was meant to do, but somehow I became a producer along the way. I like having a say in the way our shows are staged, but composing is really my business."

With the book and some of the songs ready, Dick and Oscar now went to a man they both regarded as one of the very best directors in the musical comedy business, George Abbott. They asked him to do *Me and Juliet* and he agreed on the spot, a decision he began to regret almost as soon as he started reading Oscar's libretto. It was melodramatic and sentimental, and Abbott didn't like it. He convinced himself that he must be wrong, however; Rodgers and Hammerstein were two smart men with a string of big hits behind them. Just the same, he told Dick and Oscar about his reservations concerning the book,

219

*Me and Juliet*: George Abbott, Oscar Hammerstein, Dick Rodgers, and dance arranger Trude Rittman at rehearsals with some of the cast. Used by permission of the Rodgers and Hammerstein Organization.

and Oscar told him to take it home, cut it, make notes, do what he liked. "Treat it as ruthlessly as if it were your own," he said. Abbott did just that, but it remained sentimental when it needed to be tough, mawkish when it needed to be moving.

Chorus auditions began on March 10, 1953, at the Majestic. There were parts for 17 male and 25 female singers and dancers. They were being offered $90 a week in town, $100 a week on the road. More than 1,000 wannabes turned up; Dick, Oscar, and George Abbott saw and heard every one of them. On March 19, smack on schedule, the first rehearsal was held. Rodgers and Hammerstein had a well-tried technique for presenting the story to the cast. Oscar would read from the libretto, playing different parts, then talksing the songs while Dick Rodgers played them. *Me and Juliet* was no exception, and after the "performance" — what a shame no one ever recorded one of them! — the cast gave composer and lyricist a warm round of applause before splitting up to get to work.

Singers and dancers rehearsed at the Alvin Theatre; the principals at the Majestic. Isabel Bigley, fresh from a triumph in *Guys and Dolls,* had been chosen to play Jeanie, the chorus singer with whom Larry, the assistant stage manager (Bill Hayes) falls in love. His boss Mac (Ray Walston) is having an affair with the principal dancer, Betty (Joan McCracken). Husky, tough stage electrician Bob (Mark Dawson) has had an affair with Jeanie. Mac is taken off the show. Larry and Jeanie get married secretly. Bob finds out and gets drunk, then tries to kill her during the performance of *Me and Juliet,* the "show" within the show.

A roving newspaper reporter from the *Akron Beacon-Journal* described the cast's first reading on the bare stage of the Majestic Theatre.

*Under a pair of work lights surrounded by cigarette buckets they sit in two rows, Bigley yawning frequently, Hayes a little stiff since this is his first big Broadway role, McCracken rolling her cute pert head around often — her neck seems to require limbering up. Downstage, Hammerstein, George Abbott, and their assistants watch from chairs, their backs to the dark theater. Everyone seems relaxed except Hammerstein. He's hearing his baby come to life for the first time among strangers in a cold and dark delivery room. After the lunch break, Abbott really goes to work, interrupting frequently. "Make that line wiser, Mark." "Tony, storm at him more, you know he's a complete sonofabitch." "Bill, I'm bothered by your boyish charm. Cover your emotions. Be more factual."*

221

After about a week of rehearsal, the actors began to work without scripts. The director mapped out their movements, instructing them from the auditorium in how to play the roles. The players in *Me and Juliet* were "on their feet" on the second day, blocking out their exits and entrances with chairs and makeshift props.

By mid-April the changes began. Dick and Oscar were furiously rewriting. As Rodgers remarked once, "Anybody can fix things with money. It's when things need brains that you have a little trouble." And at that point, *Me and Juliet* needed all the brains they could muster.

They took out two entire production numbers, "Wake Up, Little Theater" and "Dance," in order to speed up the action. The plan to open on a bare stage, with no overture, was abandoned. The actress playing "Juliet" in the interior play had a beautiful voice but her acting was weak; Helena Scott replaced her. On the fifth run-through there was a small audience, about 50 invited guests — friends of the management, including Josh Logan. Chorus boys and girls waiting to go on watched excitedly from the wings as Rodgers, Hammerstein, and Abbott talked from notes to groups of actors, while out in the tenth row Jo Mielziner directed the lighting via a public address system linking light crews backstage and in the balcony.

There were enormous technical difficulties, the reporter recalled.

> *A number of key scenes required the audience to see both the play-within-the-play and at the same time observe the realism of the stage manager's operations in the wings. To achieve this result and to make both elements simultaneous, the major part of the production had to be hung on specially constructed overhead steel tracks. Synchronized electric motors slowly moved the stage pictures off into the wings far enough to expose the stage manager's desk and actors and stagehands offstage awaiting their cues.*

Rodgers and Hammerstein's imaginative and daring approach to this technique of storytelling was going to set a stimulating precedent. (In fact, the enormously complicated sets for *Me and Juliet* added cripplingly to the budget, which ended up at $350,000).

There were other complications. During the first dress rehearsal, in the first act finale featuring an elaborate dance routine, someone on the light bridge had to drop the sandbag with which Bob tries to kill Bigley. The bag not only had to be heavy enough to make a loud thud, it had to fall precisely on a dance count of 19 — not 18, or 20, or somebody might really get killed. The sandbag dropped too soon, narrowly missing Bigley. Do it again. Get it right. Someone said the show looked smooth. Hammerstein didn't think so. During the first act alone he dictated eight pages of notes. Between the afternoon and evening rehearsals he and Dick cut out two minutes of "Juliet's" solo and the verse of the song "No Other Love," anxious to speed up the show.

The *Akron Beacon-Journal*'s reporter was there again when the evening rehearsal began at eight.

> *Now they are stopping frequently. Rodgers wants more light on the open-*
> *ing. Abbott wants Dawson to pick up Bigley less awkwardly. Somebody*
> *misses a light cue. "Combine nine, ten and eleven!" Mielziner yells into*
> *the squawk box. Abbott says let's fix the light cues later. No, says Rodgers,*
> *let's fix them now. The starch is going out of the show. The teaser curtain*
> *comes down too soon, then it comes down too late. More interruptions,*
> *more criticism from notes. With less than 24 hours to go the show is*
> *being stabbed to death in rehearsal. Still they go on. Stop and do it*
> *again. "Joan, you look crowded near the footlights. Try moving back."*
> *Stop and do it again.*
>
> 223
>
>    *Suddenly the whole "Keep It Gay" number falls shockingly apart.*
> *Whistles blow. Rodgers, Hammerstein, Abbott, choreographer Bob Alton*
> *race down the stage like parents racing after a kid who's fallen off his*
> *bike. They're more worried about the kid than the bike. They reassure*
> *the cast in gentle whispers. The sandbag and the lights in the first act*
> *finale are still wrong. Do it again and again and again. Energy and*
> *patience are running down, professional smiles fading. Bigley has trouble*
> *with costume and props. Suddenly she stops cold. Abbott: "What's the*
> *matter, Isabel?" Bigley: "Oh...I...oh, everything!" She seems on*
> *the verge of tears. Rodgers rushes down the aisle, says gently "Okay,*
> *sweetheart, tell us. Just take your time and tell us. We'll fix it right*
> *now." The rehearsal ends at two A.M.*

The *Beacon-Journal* reporter's merciless account continues:

> *April 20, Hanna Theatre, Cleveland. Two hours to go and they've just*
> *finished the last rehearsal. It was a less chaotic run-through but still life-*

*less. More notes again until Abbott says finally, "Okay, I love you all —
and good luck!" Bob Alton, pale and exhausted, mutters best wishes and
races out of the theater as though he wants to get lost. Rodgers kisses
McCracken and Bigley, so do Abbott and Hammerstein. Much quiet
[hand]shaking and luck wishing all around. It's now 7:25. Under the
stage, seamstresses are still sewing and pressing. On the stage, waiting to
go on, the performers seem to have turned off their nerves. They wait
quietly, like pros. Out front the theater is buzzing, full of black ties and
glittering gowns. Hammerstein sits glumly in the eighth row, ready for
more notes. Rodgers and his wife and secretary are in the back row
trying to concentrate on the program.*

On opening nights, the demeanor of both men altered completely. Rodgers was a
dynamo at rehearsal, his eye on every aspect of the production, checking, advising, ges-
turing, talking. Hammerstein would be much more aloof, sitting in the auditorium and
making copious notes. "He had very definite and fixed opinions," Abbott said, "but he
took his time about asserting them." Once the curtain was up, however, it was Rodgers
who became imperturbable while Hammerstein fumed and swore audibly beneath his
breath when things went wrong onstage. Dorothy Hammerstein said he sometimes came
out with the most awful remarks. On the opening night of *Me and Juliet*, the wayward
backdrop failed once more to come down on cue and Oscar was heard to mutter "Damn
and damn and *damn!* This is a new way: they saved it for the performance!"

The audience, however, failed to notice the fluffs and errors, and gave the show a rousing welcome. Backstage, Jerry Whyte gathered the cast around. "Thanks for a brilliant
performance," he told them. "Wonderful, wonderful." Rodgers rushed backstage, eyes
damp, his face alight with exhilaration. "Nobody could ask for more!" he shouted to anyone who wanted to listen. "Nobody could ask for more." Hammerstein was there, too.
He hugged Rodgers, the performers, shaking his head as though he couldn't quite believe
it. "We've never had an opening like this before," he said. "Never — not even *South
Pacific.*" At 3 A.M. the reviews came in. The Cleveland critics, while reserving judgment
on the weak story, liked *Me and Juliet* as much as the audience had. They called it "big"
and "beautiful" and "ingenious."

They moved to Boston's Shubert Theatre, rewriting every inch of the way. Opening
night was May 6. They won the critics by a split decision; three raves, two mildly unfa-
vorable reviews. Dick and Oscar confessed they wished they were as confident as the crit-

ics seemed to be that they could cure the weaknesses, mostly of plot. The show-within-a-show was changed yet again. Another song, "Meat and Potatoes," was dropped, lest it might be considered too raunchy (although it's difficult to imagine a really raunchy R&H song), and replaced by one called "We Deserve Each Other," which the team had written in their Cleveland hotel room. Audiences continued to love it. But would they like it in New York?

They brought *Me and Juliet* into the Majestic in New York on May 28, feeling anything but optimistic. They knew it was still flawed, and in spite of the terrific roar that greeted the final cur-

225

*Me and Juliet:* **Larry and Jeanie (Bill Hayes and Isabel Bigley).**
Used by permission of the Rodgers and Hammerstein Organization.

tain, Dick and Oscar were glum: they knew it hadn't gone well. As Dick said, "When you hear people leaving the theater raving about the sets, without a word about the rest of your show, it doesn't make you feel too confident." He was right; despite a $500,000 advance sale, despite a ten-month run (which, for anyone except Rodgers and Hammerstein, would have represented a major success), and despite an eventual profit in excess of $100,000, *Me and Juliet* has to be classed as a failure.

The show's director, George Abbott, always felt that there were two major reasons *Me and Juliet* "just died gently." One was Rodgers and Hammerstein themselves. They were the golden boys. With the honorable exception of *Allegro*, they hadn't had a flop since *Oklahoma!* They were too sure of themselves, and perhaps therefore did not try as hard as they should have. They also craved personal publicity far too much for Abbott's liking. The second was Oscar's nebulous play-within-a-play. No one had thought it out, he said, and since Oscar remained "positively Sphinx-like" on the subject, and the characters he was working with had no character, Bob Alton was at a loss to come up with the kind of *divertissement* which Jerome Robbins had done in *The King and I*. So the song and dance routines were just that, routine (at one point Dick and Oscar asked Robbins if he could "twist the dances around," and Robbins said he could, but he wouldn't do it because "it would kill Bob Alton").

The real problem lay in the very genesis of the show. It had been Dick's idea. He pushed it, he wanted it, probably even *needed* it, and Oscar — not wishing to rock the boat — had gone along with it, pretending to be as enthusiastic as Dick was. But in fact he thought the basic premise trivial and had no enthusiasm for it, and as a result ended up with the writer's nightmare: trying to make something work that he didn't believe in and didn't want to do in the first place. Cy Feuer tells an apposite story about playwright Abe Burrows, who was worried about a scene being played on a treadmill in *Guys and Dolls* and decided to ask George S. Kaufman about it. "Well," he said when he got through explaining, "that's the scene. Do you think it will work?" Kaufman pondered awhile and then said, "It all depends on what they're saying." And that, basically, is the difference between a hit and a flop. It all depends on what they're saying.

**Rodgers and Hammerstein receiving the Alexander Hamilton Award, April 4, 1956.**
Used by permission of the Rodgers and Hammerstein Organization.

There's a telling postscript to the story. Oscar, like Dick, made a point of dropping in on their shows to make sure they weren't over-running or that the actors weren't taking liberties with script or score. On his return to the office after one such visit to *Me and Juliet*, he stuck his head around his secretary's door to see if there were any messages. "How was the show?" she asked. Oscar thought about it for a long moment. "I *hate* that show," he said, and shut the door.

Even if *Me and Juliet* did not succeed in its intention to toss a bouquet to the theater they both loved, even if it had no tour and no London showing, even if, at times, the book clunked like a turkey in diving boots and the songs were at best only adequate (indeed, the ones they dropped look a damn sight more interesting than the ones they kept; you can't help wondering what the show would have been like if they'd kept that wonderful opening number, "Julius Baum Is Sweeping the Stage", the gutsy "Meat and Potatoes", the self-mocking "You Never Had It So Good"), it did accomplish one very important thing. It restored the close working relationship of Rodgers and Hammerstein to its original strong and confident state, so completely that, without the slightest indication of self-consciousness, Rodgers told Abbott, "I never want to have another collaborator as long as I live."

In 1953, Mayor Vincent Impellitteri proclaimed that the week of August 31 would be "Rodgers and Hammerstein Week" in New York. A revival of *Oklahoma!* at New York City Center had brought the total of Rodgers and Hammerstein shows in town to four; *South Pacific, The King and I*, and *Me and Juliet* completing the quartet. There were presentations of scrolls, and, later in the year, more honors: doctorates, elections to boards of trustees, directorships, awards, dinners. Dick and Oscar appeared in an MGM documentary about the Broadway stage called *Main Street to Broadway*, for which they wrote a song, "There's Music in You," which was sung by Mary Martin. There was a *Person to Person* television appearance by Dick and Dorothy Rodgers, with Ed Murrow interviewing. Both men (especially Rodgers) were honored as no songwriters in the history of the musical theater had ever been honored before. They had become an institution, and as such, they, in turn, became benefactors. The Rodgers and Hammerstein Foundation (launched the preceding year on the proceeds of the sale to *Life* magazine of a Christmas song published on December 29) was one such venture, established to provide help for talented youngsters wishing to make a career on the musical stage. (The song, by the way, was called "Happy Christmas, Little Friend." Like *Life*, it died.)

Rodgers now set up in his own name a permanent scholarship to be given annually to a talented musician. Rodgers and Hammerstein also financed a scholarship in the name of their publisher, Max Dreyfus, to be given annually to a talented singer. And more, and more. Broadway regarded these benefactions with its customary cynicism, a cynicism best expressed by Irving Berlin when Dick and Oscar established yet another annual scholarship in Berlin's name at the Juilliard School on the occasion of Berlin's 60th birthday. "They didn't do it for me," Berlin is reported to have said. "They did it for them."

Once again, Rodgers and Hammerstein began looking for a property they could make into a show. Movie director George Sidney proposed a musical film of Dickens's *A Tale of Two Cities*, but, although they liked the idea, R&H weren't interested in writing for the screen. Then, Josh Logan came back into their lives. A St. Louis lawyer named David Merrick (real name Margulois) who aspired to being a producer had acquired theatrical rights to Marcel Pagnol's film trilogy about life on the Marseilles waterfront, *Marius, Fanny*, and *Cesar*. Merrick (who would go on to bring to Broadway such resounding hits as *Gypsy, Destry Rides Again, Hello, Dolly!, I Can Get It for You Wholesale, I Do! I Do!,* and

227

*42nd Street*) asked Joshua Logan to see the movies in the hope he might be interested. Logan liked *Fanny* and he and Merrick agreed to offer it to Rodgers and Hammerstein who, in Logan's estimation, had been "put on earth to do the score."

To Logan's joy and delight, Dick and Oscar were as impressed with *Fanny* as he was. His joy and delight were quickly dissipated when they insisted that the credits begin "Rodgers and Hammerstein present..." with no other producer mentioned. *Fanny* was to be Merrick's chance to establish his name big. He had spent years persuading Pagnol to allow the adaptation, and put up the $30,000 for the rights as well as lining up backers for the production. Joshua Logan knew that Oscar wanted to do *Fanny* — "he said he had never wanted to do any show more than this one" — and he put Merrick's case as forcefully as he could to the lyricist. It was no use, Hammerstein said; Rodgers was adamant. Rodgers and Hammerstein would never share credit with an unknown.

Faced with that ultimatum, Merrick decided to go ahead alone. He enlisted Sam Behrman to work with Logan on the book, and he and the director jointly produced the show, which had a score by Harold Rome and a cast led by Ezio Pinza. It was a big hit, an ambitious and moving work that Oscar regretted to the end of his days that he had not written.

228     Rodgers and Hammerstein's next project came to them from Cy Feuer and Ernie Martin. Feuer had been head of the so-called Music Department at Republic Pictures, the renowned low-budget studio which gave the world the movies of Vera Hruba Ralston; Martin was a former television executive. After the war they teamed up and decided to get into producing musicals. They approached Howard Reinheimer and persuaded him to option them the rights of Brandon Thomas's classic farce *Charley's Aunt*, with the intention of turning it into a musical with a score by Frank Loesser.

Loesser had a big name as a lyricist (for a string of hits that included "Two Sleepy People," "I Don't Want To Walk Without You," "On A Slow Boat to China," and "The Lady's in Love With You") but hardly any at all as a composer (although he had written both words and music for "Praise the Lord and Pass the Ammunition"). Feuer and Martin were getting nowhere fast until they enlisted the aid of Rodgers and Hammerstein through lawyer Reinheimer. Dick and Oscar had enough faith in them — and especially in Loesser — to take two investment units in the projected show. Once they had the names of Rodgers and Hammerstein on their list of backers, Feuer and Martin were in business. With Ray Bolger in the lead and George Abbott directing, *Where's Charley?* was an unqualified hit, and Feuer and Martin went on to further triumphs which included *Guys and Dolls, The Boy Friend,* and Cole Porter's *Can-Can*.

All producers have ideas for shows. Some of them jell and some do not. Rodgers and Hammerstein, as we have seen, considered and rejected *Tevye's Daughters*, concluding that there wasn't a musical in it. They also considered and rejected George Bernard Shaw's *Pygmalion*, which Lerner and Loewe transformed into *My Fair Lady*, and James Michener's novel, *Sayonara*, which Joshua Logan made into a (non-musical) movie. Feuer and Martin, too, had their near misses. They worked for a long time on a show with a young composer named Meredith Willson whom Loesser had brought to them. No dice. Willson went elsewhere with what was to become *The Music Man*.

Right now, Feuer and Martin had another idea: a musical based on John Steinbeck's 1945 novel *Cannery Row*, with the author producing the libretto, and music and lyrics by Frank Loesser. Feuer recalled:

> *We thought* The Bear Flag Café *was a hell of a title and we went to John, who was a friend of ours, and said we want to do this but we're going to have to cut a lot of this stuff because the characters we're interested in are Doc and the boys and also the girls in the whorehouse… We're interested in Fauna, Doc, and the boys, we don't want all the stories about the other people, they're wonderful for you, but they're no good for us. And John said, "I've got a better idea, why don't we write a sequel [to* Cannery Row*]." So we said great and we worked on it that summer and built the story… Then, at the end of the summer, John said, "I can't write this book because that's not my business and I don't want to do it. So why don't we do this: I can lift enough of the story we've created to write a sequel to* Cannery Row*. So what I'll do is I'll write my novel and you guys will own the dramatic rights and take it wherever you want." And that was the deal.*

229

In due course, Steinbeck completed his novel, which he called *Sweet Thursday*. "We looked at this thing," Feuer said, "and we said, Jesus, this'd be perfect for Frank Loesser." But when they approached him, Loesser balked. He had a dream about his own show, something that would be closer in spirit to an opera than a musical. Based on Sidney Howard's play *They Knew What They Wanted*, it would eventually take him more than three years to write and produce it under the title *The Most Happy Fella*, but he was so preoccupied with it at the time when Feuer and Martin came to him with the Steinbeck project that he had no difficulty in turning them down. Feuer recounted the interaction:

*And he said, "You know, you should go to Rodgers and Hammerstein because they are so sensational and this is the kind of stuff they should be writing." And so we go to Oscar and we give him a copy of it [and Ernie Marlin said], "You guys have been in the sweetness and light business long enough. You need to dirty up a little the way we do." Oscar read it and said, "I think it's great" and then he called back and said, "Dick wants to do it," so we said great. So we went up to make an arrangement and he said, "Now, look, if we do it you guys are out. So if you want to turn it over to us we'll make a deal." And the deal was pretty good: 50 percent of the producers' end. And we thought, We're rich! And we turned it over to them and they destroyed it.*

In the autumn of 1953, Dick and Oscar flew to London to produce the English company of *The King and I* at the Theatre Royal, in Drury Lane. Before the show opened in London on October 8, 1953 — Valerie Hobson played Anna, Herbert Lom the King — they were already at work adapting *Sweet Thursday* for the stage. "John kept sending over installments of his manuscript typewritten on various colored papers, pink, green, yellow, and white, from New York, Sag Harbor, or wherever he went while continuing this first draft. Before *The King and I* opened and before John had finished his book, Dick and I were already at work actually writing the stage version," Oscar recalled. "By 'writing' I mean we were laying out a succession of scenes and some tentative song titles...On January 1, 1954, I started to write dialogue and lyrics."

Steinbeck's novel was published in the spring of 1954 to mixed reviews, which touched off the novelist's short fuse. "I was just having fun," he growled, "but according to some critics this is a serious crime. Some of the critics are so concerned for my literary position that they can't read a book of mine without worrying where it will fit in my place in history. Who gives a damn?"

Well, Rodgers and Hammerstein, for two, because they still had to fashion a musical out of it and the going wasn't easy. They were committed to going to Hollywood and later Arizona to work on the screen version of *Oklahoma!*, for which they were executive producers. "By that time," Oscar said, "I had written five scenes of the first act and about as many lyrics and, as I use the expression writing, I must acknowledge indebtedness to John's original book. In many cases I lifted scenes bodily from *Sweet Thursday* and manipulated, rather than adapted, them for the stage."

Before they left for the coast, he and Dick signed Harold Clurman (who had been a performer in, and the stage manager of, the original *Garrick Gaieties*) to direct the show. While at MGM, Oscar again met Helen Traubel, whom Oscar's brother Reginald had seen on a television show and recommended for a part in the forthcoming musical, some of which he had read. The former Metropolitan Opera star was in Hollywood to work on a film about the life of Sigmund Romberg called *Deep in My Heart* (which must have provided Oscar with a few chuckles, knowing what he knew about "Rommie"). To make the coincidence even more pleasant, the film was being directed by Stanley Donen, who had been in the chorus of *Pal Joey* along with Van Johnson. Oscar had seen Helen Traubel perform at the Copacabana night club in New York, and he and Rodgers were of a mind: she would be ideal in the part of Fauna, the warm-hearted madam of *Sweet Thursday*, which was now going by the Rodgers and Hammerstein title of *Pipe Dream*. The opera singer leaped at the chance they offered her.

Feuer and Martin had known from the start whom they wanted to play Steinbeck's anti-hero. Feuer said:

> *Henry Fonda was going to play the Doc. With a beard, and they didn't have beards in those days. We got hold of Hank and told him, "This is going to be a musical and you're going to have to sing." (That was in the days they had non-singing actors singing because Rex Harrison led us all astray). So we said, "You're perfect for this part and the score will be written for you to handle." And he said okay. He took some lessons here [in New York] and we made arrangements for him to go out on the road and had him practice his exercises in the hotel room and a singing teacher would come out once a week and give him a lesson. And Fonda said "I took singing lessons for about six months and at the end of it I still couldn't sing for shit."*

231

Rodgers agreed. After his (only) audition, Fonda said, "Now you can be frank. You won't hurt my feelings. Just tell me." And Rodgers said, "I'm sorry, but it would be a mistake." Cy Feuer was not amused. "So finally, after we go through all this, we turn him over to Rodgers and Hammerstein and he's out. Oscar didn't want Fonda because Fonda was his son-in-law and besides Dick said, 'I have to have singers,' and he hires Helen Traubel to play the madam and she turns out to get top billing and Doc is now the second lead!"

Throughout the summer, Oscar remained with the *Oklahoma!* crew which, true to Hollywood logic, filmed the picture near Nogales in Arizona. During this entire time,

**Judy Tyler as Suzy and Helen Traubel as Fauna, the unlikeliest brothelkeeper in history, sing "Suzy Is A Good Thing" in *Pipe Dream*.**
Used by prmission of the Rodgers and Hammerstein Organization.

232

Oscar struggled with one song, "The Man I Used to Be." "During the day and between shots, I would walk out over the prairies keeping my eyes peeled for snakes and my brain alert for rhymes. I found no snakes at all and very few rhymes. By the end of August, however, I had managed to complete one verse and one refrain of this song."

The casting of principals was not completed until August. Depending on which newspaper you check — and only one in six gets it right anyway, according to Rodgers — their original idea had been to costar Julie Andrews as Suzy with Fonda playing Doc. First they discovered Fonda couldn't sing, and then that Julie Andrews, fresh from her big success in Sandy Wilson's 1920s spoof *The Boy Friend*, had just signed a two-year contract for a new musical Fritz Loewe and Alan Jay Lerner were writing called *My Lady Liza*. It was announced in October, and opened the following March as *My Fair Lady*, setting records that even Rodgers and Hammerstein were going to have to wait a while to match.

Their next choice was Janet Leigh (an actress Rodgers had been fond of since she played his wife in the movie *Words and Music*), but she was tied up at MGM so they settled for Judy Tyler, a singer Rodgers had spotted on television in (of all things) the *Howdy Doody Show*. Doc was played by Bill Johnson, who had made a hit with Ethel Merman a couple of years earlier in *Something For The Boys* and then played the male leads in the London productions of *Annie Get Your Gun* and *Kiss Me, Kate*.

"By Christmas of 1954, the book of *Pipe Dream* was finished," Oscar said. "Dick and I now proceeded to write the songs, a job that was not finished until one week before we went into rehearsal." What no one yet knew, however, was that the partners were facing a much grimmer crisis than any which could arise out of the show. Rodgers had been suffering throughout the summer from intense pain in his lower jaw. Cancer was diagnosed and immediate surgery recommended. With quite remarkable *sang-froid,* Rodgers spent the weekend prior to his hospitalization finishing up the score for *Pipe Dream*, which, by a weird coincidence, was due to begin rehearsals the day he was admitted. He had several songs composed which needed committing to paper, and he wrote one new song. On the morning of the rehearsals, he went to the theater and played the score for the company. Then he went in for his operation, determined to survive.

And survive he did. After an operation to remove his left jawbone and some glands in his neck, Rodgers was told that the prognosis was favorable. Eight days later, he was out in the park for a ride with his wife. Ten days after the operation, still sleeping at the hospital, he was back at rehearsals. He supervised them from a wheelchair, with a handkerchief in his hands to stem the uncontrollable flow of saliva. He could not even speak properly, and his discomfort throughout the New Haven and Boston tryouts was constant. Such dedication is rare, and hard to comprehend, but the truth of the matter was that Rodgers was unhappy anywhere else than in the theater, working on a new show. Especially when that show was in trouble, and *Pipe Dream* certainly was that. When Steinbeck went up to New Haven to see the tryouts, Feuer related, "He called us and he was not excited. He said, 'Well, we'll have to wait and see.' And of course, when I heard what they had done, we'd just given up hope for it because they just didn't understand it."

There were rewrites, and then more; a song called "Sitting on the Back Porch" was cut, but still *Pipe Dream* remained weak and unconvincing. Perhaps what was wrong was that Oscar's gently tolerant and optimistic attitudes did not sit comfortably on the shoulders of the raffish denizens of Cannery Row, and in spite of a constantly charming score, *Pipe Dream* suffered, like *Me and Juliet,* from a lack of plot, a lack of dancing — although Helen Traubel's "Sweet Thursday" cakewalk with

233

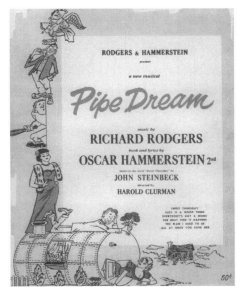

**The design for *Pipe Dream* sheet music: Not giving much away.** Author's Collection.

two Hispanic kids was a treat — and a lack of strong direction. Maybe, as Ethan Mordden says, what *Pipe Dream* needed was Abe Burrows and Michael Kidd.

They brought it, reluctantly one feels, into the Shubert Theatre on November 30, 1955, where it proceeded to lay the biggest egg in Rodgers and Hammerstein's career. The songs over which Oscar had labored so arduously in the Arizona sun (he said that his notes for "All at Once You Love Her" filled a folder thicker than the actual libretto of the show) were attractive but, for the most part, unremarkable. The book was too high-minded for such low-life people, and, as the critics were quick to point out, it was minor-key Rodgers and Hammerstein throughout. So, in spite of the largest advance sale ($1,040,000) of any show they had written thus far, *Pipe Dream* had the shortest run (seven months) and incurred the greatest financial loss. Even more ironically, Rodgers and Hammerstein, who had made almost a fetish out of *not* investing in their own shows, had put up the entire cost of the show. It cost them a fortune.

Once again there was no touring company, no British production, and no movie sale. Even the premiere of the movie *Oklahoma!* starring Gordon MacRae and Shirley Jones that October to generally good reviews and solid box office success did little to lessen their disappointment. They took their beating like the pros they were, but Oscar made no bones about his feelings. "If anybody else had produced it," he said, "we'd say that these are producers we wouldn't like to work with again." Cy Feuer says Oscar laid the blame squarely on him and Ernie Martin. "We believed your pitch and we went and did something we were never cut out to do and we should never have done it."

Much later Rodgers wryly commented that if someone in Hollywood had been writing a movie about his life at that time, they would have had him battling gamely through his illness to bring the show triumphantly to New York and, with a tearful smile, take a bow to a thunderous ovation and instant success. "Well, if there were any tears in my eyes, it was because *Pipe Dream* was universally accepted as the weakest musical Oscar and I had ever done together."

Rodgers's reaction to the failure of *Pipe Dream* was predictable: he immediately began looking for another project. He was, and always had been, the driving force of his partnerships. He had wheedled, nagged, flattered, begged, or bullied Larry Hart into putting words on paper. Even with Oscar, who was as disciplined in his work habits as any man, Dick remained the pusher. Perhaps he could not stop; perhaps, as he said, he didn't know what to do with himself if he wasn't writing for the stage. Paradoxically, it might very well have been his insistence upon their doing shows at this time which contributed to their lack of success.

234

We have seen how Rodgers vetoed a number of projects, some of which Oscar was crazy about; how they had also taken on themes to which they were far from ideally suited. Additionally, Oscar had been confiding to friends that now he was past 60, he would like to spend more time with his large and noisy family — three children by both his marriages, two stepchildren, and nine grandchildren — and less time writing. He was no longer dependent on his pen for a livelihood. There were the farm and plenty of theatrical committees if he wanted something to do. Rodgers, anxious to work, had stirred him into action twice following *The King and I* on shows which had been considerably less than successful. Maybe they both needed a rest?

Then television beckoned. There had been "spectacular" television productions of *Annie Get Your Gun, Kiss Me, Kate,* and *High Button Shoes.* Mary Martin had starred in a theatrical version of J. M. Barrie's *Peter Pan* which had been so successful that it was televised nationally early in 1955 and again in 1956. CBS Television was now looking for another children's show, and had suggested *Cinderella.* Coincidentally, Jerome Whyte, Rodgers and Hammerstein's business manager (he later headed their London operation) had bumped into Lou Wilson, Julie Andrews's American representative. Wilson's client was the hottest star on Broadway, the Eliza of *My Fair Lady,* the biggest musical sensation since *Oklahoma!* (which it would eventually outrun, as it did everything else until *Fiddler on the Roof* came along). Julie was interested in doing a television spectacular, Wilson said. Did Jerry Whyte think Rodgers and Hammerstein might be interested in writing one for her? "There's only one way to find out," Whyte said. "Ask them."

The combination of Julie Andrews, Rodgers and Hammerstein's first television musical, and *Cinderella* was a natural — hell, a bonanza — and CBS snapped it up, scheduling for it a television hookup of proportions hitherto undreamed-of in the medium. They paid Rodgers and Hammerstein's $300,000 fee without blinking, and the partners went to work on the project. Oscar decided early on that he wasn't going to "trick up" the traditional fairy tale, changing Cinderella to a Macy's shopgirl and such. It would be — except for presenting the Ugly Sisters as comic (one dowdy and the other silly), rather than cruel, characters — the traditional Perrault story with which everyone was familiar. Music would marry the characters to the dialogue in a way that had not been done before.

Creating the television show took them longer (six months in the writing, and ten more weeks of rehearsals and tryouts) and required more music (fourteen songs and various other transitional music) than a full-scale Broadway show. Prior to the broadcast, Dick and Oscar staged two full productions of the show which were recorded by kinescope (they were a year too soon for videotape). After these equivalents of New Haven and

235

**Dick and Oscar with Julie Andrews just prior to the television premiere of *Cinderella* in 1957.**
Used by prmission of the Rodgers and Hammerstein Organization.

Boston tryouts (performed without an audience, however) they did such rewriting as they felt necessary. One song, "If I Weren't King," was cut; and they were ready. The show was telecast on March 31, 1957, the 14th anniversary of the premiere of *Oklahoma!*

With Howard Lindsay (that same Howard Lindsay who had coauthored and starred in *Life with Father* and who would soon collaborate with Dick and Oscar on their last show together) in the role of the King, Dorothy Stickney (Lindsay's wife) as the Queen, Ilka Chase as Cinderella's stepmother, and Kaye Ballard and Alice Ghostley as the stepsisters, *Cinderella* was in good hands. Julie Andrews was a delightful Cinderella, Edith Adams her surprisingly young Fairy Godmother, and a newcomer aptly named Jon Cypher was her Prince Charming.

The score Rodgers and Hammerstein gave them remains one of the best they ever wrote, sparkling, witty, wistful, and, like the Prince, charming. The plaintive charm song

"In My Own Little Corner" was touchingly tailored to Andrews's gamine style:

> In my own little corner in my own little chair,
> I can be whatever I want to be.
> On the wings of my fancy I can fly anywhere,
> And the world will open its arms to me.
> I'm a young Norwegian princess or a milkmaid,
> I'm the greatest prima donna in Milan.
> I'm an heiress who has always had her silk made
> By her own flock of silkworms in Japan…

"A Lovely Night," in which Cinderella imagines what it would be like going to the ball, has a clip-clop tempo unashamedly reminiscent of "The Surrey with the Fringe on Top." "Ten Minutes Ago" is a sweeping waltz which unexpectedly, beautifully drops where you expect it to soar, while the duet "Do I Love You Because You're Beautiful?" daringly flirts with philosophy. And the Fairy Godmother's "Impossible" is full of sharper conceits than Oscar had produced in a long time.

237

> Impossible!
> For a plain yellow pumpkin to become a golden carriage.
> Impossible!
> For a plain country bumpkin and a Prince to join in marriage
> And four white mice can never be four white horses.
> The folderol and fiddle-de-dee of course is
> Imposs — ib — le!

Also, among Rodgers's instrumental pieces were a march, a gavotte, and a sweeping waltz to be played at the Ball that could hold its own against any of his very best, and that is praise indeed. If they had been aiming for a comeback, they had certainly done it in high style.

Between 8:00 and 9:00 that March night, *Cinderella* was broadcast, via a chain of stations, to what was probably the largest television audience ever assembled up to that time. According to CBS, the program was seen by 107,000,000 viewers, which was the equivalent, it was computed, of sellout performances at the Majestic Theatre eight times a week for 214 years, or of more people than had seen every one of the preceding Rodgers and Hammerstein shows combined.

**Various forms of strain, pain, and disdain during auditions for *Flower Drum Song*.** Used by prmission of the Rodgers and Hammerstein Organization.

The following year, Harold Fielding bought the rights — R&H had nothing to do with the production — adapted the show, and presented it as a traditional English pantomime at the London Coliseum for the Christmas season, with Tommy Steele as "Buttons" and three songs from *Me and Juliet* interpolated into the score, one of which, "No Other Love," became a substantial local hit. Seven years later, CBS filmed the show again, with a new cast that included Walter Pidgeon (dense) and Ginger Rogers (puddingy) as the King and Queen, Jo Van Fleet (what is Jo Van Fleet doing here?) as the stepmother, Celeste Holm (too damn *kee-yute* for words) as the Fairy Godmother, and the then-untried Lesley Ann Warren as Cinderella. All of the original score, plus "Loneliness of Evening," which had been written for *South Pacific* and cut, was used. Alas, it is this *Cinderella,* which discarded Oscar's fey never-never land script in favor of a clunky, infantile, and (unforgivably) dull one by Joseph Schrank, which has been preserved.

In 1958, another member of the theatrical Fields family came into the life of Rodgers and Hammerstein. They had worked with Herb Fields and his sister Dorothy, but never with Joe Fields, who had become a theatrical producer like his father before him. Early in 1958, Joe, who was responsible for such hit shows as *My Sister Eileen* and *Wonderful Town,* was in Hollywood trying to produce a movie based on the Peter de Vries novel *The Tunnel of Love.* Fields was having the usual trouble: both stars wanted a hundred percent of the gross, and the producer was contemplating introducing a new system, the three hundred percent gross. That way, he reasoned, the stars could have a hundred percent each and Uncle Sam could take the rest. (The movie was eventually released in 1958 starring Doris Day, Richard Widmark, and Gig Young, although it is doubtful if anyone now cares. Precious few did at the time.)

Simultaneously, Fields was negotiating the purchase of dramatic rights to a novel published the preceding autumn to much acclaim, C. Y. Lee's *The Flower Drum Song.* Chin Lee's agent, Ann Elmo, agreed to a deal, and Fields mentioned the book to Oscar

238

Hammerstein, who was in town supervising the filming of *South Pacific*. Oscar liked the sound of the title, and asked Fields to send a copy over to his hotel.

*South Pacific* was giving him more than his share of troubles. Mitzi Gaynor had won the Nellie Forbush role coveted by Doris Day. (Logan had wanted Elizabeth Taylor, but when she auditioned she was so nervous her voice was just a croak and R&H, he claimed, would not countenance her voice being dubbed, an odd decision in a movie where practically everyone else's was.) Rossano Brazzi was set for the Emile De Becque part. Unfortunately for all concerned, Brazzi believed he was God's gift to musical films and it was a long time before he could be persuaded to let Giorgio Tozzi do his singing for him. In addition, Oscar had a couple of clashes with director Joshua Logan. "He made me reshoot a scene that had cost an awful lot of money — the one where Mitzi sang 'I'm Gonna Wash that Man Right Outa my Hair' — because he thought it wasn't as effective on the screen as it had been on the stage," Logan said. "And he was right."

Oscar also rewrote the lyric for the song "My Girl Back Home" which had been dropped from the original show and which Logan wanted to reinstate in the movie "because I loved it." Logan had experimented with a technique of flooding the entire screen with a single color during some of the solos, notably "Younger than Springtime" and "Bali Ha'i," with the intention of introducing a mood matching that of the song. Oscar disliked the results intensely and Logan agreed to take the experiment out. 20th Century Fox had assured him that this could be done, but it was not.

239

The film was released in March, 1958, and, despite its treacly pace and disastrously self-indulgent direction, was well received and turned in an $18 million gross. It was not, however, a patch on the movie of *The King and I* which followed in June, starring Yul Brynner and Deborah Kerr, whose singing had been skillfully and convincingly dubbed by Marni Nixon. Director Walter Lang had taken no

Joshua Logan always said Rodgers's face "looked like a sour apple" when he was making a decision. He appears to be making one here at rehearsals of *Flower Drum Song* with producer Joseph Fields.

Used by prmission of the Rodgers and Hammerstein Organization.

**Rehearsing *Flower Drum Song:* Left to right, Larry Blyden, Gene Kelly, pianist Trude Rittman, Rodgers, and Fields.**
Used by prmission of the Rodgers and Hammerstein Organization.

240

chances, sticking to an almost carbon copy of the stage production, but giving set designers Walter Scott and Paul Fox and costume designer Irene Sharaff a blank check. The result was a stunning, a sumptuous-looking film.

Meanwhile, Oscar had agreed with Dick Rodgers that *Flower Drum Song* might be much better as a musical than a straight play, and they got together with Joe Fields on a co-production deal. Hammerstein and Fields would write the book, and Rodgers and Hammerstein would produce the show in collaboration with Fields. Oscar began work, but in July he was hospitalized for a month with a stomach ailment which required surgery. Rehearsals, which had been planned for the beginning of September, were postponed for a fortnight. Oscar was released from the hospital with a clean bill of health, and returned to the show with a "deficit" of three songs due to his absence. He professed himself unworried by this. "Both 'Happy Talk' and 'Younger than Springtime' were written in rehearsal," he told an interviewer, "and 'Getting to Know You' was written on the road. I don't prefer to do them that way, but I'm not unused to it."

His problem was behind him for now; Dick's was not. Having had no show to write for well over a year, and sinking into depression following his cancer, he had begun drinking again — drinking so heavily that he simply ground to a halt, unable to function in any meaningful way. The irony of his plight — the man who had so bitterly condemned Larry Hart's drinking as the ruination of their partnership, himself trapped by the very same demons — must have filled him with self-loathing. In his autobiography he refers obliquely to this period as something he dealt with by signing himself into the Payne

Whitney Psychiatric Clinic where "untroubled by problems and pressures…my spirits soon picked up." In fact he stayed there for almost four months.

*Flower Drum Song* was a lightweight story that took great liberties with Chin Lee's original — a sort of Chinese *Life with Father*, Oscar called it — which pointed up generation gaps in the Chinese families of San Francisco, the conflict between traditional ways and the new American lifestyles. At the behest of his parents, a "picture bride" — Mei Li — comes from the old country to marry Sammy Fong, a man she has never seen. Sammy, however, is a with-it character who isn't interested in his picture bride because he's crazy about Linda, a stripper at his club. He tries to get his friend Wang Ta married off to Mei Li, but Wang Ta isn't interested — he, too, is in love with Linda (or so he thinks). He is also blind to the love of Helen Chao, thinking of her as a friend, and his intention of marrying Linda appalls his very traditionally-minded father. It all comes out right in the end, of course.

Casting was a nightmare — there were very few Asian actors and singers working in the theater at that time. Joshua Logan had discovered a delightful Asian actress to play opposite Marlon Brando and Red Buttons in the movie *Sayonara* and suggested her to

**Rodgers and Gene Kelly at a run through of *Flower Drum Song*. Chin on hand, Miyoshi Umeki doesn't look half as thrilled as Pat Suzuki, but then, Rodgers isn't patting her on the back.**

Used by prmission of the Rodgers and Hammerstein Organization.

Rodgers for the part of Mei Li. Her name was Miyoshi Umeki and she joined a cast that already included Keye Luke (Charlie Chan's Number One Son in those far-off B-feature days) as Wang Ta's father, Wang Chi Yang; Ed Kenney as Wang Ta; Pat Suzuki as Linda; and Juanita Hall as Madam Liang. An actor named Larry Storch was given the part of Sammy Fong, but he was replaced by Larry Blyden, a college friend of stage manager Jamie Hammerstein, during the Boston tryouts, which were extended to four weeks so that the young newcomer had time to get into the part.

Rehearsals began and it became apparent fairly quickly that director Gene Kelly, who had never helmed a Broadway musical (their first choice, Yul Brynner, was unavailable), was out of his depth, lacking confidence and unable to enthuse the cast. "If he seemed more sure of basic technicalities I'd be happier, but he flounders so," Rodgers noted. An account from the *New York Morning Telegraph* painted a vivid word picture of Kelly's lack of luster. "At ten o'clock one night, after a particularly trying day, Kelly gives everyone a small smile as everyone sags into chairs, and says 'Think of the fun we're having' as he himself finally sits down. 'Look, kids, I know some of you are not used to all these notes and changes, but you must get used to them because this process goes on. The last few days have been a hodge-podge. We've had one replacement. We've had to stop to give Russell Bennett orchestrations. Some of you have been over at the Broadhurst rehearsing dances with Carol [Haney]. We're late. You're all playing very well, but now we've got to go over these readings again and again until we get them. And then I want them to stay that way.'"

Altering the staging of one song, "She Is Beautiful," consumed a good deal of time. Only when Oscar hit upon the idea of reshaping the song to make it "You Are Beautiful" could director Gene Kelly make it work. Kelly never talked much about his experiences on the show, fending off questions about it by saying, "You'd have to ask them [meaning Rodgers and Hammerstein] about that." He did remember Rodgers (whom he called Daddy Warbucks) rehearsing Pat Suzuki in singing "I Enjoy Being a Girl." "She kept on hitting the beat a little late, and Rodgers went over and over it with her until she got it the way he wanted it. 'Exactly,' he said, when she did. 'Don't ever do it better.' Don't ever change it, he meant."

Another beautiful song, "My Best Love," was cut. Keye Luke was supposed to have sung it, but it didn't work. They gave it to Hall, but that didn't work either, so they discarded it and set to work on another. Then they decided to have Sammy explain to Mei Li that he was a poor matrimonial risk. As Gene Kelly remembered: "In one afternoon, Dick wrote this song 'Don't Marry Me' and Oscar wrote the lyrics. So you see, slow as Oscar was reputed to be, he was the complete pro. Dick was always fast, but so was Oscar that day.

And Dick took me out to the ladies' room, and said, 'Listen to this,' and I said, 'It's fine, I'll stage it, I'll have it in the show tomorrow.' 'I'm glad you like it,' he said, 'because we think it's terrific.'"

Tryouts are always wearing, but they make or break a show. Once you've opened, as Joe Fields noted in Boston, the company "can't depend on the audiences anymore to tell us how we're doing. The notices were good and they'll come and enjoy themselves and laugh at *everything*. That's wonderful of course, but it's the amount of work done on the road that determines whether you have just a good show or a smash hit when you get to New York. We all intend to work very hard." And they did — Fields so hard he had a heart attack.

*Flower Drum Song* was a hit, if not a smash hit, when it opened at the St. James on December 1, 1958. Its songs were — again — good, if not top-drawer Rodgers and Hammerstein: "Grant Avenue" and "Chop Suey" being okay Eastern songs, "Don't Marry Me," "I Enjoy Being a Girl," "Sunday," and the deliberately-awful "Gliding through my Memoree" the Western ones. There were some quite beautiful numbers which are today sadly neglected, including "Love Look Away," a soaringly eloquent Rodgers melody, the winning "I am Going to Like it Here," and a song particularly dear to Oscar's heart, "A Hundred Million Miracles." In spite of Kenneth Tynan's damning description of it as "a world of woozy song," *Flower Drum Song* was a substantial success that put Rodgers and Hammerstein back upon the pinnacle to which they had become accustomed.

The show ran a year and a half on Broadway, had a 15-month tour, over a year at London's Palace Theatre, and the original cast album went gold (over one million dollars' worth). *Flower Drum Song* was filmed three years later with Nancy Kwan as Linda and James Shigeta as Wang Ta, and with Miyoshi Umeki and Juanita Hall repeating their stage roles. But even before the show opened on Broadway, Dick and Oscar had already agreed to do another. "We won't wait nearly so long between this new one and the next," he told a reporter in October, 1958. "We have an arrangement to provide Mary Martin with a new musical play next fall. It will be based on the real-life story of the Trapp Family singers. Oscar will do the lyrics for that one and Howard Lindsay and Russell Crouse will do our libretto. Naturally, we want to rest after we get *Flower Drum Song* going, so I would say that we'll get down to Mary's show next spring." Dick was feeling good again. He was looking forward immensely to working with Mary Martin. He was back on Broadway with a solid hit. He saw nothing in the future which could stop him.

243

# SO LONG,

# Farewell

*Who are we going to offend—people who like Nazis?*

—— Howard Lindsay

Vincent J. Donehue was a former actor and Tony award-winning stage director (*Sunrise at Campobello*) who had gone to work at Paramount late in 1956. One day he was asked to look at a German film called *The Trapp Family Singers* which had been a big success in Europe and South America, with a view to his directing a movie in English based upon it and starring Audrey Hepburn. The German film told the life story of Maria, Baroness von Trapp, and her beginnings as a postulant nun in Austria who was sent to be governess to the seven children of the widowed Georg von Trapp. They were later married and escaped from Austria just before the *Anschluss*, finding their way across the Alps into Switzerland and from there to the United States, where they became famous as the singing Trapps.

"It was in many ways amateurish," Donehue said of the film, "but I was terribly moved by the whole idea of it, almost sobbing." He saw it immediately as a perfect vehicle for Mary Martin, whose husband, Richard, was one of his closest friends. When Audrey Hepburn's interest in the project faded, Paramount lost its enthusiasm and let its option lapse. Donehue sent the German film to Richard Halliday. Both he and Mary Martin loved the film. "The idea was just irresistible," Mary said, "a semi-Cinderella story, but true."

Actually, it wasn't true at all. The real-life Maria Rainer had had a loveless childhood as the ward of a provincial judge and joined a monastery where, far from being a ray of sunshine, she became so ill she was sent "outside" to be a governess to one of Georg von Trapp's daughters, who was bedridden. Unlike the music-hating martinet portrayed in the Lindsay and Crouse version, von Trapp was a loving parent who encouraged his children to play instruments and sing. Nor did they escape over the Alps pursued by the Nazis; they took a train to Italy and reached America by way of England.

Nevertheless, there was not the slightest doubt in Halliday's or Mary Martin's minds that it would make a great musical, and both agreed from the outset that they wanted Rodgers and Hammerstein to produce it. But there were all sorts of obstacles to be overcome before anything like a Broadway show could be mounted. First, Halliday had to try to locate Maria von Trapp and her children, all of whose permissions would be required if they were to be portrayed live on stage. The Baroness, however, was hard to find. She was on a world tour, establishing missions in the South Seas. Letters addressed to her in Australia, Tahiti, Samoa, and other locations failed to reach her. In addition, the seven von Trapp children were scattered in various places around the world and were proving just as elusive.

At this point, Halliday's lawyer Bill Fitelson (who also represented Joshua Logan) brought in producer Leland Hayward, and Hayward became as enthusiastic as everyone else about the possibilities of the story. Together, Hayward and Fitelson chased all over Europe picking up hints and clues as to the whereabouts of the Trapp children. By the autumn of 1957, they had all the necessary permissions sewn together. The seven von Trapp children had been traced and had signed on the dotted line. The contract with Baroness von Trapp was finalized in a hospital ward in Innsbruck, where she was recuperating from malaria contracted in New

**Oscar in his workroom at Highland Farm. The bookkeeper's desk was a gift from Jerome Kern, the sampler on the wall (Oscar's lyric for "The Sweetest Sight That I Have Ever Seen") sewn by his wife Dorothy. The last thing he wrote was an apology.**

Used by permission of the Rodgers and Hammerstein Organization.

**Theodore Bikel as Captain von Trapp and Mary Martin as Maria in _The Sound of Music_. You may remember him better as Zoltan Karpathy in the movie of _My Fair Lady_. Then again, you may not.**
Used by permission of the Rodgers and Hammerstein Organization.

246

Guinea. Leland Hayward, who spoke no German, concluded his negotiations with the representative of the German film company, who spoke no English, in Yiddish!

In that same fall, Leland Hayward was contacted by Howard Lindsay and Russell Crouse, the successful team who had created _Life with Father_ and the libretto for the Irving Berlin show _Call Me Madam_. They had heard rumors about the project and were interested in writing the book for the musical. They generously offered to write a 60-page outline; if Mary Martin didn't like it, they would bow out quietly. Hayward accepted with alacrity, and Lindsay and Crouse turned in their synopsis soon afterwards. Mary liked it, but wanted to show it to Rodgers and Hammerstein. "Ever since I first worked for them," she said, "I've always asked their opinions about scripts I was thinking of doing." Although she and her husband were inclined towards Rodgers and Hammerstein as composers, Lindsay and Crouse were still thinking in terms of using the original German songs sung by the Trapp Family Singers, with perhaps just one or two new songs by Dick and Oscar.

When Halliday and Hayward brought the project to Dick Rodgers — Oscar was in the hospital — the following spring, he was excited, perhaps even more so because it was the first project he had heard Mary say she wanted to do since _Peter Pan_. When he was told about Lindsay and Crouse's idea to use a lot of the music the Trapps actually sang in their concerts, however, Rodgers demurred. "They asked me to write one new tune," he recalled. "This seemed to be most impractical. Either you do it authentically, all actual

Trapp music, or you get a complete new score. They said they would love to get a complete new score if Oscar and I would do it, but we were occupied in preparing *Flower Drum Song.* Then they said the most flattering thing in the world: if you and Oscar will do the music and lyrics, we'll wait."

Thus Rodgers and Hammerstein became coproducers with Hayward and Halliday, and while they completed the job of putting *Flower Drum Song* together, Lindsay and Crouse set to work on the book for the new show. They realized that they were going to have to fight operetta every inch of the way. "The minute you say 'Vienna' everybody thinks of chorus boys in short pants, and the minute you have a waltz, you're sunk," Lindsay said. "We had to work to keep the story believable and convincing and not letting it get into the never-never land operetta lives in."

They had their Maria from day one, but finding an actor who could make George von Trapp something more than a cipher was difficult. They went the "operatic" route first, looking for another Ezio Pinza, but Pinza was dead and there was no one else remotely like him. They heard that Leif Erickson could sing and called him in. Everyone loved him — Rodgers, who knew people always had trouble pronouncing Erickson's first name, put him at ease by telling him, "Well, life, I'll try to make leaf a little easier for you" — but the actor wasn't right for the part. Finally, they gave it to Theodore Bikel, an Israeli folksinger/actor who'd had a small part in 1957's *The Rope Dancers*, featuring Siobhan McKenna and Joan Blondell.

247

*The Sound of Music* had a "family" atmosphere almost right from the start: everyone working on it knew everyone else and the "family" conference became the accepted method for planning and discussing every aspect of the show. Dick and Oscar would play and sing the songs as they were completed for choral arranger Trude Rittman, music director Fred Dvonch, Bikel, Mary Martin, Richard Halliday, Leland Hayward, Lindsay, Crouse, or anyone else who happened to be around. Everyone attended Mary's costume fittings; she showed off Lucinda Ballard's charming gowns and the special wedding dress created for her by Mainbocher with the delight of a kid going to a party. The seven children: Lauri Peters (Liesl), William Snowden (Friedrich), Kathy Dunn (Louisa), Joseph Stewart (Kurt), Marilyn Rogers (Brigitta), Mary Susan Locke (Marta), and Evanna Lien (Gretl), made a habit of rushing Rodgers from all sides and hugging him until, he said, he felt like "a Rodgers sandwich."

The composer was at first apprehensive about writing liturgical music. He had had no problems painting musical impressions of Siam or Oklahoma or the South Pacific, but the prospect of composing a Catholic prayer was something else again, for badly done,

**Mary Martin and the children singing "Do Re Mi"; on the day Oscar died, they had to perform it just as if he hadn't.** Used by permission of the Rodgers and Hammerstein Organization.

it could easily give more offense than pleasure. For the first time in his life, he did musical research. Mother Morgan of the Manhattanville College in Purchase, New York, staged a special concert for Dick and Dorothy Rodgers at which the nuns and seminarians sang a selection of works ranging from Gregorian chants to more modern works by Fauré and others.

With this experience to guide him, Rodgers had little difficulty in composing the *Preludium* which opens the show. Indeed, the score seems by and large to have come very easily. There was one verse he cut because it sounded like "a damned five-finger exercise" but apparently few other problems, unless one counts as a problem trying to write music that gives a church flavor and at the same time creates the feeling of the national background and period in which *The Sound of Music* is set.

Mary Martin, too, got into shape in her own idiosyncratic way. Her voice teacher, William Herman, had her work out every day with boxing gloves, whacking away at a punching bag and singing while she did it. The idea was to strengthen the diaphragm and produce big tones, and anyone who ever heard her singing "The Lonely Goatherd" can attest to its efficacy. The star also visited Maria von Trapp. No longer a Baroness (she had become an American citizen in 1948), Maria von Trapp now ran an Alpine chalet-style family lodge on seven hundred acres in Stowe, Vermont. The two women became fast friends, and Maria taught Mary how to cross herself, kneel properly, and play the guitar.

Rehearsals were set for the late summer. Tryouts were scheduled at the Shubert Theatres in New Haven and Boston for the month of October, the New York opening fixed for November. The show was virtually complete within six months of the opening of *Flower Drum Song*, astonishingly fast by Rodgers and Hammerstein's painstaking standards. "This is the quickest job we've ever done. Usually, we take a couple of years," Rodgers said. "Of course, Oscar didn't have to work on the libretto in this case, so we didn't have quite so much to do."

Just how much work Howard Lindsay and Russell Crouse had done is indicated by their notes on the scenic production. These provide enormous insight into the mechan-

Same scene as on the previous page, but in the 1965 movie Julie Andrews sings "My Favorite Things" to the children. They are, from left to right, Duane Chase (Kurt), Charmian Carr (Liesl), Nicholas Hammond (Friedrich), Heather Menzies (Louisa), Kym Karath (Gretl), and Debbie Turner (Marta). British Film Institute.

ics behind the creation of the show, and since they are a remarkably prescient forecast of how the show would finally look (only two minor scenes were added) they are worth examining in detail.

### THE SOUND OF MUSIC
### NOTES ON SCENIC PRODUCTION

Since this musical does not have a dancing chorus or, in fact, a chorus as such (with the exception of the nuns who will sing) this comes closer to being a "play with music" than a musical play. We feel this demands that some of the scenes will have to have a somewhat realistic treatment, especially in the distribution of furniture, etc.

In the scene on the terrace we hope that the Captain and Elsa will dance, also the Captain and Maria. This scene also includes a "step-out" number for the children. At the same time, both the terrace and the living room, which are the two largest sets, must permit the playing of two scenes and still hold the audience. If they are too spacious in appearance the characters will have difficulty in playing intimate scenes.

In the living room in Scene 8 of Act I, there is a party of neighbors and it will probably open with an informal dance, but the furniture could probably be deliberately moved to make room for this. We liked very much the staircase which was seen in the [motion] picture. Starting on one side of the stage and running across the top of the back was a balcony but the problems of the Lunt-Fontanne Theatre may not permit this.

We are not entirely clear where all of the entrances and exits are in the various scenes. This can only be decided after the stage director and the scenic artist have all met in conference.

### Act I, Scene I: THE CORRIDORS OF NONNBERG ABBEY
We hear the nuns chanting, and we see groups of them appear and disappear through vaulted arches as different areas of the stage are lighted. Toward the end of this montage we hear the abbey bells and the movement takes on purpose and direction. A nun with a large ring of keys crosses, speaking to other nuns as she passes. Gradually we

250

hear the question they are all asking each other: "Where's Maria?," "Where's Maria?," "Where's Maria?" This builds to something of a climax as we fade out.

Act I, Scene 2:
We fade in a spot in the forest on the mountainside towards sundown, and Maria, in her nun's habit, perhaps slightly torn, is sitting on the branch of a tree, listening. She sings "The Sound of Music." Whatever staging of this number there is will be devised later. Perhaps at the end of the number we hear the abbey bells and see her hurry off.

Act I, Scene 3: THE ABBESS'S OFFICE
This calls for a desk, two chairs, a footstool and possibly a *prie-dieu*. The scene suggests the use of a window and a door. (These may be made impossible by the problems of the theater.)

Act I, Scene 4: THE LIVING ROOM OF THE VON TRAPP VILLA
We have imagined the French windows being upstage looking out on the terrace and the Alps. They would be under the balcony, if there is one. There will be, also, entrances left and right, perhaps more than one on one or the other sides.

Act I, Scene 5: OUTSIDE THE BACK DOOR OF THE VON TRAPP VILLA
We have imagined a two-step leading up to the door which has to look practical enough for Liesl to pretend to try to open it. It is, however, never opened.

Act I, Scene 6: MARIA'S BEDROOM
Here a practical window — at least one through which Liesl can crawl — is necessary. There also needs to be a bed and perhaps a wardrobe. At one side of the stage we envisioned a curtained alcove. This scene also calls for a practical door in the upstage wall.

Act I, Scene 7: THE TERRACE OF THE VON TRAPP VILLA

We have imagined the house stage right. The entrance from the house being perhaps the French window we have seen from the living room. At the back is a drop of the Alps, and perhaps this drop is continued around and downstage left for masking purposes. There can also be box hedges Stage left ... to create an entrance. There can be a marble bench to the left by the hedges, and somewhere on the stage, well down front, should be a terrace table where coffee can be served. It may be that this set should have a garden wall to make for some intimacy. There will be some remarks about this drop when we discuss Act II, Scene 1.

Act I, Scene 8: THE VON TRAPP LIVING ROOM

It is the occasion of a small party given in honour of Elsa, to which some of the neighbors have been invited. This may open with a dance.

Act I, Scene 9: WE ARE BACK IN THE ABBESS'S OFFICE, THE SAME AS ACT I, SCENE 3.

Act II, Scene 1: THE TERRACE OF THE VON TRAPP VILLA (THE SAME AS ACT I, SCENE 7)

In this scene we go into twilight, and on the mountains on the backdrop we want the effect of one or more bonfires in the shape of swastikas. This can be on St. John's Eve, June 23, or perhaps the bonfires may be a personal warning to Captain von Trapp.

Act II, Scene 2: A SCENE IN THE ABBEY

It could be the Abbess's office. It is in this scene that Maria is being dressed for her wedding.

Act II, Scene 3: A SCENE IN THE ABBEY

There is a drop of latticework behind which the nuns are looking into the church watching the wedding. The wedding is, of course, taking place where the audience is sitting.

Act II, Scene 4: THE LIVING ROOM OF THE VON TRAPP VILLA

It is in this scene that the Trapp family, including both Maria and the Captain, start to sing the song they would sing in the festival. We dim out during the song, they continue to sing and when we dim up they are singing in front of a rich velour drop which should suggest to the audience that they are now singing in the contest in the festival hall.

Act II, Scene 5: THE ABBESS'S OFFICE

We would like to see over the walls of the office again the backdrop of the Alps. It may be that we should have the same effect in Act I, Scenes 3 and 9. In this particular scene, however, we have hoped that we might see the headlights of automobiles up and down and along roads through the mountains, perhaps even suggesting that one car is being pursued and headed off by others.

Act II, Scene 6: THE FINALE

It may well be we will want to suggest that this is high in the Alps on the Swiss border.

253

With so detailed a blueprint to guide them, Dick and Oscar had no difficulty finding melodies for most of the spots they needed. The first scene opened, as Lindsay and Crouse had indicated, with the "Preludium" Rodgers had written after his sessions at Manhattanville and segued beautifully into the first major song, "The Sound of Music." In the original film, Maria had made her entrance sliding down a banister, to the dismay of the assembled nuns. For the show, the fade in on the forested mountainside, with Mary Martin in her tree, regretting that her day in the hills has come to an end, was infinitely more effective.

In the third scene, the Mother Abbess and Sisters Margaretta, Berthe, and Sophia wonder "What are we going to do about Maria?" but they can't answer their own question. "How do you catch a moonbeam in your hand?" they sigh, knowing the task is hopeless. So it is decided that perhaps Maria should go to live outside the Abbey for a while, as governess to the motherless von Trapp children. The Mother Abbess cheers Maria up by reminding her of some of the lovely things they both like in the song "My Favorite Things." (In the movie, and perhaps more effectively, Maria sings this song to the children.)

Thanks to Oscar's late-in-life decision to keep his yellow legal pad worksheets, it's possible to see the conception and realization of some of his lyrics. His legendary slowness is not in evidence here. He started on June 26 with a list of "Good Things" that included kittens, mittens, snowflakes, echoes, songs over water, and a crisp apple strudel. Next day it became 'The things that I like are all like one another." On June 28 he almost had it, but not quite:

> Raindrops on roses and whiskers on kittens,
> Curling my fingers in warm woolen mittens,
> Riding downhill on my big brother's bike,
> These are a few of the things that I like.
> Girls in white dresses with blue satin sashes,
> Snowflakes that fall on my nose and eyelashes,
> Icy cold water right out of a well,
> Tunes that I heard on an old carousel.
> Bright copper kettles and crisp apple strudels,
> Cream colored ponies and schnitzel with noodles,
> Wading a river and flying a kite,
> Waking at morning and sleeping at night.

The following day he jotted down only a few extra lines, but they were the key ones: "Brown paper packages tied up with strings," "Wild geese that fly with the moon on their wings," and — perhaps almost triumphantly — "These are a few of my favorite things."

An additional transition scene set in the corridor of the Abbey was added later between the original scenes three and four; everyone will remember the overburdened Maria, guitar around her neck, arriving at the von Trapp villa and teaching the children the rudiments of the musical scale in "Do Re Mi."

Scene five (six in the final version) had the oldest von Trapp girl, Liesl (played by Lauri Peters) secretly meeting her boyfriend behind the villa. In this scene Rolf (played originally by Brian Davies, and two years later by a newcomer named Jon Voight who would go on to fame and fortune as Ratso Rizzo's pal, the drifting *Midnight Cowboy*) and Liesl sing "Sixteen Going on Seventeen." The next sequence is set in Maria's bedroom. When a thunderstorm brings the frightened children to her, Maria tells them "Maybe if we all sing loud enough, we won't hear the thunder," and she and the children yodel the whimsical story of "The Lonely Goatherd" with ever-increasing fervor.

Scene nine, set on the terrace, provided an opportunity for Captain von Trapp, his fiancée Elsa, and their old friend Max Detweiler (Elsa was played by Marion Marlowe, Max by Kurt Kasznar) to comment on the difficulties Elsa is encountering in getting von Trapp to propose to her. The problem, Max cynically explains, is that both of them are rich, so "How Can Love Survive?" The noisy entrance of the children (dressed in clothes made from curtains) leads first to an argument between von Trapp and Maria and then a reprise of the title song.

The party in the living room contains a charming sequence where Maria and the Captain dance the *Laendler* (Rodgers's "folk-tune" is "The Lonely

Christopher Plummer (Captain von Trapp) sings "Edelweiss" (his voice dubbed by Bill Lee, who also supplied the vocals for John Kerr in *South Pacific*). He said acting with Julie Andrews was "like being hit over the head with a Valentine's Day card." Anything like that ever happened to you?

Used by permission of the Rodgers and Hammerstein Organization.

255

Goatherd" in waltz-time) and realize the growing affection between them. The children perform their party piece, "So Long, Farewell," each disappearing in order of size during its singing. In the final scene of the first act (again, Lindsay and Crouse inserted a transitional scene set in the abbey corridors), Maria has returned to the abbey, and confesses her love for the Captain. The Mother Abbess reassures her, singing the moving "Climb Ev'ry Mountain" that is the climax of the first act.

An early draft written on July 7 shows that for this song, Oscar was thinking along the same lines as "You'll Never Walk Alone" from the start: "Go forth my child /With the sun in your eyes /And the strength of life in your heart." Maria's reply emphasizes the resemblance: "On and on I will go /Till I find my life /The life I was meant to live /On and on I will go /Till I learn to give /The love I was meant to give /I will walk ev'ry road /Ford ev'ry stream /Climb ev'ry hill on the way." Ah, yes, of course. Climb ev'ry mountain.

Oscar's notes contain a second version of the song that was never used. The fact he was able to discard it shows what a consummate professional he was.

> Search ev'ry forest,
> Dark though it be.
> Follow ev'ry valley
> To its own blue sea.
> Climb ev'ry mountain,
> High though it seem.
> Never be contented
> Till you find your dream.

In the second act of *The Sound of Music* Rodgers and Hammerstein dispensed with tradition again, in their now-usual no-nonsense fashion, by adding only two new numbers — and both of them completely minor ones. Every other musical piece was a reprise of something already heard. The first scene of Act II opened with the Captain, Max, and Elsa singing "No Way to Stop It," a song really inserted to supplement the dialogue which touches (very lightly indeed) on the choices open to them: to accept the Nazi mastery of Austria (as Max and Elsa propose) or defy it (as von Trapp will).

Just before rehearsals began, they realized that although the Captain and Maria were by now obviously in love, they had no duet. "We didn't have anything until they wrote 'An Ordinary Couple,'" Mary Martin said. "And I never was happy singing it. It went downhill. I liked the lyrics but I never did like the music." She was right, but it was all they had except one of the first lyrics Oscar had written, "Love Is Not Blind," and that did not fit either the mood or the scene.

As rehearsals got under way, Oscar Hammerstein went once again into the hospital, ostensibly to be operated on for an ulcer. He had been complaining throughout the writing of the score of a recurrence of the stomach pains for which he had been operated on the preceding July. After exploratory surgery, his wife and Dick and Dorothy Rodgers were told the grim news: Oscar had a malignant cancer from which the chances of recovery were nil. It proved impossible to keep the truth from him, and once he knew it, Oscar accepted it with equanimity and told his wife and his partner that he intended to go on working as long as he could.

"It was typical of Oscar that he didn't tell anyone," Lucinda Ballard said. "I don't think he wanted anyone to know. I remember him singing 'My Favorite Things' in that darling croaky voice of his. Everyone knew he wasn't well, of course, but nobody knew that he'd been told he had six months to live. We all worked harder on *The Sound of Music* than we ever had before, because we all loved Oscar and we missed him so dreadfully."

It fell to Richard Rodgers to break the news to the cast. Mary Martin remembered how she learned of Oscar's illness:

> *They had put in the song "Sixteen Going On Seventeen" for Lauri Peters to sing and it was darling. Then, after I (as Maria) married the Captain, they wanted a moment for Lauri and I to be together. This was while we were still in rehearsal, getting ready to go on the road, and we still didn't have the scene between Lauri and myself. One day I was getting out of the car and going into the theater when I saw Oscar coming out of the stage door. He didn't see me. He was walking sort of bent over for him — and he didn't look at all well. Then he saw me and he straightened up. He had a little piece of paper in his hand, and he said, "Here are the words for the scene between you and Lauri. Dick already has the music. We're adding a verse to 'Sixteen Going On Seventeen.' I would have loved to enlarge it and make it a complete song, but we'll have to use it this way now. Don't open it yet. Just look at it when you have time." Then later on Dick Rodgers came to my dressing room and he said, "Did you see Oscar?" I said yes, and he said, "Well, Mary, you're a big girl now, and you're old enough to take things. I have to tell you that Oscar has cancer and it's really bad. He didn't want to tell you himself, so he asked me to tell you. But he's given you the lyrics?" I said he had, and Dick said, "Now, we're not going to be sad about this, Mary. We don't know how long he will be with us, but he will work to the very end. If you feel badly, stay in here for awhile, and then come out and rehearse and forget it. We're all going to forget it and that's it." I opened the piece of paper Oscar had given me. This is what it said:* A bell is no bell till you ring it. A song is no song till you sing it. And love in your heart wasn't put there to stay. Love isn't love till you give it away.

257

"It was awful, of course: everyone pretending that nothing was wrong, everyone knowing and pretending not to. It was devastating, but we all went out and carried on," she said. "New Haven, Boston, as if nothing had happened at all."

**Mary Martin with Richard Rodgers listening intently to playbacks during the recording of the original cast album of *The Sound of Music*.** Used by permission of the Rodgers and Hammerstein Organization.

The tryouts were very encouraging; the audiences responded well to the score and the story. A few minor changes were made in New Haven; the fade-out at the end of the scene envisaged by Russell Crouse and Howard Lindsay in their original book which takes the Trapp family from their home to the festival was altered to allow for a reprise of "Do Re Mi;" and in Boston, the authors took further note of a critic who complained that the ending was melodramatic, adding an extra explanatory scene and rewriting the ending. The original version had the Nazis pursuing the Trapp family — among them the treacherous boyfriend Rolf — actually coming onstage all jackbooted and swastika'd, which even post-*The Producers* sounds kind of heavy. Instead they became an offstage presence, all the more menacing because unseen.

Lucinda Ballard remembered one amusing incident during the Boston tryouts. It was very hot, and during a break in rehearsals, some of the chorus, still wearing their nuns' habits, went out to get a drink. For a long time they sat in the nearby bar, totally unaware of the fact that outside, a large crowd of very straitlaced Bostonians were gawking in appalled horror at the sight of a dozen nuns with their shoes kicked off, their habits hiked up around their knees, and their feet on tables as they smoked cigarettes, drank beer, and swapped decidedly un-nunlike anecdotes containing very un-nunlike adjectives! The "nuns" were hastily shepherded back to the safety of the theater before a riot began.

On another occasion, a party of genuine nuns was invited backstage between the matinee and evening performance to meet Mary Martin. Before they could reach her dressing room, however, musical staging director Joe Layton came bustling through, saw the nuns standing about looking understandably uncertain, and tore into them. "Goddammit!" he yelled, "You girls know you're not supposed to stand out here in the hall in your goddamned costumes! Now get back to your dressing rooms right this minute and get them off!" "But…but… but…" the nuns tried to protest. Layton would have none of it, and heckled them for about ten minutes until the real actresses emerged from their dressing rooms in their street clothes, and his face fell about four yards. Exit one chorus of nuns, giggling.

Word on the musical from New Haven and Boston was all good, and in New York the advance sale, enhanced by the reunion of the *South Pacific* dream team of Rodgers, Hammerstein, and Mary Martin, soared over $3,250,000, a record for the partnership and for the Broadway musical. There seemed little they could do to improve the show, and yet Rodgers was still unhappy with the festival sequence. He felt that Theodore Bikel needed a solo in the scene preceding the finale, in which the children slip offstage one by one in a reprise of their party piece, "So Long, Farewell," and begin their flight to Switzerland.

"Oscar was sick and couldn't come to the tryouts in Boston [he didn't see it until the October 14 Boston opening], and I felt that Bikel needed another song," Rodgers said. "In the plot there was a concert and I wrote a tune that Bikel could play on his guitar and sing. Then Oscar finally got up to Boston and I played the tune for him. He agreed Bikel should have it and he wrote the lyric." It took him just six days: the name of the song was "Edelweiss." It was the last song that Oscar Hammerstein would write.

*The Sound of Music* opened at the Lunt-Fontanne Theatre in New York on November 16, 1959. It would run for almost four years, sweep the Tony Awards, tour for another three years, and establish new records in London with an astonishing five-and-a-half years at the Palace Theatre. The critics were, in the main, kind, although some expressed dismay at the saccharine sweetness of the story. Rodgers and Hammerstein had not written it but they stepped forward, as always, to defend it as if they had.

"Sentiment," Oscar riposted, "has never been unpopular except with a few sick persons who are made sicker by the sight of a child, a glimpse of a wedding, or the thought of a happy home. *The Sound of Music* was based on the autobiography of Maria von Trapp. No incidents were dragged in or invented to play on the sentimental susceptibilities of the audience as some critics seem to feel." It wasn't strictly true, but that was how he felt. "Most of us," added Rodgers, "feel that Nature can have attractive manifestations, that children aren't necessarily monsters, and that deep affection between two people is nothing to be ashamed of. I feel that rather strongly, or obviously it would not be possible for me to write the music that goes with Oscar's words."

At the time of the show's opening, in their usual fashion, Rodgers and Hammerstein made themselves available to the press for the standard interviews about the show. One of these — among Oscar's last — had him recalling for the *New York Journal-American* the early days of his collaboration with Rodgers.

> *I was very conscious that Dick had worked for years with Larry Hart. I admired Larry's lyrics greatly. They were wittier and brighter than mine. In writing* Oklahoma! *his image was dangling in front of my face. I had to be witty, and as a result I never had or have since done funnier lyrics.*

260  "And today?" asked the reporter, never realizing the poignancy of the answer he was eliciting. "Do you think you're getting slower as you get older?"

> *I was fast in my youth — and not very good. I used to dash off lyrics on a commuter train with no trouble at all, but now I dig, dig, dig. I sometimes think that if I had a bad case of amnesia and forgot that I had been a writer of songs, I would never again do a lyric. I might start one, realizing that I had a bent for poetry, but I wouldn't think that I could ever finish it.*

It was Oscar's valedictory statement, made in full awareness of his impending death. As he had vowed, he intended to go on working as long as he was able, and that was just what he did. During the following winter he worked on new treatments of *State Fair* for a remake of that movie, and *Allegro* for a television production. He and Dick auditioned for cast replacements, talked of future things they might write together, oversaw the activities of their publishing and producing empire, even flew to London to supervise the London premiere of *Flower Drum Song* on March 24, 1960. The end, however, was very near, and Oscar was soon too sick to do any more. Rodgers immersed himself in writing the background score for another television series, this time about Winston Churchill,

called *The Valiant Years*.

They met for a final lunch one summer day in 1960. Oscar told Dick that he had given due consideration to the possibility that he might go into the hospital yet again for a battery of last-ditch attempts to arrest his cancer, and had decided against it. He said that he was going up to Highlands Farm and die there, as matter-of-factly, Rodgers said, "as if he had been discussing a set of rhyming alternatives." He hoped, Oscar told his partner, that after he was gone Dick would try working with a younger man. He was sure that would be good for him.

Halfway through the lunch,

**Julie Andrews, even *more* homespun in the movie *The Sound of Music* than Mary Martin was in the original show. Rodgers wrote a completely new song for her: "I Have Confidence In Me."**
Used by permission of the Rodgers and Hammerstein Organization.

a man seated a few tables away came over and introduced himself. After asking them to sign his menu, he ventured to ask them something else. Here were Rodgers and Hammerstein, two of the most famous men in the history of the musical theater. They were both brilliantly talented and successful. They had the biggest hit on Broadway playing in a theater around the corner. They couldn't possibly have a worry in the world, he said, so what on earth could be making both of them look so sad?

One by one, Oscar talked with his children and stepchildren, saying goodbye in his own way while he still had all his faculties. "I've had a very happy childhood," he told his son James. "I've had a good time as a young man. And I've had a terrific middle age. The only thing that I'm disappointed in is that I was looking forward to having a really good old age, too." When Jamie couldn't help but let the tears flow, Oscar got angry. "God damn it!" he yelled "I'm the one that's dying, not you!"

Oscar Hammerstein died at Highlands Farm on August 23, 1960. "It was a matinée day," Mary Martin remembered. "The phone rang and it was Dorothy Hammerstein.

**Julie Andrews and Christopher Plummer. For this scene Rodgers wrote another song, "Something Good."**
Used by permission of the Rodgers and Hammerstein Organization.

'Do the two shows, Mary,' she said, 'and do them well, because that's what Oscar would want.' It was just ghastly, but we all did it. I think I broke down on every second line, they were all so much Oscar, and he was gone and none of us wanted to believe it."

There was to be one further, total triumph ahead, one which Oscar would sadly never see — sadly, because it confirmed that his approach to the musical was what the public wanted to see and hear, confirmed Dick's oft-quoted statement to the effect that the only smart people in show business were the audiences. It was, of course, the movie version of *The Sound of Music*.

Within two years of its release, *The Sound of Music*, starring Julie Andrews as Maria and Christopher Plummer as Captain von Trapp, would gross $66 million. It went on to outdistance such box office champions as *Gone With The Wind, The Ten Commandments, Ben Hur*, and *Doctor Zhivago*, and dollar compared to inflated dollar, remains one of the most successful audience-pullers in the history of the movies. The soundtrack album, released on March 2, 1965, the same day as the film, has become the world's all-time best-selling long-playing record album. Up to 1972 alone it had sold over 14 million copies, which was more records than Frank Sinatra had then sold in his entire career. And the strange thing is that the film very nearly never got made at all.

After its $40 million debacle, the Elizabeth Taylor-Richard Burton turkey *Cleopatra*, and further losses incurred through the cancellation of Marilyn Monroe's last, uncompleted movie, *Something's Got To Give*, 20th Century Fox found itself over $60 million in the red. Irate stockholders demanded new management, and Darryl F. Zanuck was called in to put the company back on its feet. The first thing Zanuck did was fire two thousand people, and then he instituted a set of economies so swingeing that they reduced the staff on the lot to around one hundred people. He put his son Richard (later to coproduce the ultimate blockbuster *Jaws*) in charge of stopping every project in sight.

One day, Richard Zanuck ran into Irving Lazar, the agent who had sold the movie rights to *The Sound of Music* to Fox for $1,125,000 (a million for R&H, the rest for "Swifty," as he was known). Lazar was once asked by Elmore Leonard what kind of writing paid the most money. "Ransom notes," he replied. Sure that in the present climate Fox would never make the movie, Lazar told Richard Zanuck that he had someone else anxious to make it, and offered him $2 million on the spot for the return of the rights. The offer was more than tempting, but pride kept Zanuck from admitting how tight things were strapped. His father decided to go ahead on the movie, and it was a major factor in restoring Fox to profitability. Darryl Zanuck always referred to it as "the miracle movie," and from where he was sitting it's easy to see why.

Writing his own lyrics, Richard Rodgers composed two new songs for the film version, both oddly autobiographical: "I Have Confidence in Me" and "Something Good." He was unashamedly delighted by the success of the movie. "It's the most successful picture that's ever been made and that's very pleasurable," he said at the time. "It isn't just a question of money. What I enjoy particularly is what it has done for the unselfconscious people of the world — the selfconscious ones sneer a little at it. It *is* sentimental, but I

263

don't see anything particularly wrong with that. I think people have been given a great deal of hope by that picture."

Today, following hugely successful revivals in New York and London of *Carousel, The King and I, South Pacific*, and *Oklahoma!*, audiences are rediscovering Rodgers and Hammerstein all over again. The movie of *The Sound of Music* has become a sort of international treasure, inspiring astonishing devotion — there are dozens of stories of people who have seen it hundreds, in one case over a thousand — times. Then there are the multiple-visit tourists touring Salzburg by buses which stop off at locations used in the film in order to — for instance — stand on the same steps where Julie Andrews sang "Do Re Mi" and try to hit her high C. And now there is a new phenomenon called "Singalong Sound of Music" in which devotees come fancy-dressed as nuns, or parcels (brown paper packages tied up with strings), or even as a wild goose with a moon on its wings. They know every word of the screenplay (when Maria forgets her wimple they shout "Your hat, your hat!" until she remembers and runs back up the hill, at which point everyone cheers) and every note of the soundtrack. They even let off party poppers when Maria and the Captain finally kiss.

Years before Oscar died, his son Billy Hammerstein had asked him to start working on an autobiography. Oscar pooh-poohed the idea, but Billy insisted, saying that if Oscar wouldn't settle down to a formal book, what he ought to do was to write it all down in a series of letters and send them out to Billy, who was going to California to work at Paramount. Oscar agreed, and for about three months, Billy received a daily letter from his father. Some of the stories in them were hilarious, he said, especially those about Oscar's early days in show business and vaudeville. Then work intervened; there were rehearsals for *The King and I*, then another show, and another. Oscar never did get around to resuming the letter-writing, although his sons believed he always intended to.

On the night Oscar died, his family was sitting in his study at the farm. Billy Hammerstein wandered over to the old writing desk that had been a present to Oscar from Jerome Kern many years before. On it was a sheet of yellow work paper, a note to his son written by Oscar just a few days earlier. The last thing he had written was an apology for never having finished the letters.

There was a simple funeral, attended only by Oscar's family and closest friends. The words of "Climb Ev'ry Mountain" were read, and Howard Lindsay delivered the eulogy. "We shall not grieve for him. That would be to mourn him and he would not want that. On the occasion of Gertrude Lawrence's services he said, in so many words, 'Mourning does not become the theater. Mourning is a surrender to the illusion that death is final.'"

That night, in an unprecedented salute to a great theatrical talent, the lights of every theater on Broadway and in London were dimmed for three minutes while the world he had lived in all his life paid silent homage to Oscar Hammerstein. In a professional career spanning 43 years, he had written over 1500 song lyrics, an average of 37 for every single year of his life. Among them were and are some of the most popular songs in songwriting history. He had worked with every major composer in the musical theater, written the lyrics and librettos for a total of thirty-one Broadway musicals and two more in London, lyrics only for two shows (one with Romberg, one with Rodgers), and two further shows for which he wrote librettos only. He wrote lyrics and screenplays for four movie musicals, lyrics only for five more, and the screenplays of two others, plus four "straight" plays, two non-Broadway musicals, and one television musical, *Cinderella*. He was elected to the Songwriters Hall of Fame in 1971 and the Theatre Hall of Fame a year later. It's hard to think of anyone who more deserves to be there.

The most successful collaboration in the history of the musical theater was ended. The statistics it had generated were (and still are) formidable. For 15 years — from July, 1946 to July, 1961 — *Oklahoma!* held the record as the longest-running musical in Broadway history. Four Rodgers and Hammerstein musicals passed the one thousand-performance mark: *Oklahoma!, South Pacific, The King & I*, and *The Sound of Music*. The latter was — until the arrival of the Lloyd-Webber phenomenon — the longest-running American musical in London theater history. Rodgers and Hammerstein's shows occupied the Theatre Royal, Drury Lane, continuously from April, 1947 to January, 1956 inclusive; *Oklahoma!, Carousel, The King and I*, and *South Pacific* racking up a total of 3,842 performances. Collectively, the Rodgers and Hammerstein musicals earned ten Academy Awards (Oscars, indeed!), thirty-four Tony Awards, twenty-five Donaldson Awards, two Pulitzer Prizes, two Grammy Awards, and two Emmy Awards. In 1998, R&H were cited by *Time* magazine and CBS News as among the 20 most influential artists of the 20th century, and the following year they were commemorated on a U.S. postage stamp.

*Oklahoma!, Carousel, South Pacific, The King and I, Flower Drum Song*, and *The Sound of Music* were all awarded Gold Records by the Recording Industry Association of America, signifying that the soundtrack or original cast album of each of the shows had sold more than one million dollars' worth of records. In the 1950s *Variety* reported that sales of R&H records exceeded $65 million. One can only guess at what the figures must be by now, but it's probably safe to say that whatever they are, Oscar Hammerstein would have been more than pleased: he would have been satisfied.

*I want to do something good or not do anything.*

—— Richard Rodgers

For a year, Rodgers nursed his loss. "I am permanently grieved" was all that he would say, but even his grief could not keep him away from the theater forever. As he himself said, "I was only 58 at the time of Oscar's death, and while my career had been long and fulfilling, I could not imagine spending the rest of my days reliving past glories and withdrawing from the vital, exciting world that I loved."

It was never, then, a question of whether he would team up with someone else (in fact, shortly before Oscar died he had talked informally with Alan Jay Lerner about their possible collaboration), but only when. There was something else he wanted to do first, however — whether prompted by sheer need or some antic strain of perversity (because, he said, the idea simultaneously attracted him and scared him to death) we will now never know — to try his hand at writing a show for which he provided both words and music. As a sort of practice run, he used the opportunity presented by 20th Century Fox, who had decided to remake *State Fair* yet again.

The film this time starred Pamela Tiffin (whose voice, like Jeanne Crain's in the earlier version, was ghosted — this time by Anita Gordon) and Pat Boone, with Ann-Margret and Bobby Darin (Bobby *Darin?*) supporting, and Tom Ewell taking the old Charles Winninger role. Alice Faye (who had been Fox's original choice in 1945 for the Vivian Blaine part) unwisely came out of retirement to play Ewell's wife, looking throughout like a woman who knows she's made a mistake. The whole thing was awful; Tiffin as charmless as a Barbie doll, Faye looking bored, Darin lost, and some of the production numbers — notably "Isn't it Kinda Fun," performed by Ann-Margret with all the subtlety of a Barbary Coast stripper — set new lows in poor taste. Even sadder, Rodgers's additional songs, "More Than Just a Friend," "Willing and Eager," "Never Say No to a Man," "This Isn't Heaven," and "It's the Little Things in Texas," were simply not in the same league as the five retained from the original score.

Nevertheless, the experience must have started his creative juices flowing again, for he was soon deeply involved in a couple of new projects. The first was a musical for the singer Diahann Carroll, whom he had seen performing in a television show. He remembered her from the 1954 Harold Arlen musical *House of Flowers* (with a book and some of the lyrics written by Truman Capote) which, despite a superb score, had lasted only 165 performances on Broadway. He and Oscar had also considered her for *Flower Drum Song* but couldn't find a way to make her look Asian enough. And when he got to know her, he absolutely fell for her, as pictures of them together indicate. Young, gifted, and ambitious, Carroll seems to have been more than content to become his protégé.

Rodgers's idea was to put Carroll into a show as a chic, sophisticated woman of the world rather than some kind of symbol. He thought that in doing so he might possibly help in breaking down the racial stereotyping then all too prevalent along Broadway. It was a daring idea made even more daring by adding an interracial love affair. To help him realize it, he turned to his old friend Samuel Taylor, whose play *The Happy Time* Rodgers and Hammerstein had produced. Taylor had since written two additional successful plays, both later filmed: *Sabrina Fair* and *The Pleasure of His Company*.

Although Taylor had never written the libretto for a musical (and wasn't all that keen to try), Rodgers persuaded him that he could, and they set to work on the story. "All he knew was he wanted to do a show for Diahann Carroll and somehow involve Benny Goodman," Taylor said. "If we couldn't make up a good idea, we wouldn't do it."

The idea of including Benny Goodman seems to have fallen by the wayside fairly early on, although there would be a jazz combo involved. The storyline Taylor came up with involved a black girl with no problems and a white man with nothing but. He set the story in Paris rather than America, feeling the interracial love story would work better there. Barbara Woodruff (Carroll) is an American model who meets and falls in love with David Jordan, a Pulitzer Prize-winning novelist turned expatriate sponger. Barbara tries to persuade him to return to his profession, but David prefers the easy life. Finally, she makes him see that he must do it, and he reluctantly decides to return home — alone;

267

268

**Richard Kiley, left, with Diahann Carroll and Rodgers during rehearsals of *No Strings*. You don't need a magnifying glass to see he was crazy about her.** Used by permission of the Rodgers and Hammerstein Organization.

she knows their love affair would not be countenanced in a small country town in Maine. They part, as they agreed, with no strings.

Rodgers liked the idea. "Having a black actress in the starring role would give the play an extra dimension that made it unnecessary for anything in the dialogue or action to call attention to the fact," he said. But, being Richard Rodgers, he looked around for an insurance policy, something to fall back on if the idea flopped; even as he set to work on the score, he was renewing his contact with Alan Jay Lerner.

It was no secret on Broadway that Lerner and Frederick Loewe, creators of *My Fair Lady* and *Camelot*, had split up. So reverberating had been the last explosion of temper between them that Loewe had vowed he would retire and never write another note. He was sick and tired of the whole thing, he told the world. "Do you think it's living real good to be in a hotel room in New Haven — have you ever seen a typical New Haven hotel? — eating stale sandwiches and drinking cold coffee, all because there's something wrong with the second act that only God can fix?" he kvetched. No more of that, he was going to start "living real good," shuttling from his swanky penthouse at the Dorset Hotel to his yacht on the Riviera to his house in Palm Springs. He was going to drink champagne and fine wines and surround himself with beautiful girls. And he did precisely that for most of the rest of his life, which came to an end on Valentine's Day, 1988.

Broadway matchmakers saw the pairing of the witty, elegant lyrics of Lerner and the lush, melodious music of Rodgers as guaranteed sure-fire Box Office, a marriage made in Hit Parade heaven. And it has to be said that on paper, it did look good. Both men were compulsive creators — Lerner had once said, "I write not because it is what I do, but because it is what I am; not because it is how I make my living but because it is how I make my life." It could have been Rodgers speaking. So they met and discussed a couple of ideas the lyricist was mulling over. "We hit it off right away," Lerner said. "The thought he began, I'd finish, and vice-versa. We realized we had the same attitudes toward the theater, the same ideas about casting, management and breaking of theater molds." They agreed that as soon as Dick was through with *No Strings* — the title given to the Diahann Carroll show — they would team up to work on one or another of Lerner's ideas.

*No Strings* was theatrically daring in a way few Broadway shows had been up to that time. Rodgers dispensed with an overture; he disliked them anyway. The curtain opened on a darkened stage; a spotlight picked up Carroll as, accompanied only by a flute, she sang the opening (and closing) number "The Sweetest Sounds." At the end of her first chorus, another spotlight picked up her leading man, Richard Kiley, who reprised the song with a clarinet accompaniment. With Joe Layton (a former choreographer who had worked on *The Sound of Music*) as director, Rodgers worked out a way of taking the orchestra out of the pit and putting it on the stage. "I wanted them there in order to blend the orchestral sounds with the other elements so completely that they would seem to be an integral part of the proceedings, just as much as the dialogue, the lyrics, or the action. I also wanted to eliminate the chasm between the audience and the stage that has always existed because of the orchestra pit," he said.

He went even further, indulging the whimsy of actually having "no strings" in the orchestra except for a harp and a bass violin. The score contained a number of light and felicitous songs which showed that, even if he was no Lorenz Hart or Oscar Hammerstein, Rodgers could write a professional and even admirable lyric when he had to.

> *There's a vast difference in writing lyrics as opposed to writing music. Lyric writing is mosaic work. You have to pick up little bits, little syllables and put them all together painstakingly and, naturally, slowly, which accounts for the fact that lyric writing takes up so much more time. Melody writing, on the other hand, to go into another medium, is done in broad strokes and can come quickly. I found that if it didn't come quickly for me I either went away from it entirely or just put it off and tried again, and then I'd get the whole thing very rapidly.*

270

The show had a two-month tryout, first in Detroit — where theatergoers actually walked out by the dozen when Kiley and Carroll kissed onstage — followed by Toronto, Cleveland, and New Haven. Pretty soon, the word came back to New York that it was "in trouble." Layton had tried to include a couple of dance numbers which didn't work, primarily because neither of the leading players was a dancer. Too, the shine had worn off Rodgers's infatuation with his star — or more likely, vice-versa. "There was never any of that easy give-and-take and sense of camaraderie between composer and company I had experienced with Harold Arlen," Carroll wrote later. "As time passed I came to the conclusion that [Rodgers] was really incapable of hearing someone else's point of view without regarding that person as a potential adversary, and his frequent insensitivity was appalling."

"The Sweetest Sounds," with its almost autobiographical lyric, is probably the show's best-known song, but "Look No Further" deserved more recognition than it got. "Loads of Love" (more autobiography?) and an ironic waltz called "Love Makes the World Go" were the other big numbers. It was a vivacious and romantic, if not particularly adven-

**Diahann Carroll and Richard Kiley onstage in *No Strings*.** Used by permission of the Rodgers and Hammerstein Organization.

turous score, and when *No Strings* opened at the 54th Street Theatre on March 15, 1962, even if most of them were unenthusiastic about his lyrics, the critics gave it a good send-off. Insiders, who knew how much sheer guts it had taken on Rodgers's part to do the show at all, bombarded him with telegrams, sending congratulations, wishing him good luck, and he sailed on a tide of euphoria through what he later told a correspondent he had expected to be "one of the most difficult evenings of my life." Although it was never a smash hit, *No Strings* had a very respectable 17-month run (580 performances) on Broadway, and a little over four months at Her Majesty's in London, where Beverly Todd and Art Lund took the leads.

Encouraged by the show's reception, Rodgers immersed himself in a new project for Diahann Carroll, this time set in ancient Egypt and based upon the love story of Nefertiti and Akhenaton. Sidney Michaels, whose show *Ben Franklin in Paris* Rodgers had admired, was engaged to do the libretto and Jerome Robbins was called in to discuss directing, with Giorgio Tozzi (who had provided Rossano Brazzi's voice in the movie of *South Pacific*) being considered for the male lead. The whole thing fell apart when Carroll, who blamed Rodgers when she was passed over in favor of Nancy Kwan for the proposed movie of *No Strings*, put in impossible demands for her services. Rodgers didn't like the treatment Michaels turned in anyway and put the whole thing on ice. There never was a movie of *No Strings*, either. A couple of years later, Rodgers invited Hemingway biographer A. E. Hotchner to see what he could do with it, but Hotchner couldn't make it work either; it went back into the trunk for good.

Rodgers returned now to the ideas he had discussed with Alan Jay Lerner. Lerner was keen to put together a show about dress designer Coco Chanel (he would later write it with André Previn as a vehicle for Katherine Hepburn) but he couldn't get Rodgers interested. Rodgers never said why, but Arthur Laurents may have hit on the answer. He met Rodgers by chance in London and told him he was glad Dick hadn't done the show because Chanel had collaborated with the Nazis during World War II. "I'll tell you something worse," Rodgers said. "She was a part-time dyke."

Lerner then suggested (are you braced?) a musical based on a book written by the mother of Beverly Aadland, the teenaged country girl who had become the last wife of one-time movie swashbuckler Errol Flynn in his worn-out, busted-flush days. Brace yourself even further: they actually signed Joey Heatherton to play the part and called in Robert Preston, who'd starred for three years in *The Music Man*, for the Flynn character. Mercifully for all concerned, not only would Preston have nothing to do with it, he told them forcefully they were crazy to involve themselves in such a tasteless idea. They dropped Errol Flynn like a hot brick; it would be quite a few decades more until Amanda McBroom brought him back to life.

Then Lerner told Rodgers his idea about an ordinary Brooklyn girl named Daisy who is clairvoyant; she finds out under hypnosis (she wants to quit smoking) that she has had multiple previous lives. The psychiatrist who helps her discover this falls in love with the girl she was, but can't even get interested in the dull girl she is right now. Lerner must have been one hell of a storyteller because Rodgers agreed to do the story, to which they gave the tentative title *I Picked a Daisy*. Even now Rodgers hedged his bets. Hearing Lerner had called their impending collaboration "a punctuation mark in the history of the musical theater," he begged to differ; it was, he said, a question mark. "You never know how a collaboration goes until the show is on. Alan and I are not at the end of the line, you know. There is a natural qualm, when you embark upon a new phase of your life, but it doesn't frighten me. I rather take it as a challenge."

An outline, perhaps even a first draft of a libretto was completed, and Rodgers and Lerner told the papers they had decided on Barbara Harris as their leading lady, with Gower Champion directing, perhaps Richard Burton playing the shrink, and an opening in the spring of 1963. It never happened. There was — the word "inevitably" is again unavoidable — a clash of temperaments that finally resulted in the sundering of the partnership before it had even begun (Lerner would eventually complete the show, which became 1965's *On a Clear Day You Can See Forever*, with Burton Lane, who described the experience as "the worst two years of my life").

The split came about, Lerner said, because Rodgers didn't know anything about lyric writing. He had been spoiled by Larry Hart, who could "write a lyric in the middle of a cocktail party" and clearly didn't even understand why it sometimes took Hammerstein so long. "You know what Oscar would do?" Rodgers told him. "He would go to his farm in Bucks County and sometimes it would be three weeks before he would appear with a lyric. I never knew what he was doing down there. You know a lyric couldn't possibly take three weeks." For Lerner, a lyricist who sometimes took several months to write a line, this must have been a dispiriting beginning, to say the least. On top of that there was Rodgers's preoccupation with the other minutiae of the collaboration: contracts, subsidiary rights, cast albums, movie rights. "By the time we'd discussed everything, there was no more show left to discuss," Lerner said.

From Rodgers's point of view, Lerner has to have been a major disaster. His working habits were often even more erratic than Larry Hart's had been — although for entirely different reasons. Lerner was suffering from the profession's worst disease: writer's block. Worse still, he lied about it, and lied again, and then lied even more. Lyrics would be promised — by lunch time — and never materialize. He would miss appointments with the crushingly punctual Rodgers or, worse still, disappear. Unpunctuality Rodgers might have tolerated, but to him unprofessionalism was beyond the pale. When, one holiday weekend during the summer of 1963 (which Lerner had told him he was going to use to work in the country), Rodgers telephoned to find that Lerner had gone to Capri, it was the end; the partnership was dissolved, not without hard feelings.

Only a few months earlier it had been reported that Rodgers had said, *á propos* of Larry Hart, how wonderful it felt to be writing both music and the words, and "not to

273

have to search all over the globe for that drunken little fag." Although it is difficult to believe he would ever have said such a thing out loud, there can be no doubt that deep down inside, that was exactly how he felt. So no way was he going to start again with Lerner. Publicly, however, Rodgers was philosophical about the whole thing: Lerner, he explained, had been "thrown about by an awful lot of things … It was almost impossible to get him to work. Not that he didn't want to, and there was nothing about Alan that I didn't like. He's a charming fellow, bright and certainly gifted. But I couldn't get work out of him. And because of that feeling of frustration I just stopped."

**Rodgers and a young Stephen Sondheim make nice for the camera to announce their forthcoming collaboration on *Do I Hear A Waltz?***

Used by permission of the Rodgers and Hammerstein Organization.

Privately, he was incensed and said so. "How dare this young man cause me to waste a year of my life?" he said angrily to one friend. "I don't have that much time any more." And, as if conscious of its passage, Rodgers, still determined "to keep on looking for the right partner and the right property," plunged again, and again unwisely. This time it was into the idea of a musical based upon an Arthur Laurents play, *The Time of the Cuckoo*. It had originally starred Shirley Booth in its 1952 Broadway production, and was later filmed (as *Summertime*) in 1955 with Katharine Hepburn in the leading role.

Laurents had always felt it would make a good musical and had, in 1958, even interested Oscar Hammerstein in the project. Oscar had suggested leaving it a few years until people had had time to forget the Hepburn movie (which was somewhat less than a box office smash and is, in Laurents's opinion, a travesty of the original), but he had died before the project could be revived again. Rodgers knew of Oscar's former interest in the property, and was therefore very favorably inclined towards it.

Laurents's original conception had been "a small chamber musical with bittersweet melodies by Richard Rodgers, rueful lyrics by Oscar Hammerstein, and starring Mary Martin." What he got was "Dick, Steve Sondheim … but not Mary Martin. Dick thought she was too old and since he was the producer, he had the money, so he had the final say. But never mind. A score by Rodgers and Sondheim? Savor the songs, dry the martinis, cash the checks!"

It must have looked like a marvelous idea. Stephen Sondheim had been a protégé of Oscar's. He had already made a substantial reputation for himself, notably with the lyrics for *West Side Story* and *Gypsy*. Young, fresh, bursting with talent, the hottest kid on Broadway, he could put back into Rodgers's music the kind of sardonic kick that Larry Hart had once done. It should have been a dream team. Instead, it turned out to be a nightmare.

"He [Rodgers] had previously asked me to write songs with him," Sondheim said, "and although I didn't want just to write lyrics again, I told Dick I'd be honored to write with him if a project came up that excited me." Hoping against hope that such a project never would, Sondheim found himself with his back against the wall when he was pressed to do the Laurents-Rodgers show by Arthur Laurents and by Dick's daughter, Mary. He agreed to do it, and that was the first mistake. "After all," Laurents reasoned, "Dick knew Steve when Steve was a smartass whiz kid and Dick was a legend. Now this was a peer who was on the way up, and he was on the way down. Rodgers was feeling very keenly that he was old-fashioned. And he was."

They called the project *Do I Hear A Waltz?* The idea behind it was straightforward: to do something that would make a lot of money. That was the second mistake. There were to be plenty more. Elizabeth Allen was selected for the role of Leona (the lady who goes to Venice in search of love) after Anne Bancroft had been considered, and Mary Martin rejected. The male lead was played by Sergio Franchi, and John Dexter, assistant director of London's National Theatre, was brought in to direct. All these choices were nails in the show's coffin, as was the decision early on not to have any dancing in the show. It was all supposed to be a musical feast, but it never even approached that ideal.

Insecurities lurking just beneath the skin erupted; cracks which had been papered over reappeared. The show was a mess because it had no real *raison d'être*. By the time they opened in New Haven for the tryout on February 1, 1965, they knew they had to do something drastic. Herbert Ross was brought in to assist in the enormous job of putting some dances into a danceless show, but he found he could make little headway. The factions had polarized. Rodgers was insisting that the roles be played sentimentally;

**Rodgers, Sondheim, and Arthur Laurents working on three different shows called *Do I Hear A Waltz?* The man with his back to the camera is director John Dexter, who may have been working on a fourth version. Photofest.**

Laurents and Sondheim wanted a tough, dry interpretation. Liz Allen was in shreds, Franchi sterile; they had nothing to work with. When Rodgers would come into the theater, everyone would say, "Here comes Godzilla." Much, much later he told Sheldon Harnick, "In the theater it was me on one side of the aisle and all of *them* on the other. And it was a very lonely experience."

And as a result, he began drinking again. At one meeting in the Rodgers apartment, Laurents noticed that Rodgers frequently broke off the discussion and went into the men's room. Something clicked in Laurents's mind, a scene from the movie *The Lost Weekend*, in which Ray Milland played an alcoholic. When the opportunity arose, he went into the bathroom and checked. Sure enough, there was a bottle of vodka stashed in the water tank. Later, when they were trying out the show in Boston, Rodgers "drank in the men's room ... Standing guard at the door so his boss could put away the vodka undisturbed was Jerry Whyte. Jerry was Dick's man Friday, every day; he accepted with a shrug that Dick was boozing in the men's room just as he accepted that the music for the show wasn't Dick at his best or anywhere near it. He said as much to me, sensing, I think, that I still had hopes. Jerry was a fact-facer."

A haunting equivalence begins to take shape here, that of an alcoholic with a waning talent protected by his minder, his gofer and — there's plenty of evidence to support the accusation — procurer, a man whom everyone but he detests, but who is tolerated because of the respect everyone has for the alcoholic. Whyte (né Jerkowitz) was a big husky blond ex-rum runner, gambler, and womanizer, who, since the days of *Pal Joey*, had been Rodgers's shadow and closest confidant. He got him whatever he wanted: liquor, girls, anything. In other words, he was to Rodgers exactly what the loathsome Doc Bender had been to Larry Hart, and was detested for exactly the same reasons. Could anything be sadder than that?

Everything went well until the reviews came in for the tryouts and the changes began. The more they worked on them, the more tense things became. In his autobiography, Laurents captions a backstage photograph taken during rehearsals as "Dick Rodgers, Steve Sondheim, and I working on three different shows with the same title, i.e., *Do I Hear A Waltz?*" There's your trouble. Communications had broken down; Rodgers hated what he perceived as the in-crowd atmosphere being generated by Laurents, Sondheim, and Dexter, and was scathing about many of Sondheim's offerings. One day, out of town,

**Elizabeth Allen (Leona) and Sergio Franchi (Renato), the star-crossed lovers of *Do I Hear A Waltz?* (1965).**
Used by permission of the Rodgers and Hammerstein Organization.

**Norman Wisdom (Androcles) and Noel Coward (Caesar) in *Androcles and the Lion*. (1967).** Photofest.

278

Sondheim came in with a new lyric. In front of the entire company Rodgers said, "This is shit! I'm not going to let my singers sing shit like this!" *His* singers, note. Sondheim marched angrily off the stage and told Jerry Whyte he'd had it. "I'm not taking any more from him," he seethed. "I'm leaving." Whyte talked him down, told him he had to try to understand what was happening to Rodgers. Reluctantly, Sondheim allowed himself to be convinced and stayed on; but now he hated the experience too.

"It was a workmanlike, professional show," Sondheim said later. "Period. And it deserved to fail." Even so, the book is lively and there are moments when the underrated score makes the listener wish Rodgers and Sondheim had tried harder: two songs in the second scene of Act One — "This Week, Americans" and "What Do We Do? We Fly!" — have a zest and gaiety worthy of Larry Hart, while the lilting waltz which takes the show's title is both charming and unusual. They were, however, a long way from being enough in a season which also produced *Fiddler on the Roof.* One wonders whether it would have worked better had Laurents admitted then that the central character was based on him, and had the leading role been played by a man.

Since Rodgers was producer as well as composer, what he said was law, so many of the faults of *Do I Hear A Waltz?* must be laid at his door. The blame for Broadway disasters usually falls on poor direction, poor choreography, a poor score, a poor book, or poor acting. Invariably, however, it is the producer who is at the root of the trouble. A producer's job is infinitely more complex than merely raising capital. He has to see that the right people are in the right jobs, and that they get along with each other. He has to see that every fragment of the show, from the props to the lights to the costumes to the songs to the script to the actors to the electricians to the theater are absolutely correct. It is his job to ensure that when the show opens, it is ready to open. Rodgers and Hammerstein had been sensational producers. Rodgers alone appears to have been less sensational.

*Do I Hear A Waltz?* opened on March 18, 1965, at the 46<sup>th</sup> Street Theatre, and ran for 220 performances, which was far short of what was needed to pay off its $450,000 investment. Rodgers was always reluctant to talk about the experience. As late as 1973, he was asked to comment on a *Newsweek* cover story on Sondheim, in which Sondheim described Oscar Hammerstein as a man of limited talent but infinite soul and Rodgers as a man of infinite talent and limited soul. "The less said, the better," Rodgers said, and said no more.

In 1967, Rodgers was approached by NBC to write a score for a television adaptation of George Bernard Shaw's *Androcles and the Lion* — perhaps aiming for a *My Fair Lion*, as someone cynically remarked. Apparently undismayed by the bizarre casting — English pratfaller Norman Wisdom as Androcles, Noel Coward playing Caesar (basically, Noel Coward in a toga) — Rodgers produced lyrics and music for the show, which premiered on November 15 of that year. The songs were apposite but bland, and none of them has lasted — perhaps because, as one critic remarked, martyrdom and musical comedy do not mix. Rodgers devoted exactly seven lines to the show in his autobiography. We shall follow his example.

He had by now reluctantly concluded that he would never again have the kind of long-term working relationship he had once had with Larry Hart and again with Oscar Hammerstein. He filled his time by acting as overseer of the music publishing empire he and Oscar had created. If a good idea for a musical came along, he was always open to ideas. "I would like to do more," he said. "I would hate at this age to feel I couldn't do anything new, that I was not progressing, or even worse that I couldn't do anything more." In 1967 he financed a new play by Sam Taylor called *Avanti!* with Morrie Jacobs and Jerry Whyte fronting as producers and Keith Baxter playing a cheerfully amoral bisexual. It opened on January 31, 1968, and lasted 21 performances. He flirted briefly with the idea of doing a musical based on Earl Hamner's novel *You Can't Get There from Here* with a libretto by Erich Segal, but it never happened. So he did the only thing he could do: he sat and waited.

279

# Finale Ultimo

*Somebody asked Dick Rodgers what he did before he was a songwriter. He said, "I was a baby."*

—— Sheldon Harnick

Musicals had changed vastly, drastically. The revolution that Richard Rodgers had himself helped to bring about a quarter of a century earlier was now paradoxically responsible for his being unable to find another show. One of the major factors in this was the astonishing escalation in the costs of producing a new musical. Whereas in 1943, something as economically staged as *Oklahoma!* could be produced for $83,000, the more lavish *Me and Juliet*, which came ten years later, cost four times as much, and in 1960 the sumptuously spectacular *Camelot* ate up $650,000. That kind of money up front was a lot of risk to take, and backers were understandably nervous about taking it.

Nevertheless, when Rodgers announced that he would write the score for a new show based on Clifford Odets's 1954 play *The Flowering Peach* about Noah and the Flood, the auguries were again good. The libretto was to be by Peter Stone, who had worked with Rodgers on *Androcles and the Lion*, and just had a big (and unexpected) hit with *1776*, a musical about the American Revolution. The lyrics would be provided by Martin Charnin, who had done a couple of off-Broadway shows with Dick's daughter Mary, a promising composer and author (*Once Upon a Mattress, The Mad Show, Freaky Friday*).

The original idea came from Charnin. "I was very fond of the [Noah] character," the lyricist says, this "feisty, intractable 600-year-old Jew" as originally played by Menasha Skulnik. "We were six or seven years away from *Fiddler on the Roof*, so theoretically a Jewish musical — one that was indeed Biblical as well as Jewish — would maybe have a good shot. I'd known Peter [Stone] from around, although my experiences on Broadway had been minimal … and I was very fond of his work. And he cottoned to it immediately, thought it was a really nifty idea and he saw it in the same way I did … and we then went to Dick with the idea."

Rodgers liked the idea and agreed it was worth going ahead. Privately he decided that if he was going to do the show, he was going to call the shots. "A meeting or two later, Peter and I found that Dick had optioned the property," Charnin recalls. "Which meant we were not only working with him, but working for him. He had put the money up. That meant he had the veto." What could they do? They went ahead anyway.

When Steve Sondheim heard about the project, Charnin recalls, he warned him off. "In fact he went out of his way to scare the shit out of me and here's what he did. He said 'Okay, we'll improvise. You be you, I'll be Dick. Now — scribble the first lyric you've written on a sheet of paper and hand it to me.'" Charnin did as he was bid. "Okay, here's what he'll do to your first lyric," Sondheim said. He crumpled up the piece of paper, threw it in Charnin's face, then walked out of the room.

The musical, *Two by Two*, which would deal with Noah, the flood, and such then-topical themes as ecology, the generation gap, and atomic extermination, was announced in June, 1969; the following month, Rodgers was felled by a heart attack. Fortunately — for him and for all concerned — he was in the hospital having a checkup when it happened. "I never felt fear at any time," he wrote of the experience. "My attitude was not merely one of hope or expectation; just as in the case of my cancerous jaw, I was sure I'd pull through." Say what you will about his other failings, this man simply would not be stopped. He had always been a survivor, and at this time he had something to survive for: a new show. He had beaten cancer, now he put cardiac arrest behind him. As soon as they signed him out of the hospital in August he was back at work, supervising auditions, staging, casting.

One of their first steps had been to sign Danny Kaye for the role of Noah. Some were surprised: Kaye's film career, which had begun so brightly with *Wonder Man* and *Up in Arms* at Sam Goldwyn's glossy studios in the late '40s, had foundered and he had become

**Rodgers with Danny Kaye before the opening of *Two by Two* (1970). Later, Dick didn't smile anything like as much.**
Used by permission of the Rodgers and Hammerstein Organization.

a sort of roving ambassador for UNICEF. Although press reports at the time mentioned Zero Mostel, Charnin says Kaye was "the first person who came to mind. There was not a single dissent from any quarter." His and Stone's original idea had been for it to be a *Jewish* musical, with a story Menasha Skulnick could have played, but "Dick didn't want to do any of that." "That came as a bit of a surprise," Stone said. "I don't understand how the show appealed to him without that." He also found Rodgers evasive and difficult to pin down. "If you wanted to talk to the composer he had on his producer's hat," Stone recalled. "And when you wanted to talk to the producer you got the composer."

The writers went out to California and worked with Kaye on the libretto and lyrics. "We were a little bit terrified that Sylvia [Fine, Kaye's wife and acknowledged Svengali] would get into the act," Charnin said. "But she was as generous as she could possibly be. But somehow Peter and I began to 'Dannify' it, if such a word exists, putting in aspects of what he was known for, some 'stuff.' What I did was I opened the door for what came later."

The biggest problem with staging the show arose, he said, from Joe Layton's wanting to do something that would get him a credit like Jerry Robbins got for *The King and I*. Layton's "concept" was that when Noah convinces everyone there is going to be a flood, they dismantle the house board by board and carry it offstage. Then, at the opening of Act Two, there is the ark, built out of the same boards. "And as a result," Charnin smiled, "*Two by Two* is a musical about schlepping wood on and off the stage — hell, we even rehearsed in a lumber yard. My first memory of the show is wood. The whole bloody musical smelled like wood. The Shubert Theatre in Boston to this day smells of wood!"

His partnership with Rodgers, however, did not turn out to be the horror story Steve Sondheim had predicted. The fact that seven songs were abandoned before the New York opening hints at some tensions, but "it was a very pleasant collaboration, although of

282

course Dick was much older than me, so it was a formal collaboration and very much how Dick was then with everybody. And as far as I was concerned, 90 percent of those songs were splendid Richard Rodgers melodies. No matter what you say about the quality, you could identify them immediately as his — it's a really good score. It also has one of the best ballads Dick ever wrote — 'I Do Not Know A Day I Did Not Love You' — that's a glorious ballad ... but something in Dick's heart quit on the musical — and I don't know what it was. I just don't know."

"The show didn't work because every one of us was working on a different show," Stone said, oddly echoing what Arthur Laurents said about *Do I Hear A Waltz?*. "Charnin and I were doing one show, which was the Odets concept of Noah's family being a lower middle-class Jewish family from Queens. Rodgers wanted something less Jewish, less lower class, more lyrical, which was his experience. Layton wanted stage magic and brought in concepts that only hurt the show. And Danny Kaye was interested in being Danny Kaye."

*Two by Two* opened at the Imperial Theatre on November 10, 1970, and as Charnin puts it, "Danny did Danny." The show eventually ran for more than a year, but not necessarily because it was great. In February, 1971, Kaye fractured his ankle during a performance. He returned to the show with his leg in a cast, and proceeded to adapt the whole thing around his infirmity, riding around the stage in a wheelchair trying to run down the other actors, goosing the girls with his crutch, improvising lines, and altering lyrics and tempos. "He wasn't just very naughty," Charnin says, "he was outrageous. The Imperial backs on to the 46th Street Theatre — the Richard Rodgers as it now is — where Ruby Keeler was playing in *No!, No!, Nanette!* and he would race over to the proscenium and yell 'Stop that tapping!' "

At the end of his performances — and "performances" was what they were — Kaye would tell the audience that he was glad that they had come and even gladder the authors hadn't. People went to see the show for the same reasons they had many years earlier gone to see *Hellzapoppin'*: word had gotten around that you never knew what was going to happen next, except that it would be anything but what you expected. Nothing Rodgers or anyone else could do or say succeeded in making Kaye stick to the original script. He *was* the show; take him off, it was finished. In the end, they washed their hands of the whole thing, and left it alone. It is not, however, inapposite to note that Kaye never appeared on the Broadway stage again.

Troubles continued to beset Richard Rodgers. In May, 1972, in the midst of extensive plans to celebrate his 70th birthday with a "Rodgers Birthday Salute" at the Imperial Theatre, Dorothy Rodgers suffered a coronary thrombosis and, although she recovered,

283

**Danny Kaye doing his thing. One night Rodgers sent him a telegram that said "I am at the back of the theater. Wish you were here."** Used by permission of the Rodgers and Hammerstein Organization.

was hospitalized for several months. His throat was giving him constant trouble, and his voice kept petering out. He persisted, appearing before the cameras for a salute to his old partner Larry Hart when the University of Southern California devoted an evening to the memory of the lyricist, and again for Tony Palmer, who filmed Rodgers for his television series *All You Need Is Love*. He was already working on his "autobiography" — it was actually ghosted by musicologist Stanley Green — which would be published in 1975. He was also noodling with the idea of a musical version of *Arsenic and Old Lace*, coproduced by himself and Hal Prince, with Sheldon Harnick as his lyricist. Harnick recalled:

> *Dick had asked me before — while I was still working with Jerry Bock — if I would be interested in collaborating, then after I stopped working with Jerry he called and asked if I would do a version of* Arsenic and Old Lace. *We had a book by Michael Stewart but both Dick and I felt that Stewart had not left room for any music. Like any well-constructed suspense story it was very tight and there was no room for music. We called in about six other writers, Michael Stewart just gave us the book and said "Do what you want with it." And they all said "It can't be done." But Dick Rodgers was stubborn — he thought, "No, it can be done."*

285

The last writer they discussed the project with was Tom Stoppard, who took the book back to London with him, promising to come back to them in two weeks with a synopsis if he thought it could be done.

> *So two weeks later, sure enough, a synopsis arrived, and the only thing he had created that was original was that the show would begin with a musical number in which the twelve corpses in Heaven did a song and a tap-dance and then they went down to their graves in the cellar — and then the show began. And at that point Dick said "No, I guess this can't be done."*

In the spring of 1974, producer Richard Adler, no mean songwriter himself (*The Pajama Game, Damn Yankees*), called Harnick and told him he wanted to do a show about Henry VIII. Dick Rodgers would be writing the music with a book by Jerome Lawrence and Robert Lee, who had written *Mame*. According to Harnick:

> *To tell you the truth I was not too wild about the idea because Henry is not one of my heroes. But Dick Adler is a wonderful salesman and he kind of talked me into the idea that Henry is larger than life, which means that he's theatrical and as he said, hardly a year goes by that there isn't a TV show, a play, or a movie, something. He said he remains endlessly fascinating and it's high time somebody did a musical about him. But before we could even get started Dick went into the hospital for a laryngectomy and we all thought well, that's the end of that project.*

This happened in the early summer of 1974, when Rodgers's persistent hoarseness was diagnosed as cancer of the larynx and, unable to avoid the inevitable any longer, he underwent a laryngectomy. Although the operation was a success, it required Rodgers to devote a great deal of time to mastering what is known as esophageal speech, but even that was not enough to keep him away from assisting in the production of a revue conceived by his old casting director John Fearnley and Dick's cousin, Richard Lewine, called

**Sheldon Harnick and Richard Rodgers working on** *Rex:* **"Somewhere in songwriter's Heaven he's saying, 'See, I told you it was a good show!'"** Used by permission of the Rodgers and Hammerstein Organization.

*Rodgers and Hart.* Produced by Lester Osterman, Jr., this "musical celebration" opened on May 13, 1975, a bright *Babes-in-Arms*-ish presentation of some of the best-known (and also some of the least-performed) songs in the Rodgers and Hart songbook. The show was not a great success, although it was a treat to hear audiences chuckling at the felicity of some of Larry Hart's lyrics.

Despite the limitations placed upon him by his inability to talk — in an interview with me soon after the operation, all he would grudgingly say about it was "sometimes it's a bloody nuisance" — Rodgers was already deeply involved with a major new show by the time *Rodgers and Hart* premiered at the Helen Hayes Theatre. This was Richard Adler's Henry VIII musical, *Rex,* which had come back to life now that Dick had declared himself available again. Sheldon Harnick said:

> *One of the things I learned to love about Richard Rodgers was that he*
> *was the quintessential realist — whatever happened, happened. You*
> *didn't brood about it, you just got past it. So as soon as it was practical,*
> *he went to a special school to learn esophageal speech. Then we would*
> *begin to have meetings where he would have a pad and a pencil, but he*
> *was practicing his speech on us. And one time he was trying to tell an*
> *anecdote about* Oklahoma! *and he just couldn't get what he wanted to*
> *say out, and he rolled his eyes up at the ceiling. Then he wrote it on the*
> *pad, and it was "Rouben Mamoulian."*

287

Rodgers had rejected Lawrence and Lee's outline — a play-within-a-play concept that had a troupe of strolling players telling the story — and Sherman Yellen, who had worked with Harnick on *The Rothschilds,* was brought in as writer. Michael Bennett was approached to direct, but his asking price after *A Chorus Line* was too high. Hal Prince said no, so the job went to a relatively untried actor-director, Edwin Sherin. Nicol Williamson would play Henry, and Penny Fuller (who had been a big hit in the Lauren Bacall musical *Applause,* based on the movie *All About Eve*) would play both Henry's wife Anne Boleyn and his daughter Elizabeth.

*Rex* was the story of Henry VIII's quest for a male heir, his succession of wives, and his ruthless machinations to satisfy his personal desires and ambitions. Why any one of them or all of them collectively should have thought that there was anything left to say on the subject after — for it was after — Keith Michell's definitive renderings of Henry on television (followed by a further series about Elizabeth I of England starring Glenda

Jackson, and a veritable tide of tie-in books on every aspect of Tudor England) is open to conjecture. To make matters even more precarious, Rodgers had suffered a slight stroke that impaired his walking. But they went ahead. Harnick recalled that

> the notion of working with Richard Rodgers was exciting and also intimidating. Mary [Rodgers] (we'd written a few things together) alerted me. She said, "What will you do if you give my father a lyric and he says, 'I don't like it?' Or what if he writes music that you don't like, can you handle that?" I said, "I think so" but I also have to say it was difficult. What was difficult was that because of his stroke it had become impossible for him to write music unless he had words. The first lyric I took to him was the lullaby, "Elizabeth" and he looked at it and he frowned and he grunted, and I thought, "Oh, he hates it, he hates it, he hates it." But about a week later his secretary called and said, "Mr. Rodgers would like to play you the music." I went over there and he limped over to the piano and about halfway he turned around and said, "I'll probably fuck it up." And I thought, "My God, he's as nervous as I am!" Which to me was astonishing. Well, because of his physical condition he couldn't play well anymore, but he played it well enough so I could see what the song was and it was beautiful. And I said, "Oh, Dick, it's beautiful" (that was the first time I called him "Dick" and not "Mr. Rodgers") and he sort of slumped at the piano and said, "Oh, when I left the house this morning Dorothy said 'Oh, God, I hope he likes it.'" And this was such a revelation to me.

288

Later, he "began to feel that the opportunity to do another score was a gift to [Rodgers], a bonus in his life. I tell you, when we started he was a sick old man and as we worked the years just fell away from him. It was just remarkable. That was what he lived to do — to write."

On February 23, 1976, *Rex* began its tryouts in Wilmington, Delaware, and right away they saw they had problems. "We started out with a very simple concept," Harnick said. "This is a show about a man who believes that the only way to hold England together after he dies is to put a son on the throne. So he turns England upside down to get that son that he's after. And what he cannot see, is unable to see, is that he already has that son. It just happens that she's a girl, Elizabeth, and he can't accept it. And our ending was

***Rex:*** **With Rodgers at the piano, Nicol Williamson, Penny Fuller, and Sheldon Harnick meet for rehearsal.**
Photo courtesy Penny Fuller.

that he finally sees what she is and on his deathbed he accepts her. But we made a dreadful mistake. All through the first act he's saying 'I must have a son, I must have a son.' At the end of Act One he has a son, Edward. Fireworks go off. And the audience goes out thinking, 'So it's a show about a man who needs a son. He's got a son. Do we need to come back for the second act?' "

After the opening matinee performance there was a staff meeting at which a shaken Nicol Williamson observed, accurately, "They *hated* me out there!" to which Harnick beamed "Yeah! That's because he's a monster!" Williamson replied, "Sheldon, the show is called *Rex.* I'm the protagonist. They *can't* hate me. They can half-hate me if they understand why I'm doing what I'm doing, but they can't just hate me altogether. Otherwise, change the show, call it *Elizabeth* or *Catherine*, then they can hate me as much as they want, but I'm the *hero,* and you've got to give me material which makes the audience say 'Aha! Now we understand why he's doing what he's doing.'"

Penny Fuller, who played the taxing dual parts of Anne Boleyn and the young Elizabeth, recalled the fraught atmosphere. "I kept thinking this isn't working, this isn't

**Penny Fuller as Anne Boleyn in** *Rex.* Photo courtesy Penny Fuller.

290

working," she said. "My sense of what was the most dramatic thing in it, the really interesting thing, was the triangle, Henry, Anne, and Elizabeth, yet they just didn't seem to see this, everybody had to be in it, every queen. And I thought, am I crazy? Why is no one seeing this? And then I thought, Well, what do I know? There's Richard Rodgers and Sheldon Harnick and Sherman Yellen and all those people — and I concluded I must be wrong because they all know so much more than I do."

After a week they moved to Washington, rewriting, restaging, cutting, adding. The basic problem was still the book, but as Penny Fuller observed, "It was a hybrid. If it were written today, it would be much darker. It was clear to everyone that it didn't work but nobody knew what to put in its place — really what it needed was someone to take an ax to it — it was top-heavy with everything."

They also had serious problems with their King. "He was having wife trouble, show trouble — *in extremis,*" Penny Fuller said. "He was not having a good time." Harnick agreed. "Four of those six weeks [on the road] he was so worried about being accepted as a singer that he didn't act the songs as much as he should have. He was so worried about his singing and about the show that he began to give ultimatums, and it was almost like a challenge, like, If you don't like it, fire me, I'll be *happy* to leave this show. So it wound up with the tail wagging the dog and even when Hal Prince came aboard he said 'How do I handle Nicol? — he's used to having his own way.' And there was not much we could do about it. He was very difficult."

And of course, the worse it gets, the worse it gets. Even in the scenes where Yellen had given him charming dialogue — for Henry was a charmer — Williamson sulkily refused to play it that way. "He had his own conception of Henry, who was a dark soul, a dour soul, and he played him as dark and dour — and generally speaking he didn't do what we wanted him to do," Harnick recalled. At one curtain call there was a nasty incident when one of the male chorus said "Well, that's a wrap," which Williamson heard as "Well, that was crap." His frayed temper snapped and he slapped the man across the face. Whatever caused it, the incident was indefensible, and needless to say, word got out; it did neither Williamson nor the show any good at all.

Lyricist Harnick was surprised by Rodgers's lack of involvement. "It was my impression that in the past he had always, to one extent or another, gotten involved in the book, or at least made his feelings known. But as far I could see, he chose not to with this show, as though he only had so much strength and he would conserve it for the score." He needed to: in all, Rodgers would write 26 songs for *Rex*, some little better than musical exposition, a way of trying to help the audience understand Henry. At one point when Harnick apologized for imposing such demands on him, Rodgers shrugged. "This is nothing," he said. "You never worked with Danny Kaye."

In Boston, the producers panicked and called in Hal Prince, who performed major surgery. Scenes were telescoped, others scrapped, songs rewritten, others cut — including Anne's lovely lament "So Much You Loved Me" (its melody echoed in the original version by Henry's second act song to his daughter, "From Afar"). Prince restaged what everyone (now) agrees was the truest ending, jettisoning in the process the beautifully autumnal "The Pears of Anjou." "He had some wonderful ideas," Harnick said, "but everything he put in threw something else out."

On Sunday night, April 25, 1976, *Rex* opened at the Lunt-Fontanne Theatre, the same theater that had played *The Sound of Music* seven years earlier. At the end of the performance, the company signaled for Rodgers to join them onstage and the entire audience gave him a standing ovation. But the critics descended upon the show tooth and claw. *Time* magazine was typical. Henry, it said, was a "male chauvinist executioner" and "although Rodgers is incapable of writing an uningratiating tune ... several of the numbers seem more suitable for rocking a cradle than stirring a realm." *The New York Times* critic Clive Barnes was no kinder: he called it "one of the most interminable musicals in years." Williamson's reaction to the reviews was typical: "They can all stick them up their arses!" he snarled at the post-premiere party at Sardi's.

The show was a massive and catastrophically expensive failure which no effort by Rodgers or anyone else was able to prevent. Rodgers felt that his score was a good one, and indeed, several of the songs, including "Away From You" and a lilting waltz, "No

Song More Pleasing," are more than worthy of inclusion in the Rodgers songbook. Nevertheless, the show closed after only 49 performances. Although it must have hurt, Rodgers shrugged it off. "I never take success for granted," he said. "If you get up to bat often enough, it's very easy to fail. I've always known that."

Taking a longer view, perhaps he didn't fail at all. In the fall of 2000, Harnick and Yellen revised the original concept for one of James Morgan's "Musicals in Mufti" series at the York Theatre in New York, adding new scenes and restoring four good songs which had been cut. They found that the show not only "worked" but was actually the moving and powerful story they had all been trying to create. Would Rodgers have approved? Harnick thinks so. "Somewhere in songwriter's Heaven, he's saying 'See, I told you it was a good show.'"

On September 18, 1975, Rodgers's autobiography *Musical Stages* was published, and there was a party backstage at the Winter Garden Theatre attended by many of the alumni of his shows, including Edith Meiser, Vera Zorina, Constance Carpenter, and Celeste Holm. Also on hand were Armina Marshall, Joe Fields's widow Marian, Richard Adler, and, over there in the corner, someone called Frederick Nolan. Believe it or not, Rodgers even did some bookshop signings, although the autobiography itself, which failed even to mention the matter of Larry Hart's homosexuality and glossed over most of its subject's own personal problems, was a major disappointment to both its publisher and its readers.

Rodgers got a further small consolation prize in the summer of 1976 when the Circle in the Square revived *Pal Joey* as part of the 1975-6 season of plays marking its 25th Anniversary, but in that show, too, artistic temperaments clashed, and it was not the success it could have been. In 1977, Rodgers's 75th year, there was another highly successful revival of one of his biggest successes: *The King and I*, starring the original King, Yul Brynner, with Constance Towers as Anna, celebrating that show's silver jubilee. If anything, Brynner — older, heavier — was a better King now than he had been in the original: the show ran for an amazing 695 performances.

After *Rex*, nobody seriously expected Rodgers to write another show, yet astonishingly, that was exactly what he did, and this time with one of the hottest teams in town — Martin Charnin and Thomas Meehan, who had just triumphed with the "Tomorrow" musical, *Annie*.

Charnin had seen Liv Ullman in a revival of *Anna Christie* presented by Alexander Cohen and she was a sensation. He told Cohen he wanted to star her in a musical he and Meehan had written based on the John Van Druten play *I Remember Mama*. Although Charles Strouse had written the music for *Annie*, Charnin wanted to do this score himself. Cohen persuaded him that the story cried out for Richard Rodgers.

292

"I'd figured he couldn't write any more," Charnin said. "But he knew me. I was friendly with Mary. It was a pretty serviceable book. And it was safe — he didn't have to make a new connection with somebody. He wanted the show on, he wanted another show on Broadway very, very badly. So what? Believe me, he deserved every good thing that was done for him. He was frail, of course, which meant that instead of three hours we would work an hour and a half and he would retire."

It didn't take long for them to discover they had made the "classic mistake," as Cohen called it, of being in love with the idea of Rodgers writing again, and more than that, of his writing for Liv Ullman. Then, when she came to Rodgers's office, they realized her singing didn't work and was destined never to work: she couldn't even carry the tune of "Happy Birthday To You." "At the moment you know something is wrong is the moment when you should call a halt," Cohen said. Of course, no one did.

So when they got to work they had a problem from day one: "Madame Ullmann," as Charnin puts it. "Artistic differences made it impossible for me to get any work out of her. I'm not making this up, I know it for a fact, she couldn't sing the songs. She was not a Broadway musical performer. She didn't have me as a supporter and she didn't know where to turn. I don't know, I didn't know what she wanted. Ingmar Bergman, maybe."

Ullmann took her grievances to the producers claiming Charnin had "stabbed her in the back." The show was clearly heading for disaster so Cohen bit the bullet, fired Charnin and called in Cy Feuer to fix things. "Hardly the instant choice to (a) deal with Ullmann and (b) solve this piece," in Charnin's opinion. "And I did not have that moment where I went to Dick and said, 'Can you stop this?' He was weak in spirit and weak in body and he didn't fight for me, which was a great disappointment to me as a director." When Feuer also fired him as lyricist, Charnin sent wires to all his friends — a wry reworking of the automobile advertising campaign that promised "There's a Ford in your future." It said GUESS WHAT? THERE'S NO FJORD IN MY FUTURE!

"I was brought into *I Remember Mama* after it had opened in Philadelphia," Feuer says. "I realized there was something fundamentally wrong with it. I said to Alex Cohen 'I can't make a hit out of this, but I think I can keep you from getting arrested.'" Feuer saw at once that there would have to be extensive changes ("It had to be done the way the original was done," he said) and he started to make them. His first move was to replace with one actress playing both parts the two actresses who were playing the "young" Katrine who is a participant in the story and the "adult" Katrine who is the narrator. He also brought in a new choreographer, altered the ending of Act One, and threw out three songs. Dorothy Rodgers — Dick had always kept her away from his world, but

**Rodgers with Liv Ullman, the star of *I Remember Mama*.** Used by permission of the Rodgers and Hammerstein Organization.

she was on hand most of the time now — was outraged, but Dick waved her protests aside. "We're digging a ditch here," he said. "The hell with all that."

Mrs. Rodgers did put her foot very firmly down, however, when Feuer, casting around for a lyricist to replace Charnin, proposed bringing in Sammy Cahn to work with Dick. In fact, it was a brilliant idea, but even though teaming Rodgers's music with Cahn's jaunty lyrics might well have created the small miracle they needed to lift the show, Dorothy Rodgers would have none of it. Cahn, she said, was simply not "theater," not their kind of people. Feuer compromised by calling in Raymond Jessel, a television writer who had worked with the producers, but in the final analysis only four of Jessel's lyrics found their way into the finished show. In all, Rodgers created 26 melodies, half of which were dropped.

Now Feuer buckled down to his real problem. "Liv Ullman was the most magnificent Mama I have ever seen," he said. "She was made for it, with her hair done up in the traditional way. I told her we were going to make changes, major, major changes. I said there might be weeks and weeks of that, and doing it was going to be very difficult for her. She said, 'Let me think it over' and next day she came in and said, 'I'm prepared to do it if you're prepared for my temperament. I'm willing to do it but I'm going to be upset and you're going to have to contend with that.' And she was astonishing. Whatever we wrote, she played. She was quite remarkable. "But," he added — and it was a huge "but" — "Liv Ulllmann does not belong on the musical stage. She doesn't. And consequently, it didn't work."

*I Remember Mama* opened at the Majestic Theatre on May 31, 1979. "It was respectable," Feuer said, "but Liv didn't belong up there." In fact, as anyone who saw her will tell you, she did. She was no Mary Martin, of course, but she was lovely, touching, and warm; it was the show that let her down, not the other way around. As a musical, *I Remember Mama* was curiously lumpen, here mistily romantic, there heavy-handedly unfunny, with a singing family all too reminiscent of *The Sound of Music,* and never quite a thing of its own. The critical reaction was at best tepid, and although Alex Cohen tried to keep it running because Dick was approaching his 80th birthday, the audiences didn't come. The show closed after 108 performances. It had some lovely songs, notably Mama's now-loving, now-cross lament to her husband, "Lars, Lars," and the "big" love song, "You Could Not Please Me More," which Martin Charnin still thinks was a "giant" Rodgers melody.

On the testimony of his family, after *Mama* Rodgers just turned himself off. Perhaps he was partially consoled by the enthusiastic critical reception given to Billy Hammerstein's wonderful revival of *Oklahoma!* which opened at the Palace Theatre on December 13, 1979, but we will

**The program for *I Remember Mama*.** Author's Collection.

never know. Richard Rodgers died peacefully at home just one day short of the new decade, December 30, 1979. As they had when Oscar Hammerstein II died, all the theaters on Broadway and in London went dark for one minute in his memory. His body was cremated; where his ashes were scattered, no one knows. There is no grave and no memorial. Unless, of course, you count the songs — a thousand of them — and the forty-three musicals, the ten movie musicals, the television scores, a six-decade cornucopia of melody unequalled by any other American composer.

In the two decades since Richard Rodgers's death more than a few people have stepped up and kicked the dead lion. Most recently, an autobiography by Arthur Laurents cruelly exposed Rodgers's drinking problems, following which the composer's daughters revealed to the world at large what formerly only a few intimates had known: that he had suffered from frequent and severe depressions, that he was an unfeeling parent, unable to sustain meaningful relationships, a compulsive womanizer, and a lifelong alcoholic.

That all this was indeed true no one would seek to deny, but for one writer, anyway, the fact Rodgers was a deeply unhappy human being doesn't make him any the less brilliant a songwriter — if anything, it makes his melodies infinitely more poignant. We are and we will remain indebted to him for his endless melodic invention, for the true sentiment of his songs, and for the enduring pleasure they have brought into all our lives. Celebrate and applaud that giant talent, that unquenchable fount of music, and be thankful that it will be here for our children and their children, and for as long as musicals are performed and songs are sung.

One last story: on January 15, 1954, at the 1,925[th] and final performance of *South Pacific,* after the cast had taken their bows at the end of the show, they all linked arms, and with the audience joining in, sang "Auld Lang Syne." The actors then left the stage with the curtain still up, as if to say "the curtain will never come down on this show." The same could be said of both Richard Rodgers and Oscar Hammerstein: The curtain has never come down on either of them, and it probably never will.

## 1979-2002:
## Significant Richard Rodgers Milestones


KEY:

Rodgers stage, concert or movie musical

**Recording**

*Television*

Other


**1979**

> *Oklahoma!* (US National Tour, Broadway, post-Broadway tour; dir. by W. Hammerstein)
>
> *The King and I* (West End; starring Yul Brynner, Virginia McKenna)
>
> Death of Richard Rodgers (12/30)

**1980**

> *Oklahoma!* (UK tour, West End, Australia; dir. by J. Hammerstein, produced by Cameron
>   Mackintosh)
>
> *The King and I* (US National Tour; starring Yul Brynner)

**1981**

> *The Sound of Music* (West End; starring Petula Clarke)

**1982**

> *On Your Toes* (Kennedy Center, Broadway, US National Tour, West End;
>   Tony Award—Best Revival)

**1985**

> *The King and I* (US National Tour, Broadway; Yul Brynner's farewell engagement.)
>
> *South Pacific* (Los Angeles; closed prior to Broadway; starring Richard Kiley
>   and Meg Bussert)
>
> ***Rodgers & Hammerstein: The Sound of American Music*** (PBS)
>
> Wall to Wall Richard Rodgers (Symphony Space)

**1986**

> **South Pacific** (studio cast album; starring Kiri Te Kanawa, Jose Carreras)
>
> **I Remember Mama** (studio cast album)
>
> *Carousel* (Washington DC; closed prior to Broadway; dir. by J. Hammerstein,
>   choreographed by Peter Martins; Cameron Mackintosh, consultant)

**1987**

> *South Pacific* (US National Tour; starring Robert Goulet)

Carousel (studio cast album; starring Samuel Ramey, Barbara Cook, Sarah Brightman)

**1988**

*South Pacific* (West End, UK tour, Japan; starring Gemma Craven, Emile Belcourt)

Williamson Music (ASCAP) and R&H Music (BMI) brought in-house

**1989**

*The King and I* (US National Tour; starring Rudolf Nureyev)

*The King and I* (US National Tour, Japan; starring Stacey Keach; dir. by J. Hammerstein)

***Music by Richard Rodgers*** (PBS)

**The Sound of Music** (studio cast album;starring Frederica von Stade)

*Babes in Arms* (concert; Evans Haile, cond.)

**1990**

Uptown R&H office relocates to 1633 Broadway

Richard Rodgers Theatre (exhibit installation; dedication)

Fox Video releases The Rodgers & Hammerstein [six video] Collection

**Opening Night: Rodgers & Hammerstein Overtures** (recording; John Mauceri and the Hollywood Bowl Orchestra)

*The Sound of Music* (New York City Opera, Japan; starring Debby Boone; dir. by J. Hammerstein)

*Carousel* (Houston Grand Opera; dir. by Gerald Gutierrez)

*Carousel* (Chicago Lyric Opera; cond. by John McGlinn)

*The King and I* (UK tour, West End; starring Susan Hampshire; dir. by J. Hammerstein)

**1991**

*The King and I* (Australia; [Hayley Mills] dir. by Chris Renshaw; also Broadway [Donna Murphy], US National Tour [Hayley Mills], London [Elaine Paige]; Tony Award-Best Musical Revival)

Happy Talk (concert/lecture; hosted by Mary Rodgers & William Hammerstein)

*Pipe Dream* (Musicals Unlimited-New York; dir. by B.T. McNicholl)

**1992**

Rodgers & Hammerstein (book by Ethan Mordden)

**The King and I** (studio cast album; starring Julie Andrews & Ben Kingsley; John Mauceri and the Hollywood Bowl Orchestra)

*Carousel* (Royal National Theatre, London; also West End, Broadway, US National Tour, Japan; dir. by Nicholas Hytner; Tony Award-Best Musical Revival)

*Pal Joey* (Huntington Stage, Boston; book revised by Richard Greenberg)

*State Fair* (Winston-Salem, Longbeach; see below)

**1993**

R&H 50th Anniversary (Oklahoma! reunion luncheon; postage stamp;
  book, album reissues; special Tony Award)

*A Grand Night for Singing* (Rainbow & Stars; Broadway, US National Tour;
  Tony Award nominee-Best Musical)

*The Sound of Music* (UK National Tour; London/Sadlers Wells; starring Liz Roberston)

*The Sound of Music* (US National Tour; starring Marie Osmond; dir. by J. Hammerstein)

*Oklahoma!* (Troika; US National Tour)

*Cinderella* (New York City Opera)

*South Pacific* (Australia, Southeast Asia; starring Paige O'Hara, André Jobin;
  dir. by Christopher Renshaw)

**1994**

*Carousel* (Broadway; see above)

*Allegro* (Encores!)

*Oklahoma!* (UK National Tour; dir. by Christopher Renshaw)

**1995**

Oscar Hammerstein II centennial

**Some Enchanted Evening** (PBS)

Lorenz Hart centennial

*Pal Joey* (Encores!; starring Patti LuPone, Peter Gallagher)

*Cinderella* (NYCO; return engagement)

*State Fair* (US National tour, Broadway, post-Broadway tour)

**1996**

*The King and I* (Broadway; see above)

*State Fair* (Broadway; see above)

*Something Wonderful* (UK National Tour)

*Babes in Arms* (Guthrie Theatre, Minneapolis; book revised by Ken LaZebnik)

**1997**

**Cinderella** (Wonderful World of Disney/ABC-TV; starring Brandy, Whitney Houston)

The Boys from Syracuse (Encores!)

**1998**

*The Sound of Music* (Broadway, US National Tours, Australia; Tony Award
  nominee-Best Musical Revival)

*Richard Rodgers* (biography by William Hyland)

*Oklahoma!* (Royal National Theatre, London; also West End;
  dir. by Trevor Nunn; **filmed for television**)

*Babes in Arms* (1937 version; University of Cincinnati College Conservatory of Music)

**1999**

Death of James Hammerstein (1/7)

Uptown R&H office relocates to 1065 Avenue of the Americas

*South Pacific* (50th Anniversary reunion; dinner; museum exhibit; retrospective)

***Thou Swell, Thou Witty: The Rodgers & Hart Story (PBS)***

*Babes in Arms* (Encores!)

*The King and I* (Warner Bros. Animated Feature; US home video)

USPS stamp for Rodgers & Hammerstein

Sing-Along *Sound of Music*; movie karaoke phenomenon begins in UK (goes global in 2000-01)

**2000**

*The King and I* (London; see above)

*Cinderella* (US National tour)

*Rex* (Musicals in Mufti)

35th Anniversary Sound of Music promotion: DVD, VHS, CD reissue; NBC special broadcast; US premiere of Sing-Along *Sound of Music* (NY)

**2001**

300

***South Pacific*** (ABC-TV; starring Glenn Close)

*A Connecticut Yankee* (Encores!)

*Somewhere For Me: A Biography of Richard Rodgers* by Meryle Secrest.

***Richard Rodgers: The Sweetest Sounds*** (13/WNET)

RNT *South Pacific* in London.

**2002**

Richard Rodgers Centennial

RNT *Oklahoma!* on Broadway

*Rodgers & Hammerstein: The Sound of Their Music* by Frederick Nolan.

*The Boys from Syracuse* (Roundabout Theatre Co.) on Broadway

***PBS American Masters Documentary Biography of Richard Rodgers***

Carnegie Hall: Three Rodgers & Hart Concerts (Feb-May)

Carnegie Hall: *Carousel* in Concert (June)

Wall to Wall Richard Rodgers @ Symphony Space (March)

Rodgers Television Festival @ Museum of TV & Radio/NY & LA (Spring)

UK, Japan, Australia: various Centenary activities

***and the curtain is still up ...***

# Bibliographical Sources

Abbott, George. *"Mr. Abbott."* New York: Random House, 1963.

Arnaz, Desi. *A Book.* New York: William Morrow & Co., 1976.

Atkinson, Brooks. *Broadway.* New York: Macmillan, 1970.

Blum, Daniel. *Pictorial History of the American Theatre 1900-1960.* New York: Chilton, 1960.

Bordman, Gerald. *The American Musical Theatre: A Chronicle.* New York: Oxford Univ. Press, 1978.

Carroll, Diahann (with Ross Firestone). *Diahann: An Autobiography.* Boston: Little Brown, 1986.

Clurman, Harold. *All People Are Famous.* New York: Harcourt Brace Jovanovich, 1974.

De Mille, Agnes. *Dance to the Piper.* Boston: Little Brown, 1951.

— *And Promenade Home.* Boston: Little Brown, 1956.

Dietz, Howard. *Dancing in the Dark.* New York: Quadrangle, 1974.

Ewen, David. *Richard Rodgers.* New York: Henry Holt & Co., 1957.

Ferber, Edna. *A Peculiar Treasure.* Copyright renewed 1966 by Edna Ferber.

Fordin, Hugh. *Getting To Know Him: A Biography of Oscar Hammerstein II.* New York: Random House, 1977.

Furia, Philip. *The Poets of Tin Pan Alley.* New York: Oxford Univ. Press, 1990.

Green, Stanley. *The World of Musical Comedy.* New York: A. S. Barnes & Co., 1968.

— *Ring Bells! Sing Songs!* New York: Arlington House, 1971.

— (ed.) *The Rodgers and Hammerstein Fact Book.* New York: Lynn Farnol Group, 1980.

Gussow, Mel. *Don't Say "Yes" Until I've Finished Talking.* New York: Doubleday, 1971.

Harrison, Rex. *Rex.* London: Macmillan, 1974.

Hart, Moss. *Act One.* New York: Random House, 1959.

Harriman, Margaret Case. *Take Them Up Tenderly.* New York: Alfred A. Knopf, 1944.

Higham, Charles. *Ziegfeld.* London: W. H. Allen, 1973.

Hyland, William G. *Richard Rodgers.* New Haven: Yale Univ. Press, 1998.

Kobal, John. *Gotta Sing, Gotta Dance.* New York: Hamlyn, 1971.

Laurents, Arthur. *Original Story.* New York: Alfred A. Knopf, 2000.

Logan, Joshua. *Josh.* New York: Delacorte Press, 1976.

Martin, Mary. *My Heart Belongs.* New York: William Morrow & Co., 1976.

Marx, Samuel and Jan Clayton, *Rodgers and Hart: Bewitched, Bothered and Bedevilled.* New York: G. P. Putnarn's Sons, 1976.

301

Matthews, Jessie. *Over My Shoulder.* London: W. H. Allen, 1974.

Mordden, Ethan. *Broadway Babies: The People Who Made The American Musical.* New York: Oxford Univ. Press, 1983.

— *Rodgers and Hammerstein.* New York: Harry N. Abrams, 1992.

— *Coming Up Roses: The Broadway Musical in the 1950s.* New York: Oxford Univ. Press, 1998.

— *Beautiful Mornin': The Broadway Musical in the 1940s.* New York: Oxford Univ. Press, 1999.

Nolan, Frederick. *Lorenz Hart: A Poet on Broadway.* New York: Oxford Univ. Press, 1994.

Oppenheimer,George. *The Passionate Playgoer.* New York: Viking, 1958.

Palmer, Tony. *All You Need Is Love.* London: Weidenfeld & Nicolson, 1977.

Rodgers, Richard (ed.). *The Rodgers and Hart Song Book.* New York: Simon & Schuster, 1951.

— *Reminiscences of Richard Rodgers.* New York: Oral History Collection, Columbia University, 1968.

— *Musical Stages.* New York: Random House, 1975.

302     Secrest, Meryle. *Stephen Sondheim: A Life.* New York: Alfred A. Knopf, 1998.

— *Somewhere For Me: A Biography of Richard Rodgers.* New York: Knopf, 2001.

Skinner, Cornelia Otis. *Life with Lindsay and Crouse.* Boston: Houghton Mifflin, 1976.

Stagg, Jerry. *The Brothers Shubert.* New York: Random House, 1968.

Teichmann, Howard. *George S. Kaufman, An Intimate Portrait.* New York: William Morrow, 1974.

— *Smart Aleck.* New York: William Morrow, 1976.

Thomas, Tony. *Harry Warren and the Hollywood Musical.* New York: Citadel, 1975.

Wilder, Alec. *American Popular Song: The Great Innovators 1900-1950.* New York: Oxford Univ. Press, 1972.

Wilk, Max. *They're Playing Our Song.* New York: Atheneum, 1974.

Wodehouse, P. G. and Guy Bolton. *Bring on the Girls.* New York: Simon & Schuster, 1953.

Zadan, Craig. *Sondheim & Co.* Second edition. New York: Harper & Row, 1986.

# Appendix

# Index

309

317

320

322